# THE
# 100 BEST
# STOCKS
## TO BUY IN
# 2018

# THE 100 BEST STOCKS TO BUY IN 2018

PETER SANDER
AND
SCOTT BOBO

Adams Media

New York   London   Toronto   Sydney   New Delhi

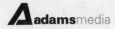
Adams Media
An Imprint of Simon & Schuster, Inc.
57 Littlefield Street
Avon, Massachusetts 02322

First Adams Media trade paperback edition DECEMBER 2017

ADAMS MEDIA and colophon are trademarks of Simon and Schuster.

For information about special discounts for bulk purchases, please contact Simon &
Schuster Special Sales at 1-866-506-1949 or business@simonandschuster.com.

The Simon & Schuster Speakers Bureau can bring authors to your live event. For
more information or to book an event contact the Simon & Schuster Speakers
Bureau at 1-866-248-3049 or visit our website at www.simonspeakers.com.

Interior design by Katrina Machado

Manufactured in the United States of America

10  9  8  7  6  5  4  3  2  1

Library of Congress Cataloging-in-Publication Data has been applied for.

ISBN 978-1-5072-0432-0
ISBN 978-1-5072-0433-7 (ebook)

# Contents

# PART I

# THE ART AND SCIENCE OF INVESTING IN STOCKS

**By Peter Sander**

# The Art and Science of Investing in Stocks

We lost.

Yes, for the first time in eight proud runs starting with the 2010 edition of *The 100 Best Stocks*, we failed to send our old nemesis—the S&P 500 Index—home empty to await for yet another shot.

Instead of the annual win to which we've grown accustomed, we ate dust. The "S&P," aided by a surprising November Trump victory at the head of the 2017 stretch, caught up and then passed us at the finish line. It won by about two lengths, a 16.4 percent year-over-year gain during our April 1 to April 1 measurement year compared to a 14.2 percent gain for our *100 Best* list.

We aren't used to seeing that horse—or very many others—in front of us.

As this opening section unfolds, we'll get to the details. You'll see how we lost and how much we lost by. You'll also see that we finished far from last. Our 14.2 percent year-over-year gain (including dividends) is hardly a reason to send us to the glue factory. You could say that we still finished easily "in the money." Yes, it fell short of the S&P's rather stunning 16.4 percent, but we think our horse did pretty well the past few years; moreover, it is ready to run again. And oh by the way, it should do better on the sloppy track of a down market if one should *ever* materialize.

Yes, "if one should ever materialize." Our publisher switched horses in late 2009 to bring us on as authors of the *100 Best* series for the 2010 edition. At that time, of course, there were buying opportunities galore. But no one, including us, ever thought the markets would rise without faltering for eight years in a row! Even with the S&P rising some 225 percent over that period (our *100 Best Stocks* rose 310 percent over the same period by the way, as Table 0.2 shows), we thought there would be at least a few down years. A few years where we could test the strength of our list against a down market; a "sloppy track."

Hasn't happened. Not yet anyway. But we're still betting that if such a down year happens, you'll still cash your ticket if you stick with us.

\* \* \*

With that, the three dominant reasons for our 2.2 percent return shortfall deserve a little explaining, so here goes:

First off, a surprisingly faster horse picked the 2017 "race" to come into its own. As we play a bit conservative, we avoid many of the truly glamorous legs on the S&P horse such as Facebook, Netflix, and Google. In doing so, we think we're more likely to win most of the races against the S&P. Just not all of them, as this year clearly demonstrated. The so-called "FANG" stocks (Facebook, Amazon, Netflix, Google) were up 30 percent for 2017 (through the end of May) while the S&P 500 index in total was up "only" 8 percent for the same five-month period. We have only one of the four customary "FANGs" on the *100 Best* list: Amazon—although if you expand just a little, "FANG" becomes "FAANG" with the inclusion of Apple, and we have that one too. All that said, we may be slower than FANG but think we're better positioned to win in the long run.

The unexpected "Trump Bump" did much to break our streak too. Say and feel what you will about the Trump administration, there's no doubt the surprise summiting of the nation's presidency gave the markets a late kick for the 2016 calendar year and beyond into 2017. Upon his election the markets overall rose 16 percent in three months (as measured by the S&P 500); that rising tide should have floated our boats higher too, and indeed it did. Where we ran into a little bit of a headwind is in regards to *which* boats it floated.

The "Trump agenda" is full of items that benefit business. Some of them, like the advance of US manufacturing and jobs and lowering corporate taxes, positively affect most or all firms in today's business landscape. But some of them, such as less regulation or changed taxation for repatriated foreign profits, affect some industries more than others: in particular, financial and tech firms. Financial and tech firms, demonstrated in Table 0.1, became the number one and number two performers among the 39 mutual fund sector benchmarks as reported by Lipper.

Here's the problem. We're especially light on financial stocks. As many of you who have followed us know, we don't have a very big appetite for financial companies. Why? Because frankly we don't really understand them. They are extraordinarily complex, and their presentation of facts and figures to investors doesn't go very far to make them any easier to understand. We "buy" businesses we can understand.

Beyond that, we don't think financial firms, in aggregate, add much value to the economy. They make their money taking crumbs off large sums of money moved around from one place to another (a metaphor used brilliantly in Tom Wolfe's 1987 observant book *The Bonfire of the Vanities*, a highly recommended read). Much of what they do is a zero-sum game; if they make money on a financial transaction, someone else loses. We're oversimplifying here, but when financial companies comprise some 22 percent of the nation's total corporate profits as they did just prior to the 2008 meltdown, look out below. When the "financials" horse took off in the wake of the 2016 election, largely due to the prospects of throwing off hobbling regulation, (which is a little scary too), we ate some dust.

While we do embrace more technology stocks (e.g., Apple, Amazon, Microchip Technology, Daktronics, Fair Isaac, Qualcomm, and now First Solar), we stop short of three of the four FANG high flyers (Facebook, Netflix, Google) largely due to valuation. We also don't go for many other tech stocks because they are (1) (again) hard to understand, (2) have high prices relative to value, and (3) often have scant investor returns, especially in the dividend department. If our book were titled *The 100 Best* Aggressive *Stocks You Can Buy*—as one derivative edition was titled in 2012—many more of these tech names would fit. But for the main *100 Best* list, we prefer to stay a bit more conservative, so as to perform well on that sloppy track when (not if) it comes to pass.

So while we picked up some of the tech tailwind for 2017, that horse left us behind as well, and the combined effects of the financial and tech stretch run contributed much to our down-the-stretch shortfall.

Finally, we were slow to pull the trigger on certain losers. Those of us who have followed our lists each year know we're sometimes early to the party. We picked automated utility smart meter maker Itron for the list some six years ago (for 2013) only to watch it underperform for five of those six years; it then became our fourth best winner in 2017. Others like Corning, Timken, State Street, Quest Diagnostics, and Microchip Technology (our biggest 2017 winner) have flatlined for a year or more before fulfilling our prophecy.

The point? Sometimes we're late to *leave* a party. The energy is gone, the lights are turning off, and the cleanup starts. Guess what—*we're still hanging around*! We've been known to hang around *too* long from time to time, waiting for certain partygoers such as IBM, HP, Ralph Lauren, and International Paper to start dancing again…but they don't! Industry shifts, marketplace shifts, Millennial shifts, organizational malaise, or who knows what get in the way—but we, as eternal optimists, hang on for one more year.

This year can serve as no better example. Among our worst performers were retailers Macy's and Target, which were handily disrupted by e-commerce and the emerging "stay-at-home" economy (more on that to follow!); we scold ourselves for underestimating that. They're off the list now, after racking up losses in excess of 30 percent. Worse still were two of our drug makers, Novo Nordisk and Perrigo, which were disrupted by Trump rallying cries to repeal the Affordable Care Act and a groundswell of disdain for drug prices. We may be totally wrong, but while we think Macy's and Target are strategically broken and should be removed, we're keeping the two drug makers, whose setback appears to fall short of breaking these businesses permanently.

Long story short, our 2017 performance was severely handicapped by the sharpness of these setbacks.

So enough ruminating and rationalizing about our 2017 defeat— although you'll hear more about it in the pages that follow (yes, we don't like to lose, even for one year!). We watched the S&P 500 take its victory lap, then got down to work figuring out which horses will stay on the track for 2018—and decided to keep all but ten of them in this year's race.

* * *

At this point we'll switch gears into one of the great debates of the day. Should you pick stocks or hire others (advisors, actively managed mutual funds) to pick stocks for you? Or should you simply buy index funds?

In this year, when a simple investment in the S&P 500 index beat our most carefully chosen, we felt we had to embrace this debate. We felt still more of an impulse to soul-search after the greatest stock picker of them all, Warren Buffett, announced in early 2017 that "both large and small investors should stick with low-cost index funds." We'll cover *why* he made that statement, and how we feel about the whole subject later in this narrative.

* * *

As we lick our wounds and move ahead (with learnings!) into 2018, we continue to embrace individual stock investing in carefully selected businesses with good track records for steady growth and shareholder returns. Unusually we had four of our 100 companies—Time Warner, Monsanto, St. Jude Medical, and WhiteWave Foods—"taken out" by mergers (that's flattering, someone else out there likes our picks too!). We acknowledge that stock prices, at the time of this writing, are at record highs, but typically we weigh longer-term business and shareholder return growth prospects more than short-term overpricing and underpricing of a stock; as such we didn't remove any companies simply because their shares were overvalued. In total, we changed ten companies, four due to acquisition and the rest due to strategic change or simply that there were better horses around for the 2018 race. We took note of possible effects of the Trump administration, the rise of Millennials, e-commerce, and the stay-at-home economy but didn't make wholesale changes to address these transitions. More to follow.

*  *  *

Again, we continue to enjoy your feedback. We've fielded many fine questions that, frankly, we enjoyed answering. Not only do we appreciate the dialogs, but we learn from them too. Keep them coming to Peter's email: ginsander@hotmail.com.

We continue to be measurement minded. "Buffettfan's" Amazon comments for *The 100 Best Stocks to Buy in 2015* continue to resonate:

> "Another plus is that they have the courage of their conviction and review the performance of their previous year's stock picks; something not seen too often in other books of this type."

It's not hard to find investment suggestions, but it's much harder to find advice—or advisors, for that matter—who regularly measure and report their successes and failures. (Maybe it's because they're continually outperformed by the indexes?) Not only is it good form (especially for us engineer types) to measure the quality of what we're providing, it also helps us understand how well our approach is working. As author Katherine Neville put it in her exquisite novel *The Eight*, "What can be measured can be understood; what can be understood can be altered."

As usual, we continue to produce this book not only to give you our annual selections (fish) but also provide a model for *how* we make our selections (teach you to fish). This Part I narrative has elements of both—and we apologize once again for parts of it that might seem repetitive, year after year—for those of you faithful enough to buy each year's edition. (For those of you who would like still more insight on how to fish, I'll point to two of my other works: *The 25 Habits of Highly Successful Investors*, from this publisher, and *All About Low Volatility Investing* from McGraw-Hill.) Anyway, for us, investing is a thought process that we hope you acquire over time—not just through our investment tenets and philosophies shared in the narrative, but also by watching us *do* it (the *100 Best* list) and ultimately through your own experience.

Finally, we continue to find investment clubs to be great forums to exchange ideas, insights, and experiences. We also enjoy evaluating investment club portfolios and comparing them to our *100 Best* list. Once again, if anyone out there wants to engage us for an investment club meeting, we can work out "consideration" (often just a free lunch; we know you've bought at least one book and we also know we aren't Registered Investment Advisors) and the means, perhaps teleconference or some such. Anyhow, the door is open; contact me (Peter) at the aforementioned email.

As always, enjoy *The 100 Best Stocks to Buy in 2018*. We hope to see you back in the winner's circle again after a disappointing 2017 finish.

Invest long and prosper!

## An Also-Ran for 2017…But a Good Track Record Still

It's hard to believe it's been four years since we created the "temporary" analysis and table comparing the performance of the *100 Best Stocks* list against major sector benchmarks as measured by Lipper, a division of Thomson Reuters and a major supplier of quality financial information and analytics especially for the mutual fund sector. While we pretty much missed the winner's circle with our 2017 picks, our "temporary" analysis is still revealing. Yes, we lost the race to the S&P 500 by a full 2.2 percentage points, but we still "stack up" in the top third of finishers for the 2017 race. Table 0.1 shows the "race" and its finishing order.

For 2017 Table 0.1 shows quite clearly how the "kick" given by the Trump victory in late 2016 beat us down the stretch. Note that Financials finished in first place, and as mentioned above, we're pretty light—deliberately so—in Financials. We also lost out to surging Science/Technology stocks (which include the heralded "FAANG" stocks), recovering Natural Resource stocks, and to Emerging Markets. But still, we beat the rest. Every horse loses a race once in a while. But we were in the running, and we still think we have the right "horses" for the vast majority of races, especially those on a sloppy (high-volatility, down market) track. Remember that our *100 Best* list is intended to be a pretty "steady-Eddie" bunch, and if you prefer tortoises to hares, we may just have the right collection of stocks for you. You'll get to cash those bets in the long run.

▼ Table 0.1: Performance Compared to Major Benchmarks

*100 BEST STOCKS 2017* COMPARED TO LIPPER MUTUAL FUND INDEX BENCHMARKS

ONE-YEAR PERFORMANCE, APRIL 1, 2016–APRIL 1, 2017

| Fund Benchmark | 1-Year Return |
|---|---|
| Financial Services | 29.6% |
| Science and Technology | 27.1% |
| Latin American | 25.3% |
| Natural Resources | 19.6% |
| Precious Metals Equity | 19.6% |
| **S&P 500 with Dividends Reinvested** | **16.4%** |
| Health/Biotech | 16.4% |
| Emerging Markets | 16.2% |
| China Region | 15.7% |
| International Small/Mid Cap Value | 15.0% |
| Global Multicap Value | 14.9% |
| Pacific Ex-Japan | 14.8% |
| *100 BEST STOCKS TO BUY 2017* | **14.2%** |
| Pacific Region | 14.2% |
| Japan Region | 14.0% |
| Global Multicap Core | 13.8% |
| Global Large Cap Value | 13.4% |
| High Yield Bond | 13.3% |
| International Multicap Value | 13.2% |
| Global Multicap Growth | 13.0% |
| Global Large Cap Growth | 12.8% |
| Global Large Cap Core | 12.6% |
| International Small/Mid Cap Core | 11.7% |
| International Large Cap Core | 11.4% |
| International Multicap Core | 11.3% |
| International Large Cap Value | 11.3% |
| Telecommunications | 10.6% |
| International Multicap Growth | 9.9% |

| Fund Benchmark | 1-Year Return |
|---|---|
| European Region | 9.8% |
| International Large Cap Growth | 9.7% |
| International Small/Mid Cap Growth | 8.6% |
| Utility | 8.4% |
| Multisector Income | 7.2% |
| General Bond | 4.4% |
| Real Estate | 3.3% |
| Inflation Protected Bond | 2.3% |
| Short US Government | 0.2% |
| Intermediate Municipal Debt | -0.3% |
| Short/Intermediate US Government | -0.4% |
| General US Government | -1.4% |
| General US Treasury | -3.3% |

Source: Lipper/Thomson Reuters, Barron's Weekly

## An Eight-Year Stretch Run

Back in 2010 we took over the publication of *The 100 Best Stocks to Buy* series from previous author John Slatter. Motivated by our own curiosity and a couple of poignant reader queries, we ask ourselves, every year: "So how well did we do?" How are we doing over the *long term*? How well did we achieve the goals of applying solid, value-based, marketplace-based investing techniques and philosophies to picking great companies, the *100 Best* of them for you to invest in? More simply stated, would you have been better off to not buy our book, not take the time to pursue individual stock investing, and throw it over the wall to a low-cost S&P 500 index fund, as so many are doing today, and as experts, even Warren Buffett himself, are now suggesting you do?

Being more sensitive now to this question than ever, for one, having endured our first losing year, and two, for now observing the groundswell toward "passive" and "index" investing (more on that in a minute), we continue to carefully monitor our long-term performance, now over an eight-year stretch. Even though we "lost" last year, upon checking the figures, we still find the long-term results pretty encouraging.

Table 0.2, another of those "temporary" tables not destined to disappear anytime soon, shows our eight-year performance—and despite coming up short in 2017, we're still pretty nicely ahead of the pack. If you had invested

$100,000 in our 2010 *100 Best* list and adjusted your portfolio according to our annual adjustments, you would have $409,097 today, compared to $326,892 if you had invested in the S&P 500 through an index fund. You'd be $82,205, or 25 percent, ahead (less, of course, the cost of buying our book each year!). Upshot: we still think we're doing pretty well despite the minor 2017 hiccup—again though losing by 2.2 percent we still gained 14.2 percent for the year! Well worth the price of a book, in our not-so-unbiased view.

## Individual Investor: This Book Is (Still) for You

If you bought this book, you're probably an astute and experienced individual investor who invests in individual stocks in individual companies. But you may also be starting out, deep in learning mode. Either way, you're not alone—you have plenty of company.

Those of you who have followed our story (and our stock picks) over the years know that we are unrelenting advocates for the individual investor. We live by the old adage: "Nobody cares about your money more than you do." While we hold this still to be an essential truth, and while a 2013 study we cited for three years bears out the fact that in the wake of the Great Recession and in light of substantial investment advisory fees, more investors were going alone than ever before. That said, we must now take more interest in *where* they were going alone. Recently, on the heels of recent recommendations of investment experts—even the Oracle of Omaha himself—and on the heels of recent investment performance, more and more investors are turning to so-called *passively* managed investments, notably index funds, as a favored alternative to stock picking or so-called *actively* managed funds, which pick stocks *for* you. In this year when even our supposedly "best" stock picks were beaten out by the S&P 500 index, we'd be foolish not to take note.

### The New Popularity of Passive Investing

Pick up any financial journal or listen to any financial commentator today and you'll soon realize there has been shift in sentiment today toward "passive," sometimes known as "index" investing. While passive investing to a large degree retains the notion that you can manage your investments better than a paid advisor can, this new "trendy" investment philosophy suggests that most if not all of you should invest in "passive" investments, that is "baskets" of stocks defined by an index, rather than trying to pick individual stocks.

We, of course, as exponents of individual stock picking, take issue with passive investing as a panacea. We do believe it has its place as an anchor or foundation of your portfolio, especially if you do not have the time or

▶ Table 0.2: Performance Compared to Major Benchmarks

**EIGHT-YEAR PERFORMANCE COMPARISON: *100 BEST STOCKS* VERSUS S&P 500**

**ANNUAL PERFORMANCE OF EACH *100 BEST* LIST AND COMPOUNDED CUMULATIVE PERFORMANCE**

| | | 2010 | 2011 | 2012 | 2013 | 2014 | 2015 | 2016 | 2017 |
|---|---|---|---|---|---|---|---|---|---|
| *100 Best Stocks* | Gain, percent | 62.5% | 20.0% | 5.5% | 19.2% | 23.8% | 15.0% | 2.65% | 14.2% |
| | Compounded | 62.5% | 94.9% | 105.6% | 145.1% | 203.5% | 249.0% | 258.2% | 309.1% |
| | $100,000 invested in 2010 | $162,500 | $194,919 | $205,639 | $245,122 | $303,461 | $348,980 | $358,228 | $409,097 |
| **S&P 500** | Gain, percent | 44.6% | 13.1% | 5.4% | 15.6% | 22.4% | 12.5% | 2.35% | 16.4% |
| | Compounded | 44.6% | 63.5% | 72.4% | 99.3% | 143.9% | 174.4% | 180.8% | 226.9% |
| | $100,000 invested in 2010 | $144,600 | $163,543 | $172,374 | $199,264 | $243,899 | $274,387 | $280,835 | $326,892 |
| Net advantage, $100K invested, *100 Best Stocks* | | $17,900 | $31,376 | $33,265 | $45,858 | $59,562 | $74,593 | $77,393 | $82,205 |

For 12-month periods beginning April 1 of previous year, dividends included after 2011 inclination to manage your own stock picks. But beyond that, we feel pretty strongly that stock picking has its place (else, would we write this book?). Let us share, in this section, the premises—and weaknesses—of passive investing.

It starts with an assessment of what it costs to "get help" with your investments. The first stop on this tour is to examine the cost of hiring a professional advisor to help you with *any* investments—passive or active. For most accounts, a professional advisor will cost 1 percent of your asset value at minimum. Trading commissions may be—and mutual fund fees and costs *will* be—additional to that figure. Mutual fund fees, some of which are hidden, can be surprisingly high; I'll get to that in a minute.

Then there are hedge funds. Those glamorous parking places for rich folks' dough in years past, which charge 2 percent in fees and 20 percent of gains—only, as widely reported in the media, there hasn't been much in the way of gains recently! The decline in hedge fund hegemony was recently brought to the forefront by none other than Mr. Buffett himself:

### The Bet: Warren Weighs In

Most of us think of Warren Buffett as the consummate stock picker. And, looking at his 50-plus-year record of picking individual stocks, who could argue? But that doesn't necessarily mean he advocates stock picking for the rest of us.

What gives?

Nine years ago, Mr. Buffett sneered at the performance of professionally managed funds—hedge funds specifically—where concentrations of investable wealth were managed by supposedly the best and the brightest professional stock pickers around: hedge fund managers. If they couldn't beat the S&P 500 index, who could? Were they worth the "2 and 20"—2 percent of assets plus 20 percent of gains—fee structure they routinely charge their clients, whether markets perform well or not?

Mr. Buffett, always eager to prove his postulations and to put his money where his mouth is, made a big bet on the notion that these high-powered funds *do* actually underperform. He bet $500,000 that five so-called "funds of funds" (funds containing other hedge funds) couldn't beat the S&P 500 index, as measured by the low-cost Vanguard S&P Index Fund over a ten-year period. Only one hedge fund manager would even step up to take this bet!

You know where this is going; Mr. Buffett won the bet handily! Over the first nine years (ending December 31, 2016) the funds of funds, hampered by a further 1 percent "funds of funds" fee on top of the "2 and 20", brought in an average of 2.2 percent return compounded annually versus 7.1 percent for the index fund! The actively managed hedge funds failed miserably, mostly due to their costs and fees.

He laments:

"A lot of very smart people set out to do better than average in securities markets. Call them active investors. Their opposites, passive investors, will by definition do about average. In aggregate, their positions will more or less approximate those of an index fund. Therefore, the balance of the universe—the active investors—must do about average as well. However, those investors will incur far greater costs....A number of smart people are involved in running hedge funds. But to a great extent their efforts are self-neutralizing, and their IQ will not overcome the costs they impose on investors."

He goes on to conclude:

- "Investors, on average and over time, will do better with a low-cost index fund than with a group of funds of [actively managed] funds." (and by association, the actively managed funds themselves);
- "The bottom line: When trillions of dollars are managed by Wall Streeters charging high fees, it will usually be the managers who reap outsized profits, not the clients";
- More than $100 billion has been wasted on bad investment advice in the past decade.
- (and thus) "Both large and small investors should stick with low-cost index funds."

The letter can be found on the Berkshire Hathaway website at www.berkshirehathaway.com/letters/2016ltr.pdf (see pages 21–24, "The Bet," for Mr. Buffett's prescient thoughts and conclusions).

And now, for a few conclusions of our own:

### Why We Think Stock Picking Still Makes Sense

Where does this leave us as exponents of individual stock picking? Did Warren Buffett, our hero, our mentor, our guiding light to picking good businesses and stocks, suddenly abandon the entire principle by which we operate (and write)?

Not so fast. Of course, Mr. Buffett clearly believes that there is room at the top, room, that is, for stock pickers who really know what they're doing and have the time. (Otherwise would he not have jettisoned his entire $122 billion stock portfolio in favor of index funds?) We see no evidence that he is following this advice—instead, he still feels he can pick stocks, and who can argue? It may not surprise you that we think we can pick stocks too, and that you and we together can ride among the elite horses in this stock-picking race.

Why do we think this? Two reasons, primarily, each of which can be summed up into a three-word statement: (1) averages are averages and (2) cost is cost.

### AVERAGES ARE AVERAGES…

What do we mean by "Averages are averages?" Simply this: in order for a population (say, a group of stocks) to have an average, *some part* of that population must be above average. When you buy a "basket" of stocks defined by a broad or a sector index, it must by definition carry both the "good" and the "bad" stocks in a group. If you buy an S&P 500 fund, you will get, by definition, the "good" and the "bad" stocks in the S&P 500. If you buy a "sector" fund, say for Financials, or more broadly, "Small Cap Value" or some such, you will get both the good and the bad (and too, the ugly!) stocks in that group.

So why not try to pick out just the "good?" Although we held on to some clunkers like Macy's and Target too long this year, we do think it's possible to pick more of the "good" than the bad as individual stock pickers. And the seven-year win streak that precedes the 2017 "downer" bears that notion out.

### …AND COST IS COST.

So what do we mean by "Cost is cost?" Simply put, you can invest "cheaply" by buying an index fund, or "expensively" by hiring an advisor to help you pick stocks (or a hedge fund manager if you're a higher roller) and/ or by buying an actively managed mutual fund.

Just how expensive *are* actively managed funds, you might ask? More expensive than most people think.

Although "active" mutual fund and asset management fees have been coming down of late, and are advertised at 1 percent or less in many cases, the true cost of mutual funds goes far beyond the well-publicized "expense ratio," which covers basic management, marketing, and distribution costs for the fund. At least three other cost factors add drag to mutual fund performance:

- *Transaction costs for trading securities*—including commissions but also the "spread" between bid and offer prices, which according to one study adds another 1–1.5 percent to costs
- *"Cash drag"*—in a fund, a certain amount of cash must be held for expenses and redemptions, another 0.8–1 percent
- *"Soft dollar" costs*—paid to professional advisory firms offering research and advice to the fund, another 0.5 percent or so

These cost factors may add another 2–3 percent to the cost of owning an actively managed mutual fund, in addition to the 1–1.5 percent "expense ratio" and another 1 percent if you're paying a professional advisor yourself to hold your account and recommend the fund in the first place.

You may be paying 5–6 percent of your asset value to achieve—what? Seven to 8 percent returns in a good year and 14–16 percent gains in an outstanding one? And what about a "down" year? Yes, you can really lose if the markets lay an egg.

Here's the bottom line:

We don't think, by any means, one bad year for our *100 Best Stocks* list should beget a change in your investing strategy.

The logic of trying to pick only the good stuff still prevails, so long as you have the time, energy, inclination, thought process, and tools to pick individual stocks. We think *The 100 Best Stocks to Buy* continues to provide you with a healthy head start in this direction, and we see no reason to abandon the individual stock picking approach as of now—for most of you anyhow. It's cheap, too: not 1 percent or 2 percent for an advisor or "2 and 20" for a hedge fund or 5–6 percent for an actively managed mutual fund—at $15.99 or less per year (and today's $4.95 discount broker commissions) you *can* actively manage your investments and win!

So now that we've made (remade) the case for the individual investor and for individual stock picking, where does *The 100 Best Stocks to Buy* really fit in? Every edition of *The 100 Best Stocks* is intended as a core tool for the individual investor, especially those investors inclined to buy individual stocks. Most of you probably aren't inclined to buy individual stocks for your entire portfolio—nor should you be unless you have the time and it's your thing to do. Sure, it makes sense to round out your portfolio with index-based funds and ETFs. It may even make sense, depending on your time and proclivity for this sort of thing, to build a base of index-based ETFs or passively managed funds, and then to "spark" it with a few individual stocks of your choosing. Either way, *The 100 Best Stocks to Buy* is designed to help.

If you accept the idea of picking individual stocks for some part of your investment portfolio, then it becomes a question of what tools and process to use. You need to start somewhere; if you're reading this, we think you've started in the right place! If nothing else, our book is far less expensive than 1 percent of your stock portfolio (we hope!).

In this vein, we'd like to share a review of *The 100 Best Stocks to Buy in 2017* recently posted by reader Aly Mawji on the literary website *Goodreads*:

"For the active stock picker, this is an amazing book giving you a quick 3-page snapshot on 100 different businesses. The data tables give you enough info for a starting point to gauge valuation. The company synopsis is terrific. I would highly recommend."

In his concise 44-word review, Mr. Mawji captures the essence of our book. Thank you, Mr. Mawji.

\* \* \*

We know that *100 Best Stocks* is hardly the only tool available. The Internet has made this book one of hundreds of choices for acquiring investing information. With the speed of cyberspace, our book will hardly be the most current source. In fact, we know, despite recent changes to the publishing schedule, that we're still at least six months out-of-date. If you check our research, you'll be able to come up with two to three calendar quarters of more current financial information, news releases, and so forth.

So does the delay built into the publishing cycle make our book a poor source? Not at all. It works because the companies we choose don't change much and because they avoid the temptation to manage short-term, quarter-to-quarter performance. We chose these companies *because* they have sustainable performance, so who cares if the latest details or news releases are included? In *The 100 Best Stocks to Buy in 2018*, as with all previous editions, we focus on the *story*—the story of each company—not just the latest facts and figures.

To that same point, *100 Best Stocks* goes well beyond just being a stock screen or a study of stocks to invest in. Analysis forms the base of *100 Best Stocks*, but it isn't the rigid, strictly numbers-based selection and analysis so often found in published "best stocks" lists. Sure, we look at earnings, cash flow, balance sheet strength, and so forth, but we'll also look far beyond those things. We'll look at the intangible and often subtle factors that make truly great businesses—that is, companies—great. That is, once again, the company's *story.*

Great companies have good business fundamentals, but what makes them really great is the presence of intangibles and subtleties—the brands, the marketplace successes, the management style, the competitive advantages, the loyal customers—that will *keep* them great or make them greater in the future. In our view, *good intangibles today lead to better business fundamentals down the road.*

*100 Best Stocks* is not a simple numbers-based stock screen like many found on the Internet and elsewhere today. It is a selection and analysis of really good businesses you would want to buy and own, not just for past results, but for future outcomes. Does "future" mean "forever"? No, not anymore. While the *100 Best Stocks* list correlates well with the notion of "blue-chip" stocks, the harsh reality is that "blue chip" no longer means "forever."

We feel that the 100 companies listed and analyzed in the pages that follow are the best companies to own for 2018, and generally, beyond. That said, the word "own" has become a more active concept these days. Gone are the days of "own forever," like the halcyon days when Peter's parents, Jerry and Betty Sander, bought their 35 shares of General Motors, lovingly placed the stock certificate in their safe-deposit box, and henceforth bought nothing but GM cars. Today, there is no forever; the economy, technology, and consumer tastes simply change too fast, and the businesses that participate in the economy by necessity change with it. Ownership is a more active concept than it was even 10 or 20 years ago.

So going forward, we offer the *100 Best* companies to own now and for 2018, those that have the best chances of not only surviving but evolving with—or even ahead of—the economy based on their current market position and approach to doing business. We think these are the best companies to (1) stay with or perhaps stay slightly ahead of business change, (2) provide short- and long-term returns in the form of cash and modest appreciation, and (3) do so with a measure of safety or at least reduced volatility so that you can burn your energy doing other things besides staring at stock quotes day and night. And—importantly—these are the picks we feel can beat the indexes, especially in the long run.

Bottom line: Our intent is simple and straightforward. We provide a list and a set of facts and stories. You take the information as it's presented, do your own assessment, reach your own conclusions, and take your own actions. Anything more, anything less, won't work. You're in charge. And we suspect that you like it that way.

## What's New for 2018

For those of you who've stayed with us over the years, this edition will take the same approach as before. For those of you reading for the first time, here are some guidelines and ideas we follow.

First and once again: no changes to the author team of Scott and Peter (we'll introduce ourselves in a minute). Once again, no significant changes to the structure or format of our presentation. Continuing is our emphasis on sustainable value, strong market position and other intangibles, and sustainable and growing cash returns to investors, in the form of dividends and share buybacks as well as share appreciation. We continue to take interest in the persistency of dividend increases above and beyond the yield itself, and we continue to stay focused on total shareholder returns. For the most part, we are playing the hand that got us here.

However, although we say every year that our investing style and presentation has remained essentially the same, the style of the best artists, writers, or even software programmers evolves over time. As with any blend of science and art, investing most certainly included, the approach evolves; the style acquires a little of this and a little of that and loses a little of something else as time goes on. Experience matters and is taken into account. Changes in the world investing context and environment factor in. And heck—we're getting older and perhaps a bit wiser. Maybe we see things a little differently than we did eight years ago…and certainly 35 years ago. All of these factors influence the mix; here are a few directions we've taken recently (or have continued with emphasis) with this edition:

- *Low-volatility bias*. We continue to think it's important to get good returns but also to sleep at night. *Steady* growth, *steady* returns, *steady* dividend increases—that's what we prefer. While we present "beta" as a measure of market correlation, we look deeper into the actual patterns and history of earnings, dividends, cash flow, and yes, share price. If it's a wild ride (or if there *are* no earnings, cash flows, etc.), we don't get on; we prefer to watch from the sidelines instead. You'll never find the likes of Twitter on our list. We know—as the markets continue to rise through the years, the chances for corrective "volatility" increase—there isn't a whole lot we can do about that except to stick to our knitting. That said, we've reached outside our normal "core" type of holding for the second year in a row to pick up a few more aggressive companies that seem at the forefront of change. Indeed, we now have four companies— CarMax, Itron, Amazon, and First Solar—that don't pay dividends. We are placing a slightly greater emphasis on identifying smaller companies for the list, to add some energy and reap the benefits of these few companies still coming into their own (more on that in a minute). We are still mostly about the steady-Eddie traditional blue-chip core, but we think a few more aggressive plays are in order as (1) change is everywhere and (2) a lot of our "core" has gotten pretty expensive.

- *Still playing defense.* While we look more for up-and-comers, we still stick to the more defensive stance taken starting in 2014 in light of market "exuberance" and in recognition of the fact that in our multi-year tenure at the reins of this book, we have yet to see a down year! We were pretty defensive in 2014 through 2016—and still managed to beat the market, though by the slimmest of margins in 2016. An improving economy and what we see as a gathering shift toward a "new" economy dominated by Millennials and the "stay-at-home" lifestyle, combined with ever-higher prices for some of our traditional favorites has led us to be just a tiny bit more aggressive with our 2018 list, removing stalwarts such as Macy's and Clorox in favor of somewhat more aggressive names like Vodafone, First Solar, Applied Materials, and Tupperware (we also added back the old stalwart Boeing). As usual, everything is done with reason, caution, and dependable returns in mind.

Our lists continue to be constructed to provide enough growth opportunity to beat the market but also to beat the market in a *down* market, that is, to be down only 5 percent if the market dropped 10 percent. Although it probably cost us a victory, at least in part, for 2017, we continue to take that position. Quite honestly, many of our *100 Best Stocks* seem fully valued at this juncture. We were—and still are—nervous about riding them any further. Our strategy for dealing with this continues to be to evaluate all of our picks carefully using our "sell if there's something better to buy" philosophy and try to visualize how they would do "on a sloppy track." And we continue to avoid "momentum" plays as they have a tendency to beat a "mo" path downward at the slightest sign of change. Thus, to our peril, we have avoided Facebook, Netflix, Google, and others (although we do have Amazon and Apple from the so-called "FAANG" list of outstanding tech performers driving today's markets: Facebook, Amazon, Apple, Netflix, Google).

- *Focus on Millennials.* The shift continues. A January 2015 *New York Times* headline summed it up perfectly: "Millennials Set to Outnumber Baby Boomers." There are now about 80 million Millennials and 79 million boomers, with Millennials counted as being born between 1982 and 1997, and more importantly, with a digital silver spoon in their mouths. Hmmm, we thought. Have we embraced this adequately in our stock picks, given that we like companies with at least steady, and preferably improving, brand strength and loyal customer bases? Millennials are typically portrayed as digitally fluent, preferring unstructured environments, having a taste for customizable products, healthy foods, immediate gratification—all with short attention spans and relatively less loyalty to companies and brands than their non-digital ancestors. We've had to ask ourselves—Do they drink Coke? Buy IBM? Shop at Target? Wash their clothes with Tide? Buy clothes emblazoned with polo ponies? Go to movie theaters?—and a thousand other questions. Are we seeing—or about to see—a major shift in consumer preferences as Millennials gradually take charge of the commercial world? Do our long-standing brands like Coke and Cheerios have cachet with these groups like they once did with us older folks?

We've seen considerable recent evidence in the retail world that the "Millennial" megatrend is large and here to stay. Online shopping is no longer just a novelty—it has captured 8.5 percent of the US retail market as of Q1 2017 and is growing 14 percent per year. Shopping malls and mall stores in particular have seen sales and traffic declines. We took Wal-Mart and Tiffany off the 2017 list and now Macy's and Target off the 2018 list (a year too late as it turns out).

The "stay-at-home" economy is growing gangbusters, and we're still not sure we've fully embraced this shift. We have, however, incorporated a review of how a company will fare with this shift, keeping retailers like Costco and Ross or Kroger on the list as they appear relatively immune to e-commerce incursion (we hope we're right!). For every retailer, we ask ourselves: Can you get it (efficiently) on Amazon Prime? If yes, we're inclined to hit the delete button.

- *New focus on "smaller" companies.* For the most part, the "typical" *100 Best* company has been large, well known, steady, profitable—a "blue-chip" stock in old investing parlance. That is still true, but good investors try to find companies for which the best years are in front of them… or more precisely, they blend some of today's successful companies with some of tomorrow's. "Invest where the puck is going, not just where it has been" hockey great Wayne Gretzky might have said about this. To that end, we've started to identify smaller companies on the *100 Best* list. Also, starting this year, we are replacing the "S&P Financial Rating" (which was largely redundant to the Value Line Financial Rating) with a size indicator in the heading for each stock. "Large Cap" companies have a total market share value (or "cap," number of shares outstanding times share price) greater than $5 billion. "Mid Cap" companies fall between $1 billion and $5 billion, and "Small Cap" companies have a total market worth of less than $1 billion. Turns out that out of our 100 companies, 11 of them are Mid Caps and two of them, Daktronics and Schnitzer Steel, are Small Caps. While we added no Mid or Small Cap companies this year, we've added four Mid Caps in the last three years. In future years we would like to have 15 or 20 Small and Mid Cap companies to add a little energy and interest to our list.

Other than that, for 2018 and beyond we continue on a value-driven track, looking for the very best businesses to invest in with an emphasis on "sell if there's something better to buy." We didn't respond too much to short-term concerns that affected everyone, like the rising dollar or falling agricultural prices. We do see the dollar stabilizing, which should help exporters. We also embraced the Trump agenda, which could bring growth in infrastructure, US manufacturing, financial deregulation, and an uptick in corporate investment if favorable tax and cash repatriation policies are enacted. While we didn't add any companies specifically due to the "Trump trade," it was always in the back of our minds as we evaluated our existing list and chose new *100 Best* candidates. Although we added two "foreign" stocks, Siemens and Vodafone, to the 2018 list, we still prefer strong exporters as a way to play the global economy, and expect a leveling dollar to make this approach look wiser going forward than it has in the past two years.

Finally, we continue to stick with a few favorites in the embattled commodity sector like Chevron and Mosaic, figuring that the current commodity cycle will reverse—and even if it doesn't, they will prosper once again as necessary efficiency measures take hold. In our view, the best businesses will survive, even thrive, in the deepest cycles. Our "good" companies will implement efficiency measures, lose competitors, and emerge ever stronger in our view. The trick, as always, is to make sure the cycle is really a cycle, rather than a sign of structural business change.

## About Your Authors

If you're a regular reader of the *100 Best Stocks* series you've probably seen the following before. It's about us, and not much has changed about us, so feel free to skip this section if it's altogether too familiar—or if it doesn't matter much to begin with.

### Peter Sander

Peter is an independent professional researcher, writer, and journalist specializing in personal finance, investing, and location reference, as well as other general business topics. He has written 50 books on these topics, as well as numerous financial columns, and performed independent, privately contracted research and studies. He came from a background in the corporate world, having experienced a 21-year career with a major West Coast technology firm.

He is, most emphatically, an individual investor, and has been since the age of 12 (okay, so Warren Buffett started when he was 11), when his curiosity at the family breakfast table got the better of him. He started reading the stock pages with his parents. He had an opportunity during a "project week" in the seventh grade to read and learn about the stock market. He read Louis Engel's *How to Buy Stocks*, then the pre-eminent—and one of the only—consumer-friendly books about investing available at the time. He picked stocks, and made graphs of their performance by hand with colored pens on graph paper. He put his hard-earned savings into buying five shares of each of three different companies. He watched those stocks like a hawk and salted away the meager dividends to reinvest. He's been investing ever since. (Incidentally, Warren Buffett bought Cities Service preferred shares, Peter bought Burlington Northern preferred shares following much the same principles, and how ironic that Mr. Buffett came to own all of Burlington Northern. Perhaps Peter will come to own a big oil company some day.)

Yes, Peter has an MBA from Indiana University in Bloomington, but it isn't an MBA in finance. He also took the coursework and certification exam to become a certified financial planner (CFP). By design and choice, he has never held a job in the financial profession. His goal has always been to share his knowledge and experience in an educational way, a way helpful for the individual as an investor and a personal financier to make his or her own decisions.

He has never earned a living giving direct investment advice or managing money for others, nor does he intend to.

A few years ago, it dawned on Peter that he has really made his living finding value, and helping or teaching others to find value. Not just in stocks, but other things in business and in life. What does he mean by value? Simply, the current and potential *worth* of something as compared to its price or cost. As it turns out, he's made a career out of assessing the value of people (for marketers), places (as places to live), and companies (for investors).

### Scott Bobo

Peter and Scott have been friends and colleagues since, roughly, tenth grade (a long time!). Scott has been part of the team for eight years now and has been huge not only in identifying the *100 Best Stocks*, but also analyzing them and explaining their pros and cons crisply and in plain English so that you can make the best use of the list. Having Scott on the team allows you to get the combined wisdom and observations of two people, not just one, in an arena where one plus one almost always equals something greater than two.

Scott has been an investor since age 14, when he made the switch from analyzing baseball box scores to looking at the numbers and charts in the business section. In his 20-plus years in engineering and technology management, he's learned that a unique product value proposition is important to the success of any company. He has also learned (the hard way) that proper financial fundamentals are critical. From a development manager's perspective, comprehending a new product's risk/reward proposition is one of the keys to a company's success. From an investor's perspective, it's also one of the keys to successful value investing in a dynamic, innovation-driven market.

Scott adds a strong analytical touch. But he is most at home as an applications engineer, explaining how a company's products work and how they apply to a customer's needs. Consequently, and in addition to analytical legwork, Scott really adds an extraordinary and very real-world sense of how a company's products "fit" in the marketplace. Determining whether a company's products are relevant, best-in-class, and have a competitive advantage over others is an oft-overlooked core skill for a value investor. Scott brings this skill to the table in a big way.

How do these diverse experiences of Peter and Scott translate into picking stocks? Just like customers or places to live, we want companies that produce the greatest return, the highest value, *per dollar invested*. And *for the amount of risk taken*. The companies we will identify as among the *100 Best* have, in our assessment, the greatest and most persistent long-term *value*, and if you can buy these companies at a *reasonable price* (a factor that we largely leave out of this analysis because this is a book and prices can change considerably), then these investments deliver the best prospects while keeping the downsides manageable.

Later we'll come back to describe some of the attributes of value that we look for.

### A "Low-Volatility" Investing Book

You've heard about—and just read about—the idea of low-volatility investing. This term means investing to minimize risk and volatility—to be able to sleep at night and count on your otherwise unpredictable retirement—and achieve decent investing returns all the same. That's the subject of Peter's book *All About Low Volatility Investing* (McGraw-Hill, 2014), and some of the "DNA" from that book has leaked into this one. But that's not what this subsection is about.

What we're getting at here is the low-volatility nature of the sequential editions of this book. We try to keep them useful and relatively simple year after year. The analysis is the same, and for the most part the presentations are the same. Each year we make a few adjustments, pruning away a few stocks and adding a few others. We do that adhering to our core principles without having any particular number of changes in mind.

When we first took over this series from John Slatter for the 2010 edition, we made 26 changes, not a revolution but perhaps a strong evolution of the philosophy toward core value principles, strong competitive advantages and intangibles, and healthy cash returns. After that first year we went back to more of a fine-tuning mode, changing 14 stocks for the 2011 list, 12 for 2012, and back to 14 for 2013. In 2014 we held the line in a measure of defense and the simple inability to find "better horses," and changed only eight stocks. For 2015 and with the heady gains in the markets (almost 24 percent) we felt that a few more of our horses might be ready to fade and brought in 13 fresh ones for that year's ride. The pattern continued mostly unchanged in 2016 when we changed ten stocks, and last year, for 2017, we changed nine.

Now with four companies (Monsanto, St. Jude, Time Warner, and WhiteWave Foods) "taken out" by acquisition, continued turmoil in the oil patch, commodity, and export businesses, and blowups in the retail and drug space this year, it might surprise you that for the 2018 *100 Best Stocks* list, we replaced just ten stocks. You can see our patience with business cycles and our "sell when there's something better to buy" principle hard at work here. For example, even though our top two losers were drug stocks (Novo Nordisk and Perrigo), we kept them on the list, figuring the "cycle"—if there is one—is short-lived and mostly a baby of the media; these are still good businesses.

The overall methodology used for analysis and selection of the *100 Best Stocks* remains largely unchanged. We continue to focus on fundamentals that really count, like cash flow; profit margins and balance sheet strength; and those intangibles such as brand, market share, channel and supply-chain excellence, and management quality that really determine success *going forward*. We continue to place more focus on dividends and more generally, investor returns. More and more, especially in today's volatile markets, we feel that investors should get paid something to commit their precious capital to a company; it's a sign of good faith to investors and provides at least some return while waiting for a larger return in the future—or if things go south later on. This year, once again, 96 of this year's *100 Best* pay at least some dividends—down from 98 in 2016 and over most previous years. The culprits are two "legacy" entries, CarMax and Itron, and two relative newcomers, Amazon and First Solar. These stocks are included because of other prospects; we can turn our heads the other way on the dividend for a while but would expect some dividends eventually as the business models mature.

A "hallmark" factor differentiating our approach is our continued preference for companies with a track record for regular dividend *increases*. A few years ago we started tracking, for each company, the number of dividend increases or *raises* (yes, you can think of them as comparable to a raise in your own wage or salary) in the past ten years. We are proud to report that of the 96 *100 Best* stocks paying dividends in 2017, fully *76* of them *raised* their dividend from 2016 to 2017 (yes, that's down from 85 in 2016—mostly due to uncertainties facing energy and commodity stocks and a continuation of buybacks as a principal shareholder return strategy). Of the 76, *41* of them have raised their dividends in each of the past ten years, and 18 more have raised them each of the past eight or nine years (most of these took a year or two off during the Great Recession), adding up to 59 stocks that can be depended on for annual raises. Pretty good stuff, in our view.

As in all editions, we review the performance of our 2017 picks in some detail, and continue with our "stars" lists identifying the best stocks in six different categories:

1. Yield Stars (stocks with solid dividend yields—Table 6)
2. Dividend Aggressors (companies with strong and persistent records and policies toward dividend *growth*—Table 6.1)
3. Safety Stars (solid performers in any market—Table 7)
4. Growth Stars (companies positioned for above-average growth—Table 8)
5. Prosperity Stars (formerly Recovery Stars—companies poised to do particularly well in a strong economy—Table 9)
6. Moat Stars (companies with significant sustainable competitive advantage—Table 10)

So, if you're an investor partial to any of these factors, such as safety, these lists are for you.

## 2016–2017: A Lackluster Showing

Now we diagnose what happened in the year gone by and try to turn that into a prognosis for the coming year. Always a challenge in any year—and especially in one where we missed our overarching goal of beating the S&P 500 index.

It was a pretty unusual year, with a far stronger, and different, election effect than we (and most others) anticipated. In years past, in anticipation of political unleashing of spending programs and new public perks, stock markets rose moderately, though this phenomenon had diminished more recently. This year we were off to a good start anyhow, as the economy improved generally and as many companies reaped the benefits of leaner, meaner cost structures put in place during and after the Great Recession. The stock market—and our *100 Best* list—were doing well but with "mere" single-digit gains. Then came the election and its unexpected outcome. The "Trump trade" went into full force, unleashing big gains particularly in financial stocks, infrastructure, defense, and some natural resource companies. For many reasons we are light on financial and defense stocks, and while we do have infrastructure and resource entries in our portfolio, we had lightened up a little on these too. The Trump trade also hurt environmental and alternative energy issues, and some healthcare stocks, particularly drug companies, as well. So we lost the race with the S&P 500 in the final stretch despite ending up the year with a pretty solid 14.2 percent return. Now, as we move forward into 2018, many factors are once again at work to consider. Will the Trump trade continue? Will new tax and spending policies put more money into individual and corporate pockets? How much will interest rates rise? And how fast will marketplace trends, such as the rise of Millennials and the decline of bricks-and-mortar retail, change the business landscape? Once again, 2018 stacks up to be a unique and interesting year—with midterm congressional elections adding to the intrigue and uncertainty.

Besides the "Trump trade," here are six factors and trends that drove, and continue to drive, the markets:

- *Higher interest rates but predictable Fed policy.* In past years we've written of an "accommodative" Fed, doing what it could to keep interest rates low, money supply high, and business and personal finances stimulated. Now the economy has recovered and employment in particular has strengthened, so the Fed, rather than providing a tailwind, is trying to raise rates gradually to control inflation and temper money supply *without* capitating growth. Given this tough balancing act, they embarked on a plan to raise rates *gradually* and *predictably*, keeping everyone informed of what they plan to do as they go. The Fed as gentle tailwind is probably over for now; interest rates are pretty much a neutral factor in the markets so long as the Fed retains its current course of moderation and transparency. We are confident they will raise rates gradually enough so as to not knock the pins out from under our income-oriented stocks: REITs, utilities, etc.

- *Economic uncertainty overseas, especially in emerging markets.* Both high- and low-growth overseas markets have become more difficult to figure. China, which accounts for such a large portion of world demand and supply for goods, has seen its growth rates drop from the high- to mid-single digits—and now the low-single digits as debt has ballooned and its credit rating has been cut. Translation: China is no longer a juggernaut, and suppliers to China and other emerging economies such as natural resource producers can no longer count on a big boost from these markets. While we think some of this is cyclical, some may be permanent as (1) we think world demand for physical goods has waned a bit (downsizing boomers, lack of space for "stuff," and emphasis on "experiences" for the world's new emerging market professionals), and (2) new raw material supplies recently turned on during the commodities boom have proven difficult to turn off.

  Now, with the Trump administration and in the wake of "Brexit," we must embrace another factor that could hamper foreign trade and cause some of our bigger exporters (and importers) to stumble again: the advance of economic isolationism. This recent populist workers' movement has reinvigorated the concept of trade protection, which of course would likely spawn trade wars thus hampering exports—which of course, ironically, would hurt the very American factory and field workers the Administration was trying to help. At this juncture we don't think *major* trade policy changes will come about, but as with most elements of this "regime change," it bears watching.

- *Continued commodity down cycle.* Tempered emerging market demand and continued oversupply spawned by recent demand peaks and new technologies like "fracking" in the energy sector continue to roil the commodity markets. In many of these markets—oil, gas, copper, iron ore, fertilizer ingredients—supply has exceeded demand for several years, but economic equilibrium suggests that eventually supply and demand will move toward a better balance as we move through

2018. A balanced commodities market will help the US markets across the board—not just the commodity producers themselves but all the financial, equipment-producing, logistical, and other companies that support them. It also helps exports as strapped foreign commodity-producing countries balance their economies, too, and have more income to use to buy US goods and services.

- *Emergence of the stay-at-home economy.* An offshoot of the Millennial emergence, CNBC's Jim Cramer and others have noted a marked shift in the propensity to carry on daily activities, whether necessary or recreational, at home "while sitting on the couch." The emergence and success of Amazon Prime is, of course, glaring evidence of this trend. More and more households elect to order food and other staples, entertain themselves, and even interact with others at home through social media. Cramer and others suggest good times ahead for TV and video content providers such as Netflix, home food and pizza delivery (Domino's), video game and video game hardware makers (Activision, NVIDIA), social media, consumer electronics, home improvement, cloud computing, small-package logistics providers—you get the idea. Of course, the trend will hurt traditional retail, mall operators, and possibly even energy and automotive interests. We've embraced the trend to a degree but not wholly in our stock picks, adding Amazon and logistics providers and removing some retailers. As the trend has already worked its way into many stock prices (Netflix, Domino's to be sure), and as video games and social media trends can prove fickle, we haven't totally jumped on board, but again it's interesting to watch.

- *US manufacturing growth—a resurgence?* For years, we've envisioned a steady, if not ground-shaking, reshoring of manufacturing to American soil. Companies finally got the memo that it isn't just about labor costs—long, inflexible supply chains and the inability to control quality negate the savings, sometimes in a big way. Chinese labor costs are going up, and improved availability and declining costs of US energy resources, especially natural gas, are helping even more. Now the Trump administration, mostly through its "bully pulpit" so far, has aimed at slowing the offshoring of jobs if not an obvious repatriation of manufacturing from overseas. True, some supply chains, especially for electronics products, simply aren't deep enough to support US manufacturing—although Apple supplier Foxconn's recent selection of a Wisconsin site for a major new plant suggests that it's not impossible to reshore such plants. For yet another year, the strong dollar has slowed reshoring a bit recently, but as dollar gains moderate or reverse, we would expect the trend to continue. Whether this "buzz" really results in a major upsurge in US manufacturing, which accounted for only 11.7 percent of GDP and 8.5 percent of employment in 2016, remains to be seen. Many of our companies, like W.W. Grainger, Illinois Tool Works, Prologis, FedEx, and others will benefit from reshoring.

- *Persistence of share buybacks.* Companies have accumulated huge hoards of cash, as they have learned how to manage expenses and leverage their infrastructure to produce more for less. Although a big chunk of that cash is parked overseas for tax reasons, companies continue to actively buy back shares, although at a slightly diminished rate, producing rather silent but persistent returns to existing shareholders.

S&P's Howard Silverblatt estimates that S&P 500 companies bought back an estimated $536 billion in 2016, compared to $573 billion in 2015 and $553 billion in 2014 (the record is $589 billion repurchased in 2007). The rise in share prices is at least partly responsible for the slight dip. More than half the companies on our *100 Best Stocks* list could be classified as "buyback aggressors," retiring 10–20 percent and as much as 50 percent of outstanding float since 2004. This, of course, serves to increase returns, both to the shareholders who sell and to those who remain to enjoy a higher rate of return on the remaining shares. Notably, Apple spent $33.7 billion on buybacks—a figure larger than the total market capitalization of most of the stocks on our list!

Tax policy changes accommodating repatriation of cash from overseas could strongly stimulate buybacks going forward.

## Report Card: Recapping Our 2017 Picks

Once again, we lost. The glowing recovery of financial stocks and strength in other sectors we're light on like Technology and Biotech, combined with unexpectedly weak retail and pharmaceutical stock performance, threw us off our horse in 2017. Well, not really off our horse—we still finished in the top third of all sectors as measured by the Lipper sector indexes (Table 0.1) and we still posted a 14.2 percent gain; nothing to cry about and certainly nothing to make you take our horse out back and shoot it.

At this juncture, we'll once again do a short refresher on how we evaluate our gains. There are many ways to evaluate the performance of a group of stocks over time. Some are simplistic, such as simply averaging the percent gain in each share price. But such a method may not weight a portfolio very realistically, for it assumes you buy the same number of shares of W.W. Grainger at $200 as you would Daktronics at $9. We feel it's better to take the approach of an investor with $100,000 to invest—who invested $1,000 in each of the *100 Best Stocks* across the board, regardless of share price. Sure, you end up with some weird quantities of shares in your portfolio, but the portfolio, and thus the performance metrics, isn't weighted in favor of more expensive stocks.

### The Bottom Line

If you had invested $100,000 in our *100 Best Stocks 2017* list on April 1, 2016—$1,000 in each of the 100 stocks—you would have ended up with $111,736 on April 1, 2017, not including dividends paid during that period for a decent 11.7 percent gain. Including dividends of some $2,425, you would have ended up with $114,161. The S&P, as measured by the buyable SPDR S&P 500 ETF Trust ("SPY"), was ahead 16.4 percent, including dividends ($116,403) during that period. We lost by $2,242 on a $100,000 investment—but we still think (modestly!) that we were winners particularly in the long term.

### Winners and Losers

The full list of the *100 Best Stocks 2017* and how they did through the comparison period can be found in Appendix A. At this point, we'll give a short overview of what really worked and what didn't within the list. First, the winners:

▼ **Table 1: Performance Analysis:** *100 Best Stocks 2017*
  **TOP 20 WINNERS, 1-YEAR GAIN/LOSS, APRIL 1, 2016–APRIL 1, 2017**

| Company | Symbol | Price 4/1/2016 | Price 4/1/2017 | % change | Dollar gain, $1000 invested (including dividends) |
|---|---|---|---|---|---|
| Microchip Technology | MCHP | $48.28 | $73.78 | 52.8% | $558.00 |
| St. Jude Medical | STJ | $55.19 | $80.82 | 46.4% | $486.86 |
| Deere | DE | $76.50 | $108.86 | 42.3% | $454.38 |
| Itron | ITRI | $41.86 | $60.70 | 45.0% | $450.07 |

| Company | Symbol | Price 4/1/2016 | Price 4/1/2017 | % change | Dollar gain, $1000 invested (including dividends) |
|---|---|---|---|---|---|
| WhiteWave Foods (*) | WWAV | $40.21 | $56.15 | 39.6% | $396.42 |
| Fresh Del Monte | FDP | $42.96 | $59.23 | 37.9% | $392.23 |
| Norfolk Southern | NSC | $82.97 | $111.97 | 35.0% | $378.33 |
| Quest Diagnostics | DGX | $72.57 | $98.19 | 35.3% | $375.78 |
| State Street Corp | STT | $58.95 | $79.61 | 35.0% | $375.57 |
| Timken Company | TKR | $33.67 | $45.20 | 34.2% | $373.33 |
| Union Pacific | UNP | $78.92 | $105.92 | 34.2% | $371.39 |
| Time Warner Inc | TWX | $72.99 | $97.71 | 33.9% | $361.01 |
| CenterPoint Energy | CNP | $21.20 | $27.57 | 30.0% | $350.00 |
| Amazon | AMZN | $659.59 | $886.75 | 34.4% | $344.40 |
| Otter Tail | OTTR | $29.44 | $38.15 | 29.6% | $338.65 |
| Apple | AAPL | $109.99 | $143.71 | 30.7% | $327.30 |
| Ormat Technologies (*) | ORA | $43.40 | $57.08 | 31.5% | $323.96 |
| Corning | GLW | $20.83 | $27.00 | 29.6% | $323.09 |
| Monsanto | MON | $87.87 | $113.20 | 28.8% | $312.85 |
| Scotts Miracle-Gro | SMG | $73.01 | $93.39 | 27.9% | $306.12 |

\* = New for 2017

Not surprisingly, our "winning percentage" picked back up to 77 out of 100 picks from 57 winners in 2016, but still off from 79 for the 2015 list and 89 for 2014. It's a better figure, but we're not terribly proud of it.

The winners hailed from many divergent parts of our list. To note first on our Top 20 Winners list (Table 1) are the four companies involved in takeovers—St. Jude, WhiteWave, Time Warner, and Monsanto. Then, though a little light on technology overall, our tech picks—Microchip Technology, Itron, Amazon, Apple, and Corning did quite well. State Street was a big winner among our lean Financials picks, and cyclical recovery became evident in the likes of our railroad stocks (Union Pacific, Norfolk Southern) and in Deere and Timken. Two of our nine new picks made this list (not as good as last year, but we'll take it).

Now, for the losers:

▼ Table 2: Performance Analysis: *100 Best Stocks 2017*

**TOP LOSERS, 1-YEAR GAIN/LOSS, APRIL 1, 2016–APRIL 1, 2017**

| Company | Symbol | Price 4/1/2016 | Price 4/1/2017 | % change | Dollar loss, $1000 invested (including dividends) |
|---|---|---|---|---|---|
| Patterson | PDCO | $46.35 | $45.23 | -2.4% | $(3.45) |
| Kimberly-Clark | KMB | $136.20 | $131.63 | -3.4% | $(6.17) |
| McCormick | MKC | $100.53 | $97.55 | -3.0% | $(12.04) |
| Starbucks | SBUX | $61.02 | $58.39 | -4.3% | $(28.35) |
| General Electric | GE | $31.93 | $29.80 | -6.7% | $(37.27) |
| Bemis | BMS | $52.16 | $48.86 | -6.3% | $(40.84) |
| Whirlpool | WHR | $183.31 | $171.33 | -6.5% | $(45.71) |
| McKesson | MCK | $157.41 | $148.26 | -5.8% | $(51.01) |
| Verizon | VZ | $54.01 | $48.75 | -9.7% | $(54.99) |
| General Mills | GIS | $64.96 | $59.01 | -9.2% | $(62.35) |
| Coca-Cola | KO | $46.83 | $42.44 | -9.4% | $(63.42) |
| Nike | NKE | $61.59 | $55.73 | -9.5% | $(84.10) |
| Campbell Soup | CPB | $65.16 | $57.34 | -12.0% | $(99.29) |
| Public Storage | PSA | $275.52 | $218.91 | -20.5% | $(177.88) |
| Kroger | KR | $38.32 | $29.42 | -23.2% | $(219.99) |
| CVS Health | CVS | $104.82 | $78.50 | -25.1% | $(234.12) |
| Macy's | M | $42.96 | $29.64 | -31.0% | $(274.67) |
| Target | TGT | $82.76 | $55.19 | -33.3% | $(304.25) |
| Novo Nordisk | NVO | $54.94 | $34.28 | -37.6% | $(355.84) |
| Perrigo | PRGO | $126.73 | $66.39 | -47.6% | $(471.47) |

* = New for 2017

Our biggest losers hit us right between the eyes in the form of Retail (Macy's, Target, Kroger) and players in the now-more-uncertain pharma industry (Perrigo, Novo Nordisk, CVS, McKesson). Other consumer-oriented firms, like General Mills, Coca-Cola, and Nike, dinged us but more likely due to overexuberance in share prices rather than real business change. At least we think so. Once again, we may have waited too long to jettison the retailers (and we retained Kroger on the list this year as we think they can sidestep the Amazon Prime thing) and we will—once again—stick with the pharma stocks, as we think the business fundamentals remain attractive and share prices are now relatively attractive too. We may cry in our beer again next year over these, but we remain committed to our "sell when there's something better to buy" mantra. In these cases, we couldn't think of anything better to buy.

Which brings us to…

## Really, It's All about Value

Those of you who take in our book every year have seen this before, but we remain steadfast in the principles of value investing.

For intelligent investors, chasing the latest fad doesn't work; buying something and locking it away forever doesn't work anymore, either. Investors must make intelligent choices based on true value and follow those choices through time and change. It all points to taking a value-oriented approach to investing and to staying modestly active with your investments.

The next obvious task is to define what we mean by a "value" approach. Essentially, it is to think of buying shares in a company as buying the company itself; it is about putting yourself in an entrepreneurial frame of mind, not just an investment frame of mind. Would you want to own that business? Why or why not?

Fundamentally, whether or not you want to own the business depends on two factors: first, the *returns* you expect to receive on your investment in the near- and long-term future, and second, the *risk* you'll take in generating those returns. Fortunately, the third factor the prospective entrepreneur must consider—"Do I have the time to run this business?"—is less of an issue for the investor.

You are looking for tangible value—tangible worth—for your precious, scarce, and hard-earned investment capital. That return can come in the form of immediate cash returns (dividends), longer-term cash returns (dividends and especially growing dividends), or as growth in the value of assets longer term. If you realize your return in the form of owning a share of a larger company eventually, that's still a legitimate return. Cash flow received later in the form of a higher share price or a takeover is still cash return; it is just less certain because of the forces of change that may take place in the interim. It is also theoretically worth less because of the nature of discounting—a dollar received tomorrow is worth more than a dollar received 20 years in the future.

The point: Many investment experts distinguish between "value" and "growth" investing; in fact, mutual funds are often classified as being one or the other. We continue to dismiss this separation; growth can be an essential component of a firm's value. That growth can come either in the form of asset values or cash returns—i.e., growing dividends.

Value also implies safety. The safety comes in three forms. First is the fundamental quality and soundness of the firm's financial fundamentals—that is, income, cash flow, and the balance sheet. Value companies have plenty of reserves, a large enough *margin of safety*, to weather downturns and unforeseen events in the marketplace. Second, they have strong enough intangibles (brands, market position, supply-chain strength, etc.) to *maintain* their position in that marketplace and generate future returns. When we say this year, as we do *every* year, that our list should fare better in a *down* market than the S&P 500 as a whole, it's these safety factors, and particularly the intangibles, that support our premise.

Third, if you're really practicing value-investing principles, you buy these companies at reduced prices, when the markets are down, when the company is out of favor. You're looking for situations where the price is less than what you perceive to be the value, although calculating the value that precisely is elusive. When you "buy cheap" you provide another margin of safety; that margin makes it less likely that the stock will drop further. It gives you room for error if you turn out to be wrong about a choice. Again, it's much like buying a business of your own—you want to pay as little as possible in case things don't turn out as you'd expect. In today's markets, admittedly it's hard to buy cheap, but many of the ten new adds for 2018 for the moment at least, appear to have value relative to the market and the other choices we could have made, although are hardly in bargain territory. Sell when there's something better to buy.

### Stay Active

What do we mean by "stay active?" Staying active means that you should remain abreast of your investment and, like any business you own, keep an eye on its performance. Periodically review the business and the stock as you would your own finances to see if it is making money and generally doing what you think it should be doing. You should keep an eye on company-related news, financials, earnings reports, and so forth—it's all part of being an individual investor and owner of companies.

Beyond that, time permitting, you should listen in on investor conference calls (usually at earnings announcements) to see what management has to say about the business. In addition, you should watch your business in the marketplace. See how many people are going to your local Starbucks and whether they are enjoying the experience, and look for other signs of excellence. See how crowded the parking lots are at Macy's and Target these days—unfortunately, not so much so as in the past, as people are truly shopping from their couches (and from work using mobile devices and so forth). We're not talking about constantly monitoring the stock price. Instead, we're suggesting an oversight of the business as though it were one you happen to own that, while professionally managed, requires an occasional glance to make sure everything is still acting according to your best interests. We also recommend a periodic review—at least annually—of whether your investments are still your best investments. Evaluate each investment against its alternatives. If you still perceive it to be the best value out there, keep it. If not, consider a swap for something new. Sell if there's something better to buy.

## The *100 Best Stocks* for 2018: A Few Comments

As we head into 2018 we expect the economy to still be growing in a generally favorable interest rate and tax environment. The Trump administration may provide a few tailwinds in the form of US manufacturing support, tax policy, and infrastructure spending, and may provide some headwinds in healthcare and other non-defense consumption industries. The jury, at this juncture, is still out. We expect a modest (emphasis on modest) recovery in energy and commodity prices as supply and demand gradually balance, a moderation or possibly a small pullback in the dollar, which will help exporters, and better news in the farm sector. We do think infrastructure spending will increase (as we did prior to the Trump administration).

Despite the enduring uncertainties, these external environmental factors should help our list achieve—and achieve better than the S&P 500 at large because we continue to tilt toward manufacturers, exporters, agriculture, and the infrastructure that supports them. We missed the boat on Financials, and may continue to, as we simply refuse to invest in companies we don't understand and that don't seem to add much real value to the economy.

But another important factor continues to play into corporate success, and thus the long-running success of the markets despite the naysayers' notion that the markets are becoming grossly overvalued. Simply put, the dire times of the Great Recession motivated most quality US companies to clean up their act and operate more efficiently. They've not only "cut the fat" but have taken a more realistic view of how and where to deploy capital— the energy industry is a good example—to produce the best returns, rather than trying to do everything. Companies are learning to "rightsize," to spin off noncongruent businesses, and to invest and invest wisely—a fact that has dragged a bit on many providers of business infrastructure like information technology products. We think both businesses and public sector spenders are reaching the end of that efficiency cycle and will start spending again, much to the aid of traditional *100 Best* entries like Oracle, GE, Itron, and Valmont and new ones such as Siemens and Applied Materials.

Still of concern is the rapid and still-uncontrolled rise in healthcare costs—and now the uncertainty created by the struggle to redefine or replace the Affordable Care Act—Obamacare. Recent data showed that almost half the jobs created since the trough of the Great Recession are in healthcare-related fields. Healthcare businesses should prosper, but healthcare also acts like a tax for the rest of us—unless we start exporting healthcare in a meaningful way (many of the companies we choose in the sector do export healthcare in the form of pharmaceutical products or healthcare technologies). Finding a balance between the escalating cost of healthcare and the drastic consequences to people who can't afford it will continue to be a challenge, and it may continue to produce some hiccups for the health insurers and providers we still carry on the list. We think (and hope) a solution is arrived at that covers the needs of our citizens while not too drastically altering the business models of our providers, but obviously some adjustments need to be made.

Another factor that has become a bit more uncertain—a variable—to consider as we move forward to commit capital to businesses (that is, buy stocks) is interest rates. Now that the Fed is in motion after eight years of unprecedented accommodation, what's next? We feel this factor will remain a non-factor, or at least in the background, so long as the Fed stays on course and continues to be "transparent." We are confident they will raise rates slowly enough so as to not knock the pins out from under our income-oriented stocks: REITs, utilities, etc.

We are very curious at exactly how far and how fast the "stay-at-home" economy will grow. We are committed to this concept especially after getting bludgeoned by Target and Macy's last year. But how big will the shift really be? Perhaps 5 percent of the population will start ordering all meals to be delivered at home (using a drone, maybe? Uber?), all at the expense of grocers and restaurants. As usual, there are early adopters, then all the rest come along at a very measured pace. We don't know where this is going or how fast it will get there, but the best companies (like the ones on our list) will adapt. That all said, we've been surprised at how fast Amazon Prime is making headway at the expense of retailers (and have climbed on board ourselves) so once again we may be underplaying this trend. Maybe it does make sense to put Domino's Pizza on the list, though the price has risen tenfold in the last ten years and doubled in the last two. I'll buy in for extra cheese and pepperoni, but I'm not sure I want to buy the stock.

All of this takes us to the usual place: We stick to companies with great business models, which have brand, marketplace, and financial strength sufficient to master the crosscurrents of change and the emergence of megatrends. We do factor in such megatrends as the couch, the cloud, the Internet of Things, the Millennial preference for experiences *over* things, the demise of paper in the workplace, the "always-on" nature of personal connectivity (and the prospect of marketers taking advantage of it), and the (for now) availability of healthcare for everyone. We've wanted to see a megatrend toward more energy wisdom; that one's been put on hold by cheap energy and new domestic energy supplies although we're still betting on it for the longer term. We continue to see a "national" economy, where large national brands gradually usurp local favorites, providing extra lift for big brands and big names like Coke and Smucker and Starbucks. (We do, however, especially with Millennials in mind, watch for localization trends in key industries like food processing; the beer industry, where local microbrews have gained significant share, provides an example.) For 2018, as ever, we look for companies with good business models, which produce high-value-add things that people (or companies) need, do it efficiently, and generate a lot of cash. Good businesses. Not just companies that make a lot of money, but good businesses with a sustainable future. We think our "core" list is still pretty good regardless of what the market does; this year the ten changes we've made take in some of the themes we've mentioned above; occasionally we switched horses where we felt it made sense. Sell when there's something better to buy. As is our custom, we'll start with the companies removed from the 2017 list:

▼ **Table 3: Companies Removed from 2017 List**

| Company | Symbol | Category | Sector |
|---|---|---|---|
| Clorox | CLX | Conservative Growth | Consumer Staples |
| Macy's | M | Aggressive Growth | Retail |
| Monsanto | MON | Aggressive Growth | Industrials |
| Patterson | PDCO | Aggressive Growth | Healthcare |
| St. Jude Medical | STJ | Aggressive Growth | Healthcare |

| Company | Symbol | Category | Sector |
|---------|--------|----------|--------|
| Target Corporation | TGT | Aggressive Growth | Retail |
| Time Warner | TWX | Conservative Growth | Entertainment |
| Verizon | VZ | Growth and Income | Telecom Services |
| Wells Fargo | WFC | Growth and Income | Financials |
| WhiteWave Foods | WWAV | Aggressive Growth | Consumer Staples |

This year's "cut" list is dominated by acquisitions; there were four this year where we typically get only one. Monsanto was acquired by Germany's Bayer AG; St. Jude Medical was acquired by Abbott Laboratories (which will circle back to our list as we added Abbott for 2018); Time Warner was acquired by AT&T (a *100 Best* stock already); and WhiteWave Foods was acquired by France's Danone. From there, we cut Macy's and Target because of dismal results and response to the e-commerce shift; in particular we were disappointed in Target's strategic response which was basically to cut prices to match online. No—wrong, 180 degrees wrong—they can't compete on price (and make any money, at least); they must compete on *experience* and *convenience* and *assortment* and *merchandising*. Though this new strategy appears to be a gaffe, we do admire Target's management and see a strong possibility that they might reverse this strategy and head in the right direction; if they do there is good opportunity for recovery. But until they do, they're off the list; that said, we're not necessarily recommending selling Target if you own it.

We cut Clorox, as we felt we had too many high-priced consumer stocks; we just lost interest in the opportunity for bleach, briquettes, and Burt's Bees. Patterson has been a laggard for years and we didn't like the headlong thrust into low-margined veterinary supplies, now more than half the business; we simply switched horses to the more dynamic and technology-based Dentsply Sirona, a purer play in the dental space. We think Verizon is strategically lost in the weeds with its acquisitions of AOL and now Yahoo!; they seem desperate to expand away from ultra-competitive mobile phone services but don't really know how to do it. We switched that horse to the relatively more growing and overseas-dominating mobile carrier Vodafone. Finally, we think Wells Fargo really laid an egg with customers (including us) with their recent scandals and general ineptitude; moreover they don't seem to be terribly contrite about any of it. They will probably recover, but financial firms, as you know, skate on thin ice with us to begin with. That horse got replaced by Prudential Financial, another same-industry switch, which we feel is well positioned with its retirement income products and especially its new corporate pension transfer products and services.

Sell when there's something better to buy. So we did that in ten cases, and here they are:

▼ **Table 4: New Companies for 2018**

| Company | Symbol | Category | Sector |
|---|---|---|---|
| Abbott Laboratories | ABT | Growth and Income | Healthcare |
| Applied Materials | AMAT | Aggressive Growth | Industrials |
| Boeing | BA | Aggressive Growth | Industrials |
| Chemed | CHE | Aggressive Growth | Healthcare |
| Dentsply Sirona | XRAY | Aggressive Growth | Healthcare |
| First Solar | FSLR | Aggressive Growth | Energy |
| Prudential | PRU | Growth and Income | Financials |
| Siemens | SIEGY | Aggressive Growth | Industrials |
| Tupperware | TUP | Aggressive Growth | Consumer Staples |
| Vodafone | VOD | Aggressive Growth | Telecom Services |

And now for the fun part—introducing our new horses for the 2018 race! We "sell when there's something better to buy" and tend to try to keep the mix of sectors relatively constant for diversification's sake and so as not to overload in any sector or industry. In some cases, like Verizon-Vodafone or Patterson-Dentsply Sirona, we switched to what we feel is a better, more strategically positioned "horse" in the same industry. As usual, we thought about Millennials (but didn't add much specifically aligned to the shift). We looked for new picks aligned to infrastructure replacement and other effects of the Trump transition. Aside from that, we continued to focus on great companies offering a great long-term value. So here goes:

Abbott Labs is the other half of the former Abbott Laboratories, an excellent company which spun off AbbVie (which we picked up last year). The Abbott half is excellent too and now includes St. Jude—it was pretty much a no-brainer. Boeing came off the list five years ago because of poor execution and business softness; neither is the case now as they have regained world leadership in commercial airliners with game-changing, more fuel-efficient products and an enormous backlog. Their defense business should also fare well under Mr. Trump. Applied Materials is coming into its own as a key supplier of semiconductor equipment just as semiconductors are becoming part of everything and are becoming less of an up-and-down, feast-or-famine business. We've started looking specifically for more promising smaller companies, and to that end Chemed is a small and little-known but interesting play in two solid and well-branded businesses in fragmented spaces: Roto-Rooter and its larger VITAS hospice care segments. First Solar is a play on really monetizing and making a profitable business out of solar energy as not only a supplier but an operator of alternative energy facilities (in the format of last year's new inclusion Ormat Technologies); we think they will prosper as more states and countries mandate that utilities buy specified amounts of alternative energy. Siemens is another infrastructure play with strong international exposure, and Tupperware is a great brand and good cash generator especially in foreign markets and may be positioned to make a comeback in the US as the stay-at-home economy advances.

As usual, we like to sum up the changes by sector after we do our picks. The sector balance is indicative at a high level of the nature of the changes we make each year. We don't like to change the sector balance too much unless there's a strong and compelling reason.

Table 5 (following) sums up this year's ten changes by sector. The biggest—and not surprising—change was the drop in Retail from eight to six companies. The addition of Boeing and Siemens (both related to infrastructure and defense) and Applied Materials (which produces semiconductor equipment), led to a net gain of three for the Industrials sector. We also added one Energy stock (First Solar). Other changes are minor or are simply replacements within the same sector. The heaviest weightings remain Consumer Staples, Healthcare, and Industrials.

▼ **Table 5: Sector Analysis and 2018 Change by Sector**
**NUMBER OF COMPANIES**

| Sector | On 2017 list | Added for 2018 | Cut from 2017 | On 2018 list |
|---|---|---|---|---|
| Business Services | 2 | | | 2 |
| Consumer Discretionary | 4 | | | 4 |
| Consumer Staples | 15 | 1 | -2 | 14 |
| Consumer Durables | 1 | | | 1 |
| Energy | 7 | 1 | | 8 |
| Entertainment | 1 | | -1 | 0 |
| Financials | 5 | 1 | -1 | 5 |

| Sector | On 2017 list | Added for 2018 | Cut from 2017 | On 2018 list |
|---|---|---|---|---|
| Healthcare | 15 | 3 | -2 | 16 |
| Heavy Construction | 0 | | | 0 |
| Industrials | 13 | 3 | -1 | 15 |
| Information Technology | 7 | | | 7 |
| Materials | 6 | | | 6 |
| Real Estate | 3 | | | 3 |
| Restaurant | 1 | | | 1 |
| Retail | 8 | | -2 | 6 |
| Telecommunications Services | 3 | 1 | -1 | 3 |
| Transportation | 6 | | | 6 |
| Utilities | 3 | | | 3 |

## Yield Signs

We continue to like dividend-paying stocks. We like stocks that pay meaningful dividends, and especially stocks that are likely to have their dividends raised over time.

With dividend-paying stocks, especially those inclined toward dividend increases, you get an attractive yield from the day you buy the stock, but you'll also get handsome raises over time. As we reported earlier, 76 of the 96 dividend-paying stocks on the 2017 *100 Best* list raised their dividends in 2016, and 41 of those have raised their dividends in each of the past ten years. We like this. We like it a lot. A company that raises its dividend 10 percent will roughly double the payout in just seven years. (Calculation? Rule of 72—divide the percent increase into 72 and you'll get the number of years it takes to double: 72/10 equals 7.2 years.) You could end up with twice the income in addition to any gains or growth in the price of the stock.

### DIVIDEND-PAYING, DIVIDEND-RAISING STOCKS—NOW AND FOREVER

The Rule of 72 and dividend-paying stocks lessons should be taken to heart by prudent investors, particularly those who fret about the effects of rising interest rates on their income-oriented investments (and who follow such fret in the financial media). When interest rates rise, bond prices fall, as the implied yield must adjust somehow; that is, a bond that generates a fixed income stream is worth relatively less in a higher interest–rate environment. Often, as we've seen, dividend-paying stocks take a tumble along with their bond brethren anytime even the rumor of rising interest rates is unsheathed. But the rising dividend provides the difference, and we feel that most of the investing world, particularly those attempting to build a comfortable retirement stream, should take note.

If you invest in a bond over a ten-year period, that bond will pay back its original principal at the end of the ten years, plus the interest as prescribed initially when the bond is sold. Nothing more, nothing less—so long as you wait ten years assuming no default—and you might not get your original principal if you decide to sell the bond sooner in a rising interest–rate environment (note that the interest payments don't go up—only that the bond value goes down).

If you invest in a dividend-paying stock with a persistent dividend raise policy and track records, as some two-thirds of the *100 Best* list represents, you enjoy the benefits of—and the protection of—the rising dividend. If your company raises its dividend 10 percent each year, the dividend will double in 7.2 years, and if it's paying 3 percent today, that implies 6 percent in 7.2 years—or a *doubling in the stock price* if the same yield is maintained (which is affected by a lot of factors besides the yield). If your company raises its dividend only 5 percent each year, it doubles in 14.4 years, but is still up roughly 70 percent in the ten-year period just described. That's still a handsome payout as well as giving solid potential for stock appreciation.

This favorable scenario simply does not exist for bonds. Bonds may be a bit safer, as the interest payments are less likely to be cut (a cut is a default) and will be paid before dividends. But when we put a stock on the *100 Best* list, we feel that not only is the dividend itself fairly secure, but so is the potential for *increase*. We should also add that most dividends receive favorable tax treatment for those of you holding investments outside of retirement accounts.

We continue to feel that investing in dividend-paying, dividend-growing stocks is the best way to save for a financially secure future.

A couple of years ago we came to the realization that we use two simple and key indicators to suggest a good stock for further analysis: (1) strong and growing yield, and (2) the persistence of share buybacks. Like that pretty face at a party, those two features suggest that we should make the effort to learn the rest of the story. We continue to focus on those healthy companies willing to not only share a portion of their profits but also to give you, the investor, a periodic raise to recognize the value of your commitment of precious investment capital. In that spirit, in our presentation format we show the number of dividend increases in the past ten years in the header right after Current Yield. We know of no other financial publication that does this.

We also present the Dividend Aggressors list in our Stars lists, which you'll see shortly. Dividend aggressors are companies with substantial payouts that are also growing those payouts at a persistent and substantial rate. They have indicated through both words and performance that they continue to do so and have the resources to do it. So it isn't enough to raise the dividend each year by just a penny; it must be substantial. It also isn't enough to raise the dividend each year but still only be yielding 0.5 percent. There are lists of "dividend achievers" floating around on the Internet, and there are even a few funds constructed around a dividend achievers index. Our Aggressors are—well—a bit more aggressive.

The climate for dividend growth continues to be favorable albeit a bit diminished from past years. Estimates call for S&P 500 dividend growth somewhere in the 6 percent range for 2017, down from 7 percent in 2015 and the 9–10 percent range for the prior two years. The slowdown is primarily due to cyclical slowdowns in the dividend-rich energy and commodity industries, which are on a cyclical low. A few have cut dividends, but many more have kept them unchanged after years of increases in some cases. On the plus side, companies are still swimming in cash ($1.5 trillion for the "500" in mid-2016)—much of which is parked overseas waiting to see what the Trump administration does with tax policy—much of this *could* turn into dividend increases or share buybacks. Appendix B shows dividend yields for all *100 Best Stocks* for 2018, which includes the number of dividend raises in the past ten years. Appendix C shows all *100 Best* companies, sorted by percentage yield, with the highest yielders at the top of the list.

## Dancing with the Stars

We continue developing and sharing our "star" categories—groups of stocks essentially the "best of the best" in categories we chose to highlight—yield stars, dividend aggressors, safety and stability stars, growth stars, prosperity stars (which we've temporarily amended to be "Trump stars"), and moat stars. We provide these stars lists because we know that every investor has his or her own preferences, and thus there are no "best" stocks within our "best" list, that is, there is no number one, two, and so on within the list.

Table 6 shows the top 20 stocks on our *100 Best* list by percentage yield as of mid-2017.

▼ **Table 6: Top 20 Dividend-Paying Stocks**

| Company | Symbol | Projected 2017 dividend | Yield % | Dividend raises, past 10 years |
|---|---|---|---|---|
| Siemens (*) | SIEGY | $5.61 | 7.8% | 8 |
| Vodafone (*) | VOD | $1.60 | 6.4% | 4 |
| Total S.A. | TOT | $2.67 | 5.3% | 7 |
| Welltower | HCN | $3.60 | 5.1% | 10 |
| AT&T | T | $1.93 | 4.6% | 10 |
| Chevron | CVX | $4.30 | 4.0% | 10 |
| CenterPoint Energy | CNP | $1.05 | 3.8% | 10 |
| Valero | VLO | $2.50 | 3.8% | 9 |
| Mosaic | MOS | $1.10 | 3.8% | 4 |
| Qualcomm | QCOM | $2.12 | 3.7% | 10 |
| Schnitzer Steel | SCHN | $0.75 | 3.6% | 3 |
| AbbVie | ABBV | $2.35 | 3.6% | 2 |
| Public Storage | PSA | $7.60 | 3.5% | 8 |
| Coca-Cola | KO | $1.42 | 3.3% | 10 |
| Daktronics | DAKT | $0.31 | 3.3% | 7 |
| Prologis | PLD | $1.70 | 3.3% | 4 |
| Novo Nordisk | NVO | $1.11 | 3.2% | 10 |
| General Mills | GIS | $1.90 | 3.2% | 10 |
| General Electric | GE | $0.94 | 3.2% | 8 |
| Paychex | PAYX | $1.80 | 3.1% | 8 |

(*) New for 2018

Table 6.1 shows our list of Dividend Aggressors for 2018:

▼ **Table 6.1: Companies with Strong Dividend Track Records**

| Company | Symbol | Estimated 2017 dividend | Yield % | Dividend raises, past 10 years |
|---|---|---|---|---|
| 3M Company | MMM | $4.51 | 2.4% | 10 |
| Abbott Laboratories (*) | ABT | $1.05 | 2.4% | 10 |
| AT&T | T | $1.93 | 4.6% | 10 |

| Company | Symbol | Estimated 2017 dividend | Yield % | Dividend raises, past 10 years |
|---|---|---|---|---|
| Boeing (*) | BA | $5.02 | 2.8% | 8 |
| CenterPoint Energy | CNP | $1.05 | 3.8% | 10 |
| Chevron | CVX | $4.30 | 4.0% | 10 |
| Cincinnati Financial | CINF | $1.94 | 2.5% | 10 |
| General Electric | GE | $0.94 | 3.2% | 8 |
| General Mills | GIS | $1.90 | 3.2% | 10 |
| Johnson & Johnson | JNJ | $2.92 | 2.3% | 10 |
| Kimberly-Clark | KMB | $3.73 | 2.8% | 10 |
| NextEra Energy | NEE | $3.59 | 2.8% | 10 |
| Paychex | PAYX | $1.80 | 3.1% | 8 |
| Prudential (*) | PRU | $2.85 | 2.7% | 9 |
| Public Storage | PSA | $7.60 | 3.5% | 8 |
| Siemens (*) | SIEGY | $5.61 | 7.8% | 8 |
| United Parcel Service | UPS | $3.17 | 3.0% | 10 |
| Valero | VLO | $2.50 | 3.8% | 9 |
| Vodafone (*) | VOD | $1.60 | 6.4% | 4 |
| Welltower | HCN | $3.60 | 5.1% | 10 |

(*) New for 2018

## REMEMBER, THERE ARE NO GUARANTEES

While dividends and especially high yields are attractive, investors must remember that corporations are under no contractual or legal obligation to pay them! Interest payments on time deposits and bonds are much more clearly defined, and failure to pay can represent default. With dividends, there is no such safety net. Companies can—and do—reduce or eliminate dividends in bad times, as most strikingly observed with BP in the wake of the Deepwater Horizon Gulf spill disaster in 2010 and most bank stocks after the 2008 dive. More recently, energy price declines have hurt many US oil producers, particularly more indebted ones engaged in the more expensive "fracking" process—and many of these players have cut or omitted dividends recently—ConocoPhillips on our 100 Best list is a current example. Phosphate/potash miner Mosaic cut theirs too. Dividend investors should there-fore keep an eye out for changes in a company's business prospects and shouldn't put too many eggs in a single high-yielding basket. On the flip side, as investors become more con-scious of returns, and as corporate management teams become more aware of such investor consciousness, we've seen a lot of companies loudly trumpet their recent dividend increases to their investors and the investing public. It's a nice sound that we hope to continue to hear.

### Safety Stars

Safety stars are companies we think will hold up well in volatile and negative stock markets as well as recessionary economies. They have stable products and customer bases, and long traditions of being able to manage well in downturns. We cut Clorox from this list because it was cut from the *100 Best* list; we replaced it with Waste Management. Several others, includ-ing the likes of Colgate-Palmolive, Coca-Cola, and Procter & Gamble from the remainder of the *100 Best* list would probably qualify.

▼ Table 7: Safety Stars: Top 10 Stocks for Safety and Stability

| Company | Symbol |
| --- | --- |
| Aqua America | WTR |
| Becton, Dickinson | BDX |
| Bemis | BMS |
| Campbell Soup | CPB |
| General Mills | GIS |
| Johnson & Johnson | JNJ |
| Kimberly-Clark | KMB |
| McCormick | MKC |
| Sysco | SYY |
| Waste Management | WM |

### Growth Stars

Looking at the other side of the coin, we picked ten stocks we feel are especially well positioned to grow, even in a negative economy and especially in a positive one. We made a couple of changes mostly to replace companies that were cut from the list or saw their growth attenuate for different but mostly temporary reasons—WhiteWave Foods (acquisition), Novo Nordisk, and Nike. We replaced them with Boeing, First Solar, and Scotts Miracle-Gro.

### ▼ Table 8: Growth Stars: Top 10 Stocks for Growth

| Company | Symbol |
| --- | --- |
| Amazon | AMZN |
| Apple | AAPL |
| Boeing | BA |
| CarMax | KMX |
| Corning | GLW |
| First Solar | FSLR |
| ResMed | RMD |
| Scotts Miracle-Gro | SMG |
| Starbucks | SBUX |
| Visa | V |

Four years ago we shifted into post–Great Recession gear, replacing our "recovery stars" list with a "prosperity stars" selection. For 2018 we'll make another temporary shift: Instead of broadbased "prosperity," we now highlight companies we think will prosper under the new Trump policies, though many of them are not firmly in place at the time of this writing. Infrastructure, defense, financial, and domestic manufacturing issues dominate this Table 9 list:

### ▼ Table 9: Prosperity Stars: Top 10 Stocks for a Growing Economy

| Company | Symbol |
| --- | --- |
| Boeing | BA |
| Caterpillar | CAT |
| General Electric | GE |
| Grainger W.W. | GWW |
| Illinois Tool Works | ITW |
| Prologis | PLD |
| Prudential | PRU |
| Schnitzer Steel | SCHN |
| Siemens | SIEGY |
| Valmont | VMI |

### Moat Stars

Finally, we get back to one of the basic tenets of value investing—the ability of a company to build a sustainable and unassailable competitive advantage. Value-investing aficionados call such an advantage a "moat," for it represents a barrier to entry for competitors that will likely preserve that advantage for some time. The moat can come in the form of technology, the use of technology, a brand, enduring customer relationships, channel relationships, size or scale, or simply a really big head start into a business that makes it hard or even impossible for competitors to catch up. The appraisal of a moat is hardly an exact science; here we give our top ten picks based on the size and strength (width?) of the moat. For 2018 we cut Monsanto due to acquisition and Stryker as we thought the new adds have wider moats. We added Boeing as we think their new products are distinctly better versus the competition and Vodafone because of their dominance in the overseas markets they serve. Once again, these are subjective picks, and good moats exist throughout our *100 Best* list.

▼ Table 10: Moat Stars: Top 10 Stocks for Sustainable Competitive Advantage

| Company | Symbol |
| --- | --- |
| Amazon | AMZN |
| Apple | AAPL |
| Boeing | BA |
| Coca-Cola | KO |
| McCormick | MKC |
| Public Storage | PSA |
| Starbucks | SBUX |
| Visa | V |
| Vodafone | VOD |
| WD-40 | WDFC |

## What Makes a Best Stock Best?

We have proclaimed that we could identify a good *100 Best* candidate on two simple features: increasing dividend and declining share counts. But these, of course, aren't the whole story: Where do we go from there? What comes next? What is it that defines excellence—*sustainable* excellence—among companies? That's been a topic of considerable debate for years, and with all the study that's gone into it, nobody has hit upon a single formula for deciphering undeniable excellence in a company. That may seem amazing at first, but when you think about it, it isn't.

That's largely because "excellence" isn't as scientific as most of us would like or expect it to be. Much like finding your "match" and life partner, it defies data and mathematical formulation. Take the square of net profits, multiply by the cosine of the debt-to-equity ratio, add the square root of the revenue-per-employee count, and what do you get? Some nice numbers, but not a clear picture of how things work together or how a company will sell its products to customers and prosper going forward. And you certainly wouldn't want to select your ideal "match" this way.

Fundamentals such as profitability, productivity, and asset efficiency tell us how well a company has done and, by proxy, how well it is managed and how successful it has been in the marketplace. Fundamentals are about what the company has already achieved and where it stands right now. If a company's current fundamentals are a mess (or your potential partner is in bankruptcy court)—stop right now; there isn't much point in going any further.

In most cases, what really separates the great from the good are the intangibles: the "soft" factors of market position, market acceptance, customer "love" of a company's products, its management, its *aura*. These features create competitive advantage, or "distinctive competence" as an economist would put it, that cannot be valued. Warren Buffett and his sidekick Charlie Munger termed these distinctive advantages as the "lollapalooza effect"—the magic or secret sauce that makes truly good businesses work as a complex *system* transcending the basic facts, figures, and resources. Most importantly, these lollapalooza factors are less about the past and more about what a company is set up to achieve in the future. When you think about it, it's the intangibles that provide the spark for most of our personal matches, too.

To paraphrase Buffett at his best: Give me $100 billion, and I could start a company; but I could never create another Coca-Cola.

What does that mean? It means that Coca-Cola has already established a worldwide brand cachet; the distribution channels, customer knowledge, and product development expertise cannot be duplicated at any cost. When companies have competitive advantages that cannot be duplicated at any cost, they have an enduring grip on their markets. They can charge more for their products. They have a moat that insulates them from competition, or makes it much more expensive for competitors to participate. They're perceived by loyal customers as having top-line products worth paying more for. They have plenty of lollapalooza.

A company with lollapalooza can control price and, in many cases, can control its costs.

## Strategic Fundamentals

Let's examine a list of strategic fundamentals that define, or keep score of, a company's success. This list can be used as a checklist, although it's hard to find a company that shows excellence in all of these areas.

### Are Gross and Operating Profit Margins Growing?

We like profitable companies; who doesn't? But what really counts is the size of the margin and especially the growth. If a company has a gross margin (sales minus cost of goods sold) exceeding that of its competitors, that shows that it's doing something right, probably with its customers and/or with its costs. But competitive analysis is elusive; there is no dependable source of "industry" gross margins, and comparing competitors can be difficult because no two companies are exactly alike; it's easy to mix apples and oranges.

We like to see what direction gross margin is moving in—up or down. A growing gross margin also signals that the company is doing something right and is gaining strength in its markets and/or its supply chain. That isn't perfect, either; as the economy moved from boom to bust, many excellent companies reported declines in gross and especially operating margins (sales minus cost of goods sold minus operating expenses) as they laid off workers and used less capacity. Still, in a steady-state environment, it makes sense to favor companies with growing margins—and more and more, we tend to do so. In a declining market, companies that can *protect* their margins will come out ahead.

### Does a Company Produce More Capital Than It Consumes?

Make no mistake about it—we like cash. Pure and simple, we also like it when a company produces more cash than it consumes.

At the end of the day, cash generation is the simplest measure of whether a company is being successful, especially over the long term. Sure, if a company buys an airplane or opens a factory or a bunch of stores in a given quarter, it will be cash-flow negative. But that should be a temporary thing; over the long haul, it should produce, not consume, cash. Companies that continually have to borrow or sell shares to raise enough cash to stay in business are on the wrong track.

So how do you determine this? You'll have to become familiar with the Statement of Cash Flows or equivalent in a company's financial reports.

"Cash flow from operations" is usually positive and represents cash booked from sales less cost of goods sold, with adjustments for noncash items like depreciation and for increases or decreases in working capital. In simple terms, is the cash going into the cash register from the daily operations of the business? Or from other sources?

"Cash used for investing purposes" or similar is a bit of a misnomer and represents net cash used to "invest" in the business—usually for capital expenditures, but also for short-term noncash investments like securities and a few other smaller items usually beyond scope. This figure is typically negative unless the company sells some part of its infrastructure. Over the long haul, cash generated from operations should well exceed cash used to invest in the business.

Companies in expansion mode may not show this surplus, and that's where "cash from financing activities" comes in. That's the cash generated from issuing debt or selling securities—or paying off debt or repurchasing shares, if things are going well—and dividends are included here as well. Again, a successful company will produce more cash—capital—from the business than it consumes, just as a successful household does the same, or else it goes into debt. Smart investors track this surplus over time.

### Are Expenses under Control?

Just like your household, company expenses should be under control, and anything else, especially without explanation, is a yellow flag.

The best way to test this is to check whether the "Selling, General, and Administrative" expenses (SG&A) are rising, and more to the point, rising faster than sales. If so, that's a yellow, not necessarily a red, flag, but if it continues, it suggests that something is out of control, and it will catch up with the company sooner or later. In a downturn, companies that are able to reduce their expenses to match revenue declines scored more points, too. Normally you won't have to dig through the financial statements for this; management usually points out its expense trends in conference calls and the "letter to shareholders" section of the annual report. It can be a little like watching children—if they're quiet on the topic, look out.

### Is Working Capital under Control?

Working capital is a hard concept to grasp—even for small entrepreneurs who live with its ups and downs on a daily basis. Insufficient working capital is one of the biggest causes of death for small businesses, and working capital and especially changes in working capital can signal success or trouble.

Using a simple analogy, working capital is the circulatory lifeblood of the business. Money comes in and money goes out, and working capital is what circulates in the veins in between. In its purest sense, it is cash, receivables, and inventory, less short-term debts. It's what you own less what you owe aside from fixed assets like plant, stores, and equipment, and long-term debt.

If receivables are increasing, that sounds like a good thing—more people owe you more money. But if receivables are rising and sales aren't, that suggests that people aren't paying their bills, or worse, the business has to finance more to achieve the same level of sales. Similarly, a rise in inventory without a rise in sales means that it costs the business more money—more working capital—to do the same amount of business. That costs twice, because unless the firm is lucky, more inventory means more obsolescence and potentially more deep-discount sales or write-offs down the road.

So a sharp investor will check to see that major working capital items—receivables and inventory—aren't growing faster than sales; indeed, a company that generates more sales with a decrease in working capital is becoming more productive.

### Is Debt in Line with Business Growth?

Like many other "fundamentals" items, you can tear your hair out looking at debt figures and trying to decide whether they're in line with asset levels, equity levels, and industry norms. A simpler test is to check and see whether long-term debt is increasing or decreasing, and in particular, whether it is increasing faster than business growth. Gold stars go to companies with little to no debt, and to companies able to grow without issuing mountains of long-term debt. It's also worth checking to make sure the company isn't simply issuing debt to buy back shares—a little of this is okay, but some companies take on expensive debt just to increase per-share earnings (and management bonuses). This isn't a good strategy; in fact, it isn't a strategy at all.

### Is Return on Equity Steady or Growing?

Return on equity (ROE) is another of those hard-to-grasp concepts, and another subjective measure when valuing assets and earnings. But at the end of the day, it's what all investors really seek: a return on their capital investments.

Like many other figures pulled from income statements and balance sheets, an ROE number, without any context, is hard to interpret. Does a 26.7 percent ROE mean, in itself, that a company is excellent? The figure sounds healthy, to be sure—it's a heck of a lot better than investing your money in a CD or T-bill. But because earnings and asset values are subjective, it may not represent true success. In fact, a company can increase ROE simply by borrowing money (yes!) and investing it into the business, even if it isn't invested as productively as other previous funds were invested. The math is complicated; we won't go into it here.

So the true test of ROE success is to check whether it is steady or increasing. Increasing—that makes sense. Why *steady*? Because if a company makes profits in a previous period and reinvests them in the business, that amount of money becomes part of equity (retained earnings). If the company reinvests productively, it will produce more returns, and ROE will at least keep up. If the company can't reinvest those earnings productively, ROE will drop—and perhaps it should be paying the earnings to you as dividends instead of investing them unproductively in the business. So if ROE is steady, the company still has good investments to make, and management is probably doing the right thing.

We should note that many investment analysts today prefer "Return on Invested Capital" (ROIC) as a metric over ROE. ROIC is return, or profit, divided by total equity *plus* debt. This gets you past the distortions that adding debt to the balance sheet might cause. Since the traditional balance sheet equation holds that "Assets = Liabilities + Capital," you can simply use total assets as the denominator—essentially the measure is "return on assets." Some analysts prefer to go farther by removing the cash balance from the asset denominator, to reflect the assets deployed and in use to generate returns and to get around the distortions of large reserve capital infusions often found at startup companies.

### Does the Company Pay a Dividend?

Different people feel differently about dividends, and as described previously, we place great emphasis on dividend-paying stocks and especially those that *grow* their dividends. After all, save for the eventual sale of the company to someone else, a dividend is the only true cash that an investor will realize from buying a stock in a corporation, other than by selling the stock. At least in theory, investors should receive some compensation for their investments once in a while.

Yet, many companies don't pay dividends or don't pay dividends that compete very effectively with fixed-income yields. Why do investors put up with this? Because, in theory anyway, a company in a good business should be able to reinvest profits more effectively than the investor can (or else why would the investor have bought the company in the first place?). Investors trust that reinvested profits will eventually bring the growth in company value that will be reflected in the share price, or eventual takeover, or an eventual payment of a dividend or, better yet, growth in that dividend.

That's the theory, anyway, but there are still lots of companies that get away with paying no dividend at all. Can we tolerate this? Yes, if a company is really doing a great job with their retained profits, like Apple before they started paying dividends four years ago, or CarMax and Itron, or, now, Amazon and First Solar. But we favor companies that offer at least something to their investors in the short term, some return on their hard-earned and faithfully committed capital. If nothing else, it keeps management teams honest and shows that management understands that shareholder interests are up there somewhere on the list of priorities. And getting an ever-*increasing* dividend—and owning a stock that has most likely appreciated because the dividend has increased—is like having your cake and eating it, too: a true favorite among investors, as noted in our previous sidebar (Dividend-Paying, Dividend-Raising Stocks—Now and Forever).

### Strategic Intangibles

When you look at any company, perhaps the bottom-line question follows the Buffett wisdom: If you had $100 billion in cool cash to spend (and we'll assume the genius intellect to spend it *well*), could you re-create that company?

If the answer is yes, it may still be a great company, but it may not be great enough to fend off competition and keep its customers forever. If the answer is no, the company truly has something unique to offer in the marketplace, difficult to duplicate at any cost. That distinctive competence, that sustainable competitive edge—whatever it is, a brand, a patent, a trade secret, a unique customer experience, a lock on distribution or supply channels—may be worth more than all the factories and high-rise office buildings and cash in the bank a company could ever have.

What we're talking about are the intangibles, the "soft" factors that make companies unique and that add up to more than the sum of their parts, the factors that ultimately drive future revenues. Intangibles not only define excellence, they define the future, while fundamentals mainly define the past. Seven key intangibles follow, although you'll think of more, and some industries may have some unique ones of their own, like intellectual property in the technology sector.

## DOES THE COMPANY HAVE A MOAT?

A business moat performs much the same role as its medieval castle equivalent—it protects the business from competition. Whatever factors create the moat, ultimately those are the factors that prevent you, with your $100 billion, from taking their business. Moats are usually a combination of brand, product technology, design, marketing and distribution channels, and customer loyalty all working together to protect a company. A moat doesn't just protect the existence of a company, it helps it command higher prices and earn higher profits.

Whether a company has a narrow moat, a wide moat, or none at all is a subjective assessment for you to make. However, you can get some help at *Morningstar* (www.morningstar.com), whose stock ratings include an assessment of the moat.

Coca-Cola has a moat because of the sheer impossibility of surpassing its brand and brand recognition worldwide. CarMax has a moat because it is farther along in putting retail-style dealerships on the ground and applying management information technologies to its business than anyone else; it would take years for a competitor to catch up. Amazon has a moat because of its immediately recognized brand, its size, and its technology leadership in delivering an industry-leading e-commerce experience. WD-40 has a moat because it's virtually the only game in town and the only recognized brand for its relatively simple product. The Moat Stars list presented earlier identifies the top ten stocks with a solid and sustainable competitive advantage.

## DOES THE COMPANY HAVE AN EXCELLENT BRAND?

It's hard to say enough about brand, especially in today's fast-moving, highly packaged, highly national and international marketplace. A strong brand means consistency and a promise to consumers, and consumers sold on a brand will prefer it over any other, almost regardless of price. People still buy Tide; Starbucks is still synonymous with high quality and ambience. Good brands command higher prices and foster loyalty, identity, and even customer "love."

Ask yourself if a company has a sought-after brand, a brand customers would pay extra to buy or align with, a brand that would be difficult to duplicate at any cost. Would customers rather fight than switch? Think about Apple, Starbucks, Coca-Cola, Allstate, Smucker's, Scotts, Southwest, or Nike, or the brands within a house, like Minute Maid (Coke), Tide

(P&G), KitchenAid (Whirlpool), iPhone (Apple), or Varathane, DAP, or Rust-Oleum (RPM International).

## IS THE COMPANY A MARKET LEADER?

Market leadership usually—but not always—goes hand in hand with brand. The trick is to decide whether a company really leads in its industry. Often—but not always—that's a factor of size. The market leader usually has the highest market share, and the important point is that it calls the shots with regard to price, technology, marketing message, etc.—other companies must play catch-up and often discount their prices to keep up. Apple is a market leader in digital music, Public Storage in self-storage units, McCormick in spices, Nike in sports apparel, and Starbucks in beverages—and so forth.

Excellent companies tend to be market leaders, and market leaders tend to be excellent companies. However, this relationship doesn't always hold true—sometimes the nimble but smaller competitor is the excellent company and *headed for* market leadership. Examples like CarMax, Valero, Columbia Sportswear, and Southwest Airlines can be found on our list.

## DOES THE COMPANY HAVE CHANNEL EXCELLENCE?

"Channels" in business parlance means a chain of players to sell and distribute a company's products. It might be stores, it might be other industrial companies, it might be direct to the consumer. If a company is considered a top supplier in a particular channel, or a company has especially good relations with its channel, that's a plus.

Excellent companies develop solid channel relationships and become the preferred supplier in those channels. Companies such as Deere, Fair Isaac, McCormick, Nike, Novo Nordisk, Procter & Gamble, Scotts Miracle-Gro, Sysco, WD-40, Visa, and Whirlpool all have excellent relationships with the channels through which they sell their product.

## DOES THE COMPANY HAVE SUPPLY-CHAIN EXCELLENCE?

Like distribution channels, excellent companies develop excellent and low-cost supply channels. They are seldom caught off guard by supply shortages and tend to get favorable and stable prices for whatever they buy. This is often not an easy assessment unless you know something about a particular industry. Fresh Del Monte, Nike, Starbucks, or Procter & Gamble again, are examples of companies that have done a good job managing their supply chains.

## DOES THE COMPANY HAVE EXCELLENT MANAGEMENT?

It's not hard to grasp what happens if a company *doesn't* have good management: Performance fails and few inside or outside the company respect the company. It's not easy for an investor to determine if a management team does a good job or acts in shareholder interests. Clues can include candor and honesty and the ability of company management to speak in accessible, easily understood terms about the company and company performance (it's worth listening to conference calls as a resource). A management team that admits errors and eschews other forms of arrogance and entitlement (i.e., luxury perks, office suites, fancy aircraft) is probably tilting its interests toward shareholders, as is the management team that can cough up some decent returns to shareholders once in a while in the form of a dividend.

This may be the most subjective and elusive assessment of all, as few investors work with these folks on a daily basis. Still, over time, you can garner a strong hunch about whether a management team is effective and on your side. We're reluctant to keep mentioning WD-40 in this section, but a trip through their website and especially their "values" page (www.wd40company.com/who-we-are/our-values/) will give you (as it gave us) comfort with their management style. Of course, be careful: It can be difficult to separate the "business B.S." from the true indicators of excellence. It becomes largely a matter of gut feel and personal assessment of what they say—again, we're back to what it takes to make that relationship "match."

## ARE THERE SIGNS OF INNOVATION EXCELLENCE?

This question seems pretty obvious, but it's not just about the products that a company sells. True, if the company is leading the industry in innovation, that's usually a good thing, for "first to market" definitely offers business advantages.

The less obvious part of this question is whether the company makes the best *use* of technology to make operations and customer interfaces as efficient and effective as possible. Southwest Airlines may have missed our list in years gone by because of the difficulty of achieving excellence in an industry where players can't control prices or costs. While airlines have enjoyed better times, we still don't like them in general—but Southwest continues to make our list today, not only because of brand and management excellence, but also innovation excellence. Why? Simply because, after all of these years, amazingly, it still has the best, simplest, easiest-to-use flight booking and check-in in the industry. Sometimes such innovations mean a lot more than bringing new, fancy products and bells and whistles to the market. You can also look to Amazon, Apple, CarMax, CenterPoint Energy, Daktronics, FedEx, Itron, Novo Nordisk, ResMed, C.H. Robinson, Starbucks, UPS, and Visa on our list for more obvious examples of companies that have deployed technology and innovative customer interfaces to achieve sustainable competitive advantage.

## Choosing the *100 Best*

With all of this in mind, just how was this year's *100 Best Stocks* list actually chosen?

The answer is more subtle than you might think. If we could give you a precise formula, you wouldn't need this book. You'd be able to do it yourself. In fact, every investor would be able to do it on his or her own. Our book would simply be the result of yet another stock screener, and every investor would invest in the same stocks. Is that a feasible or practical solution? Hardly. Everyone would scramble to buy the same 100 best stocks. The prices would be sky high, and the price of other stocks would melt to nothing.

| SIGNS OF VALUE |
| --- |
| Following are a few signs of value to look for in any company. This is not an exhaustive list by any means, but it's a good place to start: |
| » Rising dividends |
| » Declining share count |
| » Gaining market share |
| » Can control price |
| » Loyal customers |
| » Growing margins |
| » Producing, not consuming, capital (free cash flow) |
| » Steady or increasing ROE |
| » Management forthcoming, honest, understandable |

## SIGNS OF UNVALUE

» Declining margins

» No brand or who-cares brand

» Commodity producer, must compete on price

» Losing market dominance or market share

» Can't control costs

» Must acquire other companies to grow

» Management in hiding, off message, making excuses, difficult to understand, or in the news for all the wrong reasons

Fortunately or unfortunately, however you want to look at it, it isn't that simple. There are so many fundamentals, so many intangibles, and so many unknown and unknowable weighting factors to combine the fundamentals and intangibles that—well—it just wouldn't work. No screener could re-create the subtle judgment that gets applied to the cold, hard facts. It's that judgment, the interpretation of the facts and intangibles, that makes it worth spending money on a book like this.

While we didn't apply a specific formula or screener to the universe of stocks, we did take a few measurable factors into account to narrow the list from thousands to a few hundred issues. Those factors came from several sources, but at this point we must perennially tip our cap to Value Line and the research and database work they do as part of the Value Line Investment Survey. If you aren't familiar with Value Line, it's worth a look for any savvy individual investor, either online at www.valueline.com or, in many cases, at your local library. It is an excellent resource.

## When to Buy? Consider When to Sell

We've said it over and over: *Sell when there's something better to buy.*

Selling is hard. So is removing something from our *100 Best* list (unless it became part of a takeover transaction). If it's hard to figure out when to buy a stock, it's even harder to figure out when to sell. People tend to get married to their investment decisions, feeling somehow that if it isn't right, maybe time will help and things will get better. It's human nature.

Or they're just too arrogant to admit that they made a mistake. That's also human nature.

There are lots of reasons why people hold on to investments for too long a time.

Here's the fundamental truth: Buying and selling should be much the same process. Let's look at it from the point of view of selling. When should you sell? Simply, as we've said repeatedly, when there's *something else better to buy*. Something else better for future returns, something else better for safety, something else better for timeliness or fit with today's go-forward worldview; a *megatrend* as we've referred to it. That something else can be another stock, a futures contract, or a house, or any kind of investment. It can also be cash—sell that stock when...when what? When cash is a better investment. Or when you need the money, which is another way of saying that cash is a better investment—at least it's safer for the time being.

Similarly, if you think of a buy decision as a best possible deployment of capital because there's no better way to invest your money, you'll also come out ahead. It really isn't that hard, especially if you've done your homework. And it's also made easier if you avoid rash overcommitments; that is, you avoid buying all at once in case you've made a mistake or in case better prices come later down the road.

## ETFs: Different Route, Same Destination (Almost)

*The 100 Best Stocks to Buy* series continues to be about—well—the 100 best *individual companies* in which you can buy shares to build into your investment portfolio. The objective is to use these selections as a starting point to build a customized portfolio of your very own, a portfolio that earns decent, better-than-market, long-term returns from excellent companies while—because they're excellent companies—taking less risk than you would with most investments. Because you're doing it yourself, you save money on fees and expenses and come away with the pride of ownership of doing it yourself.

That said, not everyone has the time or inclination to do this this. Not everyone wants to sail through the treacherous channels of company financial information and the foggy mysteries of intangibles and marketplace performance to figure out which companies are really best to own and to keep a finger on the pulse to make sure they stay that way. You may want to own individual stocks. But just as buying a kit makes many aspects of building a new outdoor deck easier, so does buying a stock "kit": a product or package of stocks to do what you might otherwise have to struggle through on your own. If you could get such a kit product cheap enough and aligned to your needs, then why wouldn't you? It will save time, and you'll be firing up the barbecue and enjoying those outdoor parties with your friends a lot sooner. Or, perhaps at the risk of more tiring analogies, buying individual stocks is like ordering à la carte from a menu. You're not sure if what you're getting works together, so why not do a *prix fixe* to let the chef do some of the driving? Okay, enough…

Such is the impulse to find investment products—packages, *prix fixe* menus—that mimic the performance of the *100 Best* stocks. Honestly, we would *still* love it if some fund company would come to us and "buy" our index to build a fund you could buy, but that hasn't happened yet (but we as optimists never give up hope!). So in that spirit—and because we've written a lot about the merits of individual stock versus fund investing before—and because of current trends noted earlier where people are buying more passive investments and index funds—we'd like to offer this special section about using exchange-traded funds (ETFs) as a path to own portfolios crafted with many of the *100 Best Stocks* principles in mind.

### The ETF Universe

We're talking about ETFs here, not traditional mutual funds. And we're talking about ETFs built around a fairly specific index, not the S&P 500 or Russell 2000 as a broad basket. Although total traditional mutual fund assets still outweigh ETF-held assets by a factor of six to one, traditional mutual funds are more expensive and haven't performed as well as ETFs— or the market benchmarks—over time. So we will limit this discussion to ETFs, but if you're working with a professional advisor or are limited to traditional funds through your 401(k) or some other investment platform, the discussion can apply to traditional funds, too.

ETFs are packaged single securities trading on stock exchanges (rather than directly through a mutual fund company), which create a basket of securities that track the composition of specially designed indexes. With most ETFs (excluding "actively managed" ETFs) there are no fund managers making individual stock purchase or sale decisions—they are *passively managed*. The fund follows the index. It follows the good, the bad, and the ugly.

These indexes started out as broad, bland, and obvious—the first ETF, the SPDR S&P 500 ETF Trust, has tracked the S&P 500 index since 1993. Since that inception, hundreds of new indexes have been created to track everything from broad baskets of stocks to the price of certain commodities in Australian dollars. Four years ago we made an attempt to identify the indexes—and the funds built around them—that mimic *100 Best Stocks* principles.

As of early 2017, there are about 2,000 exchange-traded products traded in North America, of which about 1,800 are ETFs and 200 are so-called "exchange-traded notes," or ETNs, which are actually fixed-income securities adjusted in value to track an index without actually owning the components of the index. Growth in the ETF space has slowed as recently some funds have closed due to the lack of interest; the total number has stayed relatively constant over the past three years. Total assets were about $2.5 trillion, or 13 percent of the total "fund" market at the end of 2016. There are generalized and specialized ETFs covering stocks, bonds, fixed-income investments, commodities, real estate, currencies, and the so-called "leveraged and inverse" funds designed to achieve specialized investing objectives. Within each of those groups, the segments available could fill a chapter in and of themselves with divisions by market cap, style (growth versus value), industry, sector, strategy, country, and region—just to name a few.

### ETF Advantages

There are numerous advantages of ETFs over traditional funds—reasons why they are "where the puck is going" in packaged investments:

- *Easy to research.* ETFs are relatively easy to understand and easy to screen using commonly found screening tools at online brokers.
- *Transparency.* It's easy to learn what individual stocks an ETF owns and what comprises the underlying index, both through the online portals and through the index providers' websites. (Want to know what's in the Focus Morningstar Health Care Index? Just put the index name into a search engine, and you'll find out.)
- *Low fees, low cost.* Fees typically range from 0.1 percent for the most generic index funds to 0.2–0.8 percent for more specialized funds—about half of the typical figures found in traditional mutual funds. One fund provider—Vanguard—has traditionally been the lowest-cost provider in this regard—although Charles Schwab recently introduced a series of broad index ETFs with annual fees in the 0.03–0.06 percent range. We expect others will follow.
- *Easy to buy and sell.* It's like buying and selling an ordinary stock.
- *Easy to match your objectives and style.* New funds are showing up every day, and many match a quality, low-volatility, value-oriented style we're aligned with.

▶ Table 11: *100 Best Stocks*—ETF "Imitators"

**ETFS WITH STRONG "100 BEST" COMPOSITION AND STRATEGIES, PERFORMANCE 2016–2017**

| ETF | Symbol | Sponsor | Total assets | Expense ratio (%) | Price 4.1.2016 | Price 4.1.2017 | % gain share value | 2016-7 dividend | Yield % | Total return | What attracted us |
|---|---|---|---|---|---|---|---|---|---|---|---|
| Market Vectors Wide Moat ETF | MOAT | Van Eck | $1.1B | 0.49% | $32.34 | $38.30 | 18.4% | $0.41 | 1.3% | 19.7% | Compelling strategy |
| Powershares Buyback Achievers Portfolio | PKW | Invesco | $1.32B | 0.63% | $45.66 | $52.17 | 14.3% | $0.68 | 1.5% | 15.7% | Compelling strategy |
| iShares Dow Jones Select Dividend Index Fund | DVY | Blackrock | $16.7B | 0.39% | $82.04 | $91.50 | 11.5% | $2.76 | 3.4% | 14.9% | Growth plus income, lots of 100 Best Stocks |
| Powershares S&P 500 Low Volatility Portfolio | SPLV | Invesco | $6.6B | 0.25% | $39.04 | $43.84 | 12.3% | $0.94 | 2.4% | 14.7% | Low volatility focus, lots of 100 Best Stocks |
| First Trust Morningstar Dividend Leaders Index Fund | FLD | First Trust | $1.7B | 0.45% | $25.70 | $28.50 | 10.9% | $0.86 | 3.3% | 14.2% | Lots of 100 Best Stocks |
| 100 Best Stocks 2017 Portfolio | | | | | | | | | | **14.2%** | |
| Powershare S&P 500 High Quality Portfolio | SPHQ | Invesco | $1.2B | 0.29% | $24.70 | $27.61 | 11.8% | $0.45 | 1.8% | 13.6% | Growth and stability of dividends, lots of 100 Best Stocks |
| iShares MSCI USA Minimum Volatility Index Fund | USMV | Blackrock | $12.8B | 0.15% | $43.77 | $48.39 | 10.6% | $1.00 | 2.3% | 12.8% | Low volatility focus, lots of 100 Best Stocks |
| Spdr S&P Dividend ETF | SDY | State Street Corp | $15.1B | 0.35% | $80.69 | $88.66 | 9.9% | $2.03 | 2.5% | 12.4% | Diverse portfolio, "Dividend Aristocrats" index |

### *Dining with the* 100 Best: *A Special ETF Menu*

Our *100 Best Stocks* list doesn't really follow any investment style. It isn't just growth or value. It isn't just large cap, it isn't just high yield, nor is it just tied to certain industries or sectors of the economy. It is a blend of excellent companies in the right businesses, doing well in those businesses, with a potential for strong, steady, and growing investor returns. There is no index or any other screenable classification to select those companies. If there were, there'd be little reason to publish this book.

So as we search for ETFs that run with the same tailwinds as our *100 Best* list, we start with the name of the fund and the index that the fund follows. "Dividend Achievers" or "Buyback Achievers" tells us we're looking on the right part of the menu. Then we dig in and look at the actual portfolio composition (again, most investing portals and brokerage sites let you do this—we use Fidelity [www.fidelity.com]). If we see lots of *100 Best* stocks on the list, it confirms that we're on the right track.

Four years ago we selected eight ETFs that we thought most closely followed our *100 Best* style and principles, and could be used to build or supplement parts of your portfolio. We share the list in Table 11, and in the typical spirit of our presentations, we show the performance of these eight funds during our measurement period.

Like our overall performance, our 2017 performance against benchmark ETFs, strictly speaking, was middle-of-the-road. But looking more closely, the only two funds that really "beat" us were the more strategically focused "wide moat" and, more modestly, the "buyback achievers" ETFs; the more broadly based *100 Best* imitators finished almost in a dead heat—or worse.   Selecting ETFs is an art in itself and was covered in a now-dated but still relevant earlier book we did in this series called *The 100 Best ETFs You Can Buy 2012*. Unfortunately that book didn't find a large enough market to be updated each year, but it is still useful in its original form and is still available. There are many other ETF resources, again at your online broker or through a specialized ETF portal called ETFdb (www.etfdb.com). This portal and its classification page (www.etfdb.com/types) can be helpful in finding individual ETFs that suit your taste.

We'll leave the ETF discussion here for this year; the good news continues to be that you can invest in ETFs and still follow the *100 Best* style.

# Part II

# THE 100 BEST STOCKS TO BUY

Finally, it's post time. Let the trumpet fanfare announce the *The 100 Best Stocks to Buy in 2018* as they approach the starting gate...

## Index of Stocks by Company Name (*New for 2018)

| Company | Symbol | Category | Sector |
| --- | --- | --- | --- |
| 3M | MMM | Conservative Growth | Industrials |
| **—A—** | | | |
| *Abbott Laboratories | ABT | Growth and Income | Healthcare |
| AbbVie | ABBV | Aggressive Growth | Healthcare |
| Aetna | AET | Conservative Growth | Healthcare |
| Allstate | ALL | Conservative Growth | Financials |
| Amazon | AMZN | Aggressive Growth | Retail |
| Apple | AAPL | Aggressive Growth | Consumer Discretionary |
| *Applied Materials | AMAT | Aggressive Growth | Industrials |
| Aqua America | WTR | Growth and Income | Utilities |
| Archer Daniels Midland | ADM | Conservative Growth | Consumer Staples |
| AT&T | T | Growth and Income | Telecommunications Services |
| **—B—** | | | |
| Becton, Dickinson | BDX | Conservative Growth | Healthcare |
| Bemis | BMS | Conservative Growth | Consumer Staples |
| *Boeing | BA | Aggressive Growth | Industrials |
| **—C—** | | | |
| Campbell Soup | CPB | Conservative Growth | Consumer Staples |
| CarMax | KMX | Aggressive Growth | Retail |
| Carnival Corporation | CCL | Aggressive Growth | Consumer Discretionary |
| CenterPoint Energy | CNP | Growth and Income | Utilities |
| *Chemed | CHE | Aggressive Growth | Healthcare |
| Chevron | CVX | Growth and Income | Energy |
| Cincinnati Financial | CINF | Growth and Income | Financials |
| Coca-Cola | KO | Conservative Growth | Consumer Discretionary |
| Colgate-Palmolive | CL | Conservative Growth | Consumer Staples |
| Columbia Sportswear | COLM | Aggressive Growth | Consumer Staples |
| Comcast | CMCSA | Aggressive Growth | Telecommunications Services |
| ConocoPhillips | COP | Growth and Income | Energy |
| Corning | GLW | Aggressive Growth | Information Technology |
| Costco Wholesale | COST | Aggressive Growth | Retail |
| CVS Health | CVS | Conservative Growth | Retail |

## Index of Stocks by Company Name (continued)

## Index of Stocks by Company Name (continued)

| Company | Symbol | Category | Sector |
|---|---|---|---|
| **—M—** | | | |
| McCormick | MKC | Conservative Growth | Consumer Staples |
| McKesson | MCK | Conservative Growth | Healthcare |
| Medtronic | MDT | Aggressive Growth | Healthcare |
| Microchip Technology | MCHP | Aggressive Growth | Information Technology |
| Mosaic | MOS | Aggressive Growth | Materials |
| **—N—** | | | |
| NextEra Energy | NEE | Growth and Income | Utilities |
| Nike | NKE | Aggressive Growth | Consumer Discretionary |
| Norfolk Southern | NSC | Conservative Growth | Transportation |
| Novo Nordisk | NVO | Aggressive Growth | Healthcare |
| **—O—** | | | |
| Oracle | ORCL | Aggressive Growth | Information Technology |
| Ormat Technologies | ORA | Aggressive Growth | Energy |
| Otter Tail | OTTR | Growth and Income | Energy |
| **—P—** | | | |
| Paychex | PAYX | Aggressive Growth | Information Technology |
| Perrigo | PRGO | Aggressive Growth | Healthcare |
| Praxair | PX | Conservative Growth | Materials |
| Procter & Gamble | PG | Conservative Growth | Consumer Staples |
| Prologis | PLD | Growth and Income | Real Estate |
| *Prudential | PRU | Growth and Income | Financials |
| Public Storage | PSA | Growth and Income | Real Estate |
| **—Q—** | | | |
| Qualcomm | QCOM | Aggressive Growth | Information Technology |
| Quest Diagnostics | DGX | Aggressive Growth | Healthcare |
| **—R—** | | | |
| ResMed | RMD | Aggressive Growth | Healthcare |
| C.H. Robinson | CHRW | Aggressive Growth | Transportation |
| Ross Stores | ROST | Aggressive Growth | Retail |
| RPM International | RPM | Aggressive Growth | Materials |

## Index of Stocks by Company Name (continued)

CONSERVATIVE GROWTH

# 3M Company

Ticker symbol: MMM (NYSE) ❏ Large Cap ❏ Value Line financial strength rating: A++ ❏ Current yield: 2.4% ❏ Dividend raises, past 10 years: 10

## Company Profile

The 3M Company, originally known as the Minnesota Mining and Manu-facturing Co., is a $30 billion diversified manufacturing technology com-pany with leading positions in industrial, consumer and office, healthcare, safety, electronics, telecommunications, and other markets. The company has 81 manufacturing operations in 29 US states, and in total 132 manu-facturing operations in more than 36 countries. It serves customers in nearly 200 countries; 59.5 percent of the company's sales are international. 3M also operates 37 laboratories worldwide and spends about 5.8 percent of reve-nues on R&D. Due to the breadth of their product line and the global reach of their distribution, the company has long been viewed as a bellwether for the overall health of the world economy.

3M's operations are divided into five business segments (approximate revenue percentages in parentheses):

- The Industrial business (34 percent of 2016 sales) serves a variety of vertical markets, including automotive, automotive aftermarket, elec-tronics, paper and packaging, appliance, food and beverage, and con-struction. Products include industrial tapes, a wide variety of abrasives, adhesives, specialty materials, filtration products, closures, advanced ceramics, automotive insulation, filler and paint system components, and products for the separation of fluids and gases.
- The Safety and Graphics business (19 percent) serves a broad range of markets that increase the safety, security, and productivity of workers, facilities, and systems. Major product offerings include personal protec-tion, like respirators and filtering systems, safety and security products such as reflectorized fabrics and tapes, energy control products, traffic control products including reflective sheeting for highway signs, build-ing cleaning and protection products, track and trace solutions, and roofing granules for asphalt shingles.
- The Healthcare business (18 percent) serves markets that include medical clinics and hospitals, pharmaceuticals, dental and orthodon-tic practitioners, and health information systems. Products and services

include medical and surgical supplies, skin health and infection prevention products, drug-delivery systems, dental and orthodontic products, health information systems, and antimicrobial solutions. The Healthcare business is the most profitable, with operating margins of 31.7 percent versus margins in the low 20s for the other four businesses.

■ The Electronics and Energy segment (16 percent) serves the electrical, electronics, communications, and renewable energy industries, including electric utilities. Products include electronic and interconnect solutions, microinterconnect systems, high-performance fluids and abrasives for semiconductor and disk drive manufacture, high-temperature and display tapes, telecommunications products, electrical products, and optical film materials that support LCD displays and touch screens for monitors, tablets, mobile phones, and other products.

■ The Consumer segment (15 percent) serves markets that include retail, home improvement, building maintenance, office, and other markets. Products in this segment include office supply products such as the familiar Scotch tapes, Post-it notes, Scotch-Brite cleaning abrasives, stationery products, construction and home improvement products, home-care products, protective material products, and consumer healthcare products. This segment grew considerably with the 2012 acquisition of the Avery Dennison office products line.

Near-term strategies include streamlining the organization structure, combining 40 businesses into 26, a more general cost containment effort, and a greater emphasis on leveraging and promoting the brand across all businesses. The company has adjusted its portfolio once again with several small acquisitions and divestitures. The cost containment ("transformation" in company lingo) is intended to save $600–$700 million in costs and $500 million in working capital by 2020. A new $150 million laboratory opened in 2016 in St. Paul will help "strengthen the scientific edge." It appears that continued small acquisitions and an emphasis on fast-track R&D will continue to be themes going forward.

## Financial Highlights, Fiscal Year 2016

The usual crosscurrent of upsides including innovations, small acquisitions, and focus on higher-margined businesses swirled with the downsides of currency, emerging market headwinds, and the downshift in the energy industry; revenues dropped for the third year in a row but only 0.5 percent (0.1 percent in constant currency). Moderate gains in Safety and Graphics,

Healthcare, and Consumer segments were more than offset by a decline in the Electronics and Energy segment. Likewise, from a geographic perspective Asia-Pacific was a drag on revenues. Earnings, however, advanced on an improved business mix and cost containments by 5 percent, and per-share earnings advanced almost 8 percent aided by a 2 percent share buyback. The outlook for FY2017 and FY2018 is rosier with moderate organic revenue growth in the 1–4 percent range depending on currency effects. Margin improvements and continued share buybacks should keep per-share earnings moving forward in the 6–10 percent range annually. 3M continues to reward shareholders, with an 8 percent dividend raise and a 2 percent share buyback; the company has retired 16 percent of its float since 2011.

## Reasons to Buy

For years, 3M has served as a classic example of a "conservative growth" stock, and is a classic exercise in brand excellence, marketplace and niche strength, and steady performance. The company makes and distributes many repeat-sale products essential to manufacturing and day-to-day operations of other companies and organizations and seemingly essential to most of us, e.g., Post-it notes and Scotch tape. The company appears to do better than the markets during strong periods and also holds value better than most during downturns. There is a persistent focus on innovation here, both in its products and in its internal operations and marketing—and it's more the slow, steady variety than a flash in the pan. Pro-US manufacturing policies from the Trump administration could boost domestic businesses. Cash flows are strong and growing, and continue to be shared liberally with shareholders.

## Reasons for Caution

3M is, and always will be, vulnerable to economic cycles, but in general the business holds up pretty well in down cycles. There's plenty of pressure from the investment community to get the top line moving forward, and we worry that 3M could go on a larger acquisition rampage to boost growth, but so far we have been comfortable with the types of acquisitions the company has made. Further, profit growth has been good for such a large company, so why the angst about revenue growth? Shares have been pretty pricey recently, but we still think there's value here—once again we suggest placing a Post-it on this page to pick up a few shares when the price is right.

SECTOR: **Industrials** ❑ BETA COEFFICIENT: **1.08** ❑ 10-YEAR COMPOUND EARNINGS PER-SHARE GROWTH: **7.0%** ❑ 10-YEAR COMPOUND DIVIDENDS PER-SHARE GROWTH: **8.5%**

|  | 2009 | 2010 | 2011 | 2012 | 2013 | 2014 | 2015 | 2016 |
|---|---|---|---|---|---|---|---|---|
| Revenues (mil) | 23,123 | 26,662 | 29,611 | 29,904 | 30,871 | 31,821 | 30,274 | 30,109 |
| Net income (mil) | 3,193 | 4,169 | 4,283 | 4,445 | 4,659 | 4,956 | 4,833 | 5,050 |
| Earnings per share | 4.52 | 5.75 | 5.96 | 6.32 | 6.72 | 7.49 | 7.58 | 8.16 |
| Dividends per share | 2.04 | 2.10 | 2.20 | 2.36 | 2.54 | 3.42 | 4.10 | 4.44 |
| Cash flow per share | 6.15 | 7.43 | 7.85 | 8.35 | 9.09 | 10.02 | 10.29 | 10.93 |
| Price:  high | 84.3 | 91.5 | 98.2 | 95.5 | 140.4 | 168.2 | 170.5 | 182.3 |
| low | 40.9 | 68.0 | 68.6 | 82.0 | 94.0 | 123.6 | 124.0 | 134.6 |

Website: www.3m.com

## GROWTH AND INCOME

NEW FOR 2018

# Abbott Laboratories

Ticker symbol: ABT (NYSE) ❑ Large Cap ❑ Value Line financial strength rating: A++ ❑ Current yield: 2.4% ❑ Dividend raises, past 10 years: 10

## Company Profile

When "change" is the word of the day with one of our *100 Best* stocks, sometimes we sit out to watch the change(s) unfold before reconfirming a company's position on the *100 Best* list. Such is the case with Abbott Laboratories, a longtime stalwart, which has undergone major changes starting in 2012. In that year, it split itself in two, spinning off their research pharmaceutical firm known as AbbVie, which found its way back onto our list last year. The remaining healthcare products maker and distributor Abbott Labs, which kept the original company name, was about to make it back onto our list anyway as we thought the changes were settling out the right way. Then in 2016 Abbott announced the acquisition of cardiovascular, neuromodulation, and diabetes device maker St. Jude Medical Inc.—also a long-term *100 Best* member—making the re-inclusion decision pretty easy as we were looking for a St. Jude replacement anyway. So here we are: welcome back, Abbott Labs, to the *100 Best Stocks* list.

Abbott Labs is a leader in medicines, health diagnostics, nutrition, and cardiovascular products. Prior to the St. Jude acquisition, the company consisted of four major businesses:

■ Established Pharmaceuticals (19 percent of 2016 revenue, 16 percent of operating profit) contains a portfolio of over 1,500 established and mostly generic prescription products including flu vaccines, hormone replacements, enzyme replacements, antibiotics, and other routine remedies for common ailments (in contrast to expensive, "sexy" treatments for rare diseases). This group is particularly strong in emerging markets.

■ Nutritional Products (33 percent of revenue, 36 percent of profit) makes and markets a portfolio of baby formulas under the "Similac" brand and an assortment of nutritional supplements targeted to adults (Ensure and Glucerna are major brands), electrolyte replenishment, and other nutritional products and supplements. The company claims a number one market position in adult and pediatric nutritionals.

■ Diagnostic Products (23 percent of revenue, 26 percent of profit) makes and markets a broad line of diagnostic systems and tests for blood banks, hospitals, commercial labs, and alternate-care testing sites—this group holds a number one position in standard and advanced blood chemistry testing and monitoring. One exciting new product is the "FreeStyle Libre," a continuous electronic glucose monitoring system that eliminates finger pricks. This new product made the *Popular Science* "Best of What's New" list for 2016.

■ Vascular Products (14 percent of revenue, 23 percent of profit) is a line of coronary, endovascular, structural heart, and other physical and electronic products. This group will likely house most of the St. Jude acquisition. A new "Absorb" bioabsorbable stent was approved for sale in the US and Canada.

A fifth division of revenue ("Other") accounts for 11 percent of revenue and 0 percent of profits currently. Abbott products are sold in about 150 countries, and 42 percent of current sales occur in emerging markets.

The acquisition of St. Jude brings an assortment of structural heart repair devices, including heart valve repair and replacement technologies, heart failure remedies, cardiac rhythm management devices, cardiovascular care devices including imaging devices and stents, and neuromodulation devices to manage chronic pain and movement disorders. The St. Jude acquisition makes Abbott a number one or number two supplier into these important high-growth markets.

## Financial Highlights, Fiscal Year 2016

Global FY2016 sales rose 2.2 percent, a figure that would have been close to 5 percent without currency effects, and would also have been higher without the recent slowdowns in emerging markets. Net income rose a modest 1 percent. The numbers are hard to compare looking backward or forward, with the AbbVie split, a 2015 sale of some generic pharmaceuticals businesses to Mylan (N.V., Netherlands), and the St. Jude acquisition and others. Going forward the company projects a 25–27 percent revenue gain—almost all of it St. Jude, and a similar gain in net income. It's worth noting that per-share earnings are expected to rise 10–12 percent, significant as share counts will rise to fund the acquisition.

The company raised its dividend 7 percent in FY2016 for a 45th consecutive year of dividend increases (not counting the drop when AbbVie split off). The share count will increase about 15 percent with the St. Jude acquisition but we expect it to drop 1–2 percent annually thereafter.

## Reasons to Buy

Abbott is an established leader in important, stable, and mostly recurring healthcare markets and needs. Most of the product portfolio to date consists of products and diagnostics used over and over, including blood tests, diabetes remedies, and nutritional products. We like that position.

The St. Jude acquisition brings Abbott to a leadership position in key cardiovascular markets, a good position with today's demographics and a relatively higher-margined business. Abbott's net margins had been tracking in the 15–16 percent range; with the St. Jude acquisition, net margins in the 17–18 percent range are more likely. While the St. Jude acquisition and others will cause some pain, the "gain" lies in the greater dominance and profitability in its key markets.

## Reasons for Caution

Abbott operates with a solid business base but has been heavily involved in acquisitions since its 2012 split with AbbVie. While much of it makes sense from a strategic standpoint, it is disruptive and carries some risks—for example, in early 2016 the company made an agreement to acquire diagnostic device and service provider Alere, a deal that has gone sour and into litigation due to adverse developments since the acquisition announcement. The $23.6 billion acquisition price for St. Jude may have been too high (for a company with $6 billion in annual revenue) and will create some goodwill write-offs down the road. We don't see too many risks with the core businesses, but a company this active in the acquisition markets bears watching. That said, we expect this activity to subside somewhat as Abbott settles into its desired market position in the wake of the 2012 split. It's also worth mentioning the relative difficulty in evaluating Abbott's numbers with the large changes taking place in the past five years.

SECTOR: **Healthcare** ❏ BETA COEFFICIENT: **1.41** ❏ 10-YEAR COMPOUND EARNINGS PER-SHARE GROWTH: **NM** ❏ 10-YEAR COMPOUND DIVIDENDS PER-SHARE GROWTH: **NM**

|  | 2009 | 2010 | 2011 | 2012 | 2013 | 2014 | 2015 | 2016 |
|---|---|---|---|---|---|---|---|---|
| Revenues (bil) | 30.8 | 35.2 | 38.9 | 39.9 | 21.9 | 22.3 | 20.4 | 20.9 |
| Net income (bil) | 5.8 | 6.5 | 7.3 | 8.2 | 3.2 | 3.5 | 3.3 | 3.3 |
| Earnings per share | 3.72 | 4.17 | 4.66 | 4.99 | 2.01 | 2.28 | 2.15 | 2.20 |
| Dividends per share | 1.60 | 1.75 | 1.88 | 2.01 | 0.56 | 0.88 | 0.96 | 1.04 |
| Cash flow per share | 5.09 | 5.90 | 6.61 | 6.91 | 3.17 | 3.35 | 3.21 | 3.20 |
| Price:        high | 57.4 | 56.8 | 56.4 | 72.5 | 38.6 | 46.5 | 51.7 | 45.8 |
|               low | 41.3 | 44.6 | 45.1 | 54.0 | 31.6 | 35.7 | 39.0 | 36.0 |

Note: Figures before 2013 are for the combined company. See AbbVie, another *100 Best* stock.

Website: www.abbott.com

**AGGRESSIVE GROWTH**

# AbbVie Inc.

Ticker symbol: ABBV (NYSE) ❏ Large Cap ❏ Value Line financial strength rating: A ❏ Current yield: 3.9% ❏ Dividend raises, past 10 years: 3

## Company Profile

Spun off from the former combined Abbott Laboratories in 2013, AbbVie is a leading research-based biopharmaceutical company specializing in developing and marketing treatments and therapies for a range of complex diseases. The former Abbott was a perennial *100 Best Stock* but we wanted to give some time for the strategy and outcome of the split to become clear. The other half of the split, still called Abbott Laboratories, specializes mainly in making and distributing a line of medical supplies. AbbVie's products help treat conditions, such as chronic autoimmune diseases, in rheumatology, gastroenterology, and dermatology; oncology, including blood cancers; virology, including hepatitis C virus (HCV) and human immunodeficiency virus (HIV); neurological disorders, such as Parkinson's disease and multiple sclerosis; metabolic diseases, including thyroid disease and complications associated with cystic fibrosis, as well as other serious health conditions. AbbVie also has a pipeline of new medicines, including over 50 compounds or indications (20 in late-stage development), such as immunology, virology/liver disease, oncology, neurological diseases, and women's health. Its product portfolio includes Humira, Imbruvica, HCV products, additional virology products, metabolics/hormones products, endocrinology products, and other products.

Accounting for 63 percent of FY2016 sales and holding the title as highest-grossing drug in the world at $16.1 billion in annual sales, Humira is by far AbbVie's largest product—really, it's a franchise. As an immunological agent initially developed to treat rheumatoid arthritis, the company (and the FDA) have found it quite useful for treating other immunological diseases such as psoriasis, psoriatic arthritis, and a number of other diseases in the rheumatology, gastroenterology, and dermatology space. The patent for the "composition of matter" expired at the end of 2016—and normally with 63 percent of the business this would be a huge red flag—but the company has an extensive "patent estate" of several dozen patents for the product covering other uses, formulations, manufacturing processes, and other patents extending well into the next decade. By 2020 the company expects Humira to account for about 50 percent of sales and a large share of profits.

Other major emerging drug platforms include Imbruvica, a hematology (blood oncology) and HCV drug acquired through the 2015 acquisition of Pharmacyclics which is projected to reach 13 percent of sales by 2020, Viekira for Hepatitis C (8 percent by 2020), and the just-approved Duopa for Parkinson's disease (3 percent by 2020). As exemplified by the Humira platform, the company continually looks for ways to extend existing and modified formulations into additional disease categories with new delivery and dosage models added in where feasible (Duopa uses an implant to provide more steady levels of dopamine for advanced Parkinson's patients, for example).

More recently, the company acquired German drug maker Boehringer Ingelheim and a line of monoclonal antibodies known as risankizumab, again for immunology, and also completed the larger $5.8 billion acquisition of oncology drug maker Stemcentrx in mid-2016 to strengthen its oncology offerings using stem cell biotechnologies to address solid tumors. The company markets its products in 170 countries; about 38 percent of sales are overseas.

## Financial Highlights, Fiscal Year 2016

Making the most of its existing and new platforms, AbbVie has emerged in three short years to produce some of the best results among its research pharma peers. In part driven by acquisitions, FY2016 revenues advanced 12 percent, a figure that would have been 1.3 percent higher without currency effects. Operating margins dropped a bit due to currency and acquisition costs after a full 6 percent advance in FY2015 to end up at a still very healthy 44.2 percent, but with higher volumes and scale, net profits advanced 12 percent over 2015. Per-share cash flows advanced 13 percent supporting a 12 percent dividend increase; the dividend is up 42 percent since the company split from Abbott in 2013.

A healthy combination of organic growth and acquisitions will keep revenues rising at about a 9–12 percent clip through 2018, with per-share earnings exceeding that pace into a 13–17 percent growth range.

## Reasons to Buy

Research pharma companies are quite often too complex for our simple minds and tastes, so we take on this sector with great care, as we also did with diabetes drug specialist Novo Nordisk a couple of years back. Here, we find a bit more complexity since yes, as stated, AbbVie specializes in the treatment of complex and advanced diseases. We won't pretend to understand how its products actually work.

What we do like and think we understand is the underlying business strategy. AbbVie focuses on a few key drug platforms like Humira and Imbruvica, making the most of them while offering extendable solutions for other complex oncological, immunological, and neurological indications as well. While it's unfortunate that there are so many of these complex diseases around to treat, we like AbbVie's focus on this relatively more profitable, defensible end of the market.

The financial track record speaks for itself—any company with a 30 percent–plus net profit margin that shares its success with its shareholders comes as pretty good medicine for us.

## Reasons for Caution

Complexity is probably our number one issue—this company could fail miserably in one or more of its markets and we laymen would probably be none the wiser. The dependence on Humira naturally raises the specter of patent expirations, from which the company appears to position itself quite well to minimize the potential damage. As the policies of the Trump administration unfold, there is some concern about efforts to reduce drug prices, which would hurt AbbVie and others in the group. Finally, we do worry a bit about the growth-by-acquisition tendencies, though we do think acquisitions so far make sense and are done *on top of* a pretty sound and successful business.

SECTOR: **Healthcare** ◻ BETA COEFFICIENT: **1.54** ◻ 10-YEAR COMPOUND EARNINGS PER-SHARE
GROWTH: **NM** ◻ 10-YEAR COMPOUND DIVIDENDS PER-SHARE GROWTH: **NM**

|  | 2009 | 2010 | 2011 | 2012 | 2013 | 2014 | 2015 | 2016 |
|---|---|---|---|---|---|---|---|---|
| Revenues (mil) | — | — | — | — | 18,790 | 19,960 | 22,839 | 25,638 |
| Net income (mil) | — | — | — | — | 5,066 | 5,375 | 7,060 | 7,904 |
| Earnings per share | — | — | — | — | 3.14 | 3.32 | 4.29 | 4.82 |
| Dividends per share | — | — | — | — | 1.60 | 1.66 | 2.02 | 2.28 |
| Cash flow per share | — | — | — | — | 3.44 | 3.62 | 4.64 | 5.23 |
| Price:        high | — | — | — | — | 54.8 | 70.8 | 71.2 | 68.1 |
|               low | — | — | — | — | 33.3 | 45.5 | 45.4 | 50.7 |

Website: www.abbvie.com

## CONSERVATIVE GROWTH

# Aetna Inc.

Ticker symbol: AET (NYSE) ◻ Large Cap ◻ Value Line financial strength rating: A ◻ Current yield: 1.5% ◻ Dividend raises, past 10 years: 6

## Company Profile

Founded in 1853, Aetna is one of the nation's longest-lived insurers and a leading provider of health insurance benefits. The company's three distinct businesses are operated in three divisions. Healthcare provides a full assortment of health benefit plans for corporate, small business, and individual customers, including PPO, HMO, point-of-service, vision care, dental, behavioral health, Medicare/Medicaid, and pharmacy benefits plans. The Group Insurance business provides group term life, disability, and accidental death and dismemberment insurance products primarily to the same sort of businesses that might sign up for its health plans. The Large Case Pensions business administers pension plans for certain existing customers.

The Healthcare business is by far the largest segment and the focal point of our selection of this company. The business touches some 47 million individuals; of $63 billion in 2016 revenues, about 46 percent is Commercial (about two-thirds of that is Large Groups, one-third is Small Groups and Individuals); 43 percent is Government (including Medicare Advantage and Medicaid); the remainder is fees, investment income, and other small contributors. Driven in part by the Affordable Care Act, the Government segment has risen rapidly from 22 percent since 2010.

Aetna has proven itself to be a pacesetter among insurance providers, mainly through its support and innovations in the area of consumer-directed healthcare and preventative medicine. For example, Aetna has led the industry in developing tools, such as the Aetna Navigator price transparency tool designed to help patients evaluate the cost and outcomes of procedures in different geographies. The company also has championed patient- and doctor-accessible medical records and other techniques for making healthcare delivery more efficient—as they put it, "Industry-leading use of patient data and new connections [to help] you play a greater, more informed role in your own health." The company estimates that now 60 percent of patients want to "take charge" of their care, and 80 percent believe that "consumerism in healthcare is good for Americans."

Aetna is a big believer in the use of analytics—using a "big data" approach to predict the types of medical conditions their covered clients are likely to encounter in the coming years based on correlations among contributing factors in their large data pool. More generally, the company follows an industry trend to focus less on "episodic" care at a medical facility and more on long-term wellness—a "health plus healthcare" model. Obviously, being able to tell a particular patient how to avoid a predicted condition is a big win for both parties. A new agreement with Apple to build apps for predictive and ongoing care management was signed during the year. Aetna is also a leader in the transition of healthcare to a value-based model, where payment is based on outcomes, not activity. Some 45 percent of Aetna's healthcare spend now flows this way with a goal to increase that to 75 percent by 2020. In 2015 Aetna took a big step toward becoming a more dominant player in the industry by offering $37 billion to acquire rival health insurer Humana. Those merger plans were blocked on antitrust grounds (as was a similar merger between rivals Anthem and Cigna). We don't think that will affect AET's business or shareholder interests materially, save for freeing up some cash to increase share buybacks. The company authorized $4 billion for buybacks upon termination of the merger.

## Financial Highlights, Fiscal Year 2016

FY2016 revenues rose 4.6 percent largely due to higher premiums in most lines. Net earnings rose a somewhat healthier 7.4 percent on the back of cost containment measures. With the Humana merger prospect behind it, the company projects similar revenue gains through FY2018, while some drag from the Affordable Care Act and terminated Humana merger will keep FY2017 earnings growth in the 3 percent range (per-share earnings will rise 7 percent due to aggressive buybacks as mentioned earlier). FY2018 earnings growth is projected at 9–10 percent. A lot depends on the future of the Affordable Care Act, although the company has already pared down its 2017 participation to 242 counties from 778 in 2016. Although there was a pause in 2016 due to merger uncertainty, the company has actively raised its dividend and projects it to double by the end of 2018. It has steadily retired shares—about 33 percent of them in ten years—and should continue along this path.

## Reasons to Buy

We feel that Aetna continues to pace the pack in terms of both business and technology innovation and as such will lead the way more generally in information-driven healthcare and healthcare utilization. The company has its strategies right, is positioned to lead the way, and has declared its intentions to evolve from an "insurance" company to a "healthcare" company providing more integrated, efficient, cost-effective solutions as we move through the decade. ("Managing Risk → Managing Health"). Finally, cash returns to shareholders, once a weak spot, have improved.

## Reasons for Caution

The future of the ACA and its possible replacement adds a measure of uncertainty. Public and governmental scrutiny of health insurers has never been higher, and burgeoning healthcare costs can be difficult for even a company of Aetna's capability and influence to manage.

SECTOR: **Healthcare** ❑ BETA COEFFICIENT: **0.62** ❑ 10-YEAR COMPOUND EARNINGS PER-SHARE GROWTH: **13.0%** ❑ 10-YEAR COMPOUND DIVIDENDS PER-SHARE GROWTH: **45.0%**

|  | | 2009 | 2010 | 2011 | 2012 | 2013 | 2014 | 2015 | 2016 |
|---|---|---|---|---|---|---|---|---|---|
| Revenues (mil) | | 34,765 | 34,246 | 33,700 | 36,596 | 47,295 | 58,003 | 60,337 | 63,155 |
| Net income (mil) | | 1,236 | 1,555.5 | 1,850 | 1,658 | 2,058 | 2,330 | 2,708 | 2,908 |
| Earnings per share | | 2.75 | 3.68 | 5.15 | 5.14 | 5.86 | 6.70 | 7.71 | 8.21 |
| Dividends per share | | 0.04 | 0.04 | 0.45 | 0.73 | 0.80 | 0.90 | 1.00 | 1.00 |
| Cash flow per share | | 3.83 | 5.20 | 6.25 | 6.43 | 7.24 | 8.49 | 9.64 | 10.20 |
| Price: | high | 34.9 | 36.0 | 46.0 | 51.1 | 69.5 | 91.9 | 134.4 | 136.5 |
| | low | 16.7 | 25.0 | 30.6 | 34.6 | 44.4 | 64.7 | 97.3 | 92.4 |

**Website: www.aetna.com**

CONSERVATIVE GROWTH

# Allstate Corporation

Ticker symbol: ALL (NASDAQ) ❑ Large Cap ❑ Value Line financial strength rating: A+ ❑ Current yield: 1.8% ❑ Dividend increases, past 10 years: 6

## Company Profile

Allstate is the nation's largest publicly held, full-line "P/C" (Property/Casualty) insurance provider, offering the gamut of auto, home, renters, and business insurance, and has become a larger player in life insurance, retirement, and annuity segments as well. The company serves 16 million households through a network of 36,000 Allstate-exclusive agents with almost a billion and a half policies in force in all 50 states plus DC and Canada. It prides itself on its four-tiered brand and channel strategy for delivering choice and advice to customers where, when, and how they want it.

The company sells its own Allstate product through 9,300 exclusive agencies and its "Encompass" subbrand through independent agencies and estimates that the Allstate brand alone owns 19 percent of the traditional P/C market. The company owns and operates the e-commerce insurance portal Esurance and also sells its product directly, along with other insurance brands, through its "Answer Financial" phone portal for self-directed consumers looking for choices. That said, the lion's share of premiums ($28.8 billion, or 92 percent of policies in force) is earned through the Allstate brand, while Encompass and Esurance contribute about $1.1 billion, or about 5 percent for Esurance and 3 percent for Encompass. By product line, auto leads the way with about two-thirds of premium dollars, homeowners with 23 percent, with the rest coming from life, commercial, and other business lines. Increasingly, the company is using analytics to "microsegment" and tune the premium/cost mix.

Recent acquisitions have brought in Arity, a user of data and analytics to better manage risk, enhancing a broader strategy to deploy analytics across the business, and SquareTrade, an innovative provider of protection plans and support services for the consumer electronics buyer.

## Financial Highlights, Fiscal Year 2016

Primarily due to market share gains, Allstate's property/casualty revenue increased 3.3 percent, while investment income dropped 3.6 percent, for a combined weighted total gain of 2.5 percent. Price competition and a higher loss rate (apparently due to increased cell phone use while driving among other factors) led to a 14 percent drop in net earnings. Expected price adjustments, operational efficiencies, and a turnaround in investment income should work to increase net earnings some 25–27 percent in FY2017 followed by a 10–12 percent gain in FY2018 on revenue gains in the 4–6 percent range each year. From an operating and underwriting point of view, Allstate is one of the more efficient companies in the P/C industry, with a "combined ratio" (operating expense percentage plus loss percentage of revenue) in the 87–89 range; this "margin" measure is healthy and much improved from just a few years ago. Cash payouts to shareholders look to stabilize and increase steadily, and the company has been aggressive in reducing share counts—about 4 percent in 2016 and 46 percent since 2004.

## Reasons to Buy

We like the market position, brand strength, channel strategy, increased stability, and upside potential both in underwriting and in investment performance. The company has sold some underperforming operations and has gained a solid strategic hold on its reputation, brand, and channel strategy. Esurance and other "direct" models are gaining traction, while the company is also offering a better product mix and better cross-selling opportunities through its traditional agencies. Increased investment income will also help. Allstate has all the earmarks of a well-managed company.

The Allstate brand is ever stronger, turning from a slight negative years ago to a solid positive through stronger advertising, product offering, and general branding initiatives. The company now proudly places its name on "adjacent" businesses such as Allstate Roadside Services; another branding example is the new "Package" policy, combining auto and homeowners into a single policy sold under the Encompass brand. While Allstate has improved the top line through such initiatives, there is also clearer focus on expenses, the bottom line, stability, and overall shareholder returns going forward; in our view Allstate has become a solid blue-chip performer in a difficult industry with a pretty decent upside going forward.

## Reasons for Caution

Competition is stiff and another hurricane-infested year like 2005 could also hurt, although Allstate is more geographically diverse than some of its competitors. Higher auto claims rates, driven by smartphone use, greater mileages driven because of cheap gas, and a generally faster pace of life are also a concern but should be covered by price increases eventually. Interest rates on the industry's traditional investment instruments, while on the cusp of an improvement, are still historically weak, and another major stock or bond market correction could hurt too. For years, the brand suffered from a reputation for poor claims performance and an overly sales-y approach. Although the company is more aware of its relatively erratic past and seems to be doing something about it, the prior volatility of its results in revenues, earnings, and especially dividends paid is hard to ignore. Finally, we'll admit that we find insurers (as most Financials) difficult to understand because of terminology and somewhat different ways of measuring and reporting financial performance; you may also find this company difficult to understand well enough to commit your capital comfortably. Proceed carefully.

SECTOR: **Financials** ❑ BETA COEFFICIENT: **0.97** ❑ 10-YEAR COMPOUND EARNINGS PER-SHARE GROWTH: **4.5%** ❑ 10-YEAR COMPOUND DIVIDENDS PER-SHARE GROWTH: **-0.5%**

|  | 2009 | 2010 | 2011 | 2012 | 2013 | 2014 | 2015 | 2016 |
|---|---|---|---|---|---|---|---|---|
| Property/Casualty premiums (mil) | 26,194 | 25,957 | 25,942 | 26,737 | 27,618 | 28,929 | 30,309 | 31,407 |
| Net income (mil) | 1,976 | 1,535 | 699 | 2,143 | 2,756 | 2,379 | 2,119 | 1,785 |
| Earnings per share | 3.47 | 2.83 | 1.34 | 4.34 | 5.70 | 5.42 | 5.21 | 4.69 |
| Dividends per share | 1.01 | 0.80 | 0.83 | 1.09 | 0.75 | 1.12 | 1.29 | 1.29 |
| Underwriting inc. per share | (0.58) | (0.58) | (4.19) | 2.49 | 4.95 | 4.22 | 4.06 | 3.34 |
| Price:    high | 33.5 | 35.5 | 34.4 | 42.8 | 54.8 | 71.5 | 72.9 | 74.8 |
|           low | 13.8 | 26.9 | 22.3 | 27.0 | 40.7 | 49.2 | 54.1 | 73.0 |

Website: www.allstate.com

---

**AGGRESSIVE GROWTH**

# Amazon.com, Inc.

Ticker symbol: AMZN (NASDAQ) ❑ Large Cap ❑ Value Line financial strength rating: A+ ❑ Current yield: Nil ❑ Dividend raises, past 10 years: NA

## Company Profile

Simply put, Amazon.com makes us feel old. We can remember a mere 22 years ago when Amazon was just a retailer—a *book* retailer. A huge one, granted, but the first thought that came to mind at the mention of its name was a great place to buy a book *cheap* without having to drive somewhere to find it.

Then they started selling other stuff.

Amazon.com has become the world's largest e-commerce retailer, but the company's scope has grown beyond even that in the past several years. Amazon Web Services is now the world's largest provider of cloud computing services, with a market share larger than that of the next five largest players combined. Amazon Video is a provider of video on-demand services, competing with both traditional cable providers as well as IP (Internet)-based rivals such as Hulu. They are also producing award-winning original movies and series. Amazon Go is testing the waters in the grocery business with an eventual goal of 2,000 stores in the US, an effort that may well be accelerated with their recent purchase of Whole Foods. And in one of the more irony-laden business moves of recent memory, Amazon is now rolling out a test of retail bookstores.

## Financial Highlights, Fiscal Year 2016

Amazon reports its business in three segments: North America, International, and Amazon Web Services (AWS). Overall, FY2016 produced a 27 percent increase in revenues, with AWS leading the pack with a 55 percent gain. North America and International revenues were both up 25 percent, but while North American operations produced $2.36 billion in profits, International continues to operate at a loss, the loss expanding 70 percent in 2016 to $1.28 billion. The bulk of this loss is due to increased outlays for fulfillment capacity and additional spending on technology infrastructure and marketing in aggressively growing markets like India and Mexico.

## Reasons to Buy

There are many good reasons to own a piece of AMZN right now, as the company is at the heart of the "stay-at-home" trend, in fact, is driving it with services like Amazon Prime and the Amazon Marketplace. The Marketplace, really an online shopping mall, makes it possible for vendors and customers around the world to connect and transact business without a physical storefront. And who doesn't know about Amazon Prime's bundle of one-click ordering, free two-day shipping to most places, music, movies, free books, and other goodies? Amazon has been at the very forefront of making Internet shopping safe, secure, convenient, cost competitive for the seller and price competitive for the buyer—and it is disrupting most of the retail industry. It's a safe bet that you, or at least your neighbors, are ordering mundane household items like laundry detergent and Hershey's Kisses using Prime. We do—and no, we're not Millennials.

Okay, so it's a successful business model and a good place to shop. Does that mean it's a good stock to own? Obviously, we think so.

The single best reason to own a piece of Amazon is that it has delivered on nearly every promise made since its founding. Jeff Bezos predicted the company might take a decade to become profitable. This scared away many investors, but in retrospect, it was a brilliant piece of expectations management, having the additional benefit of being the truth. Fifteen years after making *that* statement, Bezos continued to tell investors that new Amazon projects had a five-to-seven-year horizon, on the theory that very few companies had the patience to take on projects that took that long to develop. In Bezos's view, this meant there was effectively zero competition for these longer-term opportunities. Right again.

At that time, e-commerce was growing five times faster than the over-all retail market, and Amazon was growing twice as fast as e-commerce as a whole. Fast-forward five years to today, and Amazon has carved out an enormous chunk of the US (and worldwide) retailing market by being will-ing to take on projects of enormous scale and complexity and executing on them with a vengeance. In fact, they're delivering a recent project well ahead of schedule; the Amazon Go grocery concept, built on the promise of "checkout-less" shopping, is coming online *years* before most experts in the field thought possible. "We're very stubborn," Bezos once said.

As another example, Amazon Web Services, the company's on-demand cloud computing platform, launched in 2003 as an Amazon-internal IT project for managing certain aspects of transaction data. A year later, it was launched as a service for public use. Today, AWS accounts for over $14 billion in revenue and $3.1 billion in profit, exceeding the rest of the company's profit combined.

And they're hardly done. Amazon views the Echo/Alexa personal assistant technology as a potential third large revenue stream, linking to other Amazon services for ordering of products and services or playback of music, audio books, and other media supplied by Amazon or stored on user accounts. The platform is stable and well supported, and the environment is building out quickly with tie-ins to home security services and other home-management technologies.

And finally, and not to be left out, the Whole Foods acquisition signals a head-first dive into the prospects for systematized logistics for retail, bal-ancing the dynamics of centralized and local delivery right in your neighbor-hood where it makes sense. Stay tuned.

## Reasons for Caution

As much as we like the company, its customer value proposition, and execu-tion excellence, there's no getting around the cost of these shares. With a share price approaching $1,000, up almost 50 percent in a year and a half, the valu-ation (price to earnings) is astronomical while even the forward ratio (based on

2017 projections) is around 120 (compared to 21 for the S&P 500). Although profitability is growing, and sales are growing dramatically, simply maintaining this kind of stock price may require an almost unimaginable sustained financial performance. Amazon has rewarded the bold and faithful handsomely in the past, but the timid and doubtful among us cannot be faulted for treading gingerly through the stacks of this very special bookstore.

SECTOR: **Retail** ❑ BETA COEFFICIENT: **1.10** ❑ 10-YEAR COMPOUND EARNINGS PER-SHARE GROWTH: **10.5%** ❑ 10-YEAR COMPOUND DIVIDENDS PER-SHARE GROWTH: **NA**

|  | 2009 | 2010 | 2011 | 2012 | 2013 | 2014 | 2015 | 2016 |
|---|---|---|---|---|---|---|---|---|
| Revenues (bil) | 34.2 | 48.1 | 61.9 | 74.5 | 89.0 | 107.0 | 130.0 | 136.0 |
| Net income (mil) | 1,152 | 631.0 | 130.0 | 274.0 | (241.0) | 596.0 | 2,485 | 2,371 |
| Earnings per share | 2.53 | 1.37 | 0.29 | 0.59 | (0.52) | 1.25 | 5.20 | 4.90 |
| Dividends per share | — | — | — | — | — | — | — | — |
| Cash flow per share | 3.81 | 3.77 | 5.04 | 7.68 | 9.70 | 14.60 | 18.60 | 21.99 |
| Price:           high | 185.6 | 246.7 | 264.1 | 405.6 | 408.1 | 696.4 | 685.5 | 847.2 |
| low | 105.8 | 160.6 | 172.0 | 245.8 | 284.0 | 285.3 | 474.0 | 474.0 |

Website: www.amazon.com

---

**AGGRESSIVE GROWTH**

# Apple Inc.

Ticker symbol: AAPL (NASDAQ) ❑ Large Cap ❑ Value Line financial strength rating: A++ ❑ Current yield: 1.6% ❑ Dividend raises, past 10 years: 5

## Company Profile

The Apple story of excellence and of transition from high-flying growth stock to cash-generating value stock continues unabated into 2018—with some signs of returning to its growth patterns of the past decade. The company remains an admired bellwether for consumer innovation and design for a wide swath of consumers from preteen to seniors (and a growing number of commercial customers). We hardly need to review what the company makes and sells, but we will once again anyhow; it's kind of fun.

Apple designs, manufactures, and markets computers, smartphones, tablets, portable music players, digital watches and related software, peripherals, downloadable content, and services. It sells these products through its own retail stores, online stores, and third-party and value-added resellers.

The company also sells digital content through its iTunes store. The company has become a big player in the "digital wallet" mobile payment space, with its Apple Pay apps and network. Finally, and perhaps most remarkably of all, the company continues to flirt with a move into the automobile business.

The company's products have become household names: The iPhone, iPod, iPad, and MacBook are just some of the company's hardware products. While the software may be less well-known, QuickTime, iOS, MacOS, tvOS, and WatchOS are important products. Even more important is Services, which bundles together the iCloud, iTunes, iBooks, Apple Pay, Apple Music, the Mac App Store and other content delivery, and AppleCare support services. Apple Services is a *Fortune* 500–sized business in and of itself. We haven't broken down sales figures in the past but it's well worth doing. Smartphones account for $137 billion of the $216 billion in FY2016 sales—fully 63 percent. Mac (personal computers) accounts for 11 percent, iPad 10 percent, "Other Products" for 4.5 percent and, not to be left out, Services accounts for 11 percent of revenues: $24 billon a year.

It's hard to imagine the current consumer tech landscape without Apple's presence at the top of the heap. Its product line, while comparatively narrow, is focused on areas where the user interface is highly valued, and, increasingly, where some kind of content or service can be sold after the hardware sale. The company has leveraged this focus to become one of the most profitable companies in history and continues to be the most valuable company in the world.

Apple is the flagship case study in creating extraordinary value through innovation, innovative leadership, and marketing excellence. Nowadays the company increasingly focuses on operational excellence and its Services business—Apple Pay, iCloud, Apple Music, and the like. We think the design, brand, technology, and operational excellence will gradually extend into more markets such as automotive and wearable technology.

## Financial Highlights, Fiscal Year 2016

Currency and a relative lack of significant new products led to a sales lull in FY2016. Net sales declined 8 percent, the first sales decline in years. All three hardware segments softened—iPhone by 12 percent, iPad by 11 percent, and Mac by 10 percent. But had the world ended? In a word, no. Services were up 22 percent and "Other" was up 11 percent. Net profits sagged a full 14 percent, to $45 billion, but the company still generates more profits than most companies do sales! A monstrous 240 million share buyback (4.4 percent) held per-share losses to 10 percent.

The company ends its fiscal year at the end of September, and the introduction of the iPhone 7 and 7 Plus sparked an almost immediate recovery and resurgence in revenue and earnings growth. Forecasts call for revenue growth in the 5–7 percent range annually through FY2018 with earnings growth of 4–5 percent in FY2017 and 8–10 percent in FY2018 as operational efficiencies and a shift to higher-margined Services take effect. Per-share earnings will be up in the low double digits each year as 100 million–plus share buybacks continue.

## Reasons to Buy

Innovation. Market leadership. Brand strength. Growth. Profitability. Cash flow. Cash returns. And now, the steady and growing "Services" revenue stream. Best in class across the board. How could Apple *not* be a *100 Best* stock? We certainly like the results, but mostly we continue to admire (and believe in) the business and innovation excellence that got Apple there in the first place.

Apple's best-known product, the iPhone, seems ubiquitous. You probably have one. Everyone you know has one. They're everywhere, and you can be forgiven for thinking that the market for this product is saturated. Everyone thought it was getting too expensive as lower-priced Android products started to flood the market. And everyone wondered what would happen in China. But the truth is, by improving quality, and gradually improving feature sets, Apple is once again gaining share in the smartphone market. Moreover, we seem to have come to a sweet spot on the replacement cycle as many previous iPhone customers are upgrading to the 7 and 7 Plus. New services, particularly Apple Pay and the music service, are starting to gain traction. And that's just sales—the profitability and cash-flow story is even better. Net profit margins of 20–22 percent for a company of this size alone are remarkable, and suggest that the company's products are far from becoming commoditized. On the shareholder-return front, the new emphasis on returning cash to shareholders has plenty of distance to go.

While many are concerned about Apple's ability to innovate, and while there has been something of a slowdown in the creation of whole new businesses, like iPods and tablets, we haven't given up on such innovations. We continue to feel that Apple still has room to create some blockbusters in the "wearable" technology space—smartphone technology integrated into clothing, for example, and in flexible display technologies (see Corning, another *100 Best* pick). Apple Pay, the company's venture into the financial transaction space, could also be huge, and a big driver for sales of compatible hardware. We foresee other major "vertical" applications of iPhone form and technology in cars (check out "CarPlay") and in the healthcare space for remote patient monitoring and such. Breakthrough technologies in the TV space have been talked about for some time; while not gaining much traction to date, we could still tune in to some upside in that lucrative space. Finally, we'd like to remind readers that we consider operational improvements to be innovations as well.

Last year at this time we called the below-$100 stock price dip a buying opportunity—and we were right. The P/E ratio was, stunningly, less than 12, far lower than the average company and completely ignoring growth and cash return prospects. The stock has risen some 55 percent—good for those of you who got in; now you may have to be a little more selective about entry points but at 15 times earnings and everything clicking again, we still favor Apple.

## Reasons for Caution

Our biggest concern is simple: smartphones make up 63 percent of the business. That brings a risk of saturation and competition that has made us uncomfortable in the past, but the current success of the iPhone 7 family mitigates the concern. That said, similar concerns prevail in the tablet space, where competition from Microsoft Surface and the like is getting stronger. But this segment is only 10 percent of the business—a good thing in this case. In the main, we continue to admire Apple's ability to generate income, and now, to distribute it to shareholders. The franchise is the world's most valuable in market capitalization—and deservedly so. But nobody can sit on their laurels, especially when their laurels are this high off the ground and in plain sight of every competitor. Apple must continue to feed the innovation machine.

SECTOR: **Consumer Discretionary** ❑ BETA COEFFICIENT: **1.25** ❑ 10-YEAR COMPOUND EARNINGS PER-SHARE GROWTH: **45.0%** ❑ 10-YEAR COMPOUND DIVIDENDS PER-SHARE GROWTH: **NM**

|  | 2009 | 2010 | 2011 | 2012 | 2013 | 2014 | 2015 | 2016 |
|---|---|---|---|---|---|---|---|---|
| Revenues (bil) | 36.5 | 65.2 | 108.2 | 156.5 | 170.9 | 182.8 | 233.7 | 216.8 |
| Net income (bil) | 5.7 | 14.0 | 25.9 | 41.7 | 37.0 | 39.5 | 53.4 | 45.7 |
| Earnings per share | 0.90 | 2.16 | 3.95 | 6.31 | 5.66 | 6.45 | 9.22 | 8.31 |
| Dividends per share | — | — | — | 0.38 | 1.63 | 1.82 | 1.98 | 2.18 |
| Cash flow per share | 1.02 | 2.35 | 4.26 | 6.85 | 6.96 | 8.09 | 11.59 | 10.53 |
| Price:        high | 30.6 | 46.7 | 61.0 | 100.7 | 82.2 | 119.8 | 134.5 | 118.7 |
| low | 11.2 | 27.2 | 44.4 | 58.4 | 55.0 | 70.5 | 92.0 | 89.5 |

**Website: www.apple.com**

NEW FOR 2018

# Applied Materials

Ticker symbol: AMAT (NASDAQ) ◻ Large Cap ◻ Value Line financial strength rating: A+ ◻ Current yield: 1.0% ◻ Dividend raises, past 10 years: 6

## Company Profile

Founded in 1967 in the heart of the Silicon Valley, Applied Materials is the world's leading supplier of semiconductor fabrication equipment. More precisely, they produce *machines* in the form of wafer processing equipment and *materials* in the form of raw silicon wafers, which are the starting point for nearly every discrete semiconductor product ("chips," commonly) among a wide variety of other machines and materials.

"Wafers" are thin discs made of a crystalline silicon base, upon which are constructed the electrical circuits which constitute the core of the final product. AMAT's equipment processes the raw silicon wafers (usually sliced at the foundries that produce the silicon ingots) into finished integrated circuit chips. A single 12-inch diameter processed wafer may have as many as a thousand identical finished products ("chips") etched onto its surface.

AMAT's customers are the among largest integrated circuit fabricators in the world: Intel, GlobalFoundries, Taiwan Semiconductor, Micron Technology, and others. These companies use AMAT's equipment to produce not only their own products for sale but also finished integrated circuits ("ICs") on contract for the hundreds of "fabless" (factoryless) semiconductor design houses around the world.

In 2006, AMAT entered both the display and solar panel manufacturing equipment markets, only to exit photovoltaics in 2010. The display segment is still active and is participating in the development of the organic light-emitting diode (OLED) display market. Today the company also derives significant revenue from its software and services operation, which provides management tools and technical support for its products.

## Financial Highlights, Fiscal Year 2016

AMAT posted a commendable FY2016 with strong gains in revenue (up 11 percent) and per-share earnings (up 29 percent). The Display segment shone brightly with a 152 percent increase in backlog over the prior year (backlog is very helpful in the semiconductor equipment business as sales cycles can be 6–12 months). For the company overall, backlog increased 46 percent. The company's Asia regions (Taiwan, China, Korea, and Japan) all saw increases in sales. China was particularly strong with a 35 percent increase for the year. Domestic sales fell off for the second consecutive year, down 30 percent. Sales in the US have been dropping fairly steadily, and the company now derives 88 percent of its revenue from the Asia region, which isn't surprising given its dominance of electronics manufacturing.

The first two quarters of FY2017 are notable with net income up 158 percent over the prior year's period. The worldwide market for NAND flash memory shows no signs of weakness, and AMAT's machines are in high demand in this sector.

Though the company was unable to complete a merger in 2015 with Tokyo Electron (the US Department of Justice cited irreconcilable competition issues), AMAT moved ahead with a planned inversion process, incorporating in the Netherlands. As a result, AMAT's effective tax rate fell from the 26–28 percent range from 2012–2014 to 13–15 percent in 2015–2016. This has obviously had a significant "step" impact on the reported bottom line, and financials going forward will certainly benefit as well. Current forecasts call for a 25–27 percent revenue gain for FY2017, slowing to a 4 percent gain in FY2018. Annual 3 percent share buybacks and other scale efficiencies will enhance per-share earnings gains to 65–70 percent in 2017 and about 10 percent in the following year.

## Reasons to Buy

The semiconductor equipment industry has been notoriously cyclical, with business levels rising and falling with both demand in the underlying semiconductor market as well as advancements in the state of the art of manufacturing. Demand for semiconductors tends to follow the consumer market (with a base of steadier industrial and commercial demand), while cycles in the semiconductor equipment business have been much longer, typically three to four years. The industry was at the 22-nanometer node quite a while before advancing to 14nm, but with the advent of new transistor structures, 3D fabrication, and embedded and "stacked" memory, prior metrics of the effects of node shrinks have become a bit less useful.

We mention this history only as a lead-in for the bigger picture going forward as the economics of the integrated circuit economy are about to shift in a couple of important ways. First, the type of transistors that are now approaching mainstream applications (99.99 percent of the devices on an IC are one of a dozen or so transistors) now use about 40 percent less power to operate at the same speed as earlier devices. This has a lot of implications, but in the end it will enable the possibility of many new classes of portable devices. Second, the availability of cheap computing power will further drive the ubiquity of these devices. You can buy a new "project" computer for $20 that has 300 times the computing power of our first $1,000 laptop, with far more memory, faster I/O, and better graphics. Third, momentum down the flash memory technology curve is accelerating to the point where it's no longer crazy to talk about the eventual elimination of the hard disc drive altogether. And last, the automotive market will be going through a revolution over the coming decade, with electric cars, self-driving cars, and in-car telematics and entertainment systems driving an enormous incremental demand for sensor, power, logic, and memory devices. This is all supplemental—*and much steadier*—volume in the semiconductor industry to what AMAT supports today.

Put this all together, and we think the cyclical nature of this equipment market is fundamentally changed, at least for the next four to five years. Collectively, part of this fundamental shift shows up in the market as IoT, or the Internet of Things. These new devices will demand the latest in fabrication technologies, and as a result we think the demand for fab capacity will be increasing steadily for several more years.

AMAT has few competitors, and is well positioned with fab partners in low-cost geographies, particularly in the rapidly growing Chinese market. Sales of AMAT equipment in China are growing rapidly and may soon surpass sales in the Taiwan region, long a mainstay for AMAT.

Another emerging business worth mentioning is the roll-to-roll thin film process used to make familiar packaging materials for foods like coffee beans, candies, and packaged potato chips. The process deposits flexible films that provide a gas/moisture barrier to extend the shelf life of foods. Derived from the company's vacuum deposition process, the product extends the company's applications from computer "chips" to the kind of "chips" we like to eat!

Finally, as part of the tax windfall and following the pattern set by other corporations in similar circumstances, AMAT is stepping up its dividend and stock buyback plans. In the most recent quarter AMAT returned over 40 percent of cash from operations as dividends and share repurchases. We believe this pattern will continue.

## Reasons for Caution

AMAT is the world leader in semiconductor equipment sales, but one major competitor, Lam Research, is of similar size with a solid record of growth. We feel AMAT has certain advantages in their technology and operations, but it is worth keeping a weather eye on competitors for technology announcements. That same "weather eye" should also watch to make sure the disappearance of cyclicity we're predicting actually comes true; business cycles in this industry have been the bugaboo for this stock in the past.

**SECTOR: Industrials** ◻ **BETA COEFFICIENT: 1.15** ◻ 10-YEAR COMPOUND EARNINGS PER-SHARE GROWTH: **2.5%** ◻ 10-YEAR COMPOUND DIVIDENDS PER-SHARE GROWTH: **5.7%**

|  | 2009 | 2010 | 2011 | 2012 | 2013 | 2014 | 2015 | 2016 |
|---|---|---|---|---|---|---|---|---|
| Revenues (mil) | 5,014 | 9,549 | 10,517 | 8,719 | 7,509 | 9,072 | 9,659 | 10,825 |
| Net income (mil) | 305 | 1,333 | 1,926 | 529 | 256 | 1,072 | 1,377 | 1,720 |
| Earnings per share | 0.23 | 1.00 | 1.45 | 0.42 | 0.21 | 0.87 | 1.12 | 1.54 |
| Dividends per share | 0.24 | 0.26 | 0.30 | 0.34 | 0.38 | 0.40 | 0.40 | 0.40 |
| Cash flow per share | 0.10 | 1.23 | 1.66 | 0.79 | 0.55 | 1.19 | 1.51 | 1.96 |
| Price:        high | 14.2 | 14.9 | 16.9 | 13.9 | 18.2 | 25.7 | 25.6 | 33.7 |
|              low | 8.2 | 10.3 | 9.7 | 10.0 | 11.4 | 16.4 | 13.2 | 15.4 |

Website: www.appliedmaterials.com

GROWTH AND INCOME

# Aqua America Inc.

Ticker symbol: WTR (NYSE) ◻ Large Cap ◻ Value Line financial strength rating: A ◻ Current yield: 2.3% ◻ Dividend raises, past 10 years: 10

## Company Profile

If you're like most people, by the time you landed on Water Works as you circled the Monopoly board, you had already deployed your investment capital elsewhere and weren't so excited about its modest growth and yield prospects. You can't build houses or hotels on Water Works, and the monopoly power for owning it in tandem with the Electric Company doesn't seem as powerful as other investments on the board. So you may have passed it up.

Well, times have changed since Monopoly was created. The strategic importance of water, the efficiencies of operating water utilities across a wide geography, and their stability as investments (we didn't care so much about that in Monopoly), have made water utilities a more desirable investment.

"Water Works," in this case, is Aqua America Inc., the second-largest publicly traded US water and wastewater utility. Founded 130 years ago, WTR serves approximately 3 million customers in eight states: Pennsylvania, Ohio, North Carolina, Illinois, Texas, New Jersey, Indiana, and Virginia, operating 1,460 public water and 193 wastewater treatment systems. Pennsylvania is the centerpiece, accounting for just over half of revenues and almost 75 percent of net income. Like many modern utilities, the company also owns a nonregulated subsidiary supplying industrial water and services with a new and special emphasis on the Pennsylvania, Texas, and Ohio shale industries. The company has pursued growth aggressively through acquisitions, bringing in over 200 acquisitions and growth ventures in the past ten years. Another 13 small water utilities and six wastewater systems were added in 2016 following 15 additions in 2015 and 16 additions in 2014. Over time the company has purchased some small utility services and consulting businesses as well; one example is a firm that inspects, cleans, aligns, and televises sewer and storm drain systems.

Normally we're not too thrilled with growth-by-acquisition strategies, but in this case it makes sense because a lot of local public jurisdictions and private operators see the logic in turning smaller plants over to a larger company where economies of scale and management can take effect. That, in essence, is Aqua America's strategy, and we like it—especially with the US patchwork of over 50,000 operators of small water delivery systems, most of which operate at less than prime efficiency.

## Financial Highlights, Fiscal Year 2016

Acquisitions and a few divestitures once again make true revenue and earnings trends hard to capture, but overall the company grew revenues 4.5 percent on rate increases and a 1.6 percent growth in the customer base. Per-share earnings, helped along also by rate increases and a small one-time item, grew almost 16 percent. Despite weakness in the shale industry, favorable pricing and continued economies of scale work the other way; revenues are projected ahead another 3–5 percent annually into 2018, while per-share earnings should rise in the 4–6 percent range as further economies of scale are realized. The company has raised its dividend 26 times in the past 25 years. Increases look to be in the high single digits for the next few years, strong for a utility company but well supported by cash flows.

## Reasons to Buy

You may not have played much defense in Monopoly, but it's certainly worth playing some defense in the face of today's long-term bull market, so we continue to keep Aqua on our *100 Best* list as a defensive play. The stock barely budged in the early 2016 market correction, and we always like to have a few choices that seem relatively immune to such events. That safety, plus an interest in steadily growing cash returns, fuels our interest in Aqua America. The company is a relatively small and simple business compared to a lot we look at. It occupies a strategic position in a key utility area, especially as more water works entities become available as public sector operations are trimmed. In doing so, WTR realizes a lot of operational, financial, and marketing economies of scale as it combines dozens of smaller utilities under a single management.

Aqua America is earning the maximum return on equity allowed by regulators, suggesting a "best in class" operating effectiveness; it is also beginning to expand the use and strength of its brand. The stock has a low beta of 0.48, indicating stability. The payout percentage—dividends as a percent of net profits—has trended downward, and that, along with strong cash flow, suggests continued strength on the dividend front.

## Reasons for Caution

Water distribution requires a lot of expensive infrastructure, and a lot of the current infrastructure is old; in fact, the need to replace infrastructure is one reason some smaller utilities are selling out to Aqua America. Such replacement costs, particularly with the severe winters we've been having, could be high and a drag on earnings in the short term, but the company has managed them well as evidenced by the steadiness of long-term debt as a portion of total capitalization despite these capital expenditures. Big plans made to deliver water to shale operators have been attenuated by energy price declines as well.

Overall, we chose this investment in part due to its relatively inelastic demand and steady earnings and cash flow into the future even in bad economic times; however, Aqua may participate less in economic growth and rising equity markets than other stocks we choose. Too, recent share prices may have reflected some of the optimism, making it possible that bubbly-high share prices will come out when you turn on the investing faucet.

SECTOR: **Utilities** ◻ BETA COEFFICIENT: **0.48** ◻ 10-YEAR COMPOUND EARNINGS PER-SHARE GROWTH: **8.5%** ◻ 10-YEAR COMPOUND DIVIDENDS PER-SHARE GROWTH: **8.0%**

|  | 2009 | 2010 | 2011 | 2012 | 2013 | 2014 | 2015 | 2016 |
|---|---|---|---|---|---|---|---|---|
| Revenues (mil) | 670.5 | 728.1 | 712.0 | 757.8 | 768.6 | 780.0 | 814.0 | 819.9 |
| Net income (mil) | 104.4 | 124.0 | 144.8 | 153.1 | 205.1 | 213.9 | 202.0 | 234.2 |
| Earnings per share | 0.62 | 0.72 | 0.83 | 0.87 | 1.15 | 1.20 | 1.14 | 1.32 |
| Dividends per share | 0.44 | 0.47 | 0.50 | 0.54 | 0.58 | 0.63 | 0.69 | 0.74 |
| Cash flow per share | 1.29 | 1.42 | 1.45 | 1.51 | 1.82 | 1.89 | 1.87 | 2.07 |
| Price:        high | 17.2 | 18.4 | 19.0 | 21.5 | 28.1 | 28.2 | 31.1 | 35.8 |
|                 low | 12.3 | 13.2 | 15.4 | 16.8 | 20.6 | 22.4 | 24.4 | 28.0 |

Website: www.aquaamerica.com

CONSERVATIVE GROWTH

# Archer Daniels Midland Company

Ticker symbol: ADM (NYSE) □ Large Cap □ Value Line financial strength rating: A+ □ Current yield: 2.8% □ Dividend raises, past 10 years: 9

## Company Profile

ADM is one of the largest food processors in the world. It buys corn, wheat, oilseeds, and other agricultural products and processes them into food, food ingredients, animal feed and ingredients, and biofuels. It also resells grains on the open market. Rather than the finished consumer products most food processors are known for, ADM produces and distributes intermediate components for food product manufacture and is by far the largest publicly traded company in this business. "*ADM Feeds Your Food Business*" is their motto.

Among the more important products are vegetable oils, protein meal and components, corn sweeteners, flour, biodiesel, ethanol, other food and animal feed, and now, specialty ingredients. Foreign sales make up about 47 percent of total revenue.

The company is highly vertically integrated and owns and maintains facilities used throughout the production process. It sources, transports, stores, and processes agricultural materials in 76 subsidiary countries on six continents, with 271 processing plants, 514 procurement facilities, 230 bulk storage terminals, and its own extensive sea/rail/road network. The company owns or leases 28,600 rail cars, 2,500 barges, 31 ocean vessels, and a fleet of trucks. There are 38 innovation centers worldwide.

The company operates in four business segments: Oilseeds Processing (36 percent of FY2016 sales), Corn Processing (15 percent), Agricultural Services (45 percent), and the recently acquired WILD Flavors and Specialty Ingredients and other (4 percent). The Oilseeds Processing unit processes soybeans, cottonseed, sunflower, canola, peanuts, and flaxseed into vegetable oils and protein meals for the food and feed industries. Crude vegetable oils are sold as is or are further refined into consumer products, while partially refined oils are sold for use in paints, chemicals, and other industrial products. The solids remaining from this processing are sold for a number of applications, including edible soy protein, animal feed, pharmaceuticals, chemicals, and paper.

The Corn Processing segment milling operations (primarily in the United States) produce food products too numerous to list but include syrup, starch, glucose, dextrose, and other sweeteners. Markets served include animal feeds and the vegetable oil market. Fermentation of the dextrose yields ethanol, amino acids, and other specialty food and feed products. The ethanol is processed for beverage stock or industrial use as the base for ethanol-blended gasoline and other fuels. Within this group, ADM owns a 40 percent interest in the Red Star Yeast Company.

The Agricultural Services segment is the company's storage and transportation network. This business is primarily engaged in buying, storing, cleaning, and transporting grains to/from ADM facilities and for export. It also resells raw materials into the animal feed and agricultural processing industries.

Acquired in 2015, the expanding WILD Flavors and Specialty Ingredients segment produces many existing nutrients product lines including high-fiber and nutritional supplements like natural-source vitamin E and Omega-3 DHA. This group, and the recent acquisition of Harvest Innovations, a producer of gluten-free and minimally processed soy proteins and oils, has expanded ADM's presence in the specialty corners of the food business. In mid-2016 the company divested some of its Brazil ethanol business in a strategic shift from commodity to higher value–add businesses. In total, ADM made ten moderately sized acquisitions and sales through the year.

### Financial Highlights, Fiscal Year 2016

Acquisitions, spin-offs, currency effects, fluctuating prices, and fluctuating costs of agricultural commodity inputs make any yearly comparison of ADM results challenging. After a big revenue drop in FY2015 due to the sale of the cocoa business, FY2016 again declined, this time by 8 percent mainly on lower sales prices in the wake of the commodity bust and lower volumes again from the cocoa sales as well as the disposal of South American ethanol operations. Earnings got crushed again to the tune of 31 percent for the year. We might have closed the book with continuation of these trends; however, we think things will turn around going forward: FY2017 revenues are expected to advance 4 percent and another 3 percent in FY2018, while earnings will advance 25–30 percent and 7–9 percent respectively. "Rightsizing," mix improvement, and cost containment will be priorities and will expand the naturally thin margins measurably. Steady dividend increases and modest share buybacks should continue.

### Reasons to Buy

Although near-term results have been weak, we still like ADM for the longer term. Agriculture is still a key strategic business on a global basis, and increased demand for food and especially middle-class Western diets from emerging market customers bodes well. The company is and has been a strong player in the biofuels industry. While uncertainties continue in the ethanol and biofuels segment, the company's experience and scale in ethanol and biodiesel are strong positives, and the company should win as other smaller players exit the market.

There are four major suppliers that dominate the world market for commodity foodstuffs: Archer, Bunge, Cargill, and Dreyfus—the "ABCD" of world foods. Growth through selective acquisitions is an important factor to success in this business—if you miss an attractive opportunity, you can be reasonably certain one of your competitors will not. ADM continues to grow its presence in the emerging markets of Asia, South America, and Eastern Europe. ADM's presence and extensive transportation capability give it a decided advantage over its smaller competitors, many of which are focused only in certain markets or certain industries. The company is fine-tuning its business mix, disposing of smaller low-margin product lines in favor of a higher value add in the food chain with the addition of WILD and other product lines; we like the increasing emphasis on this business. We like the solid track record for growth in dividends and overall shareholder value.

## Reasons for Caution

We've seen how agricultural cycles and production can negatively impact this company, and it will try the patience of the most patient investors. The WILD acquisition may signal a move to the "wild" side in more specialized, less commoditized business, which seems like a good strategy but does add some risk. Also the company may be late to this party though it is well positioned as a "bulk" supplier of these key ingredients. ADM is heavily invested in the corn-ethanol-fuel processing chain, which has had its own ups and downs as well as detractors. Federal government policy toward ethanol subsidies bears watching. Finally, the company does produce that nasty-sounding but in fact relatively benign high fructose corn syrup; a pickup in nutritional health sentiment in the food and especially the beverage industry won't help. There are more than the usual concerns short term for ADM, but we still consider ADM a long-term play in a healthy and vital industry.

SECTOR: **Consumer Staples** ❑ BETA COEFFICIENT: **0.89** ❑ 10-YEAR COMPOUND EARNINGS PER-SHARE GROWTH: **6.5%** ❑ 10-YEAR COMPOUND DIVIDENDS PER-SHARE GROWTH: **13.0%**

|  |  | 2009 | 2010 | 2011 | 2012 | 2013 | 2014 | 2015 | 2016 |
|---|---|---|---|---|---|---|---|---|---|
| Revenues (mil) | | 69,207 | 61,692 | 80,676 | 89,038 | 89,804 | 81,201 | 67,762 | 62,346 |
| Net income (mil) | | 1,834 | 1,959 | 2,036 | 1,496 | 1,342 | 2,248 | 1,849 | 1,280 |
| Earnings per share | | 3.06 | 3.06 | 3.13 | 2.26 | 2.02 | 3.43 | 2.98 | 2.16 |
| Dividends per share | | 0.54 | 0.58 | 0.62 | 0.69 | 0.76 | 0.96 | 1.12 | 1.20 |
| Cash flow per share | | 4.21 | 4.49 | 4.54 | 3.56 | 3.42 | 4.80 | 4.59 | 3.80 |
| Price: | high | 33.0 | 34.0 | 38.0 | 34.0 | 44.0 | 53.9 | 53.3 | 47.9 |
| | low | 23.1 | 24.2 | 23.7 | 24.2 | 27.8 | 37.9 | 33.8 | 29.9 |

Website: www.adm.com

---

GROWTH AND INCOME

# AT&T Inc.

Ticker symbol: T (NYSE) ❑ Large Cap ❑ Value Line financial strength rating: A++ ❑ Current yield: 4.6% ❑ Dividend raises, past 10 years: 10

## Company Profile

Measured by revenue, AT&T continues to be the largest telecommunications holding company in the US. Although known for years as the center of the wireline local and long-distance telecom service, it has evolved to be the largest provider of wireless, commercial broadband, and Wi-Fi services in the United States and has become a large player in consumer broadband services with its ISP service and U-verse bundle product.

In and of itself, that makes for a pretty decent business story. But the tale hardly stops here.

In mid-2015, AT&T acquired and absorbed satellite TV provider DIRECTV for about $50 billion, bringing together wireless phone and data service and satellite TV regular and on-demand offerings. The strategy: sell more bundled services and deliver more video to today's assortment of home and mobile devices.

And as if that wasn't enough, in mid-2016 the company entered into an agreement to purchase Time Warner Communications (until now, a *100 Best* stock) in a strategy to own not only the communications pipeline but also a significant chunk of content. As of this writing the deal had been approved by shareholders but not by regulators.

With the addition of DIRECTV (but not Time Warner), the company is now organized around three operating units, with Business Solutions being by far the largest, accounting for 42 percent of the $164 billion in total revenues. The Entertainment unit (which is where DIRECTV landed) includes home Internet services and the former Consumer Mobility business (translation: common cell phone service) and accounts for another 30 percent, while the remainder (28 percent) is from the International segment. While we applaud the reorganization into three clean-cut, roughly evenly sized businesses, we think the "Entertainment" segment should be renamed "Consumer" or some such—we don't all use our smartphones and Internet all the time to entertain ourselves!

Business Solutions offers both wireless and wireline services to business customers and some individual subscribers.

The Entertainment segment offers AT&T's U-verse, DIRECTV, and legacy DSL services to residential customers. They also provide legacy copper and IP-based voice services through AT&T's existing networks. The "Mobility" portion of this business provides nationwide wireless service to consumers, as well as wholesale and resale subscribers. This is the well-known consumer phone market, which offers services such as voice, text, and video.

The company estimates that more than 50 percent of its network traffic *today* is video, which is part of the justification for the DIRECTV, and now the Time Warner, acquisitions, and, almost as a footnote, the company is a major player in Latin America and dominates the lucrative Mexico wireless market.

## Financial Highlights, Fiscal Year 2016

With the large DIRECTV acquisition completed in FY2016 and another in the form of Time Warner coming in FY2017 (if approved), running revenue and profit forecasts aren't so meaningful. What we do know is that the overall business did well in FY2016, with overall revenues up 12 percent and, significantly, wireless revenues, the most competitive part of the business, up 20 percent on lower churn and net addition of 1.5 million customers. DIRECTV is a relatively more profitable business, so overall net margins were up 0.4 percent and total net income rose a full 16 percent on the year. The real story—and one goal of the DIRECTV acquisition—is cash flow, which rose to a whopping $39.3 billion (most US companies don't even have this much in sales); about $16.9 billion of that is "free" meaning not used for capital equipment purchases, dividends, etc., so there is ample cash to fund acquisitions and return to shareholders.

FY2017 is less of a blockbuster on the revenue front with a projected 1 percent growth, but acquisition synergies and a continued mix improvement will deliver 3 percent in earnings; earnings growth is projected to settle in the mid-single-digit range through FY2018 on similar modest growth. These numbers do not include the TWX acquisition. Share buybacks are off the table for now, but the regular 2 percent annual dividend increase looks likely to continue and possibly accelerate.

## Reasons to Buy

AT&T now presents itself as "a global leader in telecommunications, media, and technology." Boy, no kidding.

The two big acquisitions send a strong message that AT&T isn't just about phones and text messaging; it is about the consumer experience in all forms of access and entertainment available today. The acquisitions will increasingly bundle all forms of access and at the same time generate growth, higher margins, and thus far higher profits and especially cash flows down the road. To customers, AT&T will be a communications and entertainment machine; to investors it's a cash-flow machine.

Many investors will consider AT&T and will dismiss it as old school—too tied to old wireline operations and other traditional markets and crippled by its own size and reliance on crusty declining markets. In fact, though, AT&T has managed to innovate its way into new markets and succeed against a field of competitors who were thought to be far more nimble. The company is on a growth path that leverages its strength in broadband, mobile communications, satellite, and now, content, operations. Perhaps more than any other *100 Best* company, AT&T has weathered massive changes in its business environment and has formed itself into an agile and forward-looking company with a clear view of its future in the information era. And it has shown that it can manage and reap the benefits of large acquisitions.

And, as usual (and in spite of our worries about the acquisition), shareholder cash returns will continue to be above average, with a strong dividend payout and regular increases. We expect that once the acquisitions are paid for, the cash-flow fire hose will be aimed at shareholders in the form of better dividend raises and a resumption of buybacks—although this may take a few years to materialize.

## Reasons for Caution

As we mention every year, competition in the telecom and now, entertainment sectors, is well established and continues to be our main concern. Pricing is a key issue in AT&T's cost-sensitive consumer markets, as many of the "value" options available have, over the past year, improved their data offerings, technology, and financing options. Offsetting some of the competitive price erosion is the transition away from "subsidized" mobile contracts, where the contract revenue stream buys the phone for the customer.

But by far our biggest concern is the foray into a "vertical" merger with Time Warner. Most mergers are "horizontal," that is, between players in the same industry, and typically designed to gain operational efficiencies and market share. They're not "vertical"—between suppliers and customers. Microsoft would never buy Dell, for Dell's competitors would be turned off and do anything possible to avoid buying Microsoft products. The same situation may emerge with AT&T-TWX; other media distributors who compete with AT&T may be less likely to pick up TWX content, and other content providers (say, Sony Pictures) might be less motivated to sign good deals with AT&T as a distributor. These relationships can be complex.

We don't like vertical mergers, and if the merger occurs, these downsides definitely bear watching. Also, we wonder if this merger might be just a little too big to manage, especially on the heels of the DIRECTV acquisition.

A final thought: We hope that future narratives on AT&T will be more about the business itself and less about acquisitions.

SECTOR: **Telecommunications Services** ◻ BETA COEFFICIENT: **0.37** ◻ 10-YEAR COMPOUND EARNINGS PER-SHARE GROWTH: **4.0%** ◻ 10-YEAR COMPOUND DIVIDENDS PER-SHARE GROWTH: **4.0%**

|  | 2009 | 2010 | 2011 | 2012 | 2013 | 2014 | 2015 | 2016 |
|---|---|---|---|---|---|---|---|---|
| Revenues (bil) | 123.0 | 124.4 | 126.7 | 127.4 | 158.8 | 132.4 | 146.8 | 163.8 |
| Net income (mil) | 12,535 | 13,612 | 13,103 | 13,698 | 13,463 | 13,056 | 15,188 | 17,577 |
| Earnings per share | 2.12 | 2.29 | 2.20 | 2.33 | 2.50 | 2.50 | 2.69 | 2.84 |
| Dividends per share | 1.64 | 1.68 | 1.72 | 1.76 | 1.80 | 1.84 | 1.88 | 1.92 |
| Cash flow per share | 5.46 | 5.60 | 5.31 | 5.70 | 6.10 | 6.04 | 6.05 | 7.07 |
| Price: high | 29.5 | 29.6 | 31.9 | 38.6 | 39.0 | 37.5 | 36.4 | 43.9 |
| low | 21.4 | 23.8 | 27.2 | 29.0 | 32.8 | 31.7 | 31.0 | 33.4 |

Website: www.att.com

# Becton, Dickinson and Company

Ticker symbol: BDX (NYSE) ❑ Large Cap ❑ Value Line financial strength rating: A++ ❑ Current
yield: 1.6% ❑ Dividend raises, past 10 years: 10

## Company Profile

Gotten a flu shot or any other "delivery" of medicine lately? Chances are
the "device" used to make the delivery had a prominent "B-D" logo on the
package. "B-D" stands for "Becton, Dickinson," one of the premier medical
supply and technology companies on the planet.

Becton, Dickinson is a global healthcare technology player focused on
improving drug delivery, enhancing the diagnosis of infectious diseases and
cancers, and advancing medical lab work and drug discovery. The company develops, manufactures, and sells medical supplies, devices, laboratory instruments, antibodies, reagents, and diagnostic products through its
two segments: BD Medical and BD Life Sciences. These products are sold
to healthcare institutions, life science researchers, clinical laboratories, the
pharmaceutical industry, and the general public. With the 2015 acquisition
of CareFusion, B-D became a big player in the automated medicine delivery
market, a growing segment which reduces medicine delivery errors while
also reducing costs for medical providers. This acquisition added roughly 45
percent to the company's top and bottom lines.

International sales account for about 59 percent of the total. The B-D
brand is found throughout the range of clinics, medical offices, and hospitals
and is well recognized in the medical community.

The company now operates in two worldwide business segments: Medical
(69 percent of FY2016 sales) and Life Sciences (formerly Biosciences—31
percent). The former Diagnostics segment was folded into Medical and the
CareFusion business resides there as well.

The BD Medical segment produces a variety of drug-delivery devices
and supplies, including "sharps" (hypodermic needles and syringes) and
related disposal products, infusion therapy devices, intravenous catheters,
insulin injection systems, regional anesthesia needles, diabetes care systems,
and automated delivery and prefillable drug-delivery systems for pharmaceutical companies. The former Diagnostics unit offers system solutions for
collecting, identifying, and transporting blood and other specimens, as well
as instrumentation for analyzing these specimens. Testing systems include
those for sexually transmitted diseases, microorganism identification and

drug susceptibility, and certain types of cancer screening. The business also provides customer training and business management services.

BD Life Sciences provides research tools and reagents to accelerate the pace of biomedical discovery. Clinicians and researchers use BD Life Sciences' tools to study genes, proteins, and cells to understand disease, improve technologies for diagnosis and disease management, and facilitate the discovery and development of new therapeutics. Products include reagents, fluoroscience cell-activated sorters and analyzers, monoclonal antibodies and kits, and cell imaging and reagent solutions, among others.

## Financial Highlights, Fiscal Year 2016

With an infusion from CareFusion, FY2016 revenues advanced some 27 percent (the core business was up a respectable 6.1 percent). Both operating segments were strong, with BD Medical doing especially well in medical management solutions and diabetes care. Emerging markets turned more positive during the year with a 9 percent revenue gain in China. With the large number of shares issued for the CareFusion acquisition it's best to look at per-share earnings, which were up a substantial 20 percent for the year. Sales are expected to plateau at the $12-plus billion level in FY2017 and FY2018; a better product mix and acquisition synergies will grow earnings in the 8–10 percent range. Dividend increases should continue, but share buybacks have paused as the company pays down debt rapidly ($500 million per year) from the acquisition.

## Reasons to Buy

Becton, Dickinson continues to be a classic "blue-chip" company, as recession proof as any stock on our list. The steady upward price march, especially since 2013, is classic. Earnings, cash flow, and dividend growth have been steady and substantial, and net profit margins are both healthy (17 percent) and growing to record levels recently. The company will continue to benefit through the broadening of healthcare offerings into developing nations, from the automation of medicine delivery, and from a greater emphasis on preventative care, e.g., flu shots.

## Reasons for Caution

CareFusion was a big bet and one that lay a bit outside of the core supplies and diagnostics business presenting some additional risks, but everything seems to be going well so far. Continued strength in the dollar could weigh on performance. Changes in the Affordable Care Act also add some downside and uncertainty. Recent healthcare cost scrutiny may hurt some supplies and testing product lines but should help lines devoted to preventative care and efficient care delivery, like CareFusion. All said, Becton continues to be one of the best, safest, steadiest, and most well-managed players in the industry.

SECTOR: **Healthcare** ❑ BETA COEFFICIENT: **1.00** ❑ 10-YEAR COMPOUND EARNINGS PER-SHARE GROWTH: **9.5%** ❑ 10-YEAR COMPOUND DIVIDENDS PER-SHARE GROWTH: **12.5%**

|  | | 2009 | 2010 | 2011 | 2012 | 2013 | 2014 | 2015 | 2016 |
|---|---|---|---|---|---|---|---|---|---|
| Revenues (mil) | | 7,160 | 7,372 | 7,828 | 7,708 | 8,054 | 8,446 | 10,282 | 12,453 |
| Net income (mil) | | 1,220 | 1,185 | 1,272 | 1,123 | 1,159 | 1,236 | 1,480 | 1,869 |
| Earnings per share | | 4.95 | 4.94 | 5.61 | 5.36 | 5.81 | 6.25 | 7.16 | 8.59 |
| Dividends per share | | 1.32 | 1.48 | 1.64 | 1.80 | 1.98 | 2.18 | 2.40 | 2.64 |
| Cash flow per share | | 7.13 | 7.25 | 8.27 | 8.30 | 8.79 | 9.37 | 11.25 | 13.99 |
| Price: | high | 80.0 | 80.6 | 89.4 | 80.6 | 110.9 | 142.6 | 157.5 | 181.9 |
| | low | 60.4 | 66.5 | 72.5 | 71.6 | 78.7 | 105.2 | 128.9 | 129.5 |

Website: www.bd.com

---

CONSERVATIVE GROWTH

# Bemis Company, Inc.

Ticker symbol: BMS (NYSE) ❑ Mid Cap ❑ Value Line financial strength rating: A ❑ Current yield: 2.4% ❑ Dividend raises, past 10 years: 10

## Company Profile

You open a stick of string cheese. You pull the little tab at the end and out pops the stick of cheese, which has been happily stored in its little plastic sack through thousands of miles of trucks, warehouses, more trucks, a stockroom or two, the store, your refrigerator, and now maybe your lunch bucket or bag. You enjoy the string cheese with a sandwich made from lunchmeat packaged in a little zippered plastic bag. Afterward, you take your regular dose of allergy medication, packed up in one of those 12-tablet plastic trays.

Who makes this stuff? Did you ever stop to think about it? How it makes our lives easier, as well as those of manufacturers and distributors of these products? Neither had we, until our search for strategic and vital niche holders led us to one of the other companies in Kimberly-Clark's quiet and productive original hometown of Neenah, WI.

"Where inspired packaging solutions take shape" is the slogan, and it goes a long way to explain their value add in the food chain. Bemis makes all kinds of semirigid and flexible packaging solutions mostly out of plastic and mainly for the food, beverage, health and hygiene, building materials, and chemicals markets. Flexible packaging products include bags, wraps, and containers, many with a pressure-sensitive or zipper closure, all set up to be filled with standard packaging line equipment and all labeled for the client's products. "Raw" packaging materials roll out of 60 facilities to the end of packing lines in 11 countries. About 35 percent of sales are international (up from 33 percent in 2015); most of that is in Latin America, China, and Australia.

In 2014 Bemis sold its line of pressure-sensitive materials used in its own packaging but also sold into the printing, graphic design, and technology markets. The company had previously sold four paper-packaging plants to Hood Packaging Company—plants that make items like paper bags for pet foods. Both sales represent a sustained effort to adjust the business mix toward its higher-margin businesses—that is, high-value-add packaging solutions.

A key strategy is to help customers find economical solutions that improve product quality, safety, shelf life, and shelf presence—they attempt to differentiate a customer's product through the package. The company believes that its leadership position "rests on its strong technical foundation in polymer chemistry, film extrusion, coating and laminating, printing and converting" and that "material science continues to be the primary instrument for creating sustainable competitive advantage."

## Financial Highlights, Fiscal Year 2016
Revenue and profits for FY2016 were both down about 2 percent, although a moderate share buyback kept per-share earnings and cash flows flat. There was some price and volume erosion as food prices decrease, but we suspect that is temporary. The biggest factor affecting the company was currency headwinds; in fact, the company estimates that per-share earnings would have been ahead 8 percent without currency. Through FY2018, sales are expected to advance in the 2–3 percent range, with per-share earnings advancing 16 percent in FY2017 and 10–12 percent in FY2018 as operational efficiency measures take effect and the product mix improves with new, higher-margined "healthy, fresh, convenient" and other innovative products. Moderate share repurchases in the 1–2 percent range should continue. Dividends will rise slowly and steadily as well; we predict "steadily" because the company has increased its dividend 34 years in a row.

## Reasons to Buy
This is not an exciting company, but it is a strong niche player providing critical packaging technologies to the industries it serves. New and innovative

food-packaging designs are becoming more desired as convenience, quality, and health and safety outweigh cost as a priority in most consumer markets these days. The new packaged salads are a good example of packaging for a product not packaged before; new ziplock containers for lunchmeats, cheeses, etc., show how the package is moving up the value-add scale. The company has a significant beachhead in growing Latin American markets, China, and Australia and is investing in new technologies and applications such as package design enhancements for microwaving, easy-open packages for elderly customers (we continue to applaud this one!), new technologies to replace common plastic bottles and tin cans, and new technologies and delivery systems for the healthcare and pharmaceutical industries. We like the strategy of fine-tuning the business mix toward more profitable, higher value–add packages, and the company seems to be executing it well and getting the desired results from it. Cash flow and cash returns to shareholders have become a priority and are steady and increasing; the issue continues to have appealingly low volatility and is a good defensive play.

## Reasons for Caution

To a degree, Bemis is exposed to price volatility in both food and energy and to the economy in general. When food prices rise, consumers get more sensitive to price and may hesitate to pay for convenience packaging—I'll choose and boil my own Brussels sprouts, thank you; no boiling bags for me. Growth has been hard to come by lately, but we think new innovations in the pipeline should address that, and the efficiency measures and improved margins arising from them will lead to decent growth in earnings.

SECTOR: **Consumer Staples** ◻ BETA COEFFICIENT: **0.91** ◻ 10-YEAR COMPOUND EARNINGS PER-SHARE GROWTH: **4.0%** ◻ 10-YEAR COMPOUND DIVIDENDS PER-SHARE GROWTH: **4.5%**

|  | 2009 | 2010 | 2011 | 2012 | 2013 | 2014 | 2015 | 2016 |
|---|---|---|---|---|---|---|---|---|
| Revenues (mil) | 3,515 | 4,835 | 5,323 | 5,139 | 5,030 | 4,344 | 4,071 | 4,004 |
| Net income (mil) | 147.2 | 203.3 | 212.4 | 225.3 | 237.0 | 233.1 | 242.0 | 236.0 |
| Earnings per share | 1.38 | 1.83 | 1.99 | 2.15 | 2.28 | 2.30 | 2.47 | 2.48 |
| Dividends per share | 0.90 | 0.92 | 0.96 | 1.00 | 1.04 | 1.08 | 1.12 | 1.16 |
| Cash flow per share | 2.81 | 3.84 | 3.87 | 3.66 | 4.19 | 4.21 | 4.21 | 4.21 |
| Price:        high | 31.4 | 34.3 | 34.4 | 33.9 | 42.3 | 47.2 | 49.4 | 54.2 |
|               low | 16.8 | 25.5 | 27.2 | 29.5 | 33.7 | 34.3 | 38.9 | 42.4 |

Website: **www.bemis.com**

## AGGRESSIVE GROWTH

# Boeing Company

Ticker symbol: BA (NYSE) ◻ Large Cap ◻ Value Line financial strength rating: A++ ◻ Current yield: 3.1% ◻ Dividend raises, past 10 years: 8

## Company Profile

Way back in 2011, we "grounded" Boeing.

At the time, the airline industry was suffering from weak demand and high costs—high fuel prices in particular. They were financially strapped and weren't buying so many aircraft. Too, back then and for the next few years the company was having trouble getting its 787 Dreamliner to market, with one production delay after another. And Europe's Airbus consortium was making share gains in key aircraft markets, winning deals even with US airlines. And the military and defense market wasn't doing so well either under the Obama administration.

That was then; this is now. Boeing has navigated these air pockets, some internal, some external, with flying colors. Thanks mostly to lower fuel prices and better management, airlines have taken off and have landed order after order for modern, more fuel-efficient aircraft. Boeing has delivered on its new aircraft, including new, larger, and more efficient versions of its ever-popular 737 series. Defense spending appears to be on the rise, and Boeing is well positioned in good areas in this (aero)space, including unmanned guided weapons which appear to have strategic advantage going forward. The backlog is $473 *billion* on unfilled orders for 5,700 aircraft. The company values its potential ten-year market opportunity at $10 *trillion*. Given today's current environment and execution, there seems no place to go but up. Welcome back to your old gate on the 2018 *100 Best Stocks* list, Boeing.

Boeing is the world's largest aerospace company. Its leading commercial aircraft lines include the familiar 737, 747, 767, 777, and 787 platforms, while it also produces business jets and a variety of defense aircraft including F-15 and F/A-18 fighters, CH-47 (Chinook) and AH-64 (Apache) helicopters, Osprey vertical landing and takeoff aircraft, and Harpoon guided weapons. The company has delivered 3,483 new commercial airplanes and 1,041 military aircraft and satellites in the past five years. It also is involved in space and security systems, managing the International Space Station and selling various kinds of satellites.

The company is organized into two principal segments: Commercial Airplanes and Defense, Space & Security. Commercial Airplanes accounts for about 68 percent of 2016 revenues, while within the Defense, Space &

Security group, Boeing Military Aircraft brings in 13 percent of revenues, Network & Space Systems 7 percent, and Global Services & Support about 11 percent of revenues, respectively, giving a total of 31 percent for the DS&S group. The company is America's largest exporter and has operations in 65 countries, with foreign sales accounting for 59 percent of 2016 revenues.

Innovation and new product development are key to Boeing's success. A long-term initiative to improve fuel economy has produced results; for example, the latest 737 MAX 8 model has longer flight capabilities and a savings of at least 8 percent in fuel over its nearest competitor.

## Financial Highlights, Fiscal Year 2016

After four years of stellar growth up through FY2015, the company leveled off in most major businesses in revenue terms as new aircraft deliveries dipped slightly worldwide. However, cost efficiencies and an improved mix led to a 34 percent gain in net income adjusted for some accounting changes in the handling of R&D expenses. Net profit margins expanded to 7.3 percent from a 4.7–6.0 percent range in recent years. A 50-million share repurchase led to a full 45 percent gain in per-share earnings. An amazing performance on flat revenues! Going forward, revenues still look fairly flat, though Trump administration policies on defense spending and more commercial aircraft replacement as global airline profitability turns into new orders might make that forecast look a little conservative. Forecasts call for sales and profits to resume their upward trajectory in 2018, a result that looks likely given current backlogs and order rates.

Dividend increases have been substantial—20 percent in FY2016 and 50 percent the prior year; increases in the 20–30 percent rate going forward appear likely at least for the next two years. The company has purchased over $23 billion of its shares—18 percent of its shares—in the past five years.

## Reasons to Buy

When we "grounded" Boeing seven years ago, they were suffering from weak external markets, competition, and internal execution issues. What a difference seven years makes! New products, strong execution, and a much healthier "customer" industry have created a perfect storm for Boeing—and revenues in general and profitability in particular have responded well. Airline fleets are eager to replace aging, less fuel-efficient aircraft. Increased defense spending will also help. The company is reaping the success of massive R&D investments in recent years, and is achieving scale which also improves profitability. It also helps to have such large backlogs, as the company doesn't have to guess on production requirements, product mix, etc.

## Reasons for Caution

Throughout its history, Boeing has been subject to cyclical ups and downs as the airline industry and defense spending go through cycles of their own. Some of these cycles have been severe. That said, the current positive cycle seems to have longer legs, and the company's products in our view have a stronger and more sustainable competitive advantage in technology and scale that should help avoid the kinds of sharp downturns seen previously—if the airline business softens they will still buy new aircraft in an effort to become more efficient. Additionally, new competition has arrived at the gate in the form of new Chinese-built airliners, which have not yet been certified for US carriage but still bear watching. Finally, today's share price, too, has factored in a lot of success; we do recognize that the company's stock has tripled since we grounded it, but the business prospects and results have climbed faster than that.

SECTOR: **Industrials** ◻ BETA COEFFICIENT: **1.17** ◻ 10-YEAR COMPOUND EARNINGS PER-SHARE GROWTH: **13.0%** ◻ 10-YEAR COMPOUND DIVIDENDS PER-SHARE GROWTH: **13.0%**

|  | | **2009** | **2010** | **2011** | **2012** | **2013** | **2014** | **2015** | **2016** |
|---|---|---|---|---|---|---|---|---|---|
| Revenues (bil) | | 68.2 | 64.3 | 68.7 | 81.7 | 86.6 | 90.8 | 96.1 | 94.6 |
| Net income (bil) | | 1.3 | 3.3 | 3.6 | 3.9 | 4.6 | 5.5 | 5.2 | 6.9 |
| Earnings per share | | 1.87 | 4.46 | 4.82 | 5.11 | 5.96 | 7.38 | 7.44 | 10.84 |
| Dividends per share | | 1.68 | 1.68 | 1.68 | 1.76 | 1.94 | 2.92 | 3.64 | 4.36 |
| Cash flow per share | | 4.13 | 6.85 | 7.08 | 7.56 | 8.60 | 10.40 | 10.51 | 14.36 |
| Price: | high | 56.6 | 76.0 | 80.6 | 77.8 | 142.0 | 144.6 | 158.8 | 160.1 |
| | low | 29.0 | 54.1 | 56.0 | 66.8 | 72.7 | 116.3 | 115.1 | 102.1 |

Website: www.boeing.com

CONSERVATIVE GROWTH

# Campbell Soup Company

Ticker symbol: CPB (NYSE) ◻ Large Cap ◻ Value Line financial strength rating: B++ ◻ Current yield: 2.5% ◻ Dividend raises, past 10 years: 7

## Company Profile

Campbell Soup Company is the world's largest, as they like to say, maker of "real food that matters for life's moments." To most of the free world, that still translates to soup and the ubiquitous pop-culture-iconic Campbell's Soup can. Few brands have enjoyed such penetration and loyalty as the core Campbell's brand, and that brand still accounts for about 25 percent of the company's sales. But there is a lot more to this story—including demographic shifts toward millennial customers that the company is openly acknowledging and responding to.

After a 2015 reorganization, the company has three reporting segments: Simple Meals and Beverages (55 percent of 2016 sales), Global Biscuits and Snacks (33 percent), and Packaged Fresh (12 percent). Simple Meals includes the core Campbell's brand along with V8, Swanson, Plum Organics, and Prego. Global Biscuits contains such favorites as Pepperidge Farm, Kelsen, and Arnott's, while Packaged Fresh is built around the emerging and healthful Bolthouse Farms brand of healthy beverages, salad dressings, organic produce, and similar products. The company also acquired Garden Fresh Gourmet in 2015, bringing lines of hummus, dips, organic chips, and similar foodstuffs.

Campbell's products are distributed to 120 countries worldwide and are sold through its own sales force and through distributors. US-based operations accounted for 81 percent of revenue in FY2016. Products are manufactured in 19 principal facilities within the United States and in 9 facilities outside the country. The company's growth strategy has evolved toward greater innovation in product marketing and brand recognition and new packaging designed to broaden use in today's fast-paced economy, as well as a healthy dose of internationalization. Bolthouse, purchased in 2012 and the fastest-growing segment of the business in terms of products and revenues, gives the company better exposure to Millennials, a market not well addressed by Campbell's traditional brands.

The company recognizes "seismic shifts" in its markets—not just economic shifts but big changes in consumer needs and preferences. Consumers want healthier and fresher foods. They want greater nutrition and transparency with respect to ingredients and food origins. They want to know the impact on diet and health. They want to avoid GMOs, artificial flavors and colors, preservatives, and MSG. They want greater convenience without sacrificing diet and health. And the demographics have shifted—there are 80 million so-called Millennials and 60 million Latinos in the US market—all of whom amplify these trends. And what has happened to the business? For one, sales of soup have dropped from 42 percent of the total to 34 percent of the total, while sales of "simple meals" have risen by the same amount. We hear you, Millennials!

Generally the company is recognizing the need for marketable innovations and is answering that challenge with these noted acquisitions and other new products such as Campbell's Skillet Sauces, Slow Cooker and Oven Sauces, and various new organic products including a full line of organic canned and boxed soups, some targeted at kids. Their market research suggests the well-known desire for better nutrition and more "natural" ingredients. They are eliminating high fructose corn syrup from some and artificial flavorings and colors from all North American products. They are investing in digital advertising and e-commerce initiatives as well.

## Financial Highlights, Fiscal Year 2016

FY2016 was an "off" year for revenues; they declined about 1.5 percent on currency translations and lower volumes in key categories like soups, which were offset somewhat by the Garden Fresh acquisition and higher selling prices. Earnings, however, advanced a very healthy 10 percent on reduced costs, a streamlined organization, reduced advertising, and other expense reductions. Going forward, earnings will rise 3–5 percent annually through FY2018 as margins expand (and a 12 percent net margin in this business is pretty good), while revenues will be flat in FY2017 and are expected to rise 2–3 percent in FY2018. In the meantime, modest dividend increases and share repurchases should juice investor returns just a bit.

## Reasons to Buy

Why do we like Campbell so much? Simply: they're quite profitable compared to peers and getting more so. Another big reason is innovation. Their approach to innovation resonates with us. We think innovation is the key to survival particularly as markets evolve to the tastes of the new Millennial generation.

Then there's the usual: core brand and brand strength. Campbell owns the number one or number two position in each of the product categories in which it participates. It dominates the $4 billion US soup market and is making headway in key foreign markets too. Cash cows are always a good thing to have as you step forward into the marketing "beyond."

Campbell isn't trying to capture the remaining 40 percent of the soup market that it doesn't own. The strategy, well-known in the food industry, is to maintain and slowly grow its core brands while generating new growth, leveraging distribution and sales channels, and increasing brand presence through new products often not directly associated with the Campbell brand. The strategy sounds pretty tasty to us.

Finally, we think Campbell serves well as a defensive play in a year where playing at least some defense seems like a good idea.

## Reasons for Caution

Even with the recent emphasis on innovation, the company's brands and core customer base are aging, and adoption of new products may continue to prove slow, especially among the younger set. As others, like Coca-Cola, have found out over the years, there are risks inherent with tinkering with a long-established brand such as Campbell's. We would hope that Campbell succeeds with its new ventures without pulling the rug out from under the old ones. We still like Cream of Mushroom on a rainy day.

SECTOR: **Consumer Staples** ❑ BETA COEFFICIENT: **0.42** ❑ 10-YEAR COMPOUND EARNINGS PER-SHARE GROWTH: **5.0%** ❑ 10-YEAR COMPOUND DIVIDENDS PER-SHARE GROWTH: **6.5%**

|                     |      | 2009  | 2010  | 2011  | 2012  | 2013  | 2014  | 2015  | 2016  |
|---------------------|------|-------|-------|-------|-------|-------|-------|-------|-------|
| Revenues (mil)      |      | 7,586 | 7,676 | 7,715 | 7,707 | 8,052 | 8,268 | 8,082 | 7,961 |
| Net income (mil)    |      | 771   | 842   | 846   | 783   | 786   | 800   | 831   | 914   |
| Earnings per share  |      | 2.15  | 2.45  | 2.54  | 2.44  | 2.48  | 2.53  | 2.65  | 2.94  |
| Dividends per share |      | 1.00  | 1.05  | 1.15  | 1.16  | 1.16  | 1.25  | 1.25  | 1.25  |
| Cash flow per share |      | 2.87  | 3.25  | 3.48  | 3.35  | 3.82  | 3.53  | 3.68  | 3.97  |
| Price:              | high | 35.8  | 37.6  | 35.7  | 37.2  | 45.8  | 46.7  | 55.1  | 67.9  |
|                     | low  | 24.8  | 24.6  | 29.7  | 31.2  | 34.8  | 39.6  | 42.9  | 50.5  |

Website: www.campbellsoup.com

AGGRESSIVE GROWTH

# CarMax, Inc.

Ticker symbol: KMX (NYSE) ❑ Large Cap ❑ Value Line financial strength rating: B+ ❑ Current yield: Nil ❑ Dividend raises, past 10 years: NA

## Company Profile

"The Way Car Buying Should Be" is the appropriate slogan used by this clean-cut chain of used vehicle stores and superstores and its new big-box, retail-like model for selling cars. CarMax buys, reconditions, and sells cars and light trucks at 173 retail centers in 73 metropolitan markets in 39 states, mainly in the Southeast, Midwest, and California, but is gradually moving to a more nationwide footprint. The company specializes in selling cars that are under six years old with less than 60,000 miles in excellent condition; the cars are sold at a competitive price, typically in the $10,000 to $34,000 price range, for their condition in a no-haggle environment. The price is the price; the emphasis is on the condition of the vehicles and on a helpful and friendly sales and transaction process. Sales representatives are compensated for cars they sell but not in such a way that drives them to push the wrong car on a customer. The company sold some 671,294 used vehicles in 2016, up 8.5 percent from FY2015 and up 64 percent from the 408,080 sold in 2011. The average selling price for 2016 was $19,586, down slightly from the previous year as used car prices have softened a bit—but the average gross margin was $2,163 per vehicle, up slightly from the previous $2,109.

CarMax is gaining footholds in new markets such as Denver, Minneapolis-St. Paul, the Pacific Northwest, Philadelphia, Boston, and smaller markets such as Boise, Grand Rapids, Mobile, and El Paso. Most reports suggest they are gaining market share in the markets they serve with a high degree of customer satisfaction. CarMax opened 15 new stores 2016; and they plan to open 15 more new stores in 2017 and 13–16 new stores in 2018. From 173 stores total today, they anticipate 225 stores in place by the end of the decade, including new presence in the Seattle, New York City, and San Francisco areas and more small-format stores in smaller markets Harrisonburg, VA, and Jackson, TN—there are 10 in place already. The overall strategy is to build a national footprint and brand, achieve economies of scale, and make the most of online marketing initiatives.

The health of the economy and consumer spending have swung car buying into a higher gear, but with newfound consumer prudence. Many of these purchases are heading to the one- to six-year-old used car sector of the business, where prices are 40–60 percent lower than comparable new cars. The new car boom of recent years has led to a large number of lease returns, which, while depressing used car prices somewhat, also provides a major source of low-cost supply for CarMax's inventory. In addition to "retail" used car sales, CarMax is a big player in auto wholesaling, having moved about 382,000 units mostly taken in trade; the company is the world's largest used car buyer. The company also earns income through its financing unit, known as CarMax Auto Finance, or CAF. The unit finances about 43 percent of the company's sales.

CarMax also has service operations and sells extended warranties and other products related to car ownership. The company has state-of-the-art web-based and mobile tools as well as other aids designed to make the car selection, buying, and ownership experience more personalized, more "self-service," and generally easier. As CarMax puts it, customers expect four things when they buy a car:

1. Don't play games
2. Don't waste my time
3. Provide security
4. Make car buying fun

The company's offering is aimed at reducing these concerns and providing the right experience. The offering continues to be largely unique in the industry, and competitors would have a long way to go to catch up.

## Financial Highlights, Fiscal Year 2016

It was a good market once again for selling cars, with new car sales running at a 17 million annual rate—at the high end of the cyclical range. For the year ending February 29, 2017, which the company calls FY2017 but we will refer to as "2016" because most activity occurred in that year, same-store used vehicle sales were up about 4.3 percent (up from 2.4 percent last year); total unit volume was 8.3 percent higher but with slightly lower prices, leading to an overall revenue increase of about 4.8 percent. Success factors included a significant growth in online and mobile vehicle shopping activity, and higher conversion rates in the store with an assortment of physical and process tweaks.

The gross margin per used vehicle ticked up slightly to $2,163 from $2,109 last year as a relatively oversupplied used car market drove down prices. That with higher volumes offset slightly lower finance income, wholesaling profits, and selling prices to produce a slight 1 percent net income gain—however, per-share earnings were up 8 percent thanks to a 4 percent share buyback. FY2017 and FY2018 forecasts call for a 6–8 percent annual top-line gain mostly driven by new store openings; margins will remain about constant but the share count will come down further, perhaps another 5 percent, giving annual per-share earnings gains in the 8–10 percent range. The company announced its first share buyback program in 2012 and has pursued it aggressively every year since then, clearly set up as a shareholder return vehicle in lieu of dividends. Since then they have retired 18 percent of the float and are on track to retire a third of that 2012 225-million-share count by the end of the decade.

## Reasons to Buy

Quite simply, CarMax continues to be a buy if you believe the traditional dealer model is broken and if you believe people will continue to see value in late-model used vehicles. CarMax as a brand is gaining national recognition as a "go-to" in the car buying (and selling) process.

Additionally, CarMax brings the latest in business intelligence and analytic models to the car-marketing process, in procurement, merchandising, pricing, and selling the vehicles. Do green Jeep Cherokees sell well in Southern California? Then let's find some, put them on the lot there, and set a market-based price. KMX is well ahead of the industry in making analysis-based supply and selling decisions and has quite successfully deployed analytic tools to adjust prices and inventories quickly to market conditions. They point out the large amounts of data accumulated through selling 10.5 million vehicles, hosting 65 million customers in their history, and handling 180 million digital interactions per year—a distinct competitive advantage that bodes well for the future.

CarMax is increasingly a big player in the 40-million vehicle used car market (versus 17 million for new cars), taking market share from traditional used car dealers, but there's fertile ground to capture more. The company estimates that it has only 5 percent of the current market for zero-to-ten-year-old used vehicles in markets in which it operates, and only 3 percent of the total nationwide—all while being the largest player and twice the size of the nearest competitor.

The company is positioned well both for organic growth through market share and for geographic growth; there is still plenty of fertile ground for new growth, especially in the Northeast and Northwest and smaller metro areas. The footprint is slowly but surely becoming a nationwide one, which will not only help volumes but also brand recognition, pricing power, buying power, and cost absorption. The small-format store will probably add to this.

Earnings momentum has been strong lately, in part due to the aggressive share repurchase program.

## Reasons for Caution

CarMax will always be somewhat vulnerable to economic cycles, the availability of credit, and the availability of quality used vehicles to resell. Recent concerns about vehicle availability have morphed into concerns about oversupply as lease returns flood the market. Lease returns are an important source of supply for the company, so there is good news in this as well.

A new trend toward longer six- and seven-year new car financing periods may keep people in their cars longer, but it may also incentivize people to buy used to avoid the long financing period in the first place. As this company is still in the growth phase, and new dealerships involve putting lots of new cars on the ground, working capital needs are extensive, long-term debt has risen, and cash returns to shareholders have not met our norms; however, the share repurchase program takes a big step toward fixing that.

SECTOR: **Retail** ❑ BETA COEFFICIENT: **1.30** ❑ 10-YEAR COMPOUND EARNINGS PER-SHARE
GROWTH: **16.0%** ❑ 10-YEAR COMPOUND DIVIDENDS PER-SHARE GROWTH: **NA**

|  |  | 2009 | 2010 | 2011 | 2012 | 2013 | 2014 | 2015 | 2016 |
|---|---|------|------|------|------|------|------|------|------|
| Revenues (mil) | | 7,400 | 8,975 | 10,004 | 10,963 | 12,574 | 14,269 | 15,150 | 15,875 |
| Net income (mil) | | 281.7 | 380.9 | 413.8 | 425.0 | 492.6 | 583.9 | 628.6 | 633.8 |
| Earnings per share | | 1.26 | 1.67 | 1.79 | 1.87 | 2.16 | 2.68 | 3.05 | 3.30 |
| Dividends per share | | — | — | — | — | — | — | — | — |
| Cash flow per share | | 1.52 | 1.95 | 2.19 | 2.00 | 2.70 | 3.35 | 3.93 | 4.30 |
| Price: | high | 24.8 | 30.0 | 37.0 | 38.2 | 53.1 | 68.7 | 75.4 | 66.6 |
|  | low | 6.9 | 18.6 | 22.8 | 24.8 | 38.0 | 42.5 | 50.6 | 41.3 |

Website: www.carmax.com

## AGGRESSIVE GROWTH

# Carnival Corporation

Ticker symbol: CCL (NYSE) ❑ Large Cap ❑ Value Line financial strength rating: B+ ❑ Current
yield: 2.6% ❑ Dividend raises, past 10 years: 5

## Company Profile

Carnival Corporation is the world's largest leisure travel company, providing
cruises and cruise vacations to destinations throughout the world. The company operates under 11 individual cruise brands, or separate cruise lines in
two segments—North America, and Europe, Australia, & Asia (EAA) segments. The North America segment includes Carnival Cruise Line, Princess
Cruises, Holland America Line, and Seabourn (a luxury line) cruise brands.
The EAA segment includes Costa Cruises, Cunard Cruises, Ibero Cruises,
AIDA Cruises, P&O Cruises (UK), and P&O Cruises (Australia). Together,
these cruise lines operate over 100 modern ships (with 19 more on the way
between now and 2022) with more than 221,000 berths, and the company
claims about 48 percent of the worldwide cruise market. The company operates a few port facilities, Alaska tours, and some other adjacent travel operations. About 63 percent of revenues come from the North American brands.

The ships are modern, really, floating hotels, and the travel experience is
all-inclusive and easy for guests. The typical cruise is set up for all age groups,
with plenty of varied activities and foods for all, including new specialty restaurants and celebrity chefs on board and big names such as Crosby, Stills &
Nash in the entertainment lineup. The latest Carnival Cruise Line ship, the
*Carnival Vista*, launched in 2016, has an onboard brewery, an IMAX theater,

and an aerial "Skyride." Also launched in 2016, the Holland America Line's *Koningsdam* allows patrons to blend their own wine and enjoy Lincoln Center Stage, Billboard Onboard, and B.B. King. Fares are "all-inclusive," but travelers will find plenty of add-ons like Internet service and alcoholic beverages to run up an additional tab while on board. Cruises range from short three- and four-day "Love Boat" cruises out of Los Angeles to three- and four-week and longer passages through entire regions such as the Middle East or Southeast Asia.

Customer service is paramount and has become a recent emphasis of the Carnival lines. Live agents are available before, during, and after the cruise to answer any questions ("Can my 17-year-old bring his skateboard?" "Yes, but he'll have to stow it while on board the ship; he can access it for ports of call."). The experience is turnkey and much simpler than the typical land-based vacation, especially if multiple destinations are involved. The company and its lines have gotten smart about attracting repeat customers through loyalty programs and "perks"—some wealthier retirees might spend half a year on the company's ships as a simpler, less-expensive alternative to owning a large motor home or vacation property. Retirees have always been prime targets—but the offering is becoming more attractive to families and younger customers as well—to a degree, because cruises have become more "hip."

Recent directions include "green cruising" where ships are powered by liquefied natural gas, new cruises to Cuba (the first embarked in early 2016), and more originations and availability from China to serve the growing traveling middle class there. To that point, there are an estimated 135 million outbound travelers in China today, a figure estimated to grow to 200 million by 2020—and currently only 5 percent of the company's capacity serves China.

## Financial Highlights, Fiscal Year 2016

After many years of rocky seas, particularly during the Great Recession, Carnival has finally, through a combination of marketing and operational excellence, found calmer waters and steady tailwinds despite a slight rise in fuel costs. FY2016 was a very good year: Revenues rose just over 4 percent, while cost efficiencies and better capacity utilization drove net margins up a full 2.3 percent to 15.7 percent; net earnings were up 23 percent and per-share earnings were up 28 percent in the wake of a 3 percent buyback. Going forward, the company expects capacity increases, strong bookings, and more efficient ships to guide the course toward continued 4–6 percent annual revenue growth, stronger margins still, and earnings growth in the 10 percent range annually. A steadier and confident Carnival is also starting to return more cash to shareholders, both in the form of moderate dividend increases and share buybacks.

## Reasons to Buy

We continue to think cruising has come into its own as a mainstream regular travel alternative, not just a niche business providing a once-in-a-lifetime honeymoon or retirement cruise to Alaska. Cruises are more complete and easier than in past years, and there is something for everyone. The new ships are spectacular.

The marketing story is solid—strong brands, customer service, and customer loyalty leading the way. Millennials, who once probably would never have thought of a cruise, now are attracted to the activities, special meals, and entertainment, and the experience as a whole. It is no longer just for Grandma and Grandpa. As this group is more and more likely to shun material goods for experiences, cruise operators, especially those offering "interesting" itineraries, are in the right dock at the right time. Too, we think their strategy to capitalize on growing China tourism is on course.

Financially, we see a long-awaited return to steadier waters and more return to shareholders—all on the right heading.

## Reasons for Caution

It's hard not to think about how economic cycles can affect this industry; fancy vacations are usually the first thing to go when times turn tough. We'd counter that cruises don't have to be "exotic" and many are affordable even on a modest family budget—there's something for everyone here. High fixed costs (ships, especially today's ships, are expensive!) present some financial challenges especially in bad times. Fuel prices can be another variable, and competition in this industry is fairly intense, but we feel that Carnival has the strongest position, the best brands, and the best overall offering. You should no longer need a life jacket to buy this company, but watching the horizon is important as it is for any stock.

SECTOR: **Consumer Discretionary** ◻ BETA COEFFICIENT: **0.71** ◻ 10-YEAR COMPOUND EARNINGS PER-SHARE GROWTH: **0.5%** ◻ 10-YEAR COMPOUND DIVIDENDS PER-SHARE GROWTH: **4.0%**

|  | 2009 | 2010 | 2011 | 2012 | 2013 | 2014 | 2015 | 2016 |
|---|---|---|---|---|---|---|---|---|
| Revenues (mil) | 13,157 | 14,469 | 15,793 | 15,382 | 15,456 | 15,884 | 15,774 | 16,389 |
| Net income (mil) | 1,790 | 1,978 | 1,912 | 1,464 | 1,078 | 1,516 | 2,103 | 2,580 |
| Earnings per share | 2.24 | 2.47 | 2.42 | 1.88 | 1.39 | 1.99 | 2.70 | 3.45 |
| Dividends per share | — | 0.40 | 1.00 | 1.00 | 1.00 | 1.00 | 1.10 | 1.35 |
| Cash flow per share | 3.94 | 4.30 | 4.36 | 3.84 | 3.44 | 4.06 | 4.83 | 5.95 |
| Price:        high | 34.9 | 47.2 | 48.1 | 39.9 | 40.5 | 46.5 | 55.8 | 54.9 |
| low | 16.8 | 29.7 | 28.5 | 29.2 | 31.4 | 33.1 | 42.5 | 40.5 |

Website: www.carnivalcorp.com

GROWTH AND INCOME

# CenterPoint Energy, Inc.

Ticker symbol: CNP (NYSE) □ Large Cap □ Value Line financial strength rating: B+ □ Current yield: 3.9% □ Dividend raises, past 10 years: 10

## Company Profile

"Sell when there's something better to buy" is our guiding philosophy and mantra for removing and replacing companies on our *100 Best* list each year. Two years ago we did just that, replacing old-line utility favorite Southern Company with the more progressive, more diversified CenterPoint Energy. Part of that diversification was into the natural gas business with a 55 percent interest in Enable Midstream Partners, a natural gas master limited partnership. Given what happened in energy markets, we took a big hit (especially for a utility company) during 2015. But progressive moves to write-down losses and possibly sell the interest, combined with strength in other businesses and a secure, best-in-class yield, brought the stock back. The stock appreciated 30 percent in our 2016 measurement year, well exceeding our expectations for a utility. The positive story continues for 2017 and 2018; thus CenterPoint remains a clear-cut example of the all-important "sell when there's something better to buy" principle.

CenterPoint Energy is in the electricity delivery (not production, but delivery) business, serving more than 2.4 million customers in a 5,000-square-mile service territory in the greater Houston area, and is in the retail gas delivery business, serving more than 3.4 million metered customers in Louisiana, Arkansas, Minnesota, Mississippi, Oklahoma, and Texas (including Houston). It is the nineteenth-largest investor-owned electric utility and sixth-largest gas distribution company in the US by customer base. It is also—as of this writing—in the gas production business, with a 55 percent interest in a master limited partnership called Enable Midstream Partners, which produces and distributes wholesale gas and some oil mainly from Texas and Oklahoma. Finally, the company operates an unregulated CenterPoint Energy Services arm, which sells gas to commercial, industrial, and wholesale customers in 33 US states and provides an assortment of consulting services for other utilities.

CenterPoint intrigues us because, first, it does not own generating assets but instead distributes electricity to its customers produced by 18 providers, some green. It owns the wires, the meters, and the customer contact, while such messy problems as fuel costs and environmental risks are left to someone else. Second, in its distribution business, the company has learned to use technology to drive efficiency and improve the customer experience, with advanced implementations of smart grids, smart metering, and other technologies from companies such as Itron, Inc. (another *100 Best* pick). The company has installed smart meters for almost all of its customer base—more than 2.4 million "advanced" meters—automating meter reading and frequent readouts on electricity use. Customers are never left in the dark for long—these technologies manage the grid to reduce consumption, access the least expensive source, and keep the lights on more reliably—and when that fails, the company has also learned how to hook up with customer smartphones and media to quickly advise of service interruptions or other important announcements.

Finally, we liked the idea of a gas distributor acquiring some upstream assets to control costs and assure supplies—only it backfired as energy prices cratered in late 2014. The company took a $1.8 billion noncash write-down of the asset value of Midstream and is reconsidering its ownership—now that the pain has been taken we're good with either direction CenterPoint decides to go with this investment—sell, spin off, or retain—the decision should be made prior to 2018. Electricity transmission and distribution accounts for 41 percent of FY2016 revenues; gas distribution accounts for 32 percent, and the unregulated gas sales and services unit accounts for the rest.

## Financial Highlights, Fiscal Year 2016

With the limited partnership interest and the large unregulated sales unit, revenues and earnings can vary more widely than with most large utilities. Reported FY2016 revenues rose 2 percent and net profit dropped about 7 percent, influenced by Enable and a higher income tax rate.

Rate relief, a steady 1–2 percent rise in the customer base, expense control operating efficiency, and the predicted relative stability of Enable results are projected to bring a full 30 percent earnings gain in FY2017 on a 3 percent revenue gain; the gains return to a more "normal" but still strong 7–8 percent earnings gain on another steady 3 percent revenue gain. Depletion and depreciation allowances typically keep cash flows well ahead of earnings for this type of company. As such, cash flows are four times the indicated dividend secure despite the high percentage of reported earnings (80–90 percent) it represents.

## Reasons to Buy

We look at the electricity business as a key business anchor with decent growth prospects, and we like the deployment of leading-edge technologies in that business. We like their positioning as a low-cost producer and wholesaler in the gas business with a built-in outlet in the regulated business for their product. We think the Enable "pendulum" has swung back from "problem" to "opportunity," and that any good news in this sector, including a sale, will only help from this point forward. The dividend is still high compared to peers and appears secure and poised to grow about 4 percent a year and possibly more. CenterPoint combines the safety and yield of a quality utility with a bit of appreciation potential in the energy production and distribution business.

## Reasons for Caution

Whether eventually sold or retained, Enable still creates some uncertainty, though most of the bad news seems to be behind CenterPoint. We do worry that another slowdown in the energy economy could temper Houston's growth, creating a soft patch in its own right. CenterPoint shares have performed quite well and perhaps beyond anticipated growth; prudent investors should look for "value" entry points.

SECTOR: **Utilities** ❑ BETA COEFFICIENT: **0.55** ❑ 10-YEAR COMPOUND EARNINGS PER-SHARE GROWTH: **3.0%** ❑ 10-YEAR COMPOUND DIVIDENDS PER-SHARE GROWTH: **8.0%**

|  | | 2009 | 2010 | 2011 | 2012 | 2013 | 2014 | 2015 | 2016 |
|---|---|---|---|---|---|---|---|---|---|
| Revenues (mil) | | 8,281 | 8,765 | 8,459 | 7,452 | 8,106 | 9,226 | 7,386 | 7,528 |
| Net income (mil) | | 372 | 442 | 546 | 581 | 536 | 611 | 465 | 432 |
| Earnings per share | | 1.01 | 1.07 | 1.27 | 1.35 | 1.24 | 1.42 | 1.08 | 1.00 |
| Dividends per share | | 0.76 | 0.78 | 0.79 | 0.81 | 0.83 | 0.95 | 0.99 | 1.03 |
| Cash flow per share | | 2.94 | 3.14 | 3.43 | 3.89 | 3.54 | 3.85 | 3.40 | 3.68 |
| Price: | high | 14.9 | 17.0 | 21.5 | 21.8 | 25.7 | 25.8 | 23.7 | 225.0 |
| | low | 8.7 | 5.5 | 15.1 | 18.1 | 19.3 | 21.1 | 16.0 | 16.4 |

Website: www.centerpointenergy.com

AGGRESSIVE GROWTH

NEW FOR 2018

# Chemed Corporation

Ticker symbol: CHE (NYSE) ❑ Mid Cap ❑ Value Line financial strength rating: B++ ❑ Current yield: 0.5% ❑ Dividend raises, past 10 years: 8

## Company Profile

"Call Roto-Rooter, that's the name, and away go troubles down the drain" is the affable slogan of this well-known "root" business of the two-company conglomerate Chemed. Yes, if Roto-Rooter is the root, then those roots have sprouted a "tree" in an entirely different business: end-of-life health—hospice—care. Today's Chemed is two businesses for the price of one: the VITAS Healthcare Corporation (71 percent of FY2016 revenues) and the original Roto-Rooter, now 29 percent of revenues. Consider this new-to-our-list mid-cap company a healthcare business, one for your health at the end of life, and one for the health of your home plumbing.

As the name sounds like one of a chemical company, the name "Chemed" deserves some explanation. Its roots (sorry!) go back to a Cincinnati soap products maker (a familiar theme) known as DuBois Chemicals, which eventually made a name in the industrial cleaning products business. Chemed Corporation came on to the scene in 1971 when W.R. Grace, which had bought DuBois in 1964, spun it off as "Chemed." Chemed bought and ran Roto-Rooter franchises, and as the saying goes, liked the business so much it bought the entire company in 1980 (it had originally been founded in 1935). Chemed decided to quit the capital-intensive and environmentally sensitive commodity chemical business in 1991 and sold DuBois. The company bought VITAS in 2004. After a few other acquisitions and divestitures, we arrive at today's Chemed, a parent company of two distinct businesses. Both businesses are operated as wholly autonomous entities; the Chemed ownership or brand does not appear on either subsidiary's website except under a well-subordinated "parent company" tab at the bottom of the VITAS page (www.vitas.com/about-us) and a bare mention on Roto-Rooter's "About Us" page.

Originally founded in 1978 as a volunteer organization by a United Methodist minister and his oncology nurse wife, today's VITAS business provides non-curative hospice and palliative care services to its patients through a network of physicians, registered nurses, home health aides, social workers, clergy, and volunteers. Included are spiritual and emotional counseling to both patients and their families. In 2016, VITAS provided over 5.8 million days of care in 15 states for over 81,000 patients and their families; about 97 percent of that in their home (3 percent in dedicated inpatient units). VITAS operates in an industry dominated primarily by small, nonprofit, community-based hospices. About 97 percent of revenue is from Medicare or Medicaid sources.

The name "Roto-Rooter" is probably more familiar to most of us. Roto-Rooter originally was created to offer round-the-clock drain cleaning and maintenance services using the familiar "snake" equipment they pioneered and now manufacture and sell. Today's Roto-Rooter has expanded into providing a full line of onsite, often emergency-based plumbing and water restoration services both to residential and commercial customers; plumbing now accounts for about half of the subsidiary's revenue. The business operates through 110 company-owned branches and independent contractors and 400 franchisees. The company covers 90 percent of the US and 40 percent of Canada's population.

## Financial Highlights, Fiscal Year 2016

FY2016 revenues increased 2 percent overall, although beneath the surface Roto-Rooter revenues increased 6 percent while VITAS, hampered by a negative change in Medicare hospice reimbursement rates, advanced only 0.6 percent. That same Medicare change caused a 1.4 percent drop in net income for the year as well. However, a 3 percent share buyback led to a 2 percent gain in earnings per share. The company has only just over 16 million shares outstanding, and plans to retire as much as 4 percent of them annually.

Adjustments to the new Medicare reimbursement rates in the VITAS business, promotion of broader services in the Roto-Rooter business, and cost-savings initiatives across both businesses are expected to bring annual revenue gains in the 4–6 percent range with net earnings increases in the 10–12 percent range for FY2017 and 6–8 percent in FY2018. Steady share buybacks will keep per-share earnings increases in the 10–15 percent range.

## Reasons to Buy

With Chemed you have the opportunity to buy into not one but *two* good businesses. Both have a component of stability with ample growth opportunity. Both are leaders and recognized brands in highly fragmented industries; what other brand of plumbing services do you know aside from Roto-Rooter? Although the 15 states with current operations represent a populous cross section of the US, there is plenty of potential for geographic expansion in the VITAS business toward becoming a nationally recognized name, and possibly international. Too, increased understanding and use of home hospice services over more pricey hospitalization in end-of-life stages will help. The combined business exhibits improving margins, operating leverage, low debt, and strong cash generation and a willingness to return it to shareholders, mainly in the form of share buybacks. The small share count (16 million shares) is attractive so long as things are going well; there are relatively few shares to go around for institutional investors as the word gets out about Chemed.

## Reasons for Caution

One may always wonder about the merits of managing two such completely disparate, unrelated businesses; too, there is always a good possibility another (perhaps unrelated) company may be brought into the mix. Two disparate businesses may be manageable but as many learned in the late 1960s and early 1970s conglomerate boom, *too many* is not.

Chemed has already gained some appeal with the investment community; that and the low share count has driven recent share prices to high levels. The low share count can bring upside but also downside volatility if business conditions deteriorate. Shop carefully—else your investment results may head down the drain.

SECTOR: **Healthcare** ◻ BETA COEFFICIENT: **1.19** ◻ 10-YEAR COMPOUND EARNINGS PER-SHARE GROWTH: **14.0%** ◻ 10-YEAR COMPOUND DIVIDENDS PER-SHARE GROWTH: **14.5%**

|  | 2009 | 2010 | 2011 | 2012 | 2013 | 2014 | 2015 | 2016 |
|---|---|---|---|---|---|---|---|---|
| Revenues (mil) | 1,190 | 1,281 | 1,356 | 1,430 | 1,413 | 1,456 | 1,543 | 1,580 |
| Net income (mil) | 74.0 | 81.8 | 86.0 | 89.3 | 77.2 | 99.3 | 110.3 | 108.7 |
| Earnings per share | 3.24 | 3.55 | 4.10 | 4.62 | 4.16 | 5.57 | 6.33 | 6.48 |
| Dividends per share | 0.36 | 0.52 | 0.60 | 0.68 | 0.76 | 0.84 | 0.92 | 1.00 |
| Cash flow per share | 4.47 | 5.21 | 6.06 | 6.47 | 6.23 | 7.84 | 8.56 | 8.86 |
| Price:     high | 49.1 | 65.0 | 72.3 | 72.1 | 82.0 | 112.0 | 160.1 | 164.1 |
| low | 33.7 | 45.9 | 47.7 | 49.1 | 61.7 | 72.5 | 100.5 | 124.8 |

Website: www.chemed.com

---

GROWTH AND INCOME

# Chevron Corporation

Ticker symbol: CVX (NYSE) ◻ Large Cap ◻ Value Line financial strength rating: A++ ◻ Current yield: 3.9% ◻ Dividend raises, past 10 years: 10

## Company Profile

Over the past two years, Chevron has become a poster child for strong, stable, entrenched businesses in can't-lose industries suddenly rocked out of bed by the recent energy and commodity price crash. When the price of your chief product drops 70 percent, that forces tough decisions on "rightsizing," cost cutting, and particularly on sustaining the heretofore solid and rising dividend. For the most part Chevron stayed the course by selling some assets, issuing debt, and taking a restrained approach to capital expenditures. A moderate improvement in oil prices and a leaner, meaner cost structure is projected to lead the company to deliver net profit with oil at $60/barrel, in the ballpark if slightly below where it was four years ago with oil at $100. Thus, Chevron becomes a poster child for how to steer a large ship through a major revenue slump, and we'll keep the company on our *100 Best* list for 2018.

Chevron is the world's fourth-largest publicly traded, integrated energy company based on oil-equivalent reserves and production. It is engaged in every aspect of the oil and gas industry, including exploration and production, refining, marketing and transportation, chemicals manufacturing and sales, and power generation.

Active in more than 180 countries, Chevron has reserves of about 11.2 billion barrels of oil equivalent (55 percent liquids, 44 percent gas), with a production rate of 1.7 million barrels of oil equivalent and 5.3 billion cubic feet of gas per day. In addition, it has global refining output of more than 1.7 million barrels per day (bpd) and operates more than 16,000 retail outlets around the world. The upstream capacity is concentrated in North America (45 percent), Africa/Latin America (15 percent), Asia/Oceania (27 percent), and the Caspian Sea region (8 percent), with far less exposure to the Middle East than most larger competitors. The company is the leading producer in Kazakhstan, Thailand, and Indonesia, which rank among the highest-potential and lowest-risk non-US locations.

Although it increased the overall exposure to the 2014–15 oil price swoon, Chevron is more concentrated in oil (less in gas) than some of its competitors. That said, it has stepped up its new shale developments, particularly in gas, while reducing development costs substantially. Chevron also has active global downstream businesses in manufactured products including lubricants, specialty chemicals and additives, specialty refining units for aviation and maritime markets, and various logistics activities, including pipelines, shipping, and a global trading unit.

The company's global refining network comprises 10 wholly owned and joint-venture facilities. Gasoline and diesel fuel are sold under three well-known consumer brands: Chevron in North America; Texaco in Latin America, Europe, and West Africa; and Caltex in Asia, the Middle East, and southern Africa.

Chevron is the number one jet fuel marketer in the United States and third worldwide, marketing 550,000 barrels per day in 80 countries. The company's fuel and marine marketing business is a leading global supplier and marketer of fuels, lubricants, and coolants to the marine and power markets, with about 500,000 barrels of sales per day.

The company's traditional emphasis in oil hurt the company as prices fell almost 70 percent in 2014–15, severely affecting the bottom line and causing a rare annual net loss in 2016. While the oil price slump clearly hurt the bottom line, the emphasis on oil, lower drilling and production costs, asset adjustments, and the diversification through downstream refining and marketing is still the right position, and the recovery in oil and gas prices will act as a plus going forward—but it will take a few more years to return to where they were pre-2015.

## Financial Highlights, Fiscal Year 2016

Not surprisingly, the 70 percent oil price decline reached its nadir in January 2016, and revenues dropped another 16 percent in FY2016 after declining 35 percent in FY2015. Net earnings went negative on asset write-downs; per-share cash flow also dropped 30 percent. Assuming relatively flat oil prices in the mid-50s, Chevron forecasts an 18–20 percent rebound in revenues to about $135 billion and another 7–8 percent to $145 billion in 2018. Spending cuts, the absence of write-downs, and greater volumes will bring net profits back to $7.5 billion in FY2017 and north of $11 billion in FY2018—a bit less than half of their heyday. More than anything else to show commitment to its investors, CVX raised its dividend one cent in 2016 to keep its dividend raise record alive—no doubt the company knew we were watching(!) Raises should pick up in 2017 and beyond.

## Reasons to Buy

Not surprisingly, declining product prices, increased inventories and competition, and a relatively high fixed cost picture are not features we look for in a *100 Best* pick. We must take a long-term view of strengths and a company's response to business adversity; Chevron does quite well on both counts.

For exploration and production strength and geographic and technological diversity, few companies exceed Chevron's strengths. The company is most exposed to some of the best sectors and geographies in the business and has established a good brand and track record for discovery, production, and downstream operations. The company has made what we feel are prudent cuts in its exploration activities and its expenses in general. We like the diversification into refining, which generally benefits from lower input prices. Long term, the company has a solid record of earnings, cash generation, and cash distribution. We think shareholders will be well rewarded with growing cash returns in the long run—especially as energy prices normalize even to the diminished $60 level. With a little patience, we continue to think CVX is among the best of a hard-hit and out-of-favor industry.

## Reasons for Caution

Of course, recent energy price shifts continue to put a dent in CVX's universe. The price shifts have been an opportunity for some of the wiser—and more cash rich—players such as Chevron to streamline operations and to provide opportunities to acquire productive assets more cheaply. The biggest long-term negative is an almost doubling of long-term debt to $40 billion to keep the home fires burning. It remains to be seen how quickly, if at all, the company plans to lose that debt. This business may take some time to return to its previous glory and level of safety—but at this juncture it's probably worth the wait.

SECTOR: **Energy** ◻ BETA COEFFICIENT: **1.22** ◻ 10-YEAR COMPOUND EARNINGS PER-SHARE GROWTH: **4.0%** ◻ 10-YEAR COMPOUND DIVIDENDS PER-SHARE GROWTH: **10.0%**

| | 2009 | 2010 | 2011 | 2012 | 2013 | 2014 | 2015 | 2016 |
|---|---|---|---|---|---|---|---|---|
| Revenues (bil) | 172.6 | 204.9 | 253.7 | 241.9 | 228.8 | 212.0 | 138.4 | 114.5 |
| Net income (bil) | 10.5 | 19.0 | 26.9 | 26.2 | 21.4 | 8.9 | 4.6 | (0.5) |
| Earnings per share | 5.24 | 8.48 | 13.44 | 13.32 | 11.09 | 10.14 | 2.45 | (0.27) |
| Dividends per share | 2.66 | 2.84 | 3.09 | 3.51 | 3.90 | 4.21 | 4.28 | 4.29 |
| Cash flow per share | 10.95 | 15.99 | 19.98 | 20.05 | 18.61 | 19.17 | 13.70 | 10.05 |
| Price:          high | 79.8 | 92.4 | 111.0 | 118.5 | 127.8 | 135.1 | 113.0 | 119.0 |
| low | 56.1 | 66.8 | 102.1 | 95.7 | 108.7 | 100.1 | 69.6 | 75.3 |

Website: www.chevron.com

## GROWTH AND INCOME
# Cincinnati Financial Corporation

Ticker symbol: CINF (NASDAQ) ◻ Large Cap ◻ Value Line financial strength rating: B++ ◻ Current yield: 2.7% ◻ Dividend increases, past 10 years: 10

## Company Profile

Two years after returning Cincinnati Financial to our *100 Best* list, we continue to like the basic property/casualty ("P/C") insurer model. We continue to like the way companies that follow this model make money not only in profiting from the difference between premiums collected and costs ("underwriting income") but also by being able to invest the "float" over the years for what can be enormous gains (of course, Warren Buffett's Berkshire Hathaway carries the torch for this model). We think Berkshire is too pricey for the average shareholder, and further, it pays no dividend, but we like the model well enough to have two P/C choices on our list: Cincinnati Financial and Allstate.

Cincinnati Financial Corporation (CFC), founded in 1968, is a holding company operating several insurers engaged primarily in property/casualty insurance marketed through independent insurance agents in 41 states. The company, one of the 25 largest property and casualty insurers in the nation, operates in four segments: Commercial Lines Property Casualty Insurance, Personal Lines Property Casualty Insurance, Life Insurance, and Investments. Commercial Lines account for about 64 percent of premium revenues and are sold in 39 states; Personal Lines about 26 percent and are sold in 35 states. All insurance products are sold through independent agencies. Life insurance and other "excess/surplus" lines (specialized niche forms of insurance) are designed to allow the agents to offer a full line and account for the 10 percent remainder.

Cincinnati Financial fully or partially owns a series of subsidiary companies that actually provide and manage the insurance products marketed by the company and its agents. Its standard market property casualty insurance group includes three subsidiaries: Cincinnati Insurance, CSU Producer Resources, and CFC Investment companies. The lead subsidiary, Cincinnati Insurance, is a group that includes the Cincinnati Casualty Company and the Cincinnati Indemnity Company. This group writes a range of business, homeowner, and auto policies. Another group "member," Cincinnati Specialty Underwriters, offers the excess/surplus lines; and finally, Cincinnati Life offers life, disability, and annuity products to complete the insurance product picture.

The two noninsurance subsidiaries of Cincinnati Financial are CSU Producer Resources, which offers insurance brokerage services to CFC's independent agencies so their clients can access CFC's excess and surplus lines insurance products; and CFC Investment Company, which offers commercial leasing and financing services to CFC's agents, their clients, and other customers. Like all property and casualty insurers, CFC earns income from underwriting (premiums collected less casualty payouts) and from investing the vast pool of cash generated through premiums stored up until a loss occurs.

## Financial Highlights, Fiscal Year 2016

Somewhat higher weather-related claims led to an uptick in losses and a modest downtick in underwriting margin, leading to a moderate 13 percent drop in net income for FY2016. Premiums earned rose about 5 percent. New customers and expanded business with previous ones, strategic rate hikes, stricter underwriting guidelines, a greater use of analytics for risk management, and slightly improved investment income should all work together to produce an 8–9 percent revenue increase for FY2017 followed by a 4–5 percent increase in FY2018 and ongoing; net income will rise a modest 2–3 percent in FY2017 followed by a 5–6 percent rise in FY2018. We think these figures could be conservative especially if there are no significant disasters and if investment income (tied to interest rates) rises more quickly. Moderate dividend growth in the mid-single digits should persist through the period.

## Reasons to Buy

As mentioned at the outset, we like the basic business model. In addition, CFC enjoys both a loyal customer base and a loyal agency base. It is smaller, more nimble than Allstate and, unlike Allstate, most business is handled through agencies—with the two companies as choices, you get both ends of the spectrum. Measured by premium volume, the company is ranked as the number one or number two carrier among 75 percent of the agencies that have represented them for the past five years. The company has invested in new pricing and modeling analytics to sharpen its approach to pricing and customer relationships. CFC is on firm financial footing with a dividend covered by investment income and cash flow and a relatively low 10 percent long-term debt as a percentage of total capital. Dividend payouts have increased slowly and steadily each year. From here forward, the company is well positioned to benefit from well-managed incremental interest rate increases.

## Reasons for Caution

The current pricing environment remains less than favorable; there is a lot of competition in this business, although loyal customers and especially agents will help. Interest rates on the industry's traditional investment instruments, while rising, could continue to stay weak for some time. A large natural catastrophe could hurt. The stock price has risen with the good news; new investors should look for a pullback.

SECTOR: **Financials** ◻ BETA COEFFICIENT: **0.79** ◻ 10-YEAR COMPOUND EARNINGS PER-SHARE GROWTH: **1.0%** ◻ 10-YEAR COMPOUND DIVIDENDS PER-SHARE GROWTH: **6.5%**

|  |  | 2009 | 2010 | 2011 | 2012 | 2013 | 2014 | 2015 | 2016 |
|---|---|---|---|---|---|---|---|---|---|
| Premiums earned (mil) | | 2,911 | 2,924 | 3,029 | 3,344 | 3,795 | 4,242 | 4,480 | 4,710 |
| Net income (mil) | | 215 | 273 | 121 | 421 | 466 | 454 | 585 | 511 |
| Earnings per share | | 1.32 | 1.68 | 0.74 | 2.40 | 2.81 | 2.86 | 3.56 | 3.62 |
| Dividends per share | | 1.57 | 1.59 | 1.60 | 1.62 | 1.64 | 1.74 | 1.82 | 1.90 |
| Underwriting inc. per share | | (2.19) | (1.80) | (3.28) | (0.51) | 0.94 | 0.52 | 1.75 | 1.49 |
| Price: | high | 29.7 | 32.3 | 34.3 | 41.0 | 53.7 | 55.3 | 61.6 | 79.6 |
| | low | 17.8 | 25.3 | 23.7 | 30.1 | 39.6 | 44.0 | 49.7 | 53.6 |

Website: www.cinfin.com

# The Coca-Cola Company

Ticker symbol: KO (NYSE) ❑ Large Cap ❑ Value Line financial strength rating: A++ ❑ Current yield: 3.4% ❑ Dividend raises, last 10 years: 10

## Company Profile

The Coca-Cola Company is the world's largest beverage company. For more than 100 years, the company has mainly produced concentrates and syrups, which it then bottles or cans itself or sells to independent bottlers worldwide. Then in 2010 it took a big step to "own" the supply chain with the acquisition of bottler Coca-Cola Enterprises' North American operations; CCE still handles distribution for Europe. Independent bottlers add water (still or carbonated, depending on the product), sugar, and other (often local) ingredients, then bottle and distribute the products to restaurants, retailers, and other distributors. Now it is taking another big step—"refranchising"— selling many of these bottlers off to generate cash, to focus on the core businesses, and to dramatically increase profitability. And it is making many moves to diversify beyond its core carbonated beverage base.

Coke operates in more than 200 countries and markets nearly 500 brands of concentrate and finished beverages which are bottled into more than 3,900 different branded products, including Coca-Cola; 21 of those brands bring in over $21 billion annually. The numbers are staggering: Coke ships over 29 billion cases annually, which works out to 637 billion servings sold per year, 1.9 billion beverages consumed per day—or 21,990 servings per second. Currently it is all processed through 250 bottling partners operating 900 plants moving product through 24 million retail outlets.

In unit case volume, 80 percent of all sales are overseas—28 percent in Latin America, 29 percent in Europe, the Middle East, and Africa, and 23 percent in the Pacific. In revenue terms, the company counts about 52 percent as overseas sales.

As traditional carbonated drinks continue to go flat with today's Millennial generation, the company is moving forward in the "new world" of beverage consumption, with an investment in Keurig Green Mountain, which has now been sold to Germany's JAB Holding Co. Keurig had been working on K-Cup single servings for a recently introduced "Keurig KOLD" machine that makes single-serve soda and other chilled beverages using K-Cup servings of Coke products. It remains to be seen what will happen to this partnership and technology, but it is an indicator of one way Coca-Cola intends to expand its markets through technology and partnerships. The company has also invested in Monster Beverage and others. Some 19 of their 21 billion-dollar brands have low- or no- calorie alternatives. The new "Freestyle" machine found in a growing number of fast-food restaurants allows drinkers to customize their drinks. It's fun, and remember—customization is one of today's biggies. And did you know? It now collects data so that Coca-Cola can see what tastes are preferred; what a laboratory! (The dispenser team has its own website—check out www.coca-colafreestyle.com.) Other innovations include mass-customized cans and bottles with people's names on them, and something we've all awaited: a return to the original Coke bottle shape and format where possible.

Importantly, Coke now views their business as a total portfolio containing "category clusters," with marketing and branding strategies for each cluster. Their vision includes the following clusters and representative products:

- Traditional soft drinks—50 percent plus: Coke, Sprite, Fanta, etc.
- Energy drinks—through Monster stake—15 percent: Monster, Burn, NOS brands
- Water, enhanced water, sports—15 percent: DASANI, Smartwater, Vitaminwater, POWERADE, Schweppes
- Ready-to-drink coffee, tea—15 percent: Peak, FUZE Tea, Barista, Dunkin' Donuts Iced Coffee
- Juice, dairy, plant based—10 percent: Minute Maid, Simply Orange, Fairlife, Core Power, AdeS soy milk

The point is simple: Coke is diversifying into a comprehensive ready-to-drink beverage provider.

As mentioned previously, the company is reversing its strategy to own its US distribution channel—specifically its bottling network. Coca-Cola is embarking on a "21st Century Beverage Partnership Model," essentially a franchising model, where the company works closely with its bottling franchisees but does not carry the asset base, employee base, or the headaches of that relatively low-margin business. Commodity price risks also move over to the franchisees. The impact on margins is significant, raising net profit margins some 7–10 percent (to 27–300 percent) when fully implemented, which is supposed to occur by late 2017.

## Financial Highlights, Fiscal Year 2016

The strong dollar, weak emerging markets, and the beginning of refranchising took some of the fizz out of FY2016 results: Revenues dropped 6 percent and earnings dropped 5 percent. However, the company estimates that without restructuring, currency effects, and tax changes, net earnings would have *risen* 8 percent on cost reductions, better asset utilization, and an improved mix. Net profit margins remain in the 20 percent range, which is huge for a company this size. Projections call for a complex year in 2017 as changes are implemented—but net margins will finally improve to the tune of 23 percent. Sales will drop with refranchising some 18 percent while earnings will drop only 4 percent (you can see the margin improvement strategy starting to bear fruit)—then in 2018 earnings will *rise* 2–3 percent on another 13 percent revenue drop. If all goes according to plan, profits will advance substantially on modest revenue gains going forward from there. Cash returns to investors are decent on both the buy-back and dividend front, with dividends growing in the mid-single-digit range and share buybacks reducing share counts in the 1–2 percent range annually.

## Reasons to Buy

While the traditional fizzy drink business is becoming a bit passé in today's world, Coke is adapting to the change and in our view, continues to be solid. The company has category leadership, especially globally, in soft drinks, juices and juice drinks, and ready-to-drink coffees and teas. They're number two globally in sports and energy drinks, water, and ready-to-drink teas.

The Coca-Cola name is probably the most recognized brand in the world and is almost beyond valuation. Indeed, Mr. Buffett once uttered the classic line about its brand strength and intangibles: "If you gave me $100 billion and said take away the soft drink leadership in the world from Coke, I'd give it back to you and say it can't be done."

That's all pretty old news now; what's important is that Coca-Cola has also shown us, in today's world, that it isn't just going to sit around and go flat while we investors sit around and cry in our beer. We see signs that the company "gets it" and will not only adapt, but eventually has a chance to remain the number one brand even with a full new mix of beverages and packages for the modern world. Coca-Cola has traditionally been a steady defensive stock and offers a solid dividend with a constant track record of dividend growth. The company boasts—quite rightly—about having raised dividends in each of the past 55 years. It is also as close to a pure play on international business as you'll find in a US company.

## Reasons for Caution

Coca-Cola is under our constant scrutiny for relevance in today's increasingly Millennial-dominated market. Sales of traditional sparkling beverages in established markets—the US and Europe, and now Latin America—are in a slow decline due to interest in health and reducing obesity.

For the future, these market changes could provide some speed bumps. One wonders how the Coke culture will resonate with today's Millennial beverage requirements—less sugar, fewer artificial ingredients, more customization and transparency—and one wonders further whether the new-age consumer will adapt well to healthy or fun drinks sold by Coca-Cola. Therein lies the 64-ounce question: Can they deliver change? Fast enough? Can they get the message out? In time to make a difference as traditional sugary beverages decline? Right now, our bet is "yes."

The distribution restructuring could prove distracting, too. Overall, this is a slow, steady growth story, which may be too slow for many, with new risks the company didn't face when Mr. Buffett bought his 400 million shares years ago.

SECTOR: **Consumer Discretionary** ⬛ BETA COEFFICIENT: **0.66** ⬛ 10-YEAR COMPOUND EARNINGS PER-SHARE GROWTH: **6.0%** ⬛ 10-YEAR COMPOUND DIVIDENDS PER-SHARE GROWTH: **9.0%**

|  |  | 2009 | 2010 | 2011 | 2012 | 2013 | 2014 | 2015 | 2016 |
|---|---|---|---|---|---|---|---|---|---|
| Revenues (mil) | | 30,990 | 35,123 | 46,554 | 48,017 | 46,854 | 45,998 | 44,294 | 41,863 |
| Net income (mil) | | 6,824 | 8,144 | 8,932 | 9,019 | 9,374 | 9,091 | 8,797 | 8,354 |
| Earnings per share | | 1.47 | 1.75 | 1.92 | 1.97 | 2.08 | 2.04 | 2.00 | 1.91 |
| Dividends per share | | 0.82 | 0.88 | 0.94 | 1.02 | 1.12 | 1.22 | 1.32 | 1.40 |
| Cash flow per share | | 1.75 | 2.09 | 2.41 | 2.46 | 2.58 | 2.53 | 2.49 | 2.37 |
| Price: | high | 29.7 | 32.9 | 35.9 | 40.7 | 43.4 | 45.0 | 43.9 | 47.1 |
| | low | 18.7 | 24.7 | 30.6 | 33.3 | 36.5 | 36.9 | 36.6 | 39.9 |

Website: www.coca-colacompany.com

CONSERVATIVE GROWTH

# Colgate-Palmolive Company

Ticker symbol: CL (NYSE) ⬛ Large Cap ⬛ Value Line financial strength rating: A++ ⬛ Current yield: 2.2% ⬛ Dividend raises, past 10 years: 10

## Company Profile

For two years in a row now, we've had to ponder whether investing in Colgate-Palmolive is the right strategy. This issue isn't whether toothpaste and deodorant represent a good business—they do, and we like to build a few "defensive" (okay, boring) stocks into our portfolio just in case the markets go bad. The issue with CL is international exposure; fully 79 percent of sales originate outside North America. That, of course, brings currency risk, and there's been a lot of that lately, not to mention trade policy risk. But we think the core business is still good, and we also stick to our strategy of capturing overseas growth with domestic companies that sell a lot overseas. As such, we're sticking with Colgate.

Colgate-Palmolive is the second-largest global producer of detergents, toiletries, and other household products. The company manages its business in two straightforward segments: Oral, Personal, and Home Care; and Pet Nutrition. The Oral, Personal, and Home Care division produces and markets a number of familiar brands and products: Ajax, Palmolive, Irish Spring, Softsoap, Fabuloso, Mennen, and Speed Stick, as well as the familiar Colgate brand of oral care products. These brands are strong with substantial market share in most markets: Colgate owns 44 percent of the worldwide oral care market (easily good to keep them in the number one position), 20 percent of personal care, 19 percent of the home care, and 14 percent of the total pet nutrition markets. Other number one worldwide market positions include liquid hand soap, powdered cleanser, and pet food in US vet clinics (Hill's Pet Nutrition). Number two positions include bar soap, liquid body cleansing, and mouthwash.

Although it hurt during this most recent period of dollar strength, Colgate's real strength is in international consumer products markets, with a presence in more than 200 countries and territories. In addition to capturing almost 80 percent of its sales overseas, more than 50 percent of *that* business is in emerging markets.

## Financial Highlights, Fiscal Year 2016

Once again, Colgate's international exposure, while an asset long term, led to more currency exposure and risk than most of its brethren, which of course, we think to be a cycle, not a long-term negative, and ultimately a positive. FY2016 revenues dropped just a bit more than 5 percent, and would likely have risen 3–4 percent except for currency effects. Net income spiked higher but most of that was due to a large write-off in Venezuela during 2015, although some cost-cutting measures also took effect during the year. Operational improvements and some increased marketing efforts worldwide are projected to return the top line to 1–2 percent growth in FY2017 and 3–4 percent growth in FY2018. Net profit margins will improve dramatically as cost-savings programs take effect; in fact, the projected net margins in the 16–17 percent range are among the best in the industry and a big reason we kept the stock. Per-share earnings should grow in the 7–10 percent range through each of the two years. A faster currency turnaround would strengthen this picture. Modest dividend increases should continue: Share buybacks in the 2–3 percent range are the bigger investor return story.

## Reasons to Buy

"Focused on Global Growth" is the company's slogan—and it's an appropriate one. Colgate's brands are market leaders in most of the markets in which they operate, particularly in overseas markets where they are especially strong. They're number one or number two with many of their other brands, including Ajax and Softsoap, and have many other well-established brands. They were recently given the title of "the number one brand purchased in the world" and their products are estimated to be in half the world's households. The company's "first to market" global strategy has given it a formidable foothold in emerging markets such as China, India, and Latin America. Colgate is in a great position to benefit from the increased acceptance and use of dental care products and other toiletries in these markets, and is actively marketing to build this opportunity.

Colgate is a conservatively run company that prefers slower organic growth over quick (but expensive) acquisitions. It plows money back into the company and achieves profitability through operational excellence, rather than paying for gross margins at any price. This is a solid defensive play with a good dividend, increasing margins, real earnings growth, and solid earnings predictability. Looking at the bigger picture, Colgate is less prone to reach for new, rapidly changing markets, such as cosmetics, and less apt to try to grow through acquisitions than, say, a Procter & Gamble (another *100 Best* stock). This company is about slow, steady returns with little risk and little market volatility in bad times.

## Reasons for Caution

Colgate participates in an increasingly competitive market, requiring more frequent new-product rollouts and related marketing expenses just to keep up. As we've seen, the international exposure brings currency exposure, and sometimes pure and simple business risk, as evidenced by the Venezuela exit. New trade policies from the Trump administration may hurt directly or indirectly. Finally, the Colgate business will not stimulate more active or aggressive investors.

SECTOR: **Consumer Staples** ❑ BETA COEFFICIENT: **0.76** ❑ 10-YEAR COMPOUND EARNINGS PER-SHARE GROWTH: **5.0%** ❑ 10-YEAR COMPOUND DIVIDENDS PER-SHARE GROWTH: **10.5%**

|                    | 2009   | 2010   | 2011   | 2012   | 2013   | 2014   | 2015   | 2016   |
|--------------------|--------|--------|--------|--------|--------|--------|--------|--------|
| Revenues (mil)     | 15,327 | 15,564 | 16,734 | 17,085 | 17,420 | 17,277 | 16,034 | 15,195 |
| Net income (mil)   | 2,291  | 2,203  | 2,431  | 2,472  | 2,241  | 2,180  | 1,384  | 2,441  |
| Earnings per share | 2.19   | 2.16   | 2.47   | 2.58   | 2.38   | 2.36   | 1.52   | 2.72   |
| Dividends per share| 0.86   | 1.02   | 1.14   | 1.22   | 1.33   | 1.42   | 1.50   | 1.59   |
| Cash flow per share| 2.64   | 2.57   | 2.97   | 3.10   | 2.91   | 2.89   | 2.05   | 3.18   |
| Price:        high | 43.7   | 43.1   | 47.4   | 55.5   | 66.5   | 71.3   | 71.6   | 75.4   |
|               low  | 27.3   | 36.6   | 37.4   | 43.6   | 52.6   | 59.8   | 50.5   | 61.4   |

Website: www.colgate.com

---

AGGRESSIVE GROWTH

# Columbia Sportswear Company

Ticker symbol: COLM (NASDAQ) ❑ Mid Cap ❑ Value Line financial strength rating: B++ ❑ Current yield: 1.2% ❑ Dividend raises, past 10 years: 10

## Company Profile

As we select our *100 Best* stocks each year, among the many types of materials we use as sources we read a lot of corporate histories. The history of clothing maker Columbia Sportswear pretty much tops them all:

"Born and raised in Portland, Oregon, Columbia Sportswear Company has been making gear so that Pacific Northwesterners can enjoy the outdoors for more than 70 years. At the helm for over 40 years has been our Chairman, Gert Boyle. Her Tough Mother persona has grown Columbia into the global sportswear company that it is today—still based in Portland, still making no-nonsense apparel and footwear to keep you WARM, DRY, COOL and PROTECTED no matter what. Our unique Pacific Northwest heritage and Boyle family irreverence is what sets us apart from the competition."

Typically we don't lift content verbatim from such corporate writings. But this one not only describes Columbia's colorful past, but also quite aptly describes what the company has become today. As described—and still led by the 93-year-old Ms. Boyle (Chairperson of the Board) and her 67-year old son Timothy (President and COO)—Columbia makes a line of practical, functional, and tastefully styled activewear that is increasingly used in non-active situations. Most of you have seen a Columbia vest or jacket or two on the streets or in the woods during your daily travels. Rainwear is a specialty—given its Portland roots—but the company makes and distributes high-quality, conservatively designed shirts, pants, hoodies and fleecewear, tops and bottoms for women, shoes, and accessories among other products. The clothing and shoes are designed for outdoor wear and for skiing/snowboarding and other rugged activities, but they are casual enough and of high enough quality to fit in well for Casual Friday at work and casual anything outside of work; you won't get turned away at your favorite nice restaurant if you show up wearing Columbia. You probably won't notice Columbia—until you notice it. It's all about one of our favorite themes: "elegant simplicity."

Apparel, accessories, and equipment accounted for about 79 percent of 2016 sales, with footwear making up the rest. The company has expanded its own direct-to-consumer channel through Columbia-branded stores and through its website. US distribution is a mixed wholesale and direct model, with 3,300 wholesale customers, 91 outlet retail stores, 25 branded retail stores, and 5 brand-specific e-commerce sites (see following for some of the specialty brands). About 37 percent of sales are overseas, with Asia-Pacific and Latin America accounting for more than half of that. Through a joint venture, the company has 92 retail locations and an online sales presence in China. All apparel and footwear is manufactured by contract manufacturers to spec; the company operates no manufacturing facilities.

Columbia has also expanded into more specialty lines, like yoga clothing. Columbia also owns and distributes Mountain Hardwear, a respected line of high-end performance outerwear, and other "lifestyle" brands including SOREL (women's wear), prAna ("stylish, sustainable activewear") and Montrail (high-performance running footwear). SOREL is the largest subbrand, accounting for about 9 percent of 2016 revenues; the others account for less than 5 percent each. The Columbia brand itself accounts for just over 80 percent of revenues.

On the innovation front, a new performance technology called "OutDry Extreme," including jackets made from 21 recycled plastic bottles, has received excellent reviews in the rainwear category. A new line of performance fishing wear has also recently come to market. Comfort is a major theme; "Clothing that feels as good as it looks" is one of their mottos.

## Financial Highlights, Fiscal Year 2016

The slowdown in bricks-and-mortar retail (for example, the Sports Authority bankruptcy) and continued currency effects sent Columbia's raft on a bumpy ride in FY2016; nonetheless they came out of it fairly dry. Sales advanced just over 2 percent, while carefully managed expenses improved margins and rang up a 10 percent bottom line gain. Going forward, the company projects annual revenue growth in the 4–6 percent range through FY2018, with profits only slightly ahead in FY2017 as it invests in operational improvements, and a 10 percent earnings gain for FY2018. Dividends have been ascending to the summit slowly but surely, while share buybacks have stopped for the moment at the side of the trail.

## Reasons to Buy

Two years ago we looked for a company to replace the stumbling Ralph Lauren on our *100 Best* list, and we still think we found it in Columbia Sportswear. The brand has slowly but surely expanded its international reputation for functionality, performance, good design, quality, and value. It has the conservative, enduring qualities of Ralph Lauren products without being showy or pretentious; its understated elegance has resonated with Millennials much better than Ralph, and its appeal is much wider than just Millennials. Go out on a rainy day (or any other) and see what people are wearing.

As the brand has solidified and gone global, the company has woken up from the financial doldrums, too. Sales, margins, and profits are all on a decent uptrend in a tough retail market as the products become more standard and are distributed more widely in varying retail channels (you must no longer trek to REI to buy Columbia).

## Reasons for Caution

The clothing business is by nature notoriously cyclical and trendy, and we don't pretend to be able to follow these trends, let alone pick the companies that will ride ahead of them. That's why we like Columbia—it is trendy because it isn't trendy. That said, even this strength can fall on its ear as it has with Ralph Lauren, Eddie Bauer, and many of its brethren. (We think those two names experienced other problems, namely Ralph's hoity-toity snob appeal and Eddie's poor quality that Columbia may not experience if it stays on track.) Competition from the likes of Patagonia and Marmot is also substantial, but neither produces as complete a line nor has achieved as wide a distribution as Columbia. Oh, and about distribution—channel partners can be fickle too—or even go bankrupt. We hope they don't reach too far down market (e.g., Walmart) to boost volumes; as any mountain climber knows, it's easy to make mistakes in this industry and hard to recover.

SECTOR: **Consumer Staples** ◻ BETA COEFFICIENT: **0.75** ◻ 10-YEAR COMPOUND EARNINGS PER-
SHARE GROWTH: **3.5%** ◻ 10-YEAR COMPOUND DIVIDENDS PER-SHARE GROWTH: **9.0%**

|                     |      | 2009 | 2010 | 2011 | 2012 | 2013 | 2014 | 2015 | 2016 |
|---------------------|------|------|------|------|------|------|------|------|------|
| Revenues (mil)      |      | 1,244 | 1,483 | 1,694 | 1,670 | 1,685 | 2,100 | 2,326 | 2,377 |
| Net income (mil)    |      | 67   | 77   | 103  | 100  | 94   | 137  | 174  | 192  |
| Earnings per share  |      | 0.99 | 1.13 | 1.52 | 1.47 | 1.37 | 1.94 | 2.45 | 2.72 |
| Dividends per share |      | 0.33 | 0.37 | 0.43 | 0.44 | 0.46 | 0.57 | 0.62 | 0.69 |
| Cash flow per share |      | 1.53 | 1.71 | 2.19 | 2.07 | 1.95 | 2.74 | 3.33 | 3.61 |
| Price:              | high | 23.2 | 31.1 | 35.3 | 29.2 | 39.7 | 45.9 | 74.7 | 63.6 |
|                     | low  | 12.3 | 19.1 | 20.6 | 21.6 | 23.9 | 34.3 | 41.1 | 43.6 |

Website: www.columbia.com

**AGGRESSIVE GROWTH**

# Comcast Corporation

Ticker symbol: CMCSA (NASDAQ) ◻ Large Cap ◻ Value Line financial strength rating: A ◻ Current yield: 1.7% ◻ Dividend raises, past 10 years: 9

## Company Profile

Comcast is one of the nation's leading providers of communications services and information and entertainment content passed through those services. The core business is Comcast Cable, the familiar cable TV network that has evolved into a conduit for delivering bundled high-speed Internet services, phone services, scheduled TV, studio shows and movies, on-demand content, and even theme parks. This business serves some 23 million video subscribers and 25 million Internet subscribers in 39 states.

Comcast has been evolving its information and entertainment business gradually through its ownership of regional sports networks and national channels such as the Golf Channel, E! (an entertainment channel), Fandango (a moviegoer's website), and others. The company took a major leap forward as a content provider with the 2011–2013 two-stage acquisition of NBCUniversal, almost instantly turning the company into not only a connectivity powerhouse but a media powerhouse as well through its ownership of Universal Pictures and other assets. With that acquisition, Comcast became one of the largest integrated content development and distribution businesses in the United States.

The company built its Xfinity "X1" Internet portal brand to compete with satellite operators and such offerings as AT&T U-verse and Verizon FiOS. Customers can buy bundles of services including TV, on-demand video, and on-demand TV through Hulu, and now Netflix. With X1, customers can also get the latest high-speed Internet service, and their 50 percent connect rate with Comcast's cable customers, up from 30 percent just a few years ago makes X1 the largest high-speed broadband service in the US. In short, Comcast has evolved from being a lackluster cable TV service to a full-scale communications utility with some of the highest-performance products on the market. The company now has more Internet service customers (25 million) than it does cable subscribers (23 million), with more than 11 million phone service connections thrown in for good measure.

Comcast breaks down its business into two major segments: Cable Communications and NBCUniversal:

- Cable Communications (61 percent of total revenues and 66 percent of operating income) houses the video, high-speed Internet, and voice services (collectively, "cable services") and most importantly, the Xfinity product.
- NBCUniversal (39 percent of revenues, 34 percent of income) houses the content creation and delivery businesses, including Cable Networks (national and regional sports networks such as the Golf Channel, Comcast Bay Area, and many others—33 percent of NBCUniversal segment), Broadcast Television (NBC, 32 percent of segment), Filmed Entertainment (20 percent of segment), and Theme Parks (the noted "Universal" theme parks in Florida and Hollywood, California, and soon, China—15 percent of segment).

The vast majority of Comcast customers are residential, although the company also offers a business class service, including fiber end-user connections and cloud storage, to meet the needs of small and midsized organizations. That business segment grew 16 percent to $5.5 billion (up 41 percent over the past two years). The company also owns the Philadelphia Flyers (NHL hockey). Comcast acquired content developer DreamWorks Animation SKG for $3.6 billion in 2016.

## Financial Highlights, Fiscal Year 2016

Strength across the business and particularly in high-speed Internet, video, business services, films, the Rio Olympics, and the Super Bowl all supported an 8 percent gain in FY2016 top line revenue. Average monthly revenue per customer connection grew 4 percent to $148.26. Margins dipped slightly due to higher programming expenses, and net earnings rose only 4 percent. (Per-share earnings were up almost 7 percent supported by a 3 percent share buyback.) Revenues are projected to grow 4–5 percent in FY2017 and 6–7 percent in FY2018 with earnings ahead 5 percent and 7 percent in the two years respectively as the company gains market share and subscribers. Moderate share buybacks and dividend increases should continue.

## Reasons to Buy

The addition of Comcast to the 2013 *100 Best* list was one we debated out of concern about cable companies in general. However, it continues to pay off handsomely; the shares have tripled since our decision. We like the company's strategic and operational focus—the acquisitions make sense, and the metrics they present truly describe what's important in the business—not just size and volume, but making customer relationships better and more profitable. The different pieces of the company fit together well.

The DreamWorks Animation acquisition holds promise with several popular children's franchises to its credit including "Shrek," "Minions," and "Kung Fu Panda." We expect the Universal arm to capitalize on these properties by including them in featured theme parks and resort properties.

Comcast (and its competitors) are becoming a larger version of what the big three television networks once were. They own not only the content development and marketing, but also the content delivery infrastructure. There are no franchises or distributors to deal with, and they are free to develop independent content and compete with their own live and streamed content as they see fit. This is an extremely dynamic market model and Comcast holds a leadership position.

The growth in market dominance, improved branding, and new revenues from the increased adoption of Xfinity all bode well, as does what we think will become the eventual reality of on-demand content as a standard—and profitable—product from suppliers such as Comcast.

## Reasons for Caution

Although Comcast is certainly big enough to survive on its own, the trend toward industry consolidation brings the usual risks associated with acquisitions. The company is big and complex to manage. While recent decisions on net neutrality now look to be a positive, they aren't a done deal, and we could be left with an Internet that can't charge any extra for handling heavy loads, which with the expected expansion of such loads, could become a problem.

The company faces extreme competition in most of its markets, although it may have at least a temporary bandwidth advantage at present. It's a lucrative and growing market.

SECTOR: **Telecommunications Services** ❑ BETA COEFFICIENT: **1.01** ❑ 10-YEAR COMPOUND EARNINGS PER-SHARE GROWTH: **24.5%** ❑ 10-YEAR COMPOUND DIVIDENDS PER-SHARE GROWTH: **15.5%**

|                       |      | 2009   | 2010   | 2011   | 2012   | 2013   | 2014   | 2015   | 2016   |
|-----------------------|------|--------|--------|--------|--------|--------|--------|--------|--------|
| Revenues (mil)        |      | 35,756 | 37,937 | 55,842 | 62,570 | 64,657 | 68,775 | 74,510 | 80,403 |
| Net income (mil)      |      | 3,638  | 3,535  | 4,377  | 6,203  | 6,816  | 8,380  | 8,171  | 9,558  |
| Earnings per share    |      | 0.63   | 0.65   | 0.79   | 1.14   | 1.28   | 1.47   | 1.63   | 1.74   |
| Dividends per share   |      | 0.15   | 0.19   | 0.23   | 0.33   | 0.39   | 0.45   | 0.50   | 0.55   |
| Cash flow per share   |      | 1.79   | 1.85   | 2.22   | 2.68   | 2.83   | 3.24   | 3.45   | 3.80   |
| Price:                | high | 9.0    | 11.2   | 13.6   | 19.2   | 26.0   | 29.7   | 32.5   | 35.7   |
|                       | low  | 5.5    | 7.6    | 9.6    | 12.1   | 18.6   | 23.9   | 25.0   | 26.2   |

Website: www.comcast.com

---

GROWTH AND INCOME

# ConocoPhillips Company

Ticker symbol: COP (NYSE) ❑ Large Cap ❑ Value Line financial strength rating: B++ ❑ Current yield: 2.2% ❑ Dividend raises, past 10 years: 8

## Company Profile

Like the rest of the industry, ConocoPhillips was hit hard by the 50–70 percent haircut in the price of their main products, namely, oil and gas. You won't typically find companies that lose money, especially two years in a row, on our *100 Best* list. But we retain this company for 2018 because we think it has managed well through the downturn, taking a different approach than most in truly downsizing (or rightsizing) its business rather than borrowing its way through the trough. When the smoke clears, we think COP will be a solid bet on stabilizing and slightly rising energy prices.

Thanks to the 2012 spin-off of refiner Phillips 66, ConocoPhillips is now a pure play in the "E&P" (exploration and production) sector. Although lower oil and gas prices have turned ConocoPhillips from a $54 billion multinational "E&P" company into a $24 billion one of late (with the refining unit, it was once a $240 billion company), COP is still one of the world's largest E&P enterprises. Headquartered in Houston, TX, the company operates in 17 countries (down from 30) with about 13,300 employees (down from over 19,000).

The company's E&P operations are geographically diverse, producing most of its resources in the United States, including a large presence in Alaska's Prudhoe Bay. The company also has a large presence in US shale "fracking" regions, including Eagle Ford and Permian regions in Texas and the Bakken region in North Dakota. (Fracking was once "good"; then considered "bad" because of its relatively high cost. It's becoming "good" again as great strides in efficiency are expected to lower the breakeven cost.) As well, the company produces in Norway, the United Kingdom, western Canada, Australia, offshore Timor-Leste in the Timor Sea, Indonesia, Malaysia, China, Qatar, and Libya (but no longer Vietnam, Senegal, Nigeria, Algeria, or Russia).

Over the years, ConocoPhillips had become a strong natural gas play and a strong domestic energy player, with some 42 percent of total oil equivalents coming from the US (including Alaska). Another 19 percent originates in Canada. Recently the company has been focusing on "shorter cycle," less capital-intensive projects, selling non-producing gas assets and has been slowing deepwater exploration—all to optimize the balance sheet and cash flow. A two-thirds cut in the dividend followed these moves, and more asset sales are happening in 2017, including a $13.3 billion sale of mainly Canadian assets to Cenovus Energy which contains a provision for contingent payments if oil prices exceed $52 (Canadian) per barrel.

## Financial Highlights, Fiscal Year 2016

Once again, we don't need to delve into the details of oil prices; the story is familiar. Lower oil and gas prices and asset sales brought another 20 percent drop in 2016 revenues after a 42 percent drop in 2015; earnings went farther below the breakeven line mainly with asset sales and write-offs leading to a $3.2 billion loss. As mentioned, the dividend was cut from $2.94 to $1.00 in early 2016. Fortunately, the company is forecasting a turnaround, first in revenues with a 30–33 percent recovery in FY2017 followed by another 2–5 percent in FY2018 (at today's oil prices or slightly higher); earnings are projected back in the black to the tune of 20 cents a share in FY2017 rising to around $2.00 in FY2018. Full recovery and then some is expected in the early part of the next decade. As asset write-downs account for a good share of the loss, cash flows are still projected in the $7.00–$10.00 range per share through 2018, a positive sign. Dividend increases and share repurchases should follow suit.

## Reasons to Buy

As CEO Ryan Lance put it, "The strength of a company lies not in its ability to survive but in its ability to adapt." More than most others in the sector, COP has taken its medicine by selling assets, curbing non-core exploration, and cutting its dividend—in contrast to many of its peers who are borrowing to bridge the gap, including the dividend payment. For a company of Conoco's size, we think this is the right move.

It's highly unusual to include a company posting consecutive losses on the *100 Best* list. However, COP is strong enough to sustain itself through these tough times, and management has a good handle on the situation and the various scenarios and risks. We like the domestic slant on the production mix; it is lower cost and more stable than most. We don't have to add a measure of geopolitics into the long list of risk factors. With these factors plus the likelihood of a "leaner meaner" company emerging from the downturn, plus a still-decent dividend likely to rise substantially upon any favorable oil price movement, we think the present situation is more of a buying opportunity than a cause for concern. Drill carefully.

## Reasons for Caution

The story of ConocoPhillips has been a story of change over the past five years. The company successfully divested the refining operations to gain focus—only to gain focus on the most volatile part of the business—which has become far more volatile of late. E&P is risky by nature even with a steady oil price (although COP's domestically oriented portfolio reduces this risk); when you add in price volatility it makes for…well, a volatile mix. COP has taken its pain in stride, but continued price volatility and signs of a continuing glut as more producers come on line with lower cost production may keep the headwinds blowing for a while to come.

**SECTOR: Energy** ❑ **BETA COEFFICIENT: 1.48** ❑ **10-YEAR COMPOUND EARNINGS PER-SHARE GROWTH: 5.0%** ❑ **10-YEAR COMPOUND DIVIDENDS PER-SHARE GROWTH: 7.0%**

|  | 2009 | 2010 | 2011 | 2012 | 2013 | 2014 | 2015 | 2016 |
|---|---|---|---|---|---|---|---|---|
| Revenues (bil) | 149.3 | 189.4 | 244.8 | 62.0 | 54.4 | 52.5 | 30.7 | 23.7 |
| Net income (bil) | 4.9 | 8.8 | 12.1 | 7.4 | 8.0 | 6.2 | (1.7) | (3.2) |
| Earnings per share | 3.24 | 5.92 | 8.76 | 5.91 | 6.43 | 4.96 | (1.39) | (2.52) |
| Dividends per share | 1.91 | 2.16 | 2.64 | 2.64 | 2.70 | 2.84 | 2.94 | 1.00 |
| Cash flow per share | 9.58 | 12.50 | 15.63 | 11.47 | 12.57 | 11.79 | 5.97 | 4.77 |
| Price:     high | 57.4 | 68.6 | 77.4 | 78.3 | 74.6 | 87.1 | 70.1 | 53.2 |
|     low | 34.1 | 48.5 | 68.0 | 50.6 | 56.4 | 60.8 | 41.1 | 31.0 |

**Website: www.conocophillips.com**

## AGGRESSIVE GROWTH

# Corning Incorporated

Ticker symbol: GLW (NYSE) ❏ S&P rating: A- ❏ Value Line financial strength rating: A ❏ Current yield: 2.3% ❏ Dividend raises, past 10 years: 8

## Company Profile

When you think of Corning, you think of glass. All kinds of glass—drinking glasses, glass tableware, and that sort of thing. If you were around in the 1960s, you may remember that well-known white cookware with the little blue flowers on the side.

But things change, and so has Corning. Today's Corning is a premier technology company, more precisely, a technology materials company. If you use a smartphone, a tablet, a laptop PC, or a flat-panel television, chances are pretty good that the glass on the screen comes from Corning. A good amount of the data you see on that screen may have come through glass-based fiber-optic materials supplied by—guess who—Corning.

In fact, Corning operates in five segments, all centered on the glass business. Display Technologies (34 percent of FY2016 sales) is the world's largest producer of glass substrates for LCD displays in Japan, China, Taiwan, and South Korea for the television and computer display market. Optical Communications (formerly Telecommunications) (32 percent) makes fiber-optic cable and an assortment of connectivity and other products related to fiber for telecommunications companies, LAN, and data center applications. Specialty Materials (12 percent) provides a wide assortment of high-tech, glass-based materials, including those specialty glass screens for smartphones, tablets, etc., which it has cleverly branded as Corning Gorilla Glass for its endurance characteristics. This product is even gaining traction in automotive and architectural markets. Also out of this division comes a new bendable display substrate known as Willow Glass and a host of glass and ceramic products and formulations used in the semiconductor industry, precision instruments, and even astronomy and ophthalmology. The Environmental Technologies segment (11 percent) makes ceramic substrates and filters for emission control systems, mostly for gasoline and diesel engines. The Life Sciences segment (9 percent) makes laboratory glass and plastic wares. An "All Other" segment accounts for 2 percent.

The company competes with a number of suppliers, mostly Japanese, on a variety of fronts, and acquired the remaining 50 percent interest in a joint venture with Samsung (Samsung Corning Precision Materials) during

2014 to make it a wholly owned subsidiary with lower-cost production facilities in Korea. Corning also had a 50–50 joint venture with Dow Chemical for years, known as Dow Corning, a leader in silicon products and technologies. In 2016 Corning exchanged that interest for an equity interest in Hemlock Semiconductor Group, a producer of high-purity polycrystalline silicon used in the semiconductor and solar industries.

Promising innovations include the adaptation of its "Willow Glass," thinner than a dollar bill, for ultrathin, ultrasensitive touchscreens to improve size and weight characteristics of mobile devices. Eventually this will evolve into bendable, curved, and curvable glass displays, allowing us to literally wear our devices—an exciting prospect. Extra-strength Gorilla Glass is now in its fifth generation and found its stride in the marketplace in late 2016, with sales up 22 percent over the prior year, while double-digit revenue growth is also occurring in fiber-to-the-home solutions. The extension of Gorilla Glass beyond electronic devices into architectural and automotive designs is on track—such as the company's new "Dynamic Windows," architectural glass panels that automatically darken, reducing energy consumption, and new lighter windshields, sunroofs, and other glass products for cars.

## Financial Highlights, Fiscal Year 2016

FY2016 was kind of a transition year, especially on the earnings side. Lower LCD pricing and currency adjustments tempered sales to a modest 3 percent gain, while those factors plus expenses from the Dow Corning transaction shattered net profits to the tune of 27 percent, although the company reports a large one-time gain on the Dow Corning sale not reflected in these numbers. The company expects sales increases in the 2–3 percent range annually through FY2018, although we think this could be conservative if their more innovative products take off. Stronger demand and pricing and a more favorable product mix will drive higher margins and profits; these along with aggressive 5–10 percent share buybacks should drive per-share earnings up as much as 60 percent in FY2017 (against the weak 2016) and another 8–10 percent in FY2018. Low double-digit dividend increases also look likely, albeit on a small base.

## Reasons to Buy

As Corning puts it, we are now in the "Glass Age"—many promising new technologies are built on a foundation of high-tech glass products, and Corning is the best pure play in this niche. We like companies that stand to benefit no matter how a market plays out. Our CarMax pick benefits whether Ford or Toyota or Hyundai wins; CarMax sells used cars no matter what. At least for glass displays, Corning is in the same position—whether Samsung or Apple or LG wins the smartphone contest, Corning wins. The explosion in smart devices and the new technologies Corning is likely to bring to that space create some excitement down the road. We think the inevitable advent of wearable mobile computing devices will be a big spark for this company.

Aside from the short-term speed bump in display technologies, the core businesses like fiber optics are doing well, and we expect some of the new technologies like Gorilla Glass and the self-darkening glass products to become core businesses. Across the board, Corning continues to differentiate their products through innovation. The presence of competition, especially Japanese competition, reminds us from time to time that Corning doesn't own the "glass" niche outright, but it is close to owning the innovation in this area; for those who like pure plays in a strong and profitable technology segment, Corning is a good bet.

Finally, Corning has returned plenty of cash to shareholders both in the form of dividends and the share buybacks and appears positioned to do so going forward, especially on the buyback front. By the end of 2018, Corning will have reduced share count almost 50 percent from 2010.

## Reasons for Caution

While its product portfolio is broader than it was 15 years ago, supplying well beyond the telecom industry, the company is still subject to business and inventory cycles. Glass, without the right amount of innovation, is a commodity business with plenty of foreign competition.

SECTOR: **Information Technology** ◻ BETA COEFFICIENT: **1.38** ◻ 10-YEAR COMPOUND EARNINGS PER-SHARE GROWTH: **4.5%** ◻ 10-YEAR COMPOUND DIVIDENDS PER-SHARE GROWTH: **18.5%**

|  | 2009 | 2010 | 2011 | 2012 | 2013 | 2014 | 2015 | 2016 |
|---|---|---|---|---|---|---|---|---|
| Revenues (mil) | 5,395 | 6,632 | 7,890 | 8,012 | 7,819 | 9,715 | 9,111 | 9,390 |
| Net income (mil) | 2,114 | 3,275 | 2,620 | 1,728 | 1,961 | 2,472 | 1,339 | 1,013 |
| Earnings per share | 1.35 | 2.07 | 1.76 | 1.15 | 1.34 | 1.73 | 1.00 | 0.98 |
| Dividends per share | 0.20 | 0.20 | 0.23 | 0.32 | 0.39 | 0.52 | 0.36 | 0.54 |
| Cash flow per share | 1.86 | 2.64 | 2.49 | 1.85 | 2.12 | 2.79 | 2.15 | 2.21 |
| Price:          high | 19.5 | 21.1 | 23.4 | 14.6 | 18.1 | 23.5 | 25.2 | 25.3 |
| low | 9.0 | 15.5 | 11.5 | 10.6 | 11.6 | 16.5 | 15.4 | 16.1 |

Website: www.corning.com

AGGRESSIVE GROWTH

# Costco Wholesale Corporation

Ticker symbol: COST (NASDAQ) ❑ Large Cap ❑ Value Line financial strength rating: A+ ❑ Current yield: 1.0% ❑ Dividend raises, past 10 years: 10

## Company Profile

Every year we take a hard look at Costco, for it has become so large that we wonder how it possibly could keep growing—and how could the stock possibly keep going up—and it does. We wonder if it has any room to grow, whether it is long in the tooth as a retailing concept, too small in the margins, too expensive to buy as a stock, and too "mass" intensive to appeal to today's variety of custom-demanding Millennials. And now we have to judge it against the hard realities of e-commerce. We almost ditched our four-wheel flatbed last year and headed for the exits. But we didn't—and we're still impressed with Costco's appeal both to cost-conscious Millennials and to a whole lot of cost-conscious "old folks" like us as well. And we don't really think e-commerce has yet become a major threat to shopping that entails four-wheel flatbeds. We're keeping the company on our 2018 shopping list, once again.

Costco Wholesale Corporation operates a multinational chain of membership warehouses, mainly under the Costco Wholesale name, that carry brand-name merchandise at substantially lower prices than are typically found at conventional wholesale or retail sources. The warehouse sales model was designed to help small to medium-sized businesses reduce costs in purchasing for resale and for everyday business use, but as most know, the individual consumer has been their big growth driver. The company capitalizes on size and operational efficiencies, such as "cross-docking" shipments directly from manufacturers to stores, to deliver attractive pricing to its customers. Based on sales volume, Costco is the largest membership warehouse club chain and second-largest general retailer in the world.

Costco carries a broad line of product categories, including groceries, appliances, television and media, automotive supplies, toys, hardware, sporting goods, jewelry, cameras, books, housewares, apparel, health and beauty aids, tobacco, furniture, office supplies, and office equipment. Approximately 22 percent of sales come from packaged food and beverages, 14 percent from "fresh food," and 21 percent from "sundries"—snack foods, candy, alcohol, and cleaning supplies. Another 16 percent comes from hardlines—electronics, appliances, hardware, automotive, office supplies, and health and beauty aids—and 12 percent from softlines—primarily clothing, housewares, media, jewelry, and domestics. The rest, including gasoline, pharmacy, optical, and other services, form a catchall "other" category. The emergence of Costco as a grocer of choice cannot be missed, and the company reports particular strength in its Fresh Foods lines (meats, produce, deli, and bakery), indicating appeal to the more cost-conscious set of trend-conscious food consumers.

Additionally, Costco Wholesale Industries, a division of the company, operates manufacturing businesses, including special food packaging, optical laboratories, hearing aid centers, and jewelry distribution. The company operates 508 discount gas stations worldwide. "Ancillary" businesses such as jewelry, optometry, gasoline, and others, of course, are designed to bring people into the stores. A wide and growing variety of products are sold under its "Kirkland" private label.

Costco is open only to members of its tiered membership plan, the higher "Executive" tier at $120 annually (versus $60 for the standard membership), gaining access to reward points and other perks and discounts. (These fees were increased in mid-2017.) Executive members account for about one-third of the base and two-thirds of the sales. In all, there are 86.7 million members (up 7 percent), with a 90 percent membership renewal rate in the US and Canada.

As of the end of 2016 Costco has 723 locations: 506 in the United States and Puerto Rico (up from 492), 94 in Canada (versus 90), 36 in Mexico (unchanged), 28 in the UK (versus 27), 25 in Japan (versus 24), 12 in South Korea, 12 in Taiwan, 8 in Australia, and 2 in Spain. The company also has a significant and growing e-commerce presence at www.costco.com. Though it still accounts for only 3.5 percent of revenues, it grew 15 percent in FY2016.

## Financial Highlights, Fiscal Year 2016

Same-store sales were flat in FY2016 with many crosscurrents—food and gas price deflation, negative currency effects, higher shopping frequency but smaller average "tickets"—implying that today's urban/suburban shopper is a little less likely to stock up for the long term. Total sales increased 2 percent due to store openings. Gross margins improved slightly mostly due to lower food and gasoline input costs, leading to a slight net income gain (less than 1 percent). For FY2017 the company expects a return to stronger sales growth as deflation and currency effects subside and as new merchandising and discounting strategies take hold; sales are projected 5–7 percent higher annually through FY2018. Increased membership revenue, the switch from AMEX to Visa, and cost efficiencies should move net income comparably higher in 2017 and as much as 15 percent higher in 2018.

Membership revenues increased 4.5 percent to about $2.6 billion annually—an obviously large driver of Costco's $2 billion-plus annual net profit—and the 2017 price increase will obviously make membership revenues an even larger success factor. Dividend increases have been running in the 10 percent range, but the share buyback aisle remains closed for now.

## Reasons to Buy

Costco is in an attractive best-of-both-worlds niche: It is a price leader consistent with the attitudes of today's more frugal consumer, yet it enjoys a reputation for being more upscale than the competition. We've all heard the boast, "I got it at Costco" from even our most affluent and high-minded friends. And of course, there's everybody else.

We also continue to like the international expansion and think the formula will play well overseas—although their ambitious European and Asian plans may be tempered a bit by local preferences for small package sizes and the general lack of storage space. Any US resident who has hosted a visitor from abroad knows that Costco is a favored destination during the visit. We expect international expansion will be one of the company's primary growth drivers over the next ten years. We also applaud the recent move to switch exclusive credit card use from American Express to a co-branded Citigroup Visa credit card (in addition to accepting ordinary Visa and MasterCard debit cards). This card is less expensive and more accessible to most members, and has broadened sales appeal. Costco also gets high marks for employee pay, satisfaction, and loyalty, and for corporate citizenship in general. In all, the company has a strong brand in a highly competitive sector and is well managed.

## Reasons for Caution

The major concern today is the emergence of e-commerce. More frequent visits and lower tickets already suggest a convenience model is taking hold, and eventually these consumers could defect altogether. Or could they? True, you can buy much of what you get at Costco online. But is it really more convenient to receive huge packages on your front doorstep? Or just to go out once a week and get what you need? Time will tell, but Costco has the advantage of ease, we think, when it comes to shopping for large quantities of basic, and not so basic, needs. Another concern is the dependence on low-margin food and sundry lines. That said, food does get customers into the store and gets them there more than once a week. More store traffic means more and more regular store sales overall.

We do fret over the high share price, low margins, and dependence on membership fees for profitability. All three bring a measure of vulnerability to the stock—a misstep could be costly. On the flip side, management has shown its ability to navigate through difficult periods, the brand is strong, and the prospects for a global footprint, above all else, are encouraging for the future. There are a lot of headwinds in today's retail space, but we think Costco is unique enough and strong enough to prosper.

SECTOR: **Retail** ▫ BETA COEFFICIENT: **0.91** ▫ 10-YEAR COMPOUND EARNINGS PER-SHARE
GROWTH: **9.5%** ▫ 10-YEAR COMPOUND DIVIDENDS PER-SHARE GROWTH: **15.0%**

|  | 2009 | 2010 | 2011 | 2012 | 2013 | 2014 | 2015 | 2016 |
|---|---|---|---|---|---|---|---|---|
| Revenues (bil) | 71.4 | 77.9 | 88.9 | 99.1 | 105.1 | 112.6 | 116.1 | 118.7 |
| Net income (mil) | 1,086 | 1,307 | 1,462 | 1,741 | 1,977 | 2,058 | 2,334 | 2,350 |
| Earnings per share | 2.57 | 2.93 | 3.30 | 3.97 | 4.49 | 4.65 | 5.27 | 5.33 |
| Dividends per share | 0.68 | 0.77 | 0.89 | 1.03 | 1.17 | 1.33 | 1.51 | 1.70 |
| Cash flow per share | 4.25 | 4.85 | 5.34 | 6.13 | 6.69 | 7.05 | 7.90 | 8.24 |
| Price:    high | 61.3 | 73.2 | 88.7 | 106.0 | 126.1 | 146.8 | 169.7 | 169.6 |
| low | 38.2 | 53.4 | 69.5 | 78.8 | 98.6 | 109.5 | 117.0 | 138.5 |

Website: www.costco.com

---

**CONSERVATIVE GROWTH**

# CVS Health Corporation

Ticker symbol: CVS (NYSE) ▫ Large Cap ▫ Value Line financial strength rating: A+ ▫ Current yield: 2.5% ▫ Dividend raises, past 10 years: 10

## Company Profile

Stanley and Sid Goldstein were distributing health and beauty products in the early 1960s when they decided to branch out into retailing, opening their first Consumer Value Store in Lowell, MA, in 1963. The CVS chain had grown to 40 outlets by 1969, the year they sold the business to Melville Shoes. Melville underwent a restructuring in the mid-1990s, spinning off CVS and other retail units.

Stan and Sid should be proud. CVS is now the largest pharmacy health-care provider in the United States and ranks seventh on the *Fortune* 500 list. In keeping with its mission, two years ago it changed its name from "CVS Caremark" to "CVS Health." Its flagship Retail Pharmacy domestic drug-store chain operates 9,700 retail and specialty pharmacy stores and 1,100 walk-in healthcare clinics in 49 states, the District of Columbia, and now Brazil. The company holds the leading market share in 88 of the 100 largest

US drugstore markets, more than any other retail drugstore chain, and holds a 24 percent share of the US prescription market. Over time, it has expanded through acquiring other players in the category—Osco, Sav-On, Eckerd, and Longs Drugs. CVS's purchase of Longs Drugs in 2008 vaulted the company into the lead position in the US drug retail market, ahead of Walgreens.

Stores are situated primarily in strip shopping centers or free-standing locations, with a typical store ranging in size from 8,000–13,000 square feet. Most new units being built are based on either a 10,000-square-foot or 12,000-square-foot prototype building that typically includes a drive-thru pharmacy. Prescriptions generate over 75 percent of Retail Pharmacy sales, which in turn makes up about 46 percent of the company's total sales and is far more profitable, generating 80 percent of gross profits.

The Caremark acquisition in 2007 transformed CVS from strictly a retailer into the nation's leading manager of pharmacy benefits, the middleman between pharmaceutical companies and individuals with drug benefit coverage. The Caremark acquisition forms the core of the company's Pharmacy Benefits Management (PBM) operations, which have some 68,000 pharmacy outlets including hospitals and clinics as well as the previously mentioned retail stores. The company now manages about 1.7 billion prescriptions a year to 65 million plan members, and the Pharmacy Services segment now makes up about 54 percent of sales—but only 20 percent of gross profit. This is a low-margin business, with gross profit of about 5 percent of revenue versus more than 30 percent for the Retail Pharmacy segment. CVS estimates that they own 30 percent of the US PBM market.

Part of the Retail Pharmacy segment, the company's MinuteClinic concept is especially interesting in today's climate of managing healthcare costs. CVS now has 1,135 clinics (including 80 new clinics in Target stores—see following) in 33 states and DC, offering basic health services like flu shots given by 2,200 nurse practitioners and physician's assistants in a convenient retail environment. Plans are to grow MinuteClinic into 1,500 locations in 35 states by 2018. The concept gradually is gaining mainstream acceptance with 28 million patient visits to date—and of course, those clinics located in CVS stores bring traffic to those stores. The company also operates mail order and online pharmacies for regular and chronically ill patients.

Two recent acquisitions are worth noting. First, in 2015 it became the operator of 1,674 pharmacies located in Target stores, filling some 100 million prescriptions annually. There is also a network of 80 health clinics within these stores. Second was the 2016 purchase of Omnicare to serve the skilled nursing and long-term care markets.

## Financial Highlights, Fiscal Year 2016

FY2016 sales rose almost 16 percent, helped along—to what extent we don't know—by the Target and Omnicare acquisitions, which closed during the year. This growth figure was a bit under forecast, which had been 17–18 percent. Net income also lagged, up only 8 percent, suggesting some drug price erosion felt across the rest of the industry and also suggesting that the acquired properties are a bit less profitable. Per-share earnings were up over 9 percent however, due to a healthy 3.6 percent share buyback. Through FY2018, revenue growth will settle into the 4–6 percent range, with earnings actually down 2 percent in FY2017 as more drug price competition takes hold and as the company deals with the effects of losing some PBM contracts to rival Walgreens. Per-share earnings should resume high single-digit growth in 2018 with aggressive buybacks continuing; CVS targets buying back 30 percent of its shares between 2008 and 2018. Dividend growth in the mid–double digits (15 percent annually) sweetens the pot.

## Reasons to Buy

We don't much care for retail in today's modern "stay-at-home" economy, but CVS is a notable exception mainly due to its convenience and its health offerings, both which are difficult to match on Amazon Prime. What's more, its "retail" location in the healthcare food chain positions it perfectly to capitalize on favorable demographics: an aging population, one also ever more willing to pay for convenience, and a growing acceptance of CVS as a local convenience store for needs beyond health and personal care products.

CVS is clearly a smartly diversified market leader. The overall strategy seems to be to grow market share and scale both with its retail operations and with its pharmacy benefits businesses. Cross-selling of prescriptions, retail products, and health services all seems to be working well and is an important part of the strategy.

There has been plenty of return for shareholders in the form of cash dividends and steady and large share buybacks. Share price appreciation has taken a momentary pause due to uncertainties in the drug and retail industries and in the future of the Affordable Care Act, but we think the company is well positioned to avoid the downsides; the pause probably represents a buying opportunity.

## Reasons for Caution

Some of the features of the Trump administration agenda create new uncertainties for CVS, including drug pricing and the Affordable Care Act. The effects at the time of this writing remain to be seen. Competition has heated up in the all-important PBM industry, and the new tendency for people to stay home and stay away from Target stores may also hurt. All together, the environment CVS is operating in has become less stable than years past, but we think the company has the footprint, the resources, and the management qualities to effectively manage through the change.

SECTOR: **Retail** ❑ BETA COEFFICIENT: **0.82** ❑ 10-YEAR COMPOUND EARNINGS PER-SHARE GROWTH: **14.5%** ❑ 10-YEAR COMPOUND DIVIDENDS PER-SHARE GROWTH: **24.0%**

|  |  | 2009 | 2010 | 2011 | 2012 | 2013 | 2014 | 2015 | 2016 |
|---|---|---|---|---|---|---|---|---|---|
| Revenues (bil) |  | 98.7 | 98.0 | 107.2 | 123.1 | 126.7 | 139.4 | 153.2 | 177.5 |
| Net income (mil) |  | 3,803 | 3,700 | 3,766 | 4,394 | 4,902 | 5,255 | 5,810 | 6,300 |
| Earnings per share |  | 2.63 | 2.67 | 2.80 | 3.43 | 4.00 | 4.51 | 5.18 | 5.84 |
| Dividends per share |  | 0.30 | 0.35 | 0.50 | 0.65 | 0.90 | 1.10 | 1.40 | 1.70 |
| Cash flow per share |  | 3.73 | 3.75 | 4.10 | 4.99 | 5.74 | 6.30 | 7.18 | 8.27 |
| Price: | high | 38.3 | 37.8 | 39.5 | 49.8 | 72.0 | 98.6 | 113.6 | 106.7 |
|  | low | 23.7 | 26.8 | 31.3 | 41.0 | 49.9 | 64.9 | 81.4 | 69.3 |

Website: www.cvs.com

---

**AGGRESSIVE GROWTH**

# Daktronics, Inc.

Ticker symbol: DAKT (NASDAQ) ❑ Small Cap ❑ Value Line financial strength rating: B+ ❑ Current yield: 3.0% ❑ Dividend raises, past 10 years: 7

## Company Profile

You're driving down the highway. You're thinking about getting rid of a month's worth of grime and dirt and crud from your car. Suddenly, in vivid Technicolor, you see a billboard ahead on your right. Not just any old indifferent and ignorable billboard displaying the same old thing months on end. It's brightly lit. It flashes an offer. Five Star Car Wash, at this exit, has a "Today Only—25 Percent Off" special. A few minutes ago you passed an electronic sign flashing "Road Work Ahead—Current Delay 30 Minutes." So, you tap the brakes, hit the right lane, and off the interstate you go. A win-win—you have a clean car, and the car wash, having a lighter day than usual and temporarily pricing its services accordingly, gets another unit through their system.

Hockey great Wayne Gretzky made famous the idea of "skating where the puck is going," and it's still one of our favorite investing maxims. Like it or not, we think such real-time, highly visual signage is where the puck is going in marketing: real-time visual displays to complement your real-time mobile devices. Give it time, and it will come. Give it time, and there will be real-time visual graphic displays on park benches and subway entrances. Give it time, and there will be "digital street furniture" and such just about everywhere. Give it time, and there will be large video displays in entertainment venues, gambling casinos, and the like. Give it time, and vividly colorful video displays will become standard architectural elements on modern office buildings.

So how do you invest in this looming megatrend? There's a small company located almost literally in the middle of nowhere—Brookings, South Dakota—that makes this stuff. Chances are this company made both of the signs mentioned above. "Digital Street Furniture" is actually one of their product lines. Their core and founding business is really the large multimedia scoreboards in place in a growing number of sports arenas. The company, Daktronics, has a hand in an assortment of places where digital display technology can make a difference in outdoor environments, from $40 million scoreboards to the variable dollars-and-cents-per-gallon digital displays outside your local gas station.

Daktronics is the world's leading supplier of electronic scoreboards, large electronic display systems, digital messaging solutions, and related software and support services for sporting, commercial, and transportation applications. The company offers everything from small signs and scoreboards costing under $1,000 to the large $40 million sports-complex scoreboards mentioned above.

Business segments include Commercial, Live Events, High School Parks and Recreation, Transportation, and International: These groups are organized around customer segments and are all set up to create and sell unique applications of the core product lines of the company, which include video display systems, scoring and timing systems, digital billboards, digital street furniture, and simpler message displays like price, time, and temperature displays. Most of the company's products are based on LED technology with low to high resolution and embedded digital controllers. Here is a bit more "color" on the five segments:

- Commercial (26 percent of FY2016 revenue) sells a variety of digital signage to auto dealer, restaurant, gaming, retail petroleum (gas stations, mainly), and shopping center markets. Vivid video displays used for architectural or commercial purposes as part of the full building design is another emerging subsegment of this business.
- Live Events (36 percent of revenue) produces the traditional and some highly customized scoreboards, as well as signs for entertainment

venues, including programmable displays, parking information signs, and even specialized signs for places of worship.

- High School Parks and Recreation (12 percent) includes not only digital-age marquee signs for theaters and other venues but also for the box office, merchandise sales areas, and others.
- Transportation (9 percent) covers the freeway signs; there is also plenty of digital signage in airports, train stations, public parking areas, and other public transit facilities.
- International (17 percent) sells all applications into international markets.

Overall, Daktronics has about a 30 percent share of the LED video display market, making it the number one player. In early 2016 the company acquired Canadian digital media solutions provider ADFLOW Networks, signaling a greater emphasis on providing complete solutions, not just LED hardware. In early 2017 the company rolled out new lines of ultra–high definition visual displays.

The company has about 2,785 employees—including, somewhat unusually, about 400 interns and students on the payroll mostly from the local South Dakota State University. Retired cofounder and chairman Aelred J. Kurtenbach, a PhD electrical engineer and professor at SDSU, owns 5.1 percent of the shares. His son, Reece A. Kurtenbach, runs the company. The website, at www.daktronics.com, is a fun and instructive ride.

## Financial Highlights, Fiscal Year 2016

Several crosscurrents affected the business again in FY2016, as the different segments turned in mixed results. The strong dollar hurt and the timing of delivery of big projects varied as usual. The good news is that total orders and the backlog were up. Relatively flat volumes in other segments, in part due to competition, reduced throughput, which increased unit costs. Revenues declined just over 4 percent, while net income dropped about 50 percent. FY2017 and FY2018 bring higher backlogs and decent prospects in all businesses. Revenues should rise in the 4–5 percent range annually. More volume to absorb fixed costs, less subcontracting, improved mix, and reduced warranty costs should bring FY2017 earnings back to near previous levels, with a 50 percent improvement to $17 million for FY2017 and another 11–12 percent gain in FY2018 on improved volumes, reduced warranty expenses, and higher net margins. The regular dividend was cut from 40 cents to 24 cents per share annually, but special dividends will (and have been) paid. Share buybacks are about a million shares per year regularly—2.5 percent of the float.

## Reasons to Buy

Since beaches and surf weren't part of the landscape when we were growing up in the Midwest, like any normal kids we were fascinated with signs of all kinds. Daktronics takes signs to a new level.

We continue to feel that such digital signage is a big part of the future of mass, real-time marketing communications—a "system" including your mobile device plus electronic signage—like it or not. Overall, we like situations where a core technology is applied successfully to an ever-larger number of end markets. Too, we think as such digital signage becomes more mainstream, the company will be able to produce in larger volumes, even mass-produce more of their applications, which should drive down unit costs and increase profitability. We see advantages in the location, too—a dedicated work force and low cost of doing business. Too, the company has virtually no debt.

All this said, Daktronics hasn't performed as well as hoped for when we added it to our *100 Best* list in 2015 in an attempt to get a bit of niche technology and small-cap growth "energy" into the mix. The company just hasn't hit its stride (nor its own production capacity) with its business, though backlogs and order flows are getting stronger. We hope to see a significant near-term advance in Transportation and Commercial applications—this is where we think the bulk of future expansion really lies. Our patience is paid for in part by the attractive dividend (though it was cut in mid-2016), and we hope for an eventual "breakout" in this enticing market. We may not be wrong, just early.

## Reasons for Caution

While the company is the top player in its market, there is plenty of product and price competition in the form of major Japanese firms like Mitsubishi (and if you've been to Tokyo, you know how mainstream digital signage can be). We do also wonder if environmental movements will rise up to quell what could easily become overstimulating visual "pollution," but so far to our knowledge this hasn't happened on a large scale.

More conventionally, Daktronics clearly has a riskier profile than most of our picks. Order flow and delivery timing can vary considerably especially in the Live Events segment, but we continue to think the business will smooth out considerably once electronic commercial signage becomes more mainstream.

SECTOR: **Information Technology** ◻ BETA COEFFICIENT: **1.50** ◻ 10-YEAR COMPOUND EARNINGS PER-SHARE GROWTH: **-2.5%** ◻ 10-YEAR COMPOUND DIVIDENDS PER-SHARE GROWTH: **27.0%**

|  |  | 2009 | 2010 | 2011 | 2012 | 2013 | 2014 | 2015 | 2016 |
|---|---|---|---|---|---|---|---|---|---|
| Revenues (mil) | | 393 | 442 | 489 | 518 | 552 | 616 | 570 | 590 |
| Net income (mil) | | (7.0) | 14.2 | 8.5 | 22.8 | 20.9 | 2.1 | 2.10 | 10.3 |
| Earnings per share | | (0.17) | 0.34 | 0.20 | 0.53 | 0.51 | 0.47 | 0.05 | 0.25 |
| Dividends per share | | 0.10 | 0.10 | 0.22 | 0.23 | 0.39 | 0.40 | 0.40 | 0.27 |
| Cash flow per share | | 0.37 | 0.81 | 0.62 | 0.91 | 0.85 | 0.82 | 0.43 | 0.85 |
| Price: | high | 10.5 | 17.3 | 16.7 | 11.9 | 16.1 | 15.6 | 13.2 | 10.9 |
| | low | 5.9 | 7.1 | 8.0 | 6.3 | 9.4 | 10.8 | 7.2 | 5.9 |

Website: www.daktronics.com

---

AGGRESSIVE GROWTH

# Deere & Company

Ticker symbol: DE (NYSE) ◻ **Large Cap** ◻ **Value Line financial strength rating: A++** ◻ **Current yield: 2.2%** ◻ **Dividend raises, past 10 years: 9**

## Company Profile

We finally got our way with Deere.

For five years, and especially the past two, Deere & Co. has been testing our mettle and conviction as long-term investors. The brand and business are best in class, but current business conditions including agricultural surpluses, a strong dollar, declining exports, low farm prices, and low farm incomes had Deere and most other ag-related companies stuck in the knee-deep mud of cyclical lows. Inventories of both new and used product were piling up at dealerships. But due to brand strength, loyalty (ours and its customers'), the propensity of good companies to use downturns to become more efficient, and our long-term belief in agriculture, we hung on to Deere. We're glad we did. Founded in 1837, Deere & Company grew from a one-man blacksmith shop into a worldwide corporation that today does business in more than 160 countries and employs more than 57,000 people around the globe. Deere has a diverse base of operations reporting into three segments: Agriculture and Turf, Construction and Forestry, and Financial Services.

Deere has been the world's premier producer of agricultural equipment for nearly 50 years. The Agriculture and Turf segment produces and distributes tractors, loaders, combines, harvesters, seeding, mowers, hay baling, tilling, crop care and application, and other equipment. If it's used on a farm and requires an engine, Deere likely offers it.

Additionally, over the years, the company has developed and expanded lines of turf and utility equipment, including riding lawn equipment and walk-behind mowers, golf course equipment, utility vehicles, and commercial mowing and snow-removal equipment. Deere also offers a broad line of associated implements: integrated agricultural management systems technology and solutions; precision agricultural irrigation equipment and supplies; landscape and nursery products; and other outdoor power products.

With the Construction and Forestry segment, Deere is also the world's leading manufacturer of forestry equipment and a major manufacturer of heavy construction machines (Caterpillar is still the market leader in this segment). Major lines include construction, earthmoving, material-handling, and timber-harvesting machines including but not limited to backhoe loaders; crawler dozers and loaders; four-wheel-drive loaders; excavators; motor graders; articulated dump trucks; landscape loaders; skid-steer loaders; and log skidders, feller bunchers, log loaders, log forwarders, log harvesters, and related attachments.

As the company reports it, revenue for the Agriculture and Turf segment is about 79 percent of the $23.4 billion in FY2016 revenue; the Construction and Forestry segment makes up the remainder. The Financial Services segment rolls its revenue into the other segments, and only segment profits are reported, but that segment produces about 20 percent of total net profit.

The Financial Services segment includes John Deere Credit, which is one of the largest equipment finance companies in the United States, with more than 1.8 million accounts.

Overall, international sales continue to account for 36 percent of the total.

## Financial Highlights, Fiscal Year 2016

Declining equipment sales resulting from poor farm incomes and oil industry and general construction softness resulted in an 8 percent drop in FY2016 revenues. Earnings dropped 21 percent as factory utilization declined and the Construction and Forestry segment actually lost money. Per-share cash flows remained north of $7.00, signaling continued fundamental business health. The upturn the company visualized last year for 2017 has started to materialize (hence the strong recent stock price) and FY2018 should bring a roughly 10 percent growth in earnings on a 3 percent growth in sales. The company has chosen not to increase the dividend and to curtail buybacks until a more certain recovery, probably after 2018, but that said, Deere has retired 20 percent of its float since 2011. Deere may become a classic case study in managing a down cycle for better days ahead; we'll see.

## Reasons to Buy

Even with the business passing its nadir, Deere continues to be a tough call. As the saying goes, "Everything is a cycle"—and we're placing our bets that this, too, has passed and the aforementioned heavy use of Deere machinery, coupled with the inevitable long-term growth in agriculture will put the company back on top of its game in just a few short years. Who can argue about the long-term growth in agriculture, as the global population is predicted to increase 30 percent by 2050 and as global standards of living increase on top of that? Indeed, the company reminds us that global grain demand has already increased 35 percent just from 2000 through 2015.

We're also big fans of the brand and historic excellence. "Nothing runs like a Deere" is the company's apt slogan, and as far as industrial companies go, Deere continues to be a poster child for US industrial ingenuity and excellence. It has an outstanding brand (and one of the most popular logos for hats, jackets, and so on, worn by people who have barely seen a farm field!) and reputation in the agriculture industry, and we see the ag industry as strong and strategic far into the future as global living standards improve and emerging markets develop.

Longer term, farm incomes should rise worldwide, and the company continues to invest in developing markets. Too, we think that innovation is a plus—Deere leads its competitors in R&D investment (5.9 percent of sales), bringing the Internet and GPS to farming and farming machines; new engines also promise greater fuel economy and reduced emissions.

Beyond its products, Deere has established an almost unassailable brand leadership with its services and customer-centered innovations. Deere, more than others, puts its people in the field (literally) to figure out what agriculture professionals really need, and they work with their customers closely to sell their products through a solid dealer network.

"Sell when there's something better to buy"—and we still can't come up with anything better in this important manufactured goods segment.

## Reasons for Caution

The company has plowed through an extraordinarily difficult period giving us a test of our long-term commitment. Now the stock price has jumped 25 percent—too much, too soon given the slow, steady recovery?

Deere is, and always will be, vulnerable to cycles in the farm sector. The normal cycle, and in particular indelible memories of 1980s farm difficulties, can cause the farmers who buy this stuff to get cautious pretty quickly. All in all, farming will always be with us, both in the US and overseas, and there will always be a demand for machines and especially smarter, more efficient ones—Deere has an enormous brand and long-term track record.

SECTOR: **Industrials** ◻ BETA COEFFICIENT: **0.73** ◻ 10-YEAR COMPOUND EARNINGS PER-SHARE GROWTH: **6.0%** ◻ 10-YEAR COMPOUND DIVIDENDS PER-SHARE GROWTH: **14.0%**

|  |  | 2009 | 2010 | 2011 | 2012 | 2013 | 2014 | 2015 | 2016 |
|---|---|---|---|---|---|---|---|---|---|
| Revenues (mil) | | 20,756 | 23,573 | 29,466 | 33,501 | 34,998 | 32,961 | 25,775 | 23,387 |
| Net income (mil) | | 1,198 | 1,865 | 2,799 | 3,065 | 3,533 | 3,162 | 1,937 | 1,524 |
| Earnings per share | | 2.82 | 4.35 | 6.63 | 7.64 | 9.08 | 8.53 | 5.76 | 4.81 |
| Dividends per share | | 1.12 | 1.16 | 1.52 | 1.79 | 1.99 | 2.22 | 2.40 | 2.40 |
| Cash flow per share | | 4.05 | 5.72 | 8.34 | 9.56 | 11.45 | 11.45 | 8.62 | 7.39 |
| Price: | high | 56.9 | 84.9 | 99.8 | 89.7 | 95.6 | 94.9 | 98.2 | 104.6 |
| | low | 24.5 | 46.3 | 59.9 | 69.5 | 79.5 | 76.9 | 71.9 | 70.2 |

Website: www.deere.com

**AGGRESSIVE GROWTH**

NEW FOR 2018

# Dentsply Sirona

Ticker symbol: XRAY (NASDAQ) ◻ Large Cap ◻ Value Line financial strength rating: B++ ◻ Current yield: 0.6% ◻ Dividend raises, past 10 years: 9

## Company Profile

We switched horses. Whether or not it was midstream remains to be seen, and whether or not we will fall off and get wet also remains to be seen.

There are basically two medium-sized publicly traded dental supply operations behind market leader Henry Schein, which distribute to all medical and veterinary trades as well as dental. The two companies are Patterson Companies (PDCO) and Dentsply Sirona. We've had Patterson Companies on our *100 Best* list since the beginning of (our) time in 2010. We've always liked the steady and repeatable business of dental suppliers, and not too long ago we had Dentsply on our list as well. However, a few years back we decided we didn't need two companies in the same business and picked PDCO because of higher cash returns to shareholders—dividends and stock buybacks.

So why now the switch of horses? Both companies had some pretty bad cavities in their growth trajectory; neither have gained much traction recently as the recession and diminished dental plan coverage have resulted in a fair amount of dental procrastination on the part of patients. Both companies undertook initiatives to spur growth, which in this steady industry, means making acquisitions. Patterson acquired Animal Health International, a large veterinary supplier that is actually larger than the original business, in 2015. Dentsply acquired Sirona Dental Systems, formerly a unit of Siemens and the world's largest dental equipment (not supplies) manufacturer, in early 2016.

We feel that Sirona is a good (and high-margined) complement to XRAY's existing dental business, while Animal Health targets a completely different customer base and is a far lower-margin business to boot. To that point, Dentsply's net profit margins will increase 2–4 percent to about 15 percent while Patterson's net margins will decrease almost that much to 3–4 percent total—a dramatic shift. To a large degree, this drove the shift on our list.

With the merger, Dentsply Sirona is now the world's largest maker of professional dental products and technologies and offers a complete solution ("The Dental Solutions Company" is their slogan) of equipment and consumables to cover the needs of any dental practice, clinic, lab, or distributor in the field.

The Sirona acquisition brought among other things a core competency in new dental technologies like digital and 3D imaging systems, CAD/CAM tools for custom manufacture of lab products, and the single-visit "CEREC" crown making system. It added about 50 percent to Dentsply sales and a strong international footprint.

Prior to the Sirona acquisition, Dentsply's sales breakdown was about 50 percent dental specialty products, including root canal instruments and materials, digital scanning and x-ray products, and implant materials, 29 percent ordinary dental practice consumables, 10 percent dental lab materials such as crown and bridge materials, and 12 percent consumable medical device products such as drills and catheters. We don't know the exact breakdown after the Sirona acquisition, but Sirona surely raised the percentage brought in under the "specialty products" category—instruments and technologies—and also vastly increased the overseas presence. The combined company has 40 distributors and a sales presence in 120 countries accounting for 66 percent of sales overseas.

## Financial Highlights, Fiscal Year 2016

Financial comparisons aren't too meaningful here due to the large acquisition; FY2016 revenues jumped about 40 percent, or a billion dollars, to just under $3.8 billion while earnings experienced a similar jump. Of greater interest are the forward projections, which call for a 10 percent revenue gain in FY2017 and a stronger 13 percent rise in FY2018, while acquisition synergies and margin improvements will bring a 30 percent rise in net income in FY2017 and a more moderate 10 percent gain in FY2018. The dividend, while still small, is slated to grow about 10 percent annually.

## Reasons to Buy

Dentsply Sirona is well positioned to capitalize on several growth vectors in the dental industry. First, there's the international and emerging market opportunity, as modern dental health becomes a standard in overseas and especially developing markets. Second is the greater integration of digital technologies in the dental practice, from x-rays to 3D and CAD/CAM automation of lab work such as crowns to the management of patient records; the company is well positioned in all parts of this operational food chain. Third is the increased presence of single-visit outcomes, where a crown can be mapped, created, and installed in one day using the CEREC technologies. Fourth is the stream of licensee revenue other distributors bring in for deploying Dentsply technologies like CEREC. (As an example, Patterson also offered CEREC as a licensee.)

Of course, these geography and technology-related growth vectors are additional to the growth already slated for the industry coming in the form of an aging population, greater and longer retention of natural teeth, greater acceptance and practice of dental implants, and the gradual automation and digitization of dental practices.

We like the stronger positioning of the combined company as a one-stop shop for all technology and consumables needed to run any kind of dentistry-related practice, as well as the greater extension into higher-margined technology products and the greater presence overseas. And of course we like the higher gross and net margins all of this is bringing to the bottom line.

## Reasons for Caution

Dental markets can be cyclical, as we found out during the Great Recession as patients put off more elective procedures and dental practices stopped spending on equipment and supplies. As pointed out above, we take a little hit with Dentsply Sirona on shareholder returns—dividends and share repurchases—at least for now. In fact, the company increased its float 50 percent albeit to bring in a 50 percent sales increase with the acquisition. The good news: XRAY plans to retire 5 million of the 85 million new shares issued each year for the foreseeable future.

SECTOR: **Healthcare** ❑ BETA COEFFICIENT: **1.21** ❑ 10-YEAR COMPOUND EARNINGS PER-SHARE GROWTH: **7.5%** ❑ 10-YEAR COMPOUND DIVIDENDS PER-SHARE GROWTH: **9.5%**

|  | 2009 | 2010 | 2011 | 2012 | 2013 | 2014 | 2015 | 2016 |
|---|---|---|---|---|---|---|---|---|
| Revenues (mil) | 2,160 | 2,221 | 2,537 | 2,928 | 2,951 | 2,922 | 2,674 | 3,765 |
| Net income (mil) | 275.8 | 277.2 | 290.9 | 319.2 | 340.7 | 360.4 | 373.0 | 500.0 |
| Earnings per share | 1.84 | 1.90 | 2.02 | 2.22 | 2.35 | 2.50 | 2.62 | 2.75 |
| Dividends per share | 0.20 | 0.20 | 0.21 | 0.22 | 0.25 | 0.27 | 0.29 | 0.30 |
| Cash flow per share | 2.32 | 2.42 | 2.56 | 3.20 | 3.33 | 3.51 | 3.62 | 3.40 |
| Price:          high | 36.8 | 38.2 | 40.4 | 41.4 | 51.0 | 56.3 | 63.4 | 65.8 |
|                  low | 21.8 | 27.8 | 28.3 | 34.8 | 39.4 | 43.0 | 49.4 | 53.4 |

Website: www.dentsply.com

---

## GROWTH AND INCOME

# E. I. du Pont de Nemours and Company (DuPont)

Ticker symbol: DD (NYSE) ❑ Large Cap ❑ Value Line financial strength rating: A++ ❑ Current yield: 2.0% ❑ Dividend raises, past 10 years: 5

### Company Profile

We don't normally stick around when companies do what DuPont is doing. When a company goes through the kinds of changes that DuPont has gone through and is planning for the future, we normally take a back seat until the dust settles. If we like the resulting business structure, we're back in. We've gone to the sidelines with Abbott Laboratories and others as they have split and reorganized. It is usually too difficult to size up the outcome.

We could very easily adopt the same stance with DuPont. The company first came into doubt in 2015 as a proxy fight led to the spin-off first of a coatings business, then of the lower-margined commodity chemical businesses into "Chemours," which makes mainly pigments and refrigerants. The spin-offs are reflected in the numbers below. That was followed with the 2016 blockbuster mega merger announcement between two large equals— DuPont and Dow Chemical. As if that wasn't enough, the merger plan includes a split of the combined company into three separate businesses: a materials science business centered on plastics, an agricultural chemicals business, and a specialty chemicals business 18 months after the late 2017 completion of the merger.

"When in doubt, reorganize." This popular satire about Corporate America has enjoyed no finer hour than with DuPont. But in this case, we like the direction and think the ultimate outcome could be worth the wait and uncertainty. Meanwhile, the current DuPont business has also fared well after the Chemours spin-off; that's what most of the rest of this narrative is about. "The miracles of science" is the slogan and rallying cry of DuPont, the $25 billion science and technology market leader originally founded in 1802 to make gunpowder.

Although the company is still known to many as a cyclical diversified chemical company making a host of lifeless chemical products and ingredients, many by the tank car–load, with recent changes today's DuPont continues to take the lead in science and technology with important end-product ingredients in a range of disciplines, including biotechnology, electronics, materials and science, safety and security, and synthetic fibers. The company has always been a technology leader with such well-known inventions as Nylon and Rayon in earlier years, and Teflon and Kevlar more recently. The vision and guiding philosophy for the core DuPont business is still "market-driven science," and it has delivered successfully on that vision.

Today's DuPont looks at itself as a leader in three fields: Agriculture & Nutrition, Industrial Biosciences, and Advanced Materials.

- Within the Agriculture & Nutrition segment is the Agriculture business unit itself. Agriculture delivers a portfolio of products and services specifically targeted to achieve gains in crop yields and productivity, including Pioneer brand seed products and well-established brands of insecticides, fungicides, and herbicides. Pioneer develops, produces, and markets corn hybrid and soybean varieties and sells wheat, rice, sunflower, canola, and other seeds under the Pioneer and other brand names. DuPont also sells a line of crop protection products for field and orchard agriculture. The smaller Nutrition and Health unit consists of the recently acquired Danisco's specialty food ingredients business and Solae, a majority-owned venture with Bunge Limited, which is engaged in developing soy-based technologies. The unit provides solutions for specialty food ingredients, health, and safety. Products include cultures, emulsifiers, gums, natural sweeteners, and soy-based food.

- The Industrial Biosciences unit is engaged in developing and manufacturing a wide range of enzymes, the biocatalysts that enable chemical reactions, on a large scale. The segment's enzymes add value and functionality to a broad range of products and processes, such as animal nutrition, detergents, food manufacturing, ethanol production, and industrial applications.

■ The Advanced Materials segment is made up of Electronics and Communications, which makes a line of high-tech materials for the semiconductor industry, including ceramic packages and LCD materials. E&C supplies differentiated materials and systems for photovoltaics (solar), consumer electronics, displays, and advanced printing. It also includes the Performance Materials business unit, which supplies high-performance polymers, films, plastics, and substrates to a variety of industries from automotive to aerospace and consumer durable goods manufacturers and many others, and the Safety and Protection unit, maker of protective fibers and clothing, including bulletproof apparel; disinfectants; and protective building surfaces—Tyvek house wrap is one of the bigger brands here.

Thus concludes the description of DuPont as a standalone entity. The combined company will be called "DowDupont," and the merger brings a vast array of basic chemicals and materials, many in the plastics space such as polyethylene, polystyrene, polypropylene, and various related monomers and commodity chemicals. Dow had previously merged with diversified chemical producer Union Carbide. To gain regulatory approval, the combined company divested a pesticide and herbicide line to FMC. The spin-off into the three separate companies will become clearer in 2018 and certainly bears watching, but should unlock value if the Chemours experience serves as an example.

### Financial Highlights, Fiscal Year 2016

With all of these changes in the air, a review of FY2016 performance seems almost anticlimactic, and projections forward are difficult to make as well. Currency, some softness in international markets, and effects of the Chemours divestiture affected FY2016 performance. Revenues dropped just over 2 percent, but the real story has been a near 5 percent increase in operating margins—from roughly 14 percent to 19 percent—resulting from the divestiture. As a consequence, net profit was up almost 18 percent despite the revenue shortfall. When strategic changes support higher margins and profits, we like the story and it is one of the reasons we hang on to DuPont despite the change. FY2017 and FY2018 revenues (DuPont only) are expected to rise 3–5 percent each year, with continued strength in profits, up 7–9 percent annually.

### Reasons to Buy

The transformation, long waiting in the wings, looks anything but tentative and should allow DuPont (and its brother Dow) to unlock value and settle into an effective alignment for the long term. The product pipeline continues to be full, individual product margins remain strong, the product mix is improving, and the company's biggest moneymakers still dominate their markets. Exits from commodity businesses, lower commodity costs, and a large slate of cost cuts, totaling $3 billion annually according to current projections, should help the bottom line.

The company—and its descendants—will continue to capitalize on "global megatrends": population growth, alternative energy production, and so forth, and should also get a boost from Trump administration "made in America" initiatives. The improvement of worldwide food production is at the center of the all-important agricultural products business. The combined businesses have brand leadership in many important categories and have been committed to total shareholder returns with a good dividend track record (and Dow has typically paid a higher yield than DuPont) and an aggressive share buyback program.

## Reasons for Caution

Mergers and reorganizations are complex, and DuPont is taking on both in a big way. Things could change or fall apart, and the list of possible distractions is long—there is some risk here. DuPont is no longer a "quiet" stock suitable for buying and putting away for the long term. While we do think there is unrealized value down the road, new and existing shareholders will have to keep track of the situation as it develops. It's way too soon to declare "success."

SECTOR: **Materials** ◻ BETA COEFFICIENT: **1.71** ◻ 10-YEAR COMPOUND EARNINGS PER-SHARE GROWTH: **5.5%** ◻ 10-YEAR COMPOUND DIVIDENDS PER-SHARE GROWTH: **2.5%**

|  | | 2009 | 2010 | 2011 | 2012 | 2013 | 2014 | 2015 | 2016 |
|---|---|---|---|---|---|---|---|---|---|
| Revenues (mil) | | 26,109 | 31,505 | 37,961 | 34,812 | 35,734 | 34,723 | 25,130 | 24,594 |
| Net income (mil) | | 1,853 | 3,032 | 3,698 | 3,137 | 3,632 | 3,703 | 2,503 | 2,951 |
| Earnings per share | | 2.04 | 3.28 | 3.93 | 3.33 | 3.68 | 4.01 | 2.77 | 3.35 |
| Dividends per share | | 1.64 | 1.64 | 1.64 | 1.70 | 1.78 | 1.84 | 1.72 | 1.52 |
| Cash flow per share | | 3.70 | 4.80 | 5.67 | 5.19 | 5.65 | 5.87 | 4.54 | 4.87 |
| Price: | high | 35.6 | 50.2 | 57.0 | 57.5 | 65.0 | 75.8 | 80.6 | 75.9 |
| | low | 16.0 | 31.9 | 37.1 | 41.7 | 45.1 | 59.3 | 47.1 | 50.7 |

Website: www.dupont.com

# Eastman Chemical Company

Ticker symbol: EMN (NYSE) ❑ Large Cap ❑ Value Line financial strength rating: A ❑ Current yield: 2.5% ❑ Dividend raises, past 10 years: 7

## Company Profile

Spun off in 1993 from the recently bankrupt Eastman Kodak, Eastman Chemical is one of those "better living through chemistry" companies with a history of solving problems and providing standard, high-tech, and high-precision materials to industries ranging from food and beverage to toys to medical equipment to computers and electronics. The Eastman mission could almost be refined into "better living through *polymer* chemistry"— the chemical building blocks, mostly sourced from petroleum and other feedstocks known as hydrocarbons, that turn into all things useful such as plastics, paints, coatings, inks, and the like. Many of their products are "intermediaries," used to manufacture *other* chemicals and products. When speaking the language of the company you quickly pick up expressions like "olefin cycle" and "phthalate," among the more difficult concepts and spelling challenges, like "ophthalmology." We aren't chemists but have enough understanding of basic chemistry to feel comfortable reading their reports; if you don't, you may want to look elsewhere.

The company is organized into five product segments, all of which have remained roughly the same size and have something more or less to do with petrochemicals:

- *Advanced Materials* (23 percent of 2016 sales) produces and markets specialty plastics, interlayers, and films, including copolyesters, cellulose esters, and safety glass, plastic, and window film products for the automotive and transportation, building materials, LCD and display manufacturing, health and wellness, and durable goods industries.
- *Additives & Functional Products* (21 percent) produces chemical products for the coatings industry and for tires, paints, inks, building materials, durable goods, and consumables markets. Key technology platforms include rubber additives, cellulosic polymers, ketones, coalescents, polyester polymers, olefins, and hydrocarbon resins.
- *Fibers* (15 percent) produces acetate tow, triacetin, and solution-dyed acetate yarns for the apparel, filtration, tobacco (filters), fabric, home furnishings, medical tape, and other industries.

- *Additives & Plasticizers* (15 percent) produces intermediary products, mainly adhesive resins and plasticizers, sold into the consumables, building materials, health and wellness, industrial chemicals, and durable goods markets.

- *Specialty Fluids and Intermediates* (26 percent) is a catchall for other products that don't fall into the other segments, including new or custom-made polymer-based products for key customers. Acetic acid, ethylene, paint and building materials intermediaries, agrichemicals, and aviation hydraulic fluid are among the many products in this group.

Obviously there could be considerably more detail in these descriptions, but it would only engage those with a strong chemistry or materials background. A trip through their "Products" page on their website is fascinating. Bottom line: Eastman makes a lot of strategically important materials that support a lot of manufacturing processes for common and fairly high-volume items, such as beer bottles, automotive glass, and LCD displays. By end use market, sales divide into Transportation (20 percent), Consumables (16 percent), Building & Construction (14 percent), Tobacco (11 percent (!)), Industrial Chemicals & Processing (10 percent), Personal Care/Health (7 percent), Consumer Durables (7 percent), Food, Feed, and Agriculture (6 percent), Energy, Fuels, & Water (4 percent), Electronics (3 percent), and Other (2 percent). Additionally, these materials are used in considerable amounts in overseas manufacturing. Eastman has adapted by setting up plants in 16 countries and driving foreign sales to 57 percent of the total. By region, sales are 46 percent from North America, 27 percent Asia-Pacific, 22 percent EMEA, and 5 percent Latin America.

Acquisitions of adjacent or related technologies are an important part of Eastman's strategy, with recent acquisitions of BP plc's turbine engine oil business, Knowlton Technologies (fibers), and specialty chemical and performance material maker Solutia. Many expect Eastman to continue to be active in the acquisition market especially in light of the DuPont-Dow combination.

## Financial Highlights, Fiscal Year 2016

The strengthening dollar, continued slowing of manufacturing in emerging markets, and weakness and price competition in the Fibers segment (acetate yarns, cigarette filters, and others) combined to take a 6.6 percent bite out of revenues; however, cost reductions and a better product mix led to higher margins and kept net earnings roughly flat and per-share earnings up just shy of 2 percent. Going forward, the company expects improvements in overseas volumes, particularly from emerging economies, a weaker dollar, cost reductions, and a further improved product mix to lead to revenue gains in the 2–4 percent range annually with substantial net profit gains in the 20 percent–plus range in FY2017 and 10 percent in FY2018 as margins improve sizably. Strong cash flows came back to investors in the form of a 15 percent dividend raise this year; 10 percent raises going forward look likely, with modest share buybacks in the mix as well.

## Reasons to Buy

Like many *100 Best* picks, this well-managed enterprise has used the lag period to increase efficiency and gain ground on weaker players and should emerge quite well eventually.

Although Eastman lies on the edge of the "buy businesses you understand" test, the company really does produce things vitally important to manufacturing mainstream and advanced products. Successful product development has always been a key strength for Eastman. Eastman will benefit from the continued strength in domestic manufacturing, although its international operations, particularly in Asia, are also a source of strength. Eastman continues to position itself for continued moderate organic growth with a strong base of repeat business, a more favorable cost structure, and excellent cash flow.

## Reasons for Caution

Eastman's fortunes will follow those of the larger manufacturing sector in general and, to a lesser extent, the feedstock (petroleum) market more specifically. Too, their fourth-largest end market by sales volume is tobacco (filter materials) at 11 percent of sales—although it is getting replaced by other product categories, it will be a drag on growth (the good news, for socially responsible investors anyway, is that this segment accounted for 15 percent recently). There is also some concern about the health effects of phthalates, one of their key plasticizer products, although they do sell a line of non-phthalate plasticizers.

Eastman did take on a lot of debt with the Solutia and other acquisitions but is deploying cash to pay down this debt. We are a bit more concerned with the debt level (at 59 percent of total capital recently, down from 65 percent last year), but projections call for that to be reduced to 46 percent, closer to its long-term norm. The prospect of acquisitions, particularly a large one to keep up with DuPont/Dow, does add some risk. That said, Eastman has all the earmarks of a well-managed and well-positioned company.

SECTOR: **Materials** ▫ BETA COEFFICIENT: **1.37** ▫ 10-YEAR COMPOUND EARNINGS PER-SHARE
GROWTH: **9.5%** ▫ 10-YEAR COMPOUND DIVIDENDS PER-SHARE GROWTH: **6.0%**

|  | 2009 | 2010 | 2011 | 2012 | 2013 | 2014 | 2015 | 2016 |
|---|---|---|---|---|---|---|---|---|
| Revenues (mil) | 5,047 | 5,842 | 7,178 | 8,102 | 9,350 | 9,527 | 9,648 | 9,008 |
| Net income (mil) | 265 | 514 | 653 | 802 | 1,008 | 751 | 848 | 854 |
| Earnings per share | 1.82 | 3.48 | 4.56 | 5.38 | 6.45 | 4.95 | 5.66 | 5.75 |
| Dividends per share | 0.88 | 0.90 | 0.99 | 1.08 | 1.25 | 1.40 | 1.60 | 1.84 |
| Cash flow per share | 3.72 | 5.62 | 6.76 | 7.55 | 9.45 | 8.08 | 9.60 | 9.79 |
| Price:     high | 31.0 | 42.3 | 55.4 | 68.2 | 83.0 | 90.6 | 83.9 | 78.8 |
| low | 8.9 | 25.9 | 32.4 | 39.2 | 63.5 | 70.4 | 62.8 | 56.0 |

Website: **www.eastman.com**

---

## GROWTH AND INCOME

# Empire State Realty Trust

Ticker symbol: **ESRT** (NYSE) ▫ **Large Cap** ▫ **Value Line financial strength rating: NR** ▫ **Current
yield: 2.0%** ▫ **Dividend raises, past 10 years: 2**

## Company Profile

Nobody would dispute that the Empire State Building is a national treasure. Beautifully designed, it is an emblem of New York business well known to the world. It is such an emblem that more than 4 million people came to visit it last year, just to go up to the observation deck; 65 percent of them were from overseas. That observation deck is a $125 million annual icing on the cake for what we still think is an exciting new REIT built around the Empire State Building. But is this REIT just the Empire State Building? No—it has diversified to hold 14 office buildings in key locations across the New York area, nine in Manhattan and five others in or near major transportation hubs in White Plains, NY, and Stamford and Norwalk, CT. ESRT also owns six standalone retail properties, four in Manhattan and two in Connecticut. The Empire State Realty Trust is a pure play on real estate in the most dynamic and sought-after real estate market in the world.

The Empire State Realty Trust was formed in 2011 and went public in October 2013. As a REIT, ESRT is relatively small in comparison to other real estate trusts, but they make up for that in their strengths, which they call out quite clearly in their presentations:

- *Unique, irreplaceable properties.* ESRT is a pure play in the New York area, one of the world's most prized office markets; the cornerstone of their base, the Empire State Building, is one of the most recognized icons in the world. Another concentration of office properties is in the revitalizing 34th Street and Broadway area, home of the Macy's flagship store.
- *Expertise in reconditioning such properties.* The Empire State Building is beautiful, particularly for you fans of classic Art Deco architecture. But it needed a facelift—and got a big one from ESRT. In addition to managing properties, ESRT has a construction arm specializing in reconditioning and repurposing buildings and spaces for tenant use. The Empire State Building got a major energy retrofit; it is a showcase project and is estimated to save some tenants 38 percent and as much as 57 percent on energy costs (check out www.esbsustainability.com for details); it got a new fitness center for tenants also. ESRT will lease you "white box" space—or spaces tailored to your needs. ESRT is performing energy and functionality upgrades to other vintage buildings as well. It is part of their strategy to increase attractiveness...and of course, rents.

In area, ESRT owns and manages about 10 million rentable square feet; 75 percent of that is Manhattan office space, 18 percent is Greater New York space, and 7 percent is dedicated retail, mostly in Manhattan. The Empire State Building itself is about 2.7 million square feet, or about 27 percent of the rentable space in the trust. The client list is a corporate who's who, with older companies like Macy's, Bank of America, Johnson Controls, and Bulova mixed in with latter-day names like LinkedIn, Expedia, and Shutterstock. The client base is diverse, with just 18 percent being the "typical" New York financial industry names. About 88 percent of current office space is leased; 90 percent of retail is also rented. Most clients sign long-term leases of ten years or so, and the company is trying to move to large block or entire floor leases.

For 2017, the roughly $678 million in annual revenue breaks down as follows: 65 percent Manhattan office, 14 percent Greater New York Metro office, and 3 percent standalone retail. What about the other 18 percent? you may ask. Look up, please. It's from the Observatory, split between the 86th and 102nd floor of the Empire State Building. We mentioned it at the beginning of this narrative—the Observatory brought in $126 million in FY2016, a nice "kicker" business, one that most REITs don't have.

Financially, ESRT touts what they refer to as "embedded, derisked growth." The "embedded" part refers to loyal tenants and a carefully managed "laddering" of lease expirations; the company attempts to have 5–10 percent of its lease base expire each year. Those expirations will be renewed at higher rates, to include not just inflation but also to cover improvements. ESRT estimates that rents will grow overall 8 percent to as much as 63 percent per year through 2021 as leases expire. "Derisked" refers to this smooth steady upward path but also to the location and desirability of the properties they own. They also present "best in class" financial fundamentals, with Manhattan leasing spreads (roughly comparable to gross margin—lease less mortgage obligations) of 22 percent versus 9 percent for their peer group. The "debt to enterprise value" ratio is 15 percent versus 38 percent for peers. Only about 41 percent of the portfolio is encumbered by mortgages—down from 99 percent at IPO. Less debt, less leverage, greater profitability.

As investments REITs are typically good income producers, since they are required by law to pay a substantial portion of their cash flow to investors. The accounting rules are different, and REIT investors should focus on Funds From Operations (FFO), which is analogous to operating income; net income figures have depreciation expenses deducted, which can vary in timing and not always be realistic. Funds From Operations (FFO) support the dividends paid to investors.

## Financial Highlights, Fiscal Year 2016

As ESRT only went public in the fall of 2013, we still do not have a well-developed financial presentation for the company or its financial history. Total Funds From Operations (FFO) increased 5 percent to $268 million. The fourth quarter of FY2016 saw 54 new leases executed with an average duration of 7.4 years and an average 11 percent per square foot rent increase. Observatory revenue grew 11.6 percent over FY2015. The REIT estimates that it has completed its $700 million spending plan to redevelop and restore its Manhattan buildings (the largest, of course, being the Empire State Building). The completion of that spend should enhance reported net income going forward—and in turn, shareholder payouts, since REITs are legally required to pay out 90 percent of reported income.

As yet, we have not been able to obtain projections into FY2017 and FY2018.

## Reasons to Buy

ESRT exhibits most of the traits we like to see when we consider buying a real estate investment trust. It has good real estate, yes, but it isn't just the real estate—it's a good business, too. It adds value in the form of redevelopment services, and the observation deck is a nice bonus. We don't depend solely on the rising value of the underlying real estate, and we don't depend too much on increasing the rent. That said, the prime locations they own and the exclusive focus on the New York area make for an excellent opportunity to raise rents—which is, in fact, happening at a good pace.

And who wouldn't want to own a piece of the Empire State Building? The energy and whole-building retrofit of the Empire State Building has won considerable acclaim with green building advocates and others; a search on "empire state building energy retrofit" gives several angles to this story. The building was once felt to be in an irreversible decline; the retrofit, energy, and publicity around it have returned it to its classic status as a prestige address. ESRT is using it wisely as a brand centerpiece for events, social media, and general marketing—even as a visual scoreboard for the results of the 2016 presidential election.

In short, not only do we like the fundamentals, we also admire the overall value creation strategy. As retrofits and other investments in the portfolio are now mostly paid for, ESRT will become a much stronger cash machine, and with REIT distribution rules, that cash will end up in the pockets of shareholders in the not too distant future.

## Reasons for Caution

ESRT is new and less proven than most of our choices, although it has a seasoned management team from its roots as a private equity trust. We can't give you as much historical analysis as we would with most *100 Best* stocks investments. Too, the short-term future of retail real estate in general is not too bright, as many major tenants are reviewing their space commitments—that said, we don't think this concern affects New York real estate so much. All in all, ESRT still appears an opportunity to "get in on the ground floor" of what we think will be a strong investment for years to come.

SECTOR: **Real Estate** ◻ BETA COEFFICIENT: **1.00** ◻ 10-YEAR COMPOUND FFO PER-SHARE GROWTH: **NM** ◻ 10-YEAR COMPOUND DIVIDENDS PER-SHARE GROWTH: **NM**

| | 2009 | 2010 | 2011 | 2012 | 2013 | 2014 | 2015 | 2016 |
|---|---|---|---|---|---|---|---|---|
| Revenues (mil) | — | — | — | — | — | 635.3 | 657.6 | 677.7 |
| Net income (mil) | — | — | — | — | — | 70.0 | 73.8 | 51.5 |
| Funds from operations per share | — | — | — | — | 0.84 | 0.97 | 0.97 | 0.94 |
| Real estate owned per share | — | — | — | — | — | 8.42 | 8.55 | 6.55 |
| Dividends per share | — | — | — | — | — | 0.34 | 0.34 | 0.42 |
| Price:   high | — | — | — | — | 15.6 | 18.1 | 19.0 | 22.3 |
| low | — | — | — | — | 12.6 | 14.1 | 14.6 | 17.2 |

Website: www.empirestaterealtytrust.com

---

## AGGRESSIVE GROWTH

# Fair Isaac Corporation

Ticker symbol: FICO (NYSE) ◻ Mid Cap ◻ Value Line financial strength rating: B++ ◻ Current yield: 0.1% ◻ Dividend raises, past 10 years: 0

## Company Profile

Ordinarily when a share price triples in four years and outpaces sales and earnings growth by a considerable margin, we take a very hard look at whether there's any room to run despite the excellence of the company. Fair Isaac is a clear case, having run from the low 40s in 2013 to the 120s in early 2017. But can we run from such an 800-pound gorilla in today's most valuable space of Big Data and analytics? Fair Isaac has become the Apple, the Google, the Amazon of this key space, a pure play in this ever-expanding and lucrative niche. We think the compounded growth of the company's native market—analytics—plus the growth of the company's business *within* the market will continue to make this company stand out. FICO stays on the list for 2018.

"Making Every Decision Count" is the motto of the Fair Isaac Corporation, which provides decision support analytics, software, and solutions to help businesses improve and automate decision making and risk management. The most well-known and best example of these solutions is the FICO score—an analytic single-figure estimate of a consumer's creditworthiness used mainly in the credit industry but also for other purposes such as employment and insurance.

FICO provides its analytic solutions and services to a variety of financial and other service organizations, including banks, credit-reporting agencies, credit card–processing agencies, insurers, telecommunications providers, retailers, marketers, and healthcare organizations. It operates in three segments: Applications, Scores, and Decision Management Software. The Applications segment provides decision and risk management tools, market targeting and customer analytics tools, and fraud detection tools and associated professional services, all now under an umbrella called Enterprise Fraud Management. (If you've had a credit card fraud alert recently, it probably came from FICO's "Falcon" suite of fraud prediction and protection services, which are currently deployed to protect some 2.5 billion credit cards.) The Scores segment includes the business-to-business scoring solutions; myFICO solutions, delivering FICO scores for consumers; and associated professional services. The Decision Management Software (formerly "Tools") segment provides software products and consulting services to help organizations build their own analytic tools. Many of these analytics and scores are packaged to be available through their "Analytic Cloud" as "SaaS"—Software as a Service—applications, providing an ongoing revenue stream tied to their use.

The company actively works with customers in a variety of vertical markets to identify and apply their tools and applications; these analytics go beyond traditional financial applications into marketing and operational optimization. FICO's analytics are not only used to manage risk and fraud but also to build more profitable customer relationships, optimize operations, and meet government regulations. The company promotes its vertical applications in the grocery, retail, pharmaceutical and life sciences, insurance, financial services, consumer packaged goods industries, and in education and public sector applications as well.

## Financial Highlights, Fiscal Year 2016

Led by the Scores segment, total revenues advanced 5.1 percent in FY2016. The largest segment, Applications (at 60 percent of the business) grew at 1 percent. The Scores segment, which now contributes 27 percent of the business, grew 16 percent, while the Decision Management Software business, accounting for 13 percent of the business, moved forward at a 2 percent rate. Earnings jumped ahead some 26 percent after a flat FY2015 on higher margins related to an improved mix, some expense reductions, and a write-off in 2015. Expectations call for a 10 percent rise in FY2017 earnings on a 6 percent rise in revenues as the company profits from a broadening base of applications outside the financial services industry.

We should note that the company's very modest dividend policy is offset by aggressive share buybacks; the company bought back some 1.3 million shares in FY2016 (out of about 30 million outstanding) and has reduced share counts some 50 percent since 2005. Plans call for another 10–15 percent reduction over the next few years—a very deliberate approach to returning cash to shareholders.

## Reasons to Buy

"Big data" and related analytics are gaining strength right now as more vertical industries (banking, retail, utilities, pharma, medical devices, health insurers, etc.) learn how to use them more efficiently and effectively to manage different parts of their business. The market is growing both deeper (more analytics being used) and wider (more companies in more industries using them)—a very good scenario as pointed out above.

There are a number of companies, large and small, in the analytics business, but few have the brand reputation, product packaging, and leadership enjoyed by FICO, which serves more than 95 percent of the largest financial institutions in the US. The company is a pure play and is considered to be the gold standard for this type of product. It is more turnkey and easy for customers who don't have advanced mathematicians and software engineering staffs to buy. As a consequence, and with the brand recognition of the FICO score, the company has attained a large moat on its brand and is a good example of how packaging and market definition can be as important as the product.

FICO's modeling approaches are now being used to analyze customer behavior and provide decision support for insurability, employability, acceptance into schools, and even customer behaviors in stores or online, other areas well beyond a consumer's ability to repay extended credit. International demand for FICO's products continues to grow, too, notably in China, where fraud protection continues to be a big business.

The dividend remains inconsequential, but it doesn't take a genius (or analytics) to appreciate the company's policy of providing shareholder returns in the form of share buybacks.

## Reasons for Caution

There continues to be some competition on the scoring front, but the forefront FICO brand keeps serious competition at bay. Software companies always run a certain amount of technology risk. The ability to sell in a "cloud" environment and to maintain or increase margins by selling the right mix of products and channels will be key. There is some public concern that scoring models oversimplify lending and insurability decisions and should not be used or relied on so heavily.

But mainly we're concerned about how much investors have already loved this stock and have priced FICO's excellent market position to perfection. This not only creates some downside price risk but also makes the company's share buybacks expensive. "Score" your purchases carefully.

SECTOR: **Business Services** ❑ BETA COEFFICIENT: **1.24** ❑ 10-YEAR COMPOUND EARNINGS PER-SHARE GROWTH: **6.0%** ❑ 10-YEAR COMPOUND DIVIDENDS PER-SHARE GROWTH: NM

|  | | 2009 | 2010 | 2011 | 2012 | 2013 | 2014 | 2015 | 2016 |
|---|---|---|---|---|---|---|---|---|---|
| Revenues (mil) | | 630.7 | 605.6 | 619.7 | 676.4 | 743.4 | 789.0 | 839.0 | 881.4 |
| Net income (mil) | | 65.1 | 64.5 | 71.6 | 92.0 | 90.1 | 94.9 | 86.5 | 109.4 |
| Earnings per share | | 1.34 | 1.42 | 1.79 | 2.55 | 2.48 | 2.72 | 2.65 | 3.39 |
| Dividends per share | | 0.08 | 0.08 | 0.08 | 0.08 | 0.08 | 0.08 | 0.08 | 0.08 |
| Cash flow per share | | 2.15 | 2.36 | 2.58 | 3.20 | 3.54 | 3.98 | 3.85 | 4.56 |
| Price: | high | 24.5 | 27.0 | 38.5 | 47.9 | 63.5 | 74.4 | 97.6 | 133.0 |
|  | low | 9.8 | 19.5 | 20.0 | 34.6 | 41.3 | 50.3 | 69.4 | 80.2 |

Website: www.fico.com

## AGGRESSIVE GROWTH

# FedEx Corporation

Ticker symbol: FDX (NYSE) ❑ Large Cap ❑ Value Line financial strength rating: A++ ❑ Current yield: 0.8% ❑ Dividend raises, past 10 years: 9

## Company Profile

FedEx Corporation is the world's leading provider of guaranteed express delivery services and a major player in the overall small shipment and small-package logistics market. The corporation is organized as a holding company, with four individual businesses that compete collectively and operate independently under the FedEx brand, offering a wide range of express delivery services for the time-definite transportation of documents, packages, and freight:

- The familiar FedEx Express operation offers overnight and deferred air service to 60,000 drop-off locations, operating 643 aircraft through ten air express hubs and approximately 157,000 ground vehicles to support this business, and estimates that it reaches markets that comprise about 90 percent of global GDP.

- FedEx Ground offers overnight service from 575 pickup/delivery terminals for up to 400 miles anywhere in the United States for packages weighing up to 150 pounds. Ground serves 100 percent of US residences, and now features the so-called "SmartPost" operation, where small and less urgent packages are delivered "last mile" to local addresses by the US Postal Service and newly acquired reverse logistics provider GENCO—both key offerings for the e-commerce business. The unit now includes ground services of TNT mainly in Europe.

- FedEx Freight offers standard and priority LTL (less than truckload) service across North America mainly for business supply-chain operations with 370 terminals and service centers.

- FedEx Services, which includes 1,800 former Kinko's copy and office centers, now operates under the FedEx/Office brand, and FedEx Tech-Connect provides solutions to integrate supply-chain management IT tools with FedEx's systems.

The company has about 340,000 "team members"—employees and contractors. They serve more than 375 airports in over 220 countries. Except for the number of countries served, all of these figures are slightly attenuated from previous years as the company weeds out unproductive and redundant locations in a drive for efficiency.

In FY2016, the Express segment accounted for 52 percent of revenues, Ground 33 percent, Freight 12 percent, and Services 3 percent. The mix shifted somewhat toward ground (6 percent higher for Ground, 5 percent lower for Express) mostly due to last year's incorporation of worldwide logistics provider TNT Express into the mix—much of this increase was in Europe. To a degree it also reflects a sharp rise in e-commerce–related business-to-consumer shipments as well. The company estimates that over 96 percent of its customers use two or more of these services, attesting to the fact that FedEx's business is increasingly tuned to providing a total and flexible logistics solution.

The company just signed a deal to offer pickup and drop-off at all Walgreens store locations, pickup being especially important in this modern era of doorstep theft of e-commerce shipments. To accommodate higher e-commerce volumes (which the company projects to grow at 15 percent annually for the foreseeable future) FedEx recently opened four major hubs and 19 new sorting centers in the Ground network.

## Financial Highlights, Fiscal Year 2016

Stronger e-commerce and global commerce in general fueled an overall 6 percent growth in revenues, with net profits up some 17 percent with price increases, better capacity utilization, and operational improvements. Recently, the large rise in home-delivered e-commerce has hurt margins somewhat (it takes more resources to deliver many one-off small packages to individual residential addresses). Combining that margin pressure with a 20 percent TNT-driven revenue rise, net earnings are forecast to rise only 4–5 percent. Price increases and more synergies from TNT will improve margins once again; estimates call for an 11 percent earnings rise on a 5 percent increase in revenue for FY2018. Cash flows continue strong, making moderate buybacks and dividend hikes likely.

## Reasons to Buy

FedEx has several tailwinds now—lower fuel costs, customer-driven logistics fine-tuning, and the growth of e-commerce.

The growing e-commerce business and greater need for a complete, economical, and partially time-sensitive logistics mix makes FedEx the right place to be as American manufacturing activity and local sourcing increase—although this will dampen international shipments. With SmartPost and other business expansions, the Ground segment is approaching a 30 percent market share for such services, a position from which it can start to call the shots in the marketplace for lucrative e-commerce and time-sensitive ground business. Indeed, of late, the company has been able to raise prices while also gaining market share.

The continued resurgence in the economy and growth in online shopping and delivery will certainly help volumes. The logistics business is always ripe for innovation, and FedEx has long been an innovator in the transportation and small-package shipment business, not only with new transportation services, but also with new tools to help customers track shipments and manage their supply chains in real time; we expect this to continue.

## Reasons for Caution

The company is always vulnerable to economic downturns and fuel prices, particularly if cost increases come faster than they can be recovered in rates and fuel surcharges—as is often the case. It remains to be seen how much the Trump administration's trade policies will affect international trade, which could hurt international volumes and pricing with some offsetting gains in domestic business. Export traffic—which fills empty outbound planes—continues to be hampered by the strong dollar. While cash flows are strong, this company must occasionally purchase or lease aircraft, and this and other capital expenditures can put a big dent in cash flows (although recent new aircraft purchases are said to save 30 percent in fuel). While the company has done a good job of carving out its "full service" niche, it is always vulnerable to competition in both domestic and overseas markets; that said, its size and scale are an advantage in most cases.

While payouts are increasing steadily, they are still less than we think they could be given the strong cash flow.

SECTOR: **Transportation** ❏ BETA COEFFICIENT: **1.14** ❏ 10-YEAR COMPOUND EARNINGS PER-SHARE GROWTH: **6.5%** ❏ 10-YEAR COMPOUND DIVIDENDS PER-SHARE GROWTH: **11.0%**

| | | 2009 | 2010 | 2011 | 2012 | 2013 | 2014 | 2015 | 2016 |
|---|---|---|---|---|---|---|---|---|---|
| Revenues (mil) | | 35,497 | 34,734 | 39,204 | 42,680 | 44,287 | 45,567 | 47,453 | 50,365 |
| Net income (mil) | | 1,173 | 1,184 | 1,452 | 2,032 | 1,561 | 2,097 | 2,572 | 3,016 |
| Earnings per share | | 3.76 | 3.76 | 4.90 | 6.41 | 6.23 | 6.75 | 8.95 | 10.80 |
| Dividends per share | | 0.44 | 0.44 | 0.48 | 0.52 | 0.56 | 0.60 | 0.80 | 1.00 |
| Cash flow per share | | 10.09 | 10.01 | 11.13 | 13.08 | 12.41 | 16.32 | 18.35 | 21.27 |
| Price: | high | 92.6 | 97.8 | 98.7 | 97.2 | 144.1 | 183.5 | 185.2 | 201.6 |
| | low | 34.0 | 69.8 | 64.1 | 82.8 | 90.6 | 128.2 | 130.0 | 119.7 |

Website: www.fedex.com

## AGGRESSIVE GROWTH

NEW FOR 2018

# First Solar, Inc.

Ticker symbol: FSLR (NASDAQ) ❏ Mid Cap ❏ Value Line financial strength rating: A- ❏ Current yield: Nil ❏ Dividend raises, past 10 years: NA

## Company Profile

First Solar is the largest US-based provider of photovoltaic (solar) energy solutions. It is a vertically integrated business, producing the core building-block solar panels as well as large-scale generation systems that utilize these same panels. They also provide Operations and Management (OM) services for utility-scale installations, and sell these OM services for any installation worldwide. They are the world's largest OM provider, with over 3 percent of the global market under their management.

The company's panels employ a proprietary thin-film cadmium-telluride chemistry which, while less efficient than the highest-grade mono-crystalline silicon, is competitive with polycrystalline, the most commonly used form for energy generation. The technology also has certain other advantages in production and application which make it very attractive in terms of its cost and longevity. Founded in 1990 as an R&D-focused endeavor and renamed in 1999, FSLR began commercial operations in 2002 and now designs, manufactures, operates, and maintains all elements of the solar power chain across residential, commercial, and utility-scale applications.

## Financial Highlights, Fiscal Year 2016

Several passing clouds threw shade on First Solar's ballgame in 2016, resulting in their first losing season since shares began trading in 2002. Revenues saw a decline of nearly 18 percent which, by itself, probably would not have put the results in the red, but the company used 2016 to do a significant amount of restructuring as they decided to scrap a "Series 5" iteration of their technology in favor of moving straight on to Series 6. The company accelerated inventory and tooling write-offs, initiated a 20 percent workforce reduction, and closed some smaller production facilities (primarily in Germany, where many local tax incentives expired). They also incurred extra costs to accelerate Series 6 production. In the end, the $360 million loss looks worse on paper than it actually is as an indicator for the health of the business going forward; it will become mostly a timing issue burdening 2016 with extra costs for revenues received in 2017 and beyond. That all said, in the midst of an off year, the company still paid off 40 percent of its long-term debt.

## Reasons to Buy

Patience is a virtue, and perhaps no one knows this better than solar energy investors. After nearly a decade of great promise and so-so performance on the part of solar panel producers in the mid-2000s, investors were treated to a glut of relatively inexpensive panels that came along at the worst possible time—the Great Recession—when the domestic housing market was on the verge of collapse. Industry wide, sales plummeted and share prices followed suit (FSLR shares fell over 66 percent in six months in 2008). R&D investments were cut deeply, reflected in the nearly flat solar cell efficiency improvements over the following six years.

Fast-forward to 2017, and we see a far more encouraging environment for solar investors. Consumer tax incentives, once reviled by conservative taxpayers, are now celebrated and remain in place across most of the US. Improvements in production processes have driven costs down and renewed research investments have bolstered the performance of most panel technologies.

FSLR's proprietary photovoltaic cell technology requires no silicon; instead it uses a thin cadmium-telluride film over glass. FSLR is thus not exposed to the vagaries of the worldwide market for polycrystalline silicon. The volatility of this "poly" market played a large role in the whipsaw pricing for panels in the late 2000s and was a major factor in the elimination of many of FSLR's early competitors.

From a business-management perspective, First Solar shines, particularly when compared to some of their "wildcat" competitors. Rather than living on the edge of thin margins and low capitalization, First Solar's balance sheet is very strong. Despite posting a $358 million loss last year, the company has more cash than total liabilities and a debt-to-equity ratio of just 4 percent.

Finally, the biggest 2018 story for First Solar will be the performance of their latest Series 6 panel technology. The company continues to ship older Series 4 product, and the cancellation of Series 5 means that First Solar has had a great deal of time to optimize the cost and performance of the Series 6 modules. Early data indicates a 35 percent reduction in cost per watt and an efficiency improvement from 17–18 percent when compared to Series 4 product. Series 6 production tooling will come online at the Perrysburg, Ohio, manufacturing facility in early 2018. First Solar's higher-volume facility (in Malaysia) will follow six months later.

As mentioned, First Solar is the largest provider of OM services for the solar industry. This is an attractive business, as most traditional utilities have little experience and/or expertise with the technology and welcome a turn-key solution for their state-mandated renewable energy quotas. The global OM market is expected to triple by 2020, and it serves to steady the revenue and profit stream which would otherwise be more volatile if the company simply built and sold photovoltaic products.

## Reasons for Caution

The skip of the Series 5 technology, while likely a positive long-term move, has disrupted some of FSLR's order and production flows. Many US-based utilities pulled orders into 2017, uncertain about the status of industrial tax incentives under the new administration—and due before the 2018 Series 6 production ramps up. Also, there is some technology "ramp" risk here as the Series 6 product is not yet proven in production quantities; too, the Malaysia facility will not come online until much later in the year. Also, polysilicon advances continue apace, and further improvements in the technology will continue to pressure First Solar's competitive advantages. All of these are fairly typical risks in the rapidly evolving solar industry.

SECTOR: **Energy** □ BETA COEFFICIENT: **1.60** □ 10-YEAR COMPOUND EARNINGS PER-SHARE GROWTH: **NA** □ 10-YEAR COMPOUND DIVIDENDS PER-SHARE GROWTH: **NA**

|  | 2009 | 2010 | 2011 | 2012 | 2013 | 2014 | 2015 | 2016 |
|---|---|---|---|---|---|---|---|---|
| Revenues (mil) | 2,066 | 2,564 | 2,766 | 3,369 | 3,309 | 3,392 | 3,579 | 2,951 |
| Net income (mil) | 640 | 664 | 484 | 430 | 353 | 397 | 546 | (358) |
| Earnings per share | 7.53 | 7.68 | 5.55 | 4.90 | 3.70 | 3.91 | 5.37 | (3.48) |
| Dividends per share | — | — | — | — | — | — | — | — |
| Cash flow per share | 9.03 | 9.56 | 8.31 | 7.95 | 5.90 | 6.40 | 7.90 | (1.22) |
| Price:    high | 207.5 | 153.3 | 175.4 | 50.2 | 66.0 | 74.8 | 67.8 | 74.3 |
| low | 100.9 | 98.7 | 29.9 | 11.4 | 24.5 | 40.5 | 39.2 | 28.6 |

Website: www.firstsolar.com

## CONSERVATIVE GROWTH

# Fresh Del Monte Produce Inc.

Ticker symbol: FDP (NYSE) □ Mid Cap □ Value Line financial strength rating: B++ □ Current yield: 1.0% □ Dividend raises, past 10 years: 5

## Company Profile

Founded in 1892, Del Monte originated as a brand for coffee packaged for the prestigious Del Monte hotel in Monterey, CA. The original firm expanded its business and selected Del Monte as the brand for a new line of canned peaches, and the rest, as they say, is history. The company has grown—in a large part based on acquisitions particularly of tropical fruits and food producers—into the one of the largest vertically integrated producers and distributors of fresh and fresh-cut fruits and vegetables, as well as prepared fruits and vegetables, juices, beverages, and snacks, in the world.

The company has 90,000 acres in production, and its products are available in 100-plus countries through 40-plus distribution centers and 18 "fresh cut" centers. Products include bananas (the largest product line at 45 percent of 2016 sales), an all-important "other fresh produce" category (46 percent of sales), and prepared food (9 percent). The "other fresh produce" category deserves further breakout, and in some cases, description:

- Fresh-cut produce (13 percent)—this is the fastest-growing segment and the category we're most excited about (it was 12 percent last year and 10 percent in 2015). It offers fresh-cut fruits—pineapples, melons, grapes, citrus, apples, mangos, kiwis, and others—and vegetables for salads packed in convenient, safe, and branded plastic containers; so far sold only in the US, Canada, UK, Japan, and the Middle East. These products are gaining traction in foodservice and convenience store end markets.
- Gold pineapples (12 percent)—the branding is "Del Monte Gold Extra Sweet."
- Nontropical fruit (6 percent)—includes grapes, apples, pears, peaches, plums, nectarines, cherries, citrus, and kiwis.
- Avocados (6 percent)
- Melons (3 percent)
- Tomatoes (2 percent)
- Vegetables (1 percent)
- Other fruit, products, and services (3 percent)

A big part of why we like Fresh Del Monte is that it's not just a producer but is also a logistics company specializing in fresh packaging and transport, really for all parts of the fresh-food supply chain. It runs from farm to store shelf, including sophisticated refrigerated storage and transport, all the way to helping end-store operators with market research, promotion, display, stocking decisions, and other logistical support. The company owns a fleet of 20 ocean-going refrigerated vessels and manages a network including 4,500 refrigerated containers, refrigerated port facilities, and the aforementioned distribution and "fresh cut" centers. Too, the company has innovated in such areas as Controlled Ripening Technology for bananas, which it licenses to other producers.

By geography, 55 percent of sales are in North America, 17 percent in Europe, 12 percent in Asia, and 14 percent are in the Middle East and North Africa. This supply-chain leadership gives the company a distinct advantage and a laboratory within which they can produce and distribute all sorts of new products and packages to a large part of the world, a big advantage over the world's many, many small producers. See a market for fresh fruit snacks in special packages in Japan? Fresh Del Monte can produce it and get it there.

## Financial Highlights, Fiscal Year 2016

FY2016 showed favorable volume trends in many key segments including avocados and fresh cut; stronger pricing, volume-based efficiencies, and operational improvements led to a dramatic increase in net profit margins, from 3.3 percent in 2015 to 5.5 percent in 2016. Total revenues slipped about 1 percent due to volume shortfalls in bananas and pineapples and due to currency effects, but net profit was almost 70 percent and per-share earnings were up almost 75 percent for the year. For FY2017 and FY2018, strength in the fresh-cut segment, market share gains, and stronger international sales should bring 4–6 percent sales advances annually through FY2018, while earnings are projected to stay flat (after a great FY2016) in 2017 and rise 4–6 percent in 2018. Operating and net profit margins should stay in the 6–7 percent range and 5–6 percent range through the period and should be more consistent as worldwide scale grows. After a large 8 percent share buyback in 2014 the pace has been more modest but steady at about 1 percent. We feel that all of these forecasts are conservative, particularly as the fresh-cut product lines gain traction in a widening set of markets.

## Reasons to Buy

What brought us to Fresh Del Monte two years ago wasn't just the pineapple, or even the bananas. It is their emerging leadership in healthful and especially innovative and modern fresh packaged foods, items we think will play well with today's demographic, who demand fresh, convenient, natural, unique, and customizable foods and "fresh-cut" food packages. More fundamentally, we're attracted to the brand, the logistics network, "fresh-cut" opportunities, increased scale, and operating efficiency. The company claims that "Del Monte" is one of the two top-of-mind brands in the fresh produce space with over 90 percent awareness; that not only supports higher prices but also makes it easier to enter new markets.

We like the vertical integration, which gives it control of its supply chain, and most of all, we like Fresh Del Monte's competitive advantage in distribution, and we see this playing well with what we expect to be a growing demand for smartly packaged fresh and fresh-cut food offerings, which are currently only 13 percent of the business. This category is starting to take off, and combined with packaged salads and such, become a major category in groceries and mass distributors of food products. People want convenience and variety, and these prepackaged items fit in—and when you take into account storage and spoilage, they actually become cheaper than their unpackaged equivalents. They can be mixed any way the markets want, as we've seen with prepackaged salads. Like pineapples, blueberries, and mangos together? Fresh Del Monte can produce and distribute just such a medley. You don't have to buy a pineapple, cut it up, buy a bag of blueberries; you get the idea.

All of that, plus a helping of financial strength (debt is only 11 percent of total capital) and a bias toward shareholder returns, makes this mid-cap offering a worthwhile recipe to play emerging trends in the food industry.

## Reasons for Caution

Past results have been volatile, and the still-thin margins reflect a company that is more of a "commodity" producer than anything else. We think the "fresh-cut" offerings will continue to help grow Fresh Del Monte out of this low-margin category. As a logistics company, particularly one with a moderate amount of air cargo in its mix, it is vulnerable to fuel price shocks. There is also strong competition in most parts of this industry.

SECTOR: **Consumer Staples** ❑ BETA COEFFICIENT: **0.37** ❑ 10-YEAR COMPOUND EARNINGS PER-SHARE GROWTH: **3.0%** ❑ 10-YEAR COMPOUND DIVIDENDS PER-SHARE GROWTH: **NM**

|  |  | 2009 | 2010 | 2011 | 2012 | 2013 | 2014 | 2015 | 2016 |
|---|---|---|---|---|---|---|---|---|---|
| Revenues (mil) | | 3,496 | 3,552 | 3,590 | 3,421 | 3,684 | 3,928 | 4,057 | 4,012 |
| Net income (mil) | | 144 | 62 | 93 | 143 | 87 | 144 | 132 | 222 |
| Earnings per share | | 2.26 | 1.02 | 1.56 | 2.46 | 1.54 | 2.73 | 2.49 | 4.33 |
| Dividends per share | | — | 0.05 | 0.30 | 0.40 | 0.50 | 0.50 | 0.50 | 0.55 |
| Cash flow per share | | 3.58 | 2.40 | 2.87 | 3.69 | 2.79 | 4.12 | 3.89 | 5.85 |
| Price: | high | 26.7 | 25.2 | 28.6 | 26.9 | 30.8 | 35.0 | 47.5 | 66.9 |
| | low | 12.2 | 19.2 | 21.3 | 21.6 | 24.7 | 24.0 | 32.0 | 36.7 |

Website: www.freshdelmonte.com

---

GROWTH AND INCOME

# General Electric Company

Ticker symbol: GE (NYSE) ❑ Large Cap ❑ Value Line financial strength rating: B++ ❑ Current yield: 3.3% ❑ Dividend raises, past 10 years: 7

## Company Profile

Everyone knows GE, and most know the recent story of GE—the colossal conglomerate built mostly around things that use or produce electricity and a few other things like jet engines and railroad locomotives. Oh yes, and built around that colossal finance arm—GE Capital—that morphed into a $300 billion giant that dominated the business and almost took down the company in the Great Recession. That's the "old" GE, and today's GE is ripe with the results of transformation—a transformation back to its previous industrial roots—now with a strong technology footprint.

Today's GE now describes itself, quite aptly, as the "Digital Industrial" company. GE is already industrial at its core, for it makes all kinds of capital equipment and end products mostly sold to industrial customers. And it's now "digital" because of a growing emphasis on products and machines controlled by software and by the Internet. The company positions itself as a leader in the "Industrial Internet of Things," the "next great wave of productivity," and also is selling an ownership ecosystem for many of its products called "Predix," which connects with GE to optimize service and performance of industrial machines, jet engines, etc.

Oh, and GE Capital? Most of it is gone now, sold off to better and greener pastures such as Wells Fargo and Blackstone, where good and not-so-good financial assets belong. Enough gone that the company is no longer considered a "systemically important financial institution" (a.k.a. "too big to fail") and so regulations governing share repurchases and dividend increases no longer apply.

With or without its finance unit, General Electric is still colossal. Formed in 1892 as a major producer of all things electric in the wake of the commercial harnessing of electricity, the company evolved over the years into a massive conglomerate producing aircraft engines, power generation, railroad locomotives, household appliances, energy infrastructure, alternative energy equipment, medical imaging equipment, oilfield service equipment, and a vast array of other mostly industrial products—in addition to its departing General Electric Capital Services, or "GE Capital" financial arm.

GE sold its household appliance business to China's Haier for $5.6 billion in 2016, leaving the following operating segment mix (by segment and percent of FY2016 revenues): Power (22 percent), Oil & Gas (10 percent), Renewable Energy (7 percent), Aviation (21 percent), Healthcare (15 percent), Transportation (4 percent), and Energy Connections & Lighting (formerly Appliances & Lighting, 12 percent). GE Capital accounts for about 9 percent but once produced 30 percent of revenue and a third of profits...and a lot of headaches and risks that both management and investors—for the most part—are glad to be rid of.

International sales account for about 57 percent of revenues, a number that is likely to rise steadily with the return to the industrial base. The GE Capital divestiture is estimated to be about three-quarters complete; most of the remainder, to be closed out by the end of 2017, will fund more share buybacks, acquisitions, and strengthening of business in other segments. Currently the company is adding to its Oil & Gas segment with an in-progress acquisition of Baker Hughes—the timing of which initially looked poor but may prove quite adept as the energy industry slowly recovers. The rearrangement of GE's businesses, is thought to be largely complete; this should allow the company to move forward without distraction into its new future.

## Financial Highlights, Fiscal Year 2016

The seas of change continue to make comparisons and forward estimates difficult. In general, while earnings and revenues have declined sharply starting in FY2015 due to the GE Capital divestitures, they should stabilize by 2018.

FY2016 revenues dropped again—but we consider that a good thing in this case as it was largely driven by the Financial divestiture. The Oil & Gas segment was also weak and currencies added some weight but were offset by strength in Power, Aviation, and Healthcare. Revenues and profits going forward are becoming easier to predict and are showing the way to "bringing good things to life" in FY2018, but there are still a lot of moving parts. Current projections call for FY2017 revenues to advance in the 1–2 percent range followed by a 6–8 percent rise in FY2018: Cost containment and business mix improvements will light the way to a 4–6 percent net earnings gain in FY2017 and a more robust 14–15 percent gain in FY2018. Steady and large buybacks and dividend increases are clearly in the cards; we applaud the company for taking some 2 *billion* shares off the table since 2010 but the 8.6 billion out there still provide plenty of opportunity.

## Reasons to Buy

Finally. A light at the end of the tunnel for 2018. As so much has changed, our "Reasons to Buy" remain largely the same:

At heart, GE is simplifying and returning to its roots as a top-grade industrial infrastructure play. It is downsizing, rightsizing, remixing, and trimming businesses all over—not just its financial services arm—and happily, that process is approaching completion so far as the Finance business is concerned. The value unlocked—not to mention the reduction of risk and the decreased consumption of management bandwidth—should be huge pluses in our view. We should note again that the company will keep some of its financial business intact—the part that finances acquisition *of GE products*—a move that makes a lot of sense to us.

Beyond the finance divestiture, the company continues to tout its "look of a simpler company." It is nearing the end of a five-year plan to increase operational efficiency by such actions as reducing HQ operations and reducing the number of resource planning software systems (by 77 percent was the goal for that one). Now the goal shifts to reducing production costs and increasing operating margins by a half percent each year (huge for a $125 billion company) and also to integrating certain cross-functional services such as engineering and plant capacity between the various businesses.

We also like the new positioning as a high-tech industrial supplier. The company's visions on the Industrial Internet of Things and on tying products back to the mother ship during their life cycle, creating more post-sale business opportunities, make a lot of sense to us.

Cash returns to shareholders will remain significant as divestitures continue, regulation subsides, and profitability and cash flows increase. These factors will likely eliminate hundreds of millions more shares from the share count and get the dividend back up to its historical levels approaching 5 percent.

All in all, we think the company is getting back to what it does best, and we also think the brand image will improve as well as it retrenches into its core businesses. There is considerable need to replace infrastructure, now a focus of Trump administration policy, and GE is right at the heart of this trend. GE is a strong force in its markets, likely to get stronger without the distractions of managing one of the largest financial businesses in the world. We hope we can devote more of this narrative in the future to describing GE's *businesses*, not its business *change*.

## Reasons for Caution

The efforts and distractions of the GE Capital divestiture are diminishing but are still present. The company is still active in the acquisitions and dispositions market and as a whole is still extraordinarily complex, and one now has to hope even more for better times in the oil and gas business. Although the company has plans to retire a billion more shares, the billions remaining are somewhat of a negative. It's hard to generate meaningful per-share gains when new sales and profits are divided up into so many little slices. The divestitures and their proceeds will continue to help fix this.

SECTOR: **Industrials** ❑ BETA COEFFICIENT: **1.18** ❑ 10-YEAR COMPOUND EARNINGS PER-SHARE GROWTH: **-1.5%** ❑ 10-YEAR COMPOUND DIVIDENDS PER-SHARE GROWTH: **-2.0%**

|  | | 2009 | 2010 | 2011 | 2012 | 2013 | 2014 | 2015 | 2016 |
|---|---|---|---|---|---|---|---|---|---|
| Revenues (bil) | | 156.8 | 150.2 | 147.3 | 147.4 | 146.0 | 148.6 | 127.7 | 123.7 |
| Net income (bil) | | 11.4 | 12.6 | 14.9 | 16.1 | 16.9 | 16.6 | 13.4 | 13.6 |
| Earnings per share | | 1.03 | 1.15 | 1.31 | 1.52 | 1.64 | 1.65 | 1.32 | 1.49 |
| Dividends per share | | 0.61 | 0.46 | 0.61 | 0.70 | 0.79 | 0.88 | 0.92 | 0.92 |
| Cash flow per share | | 2.07 | 2.13 | 2.28 | 2.44 | 2.65 | 2.60 | 1.94 | 2.05 |
| Price: | high | 17.5 | 19.7 | 21.7 | 23.2 | 28.1 | 27.6 | 31.5 | 33.0 |
| | low | 5.7 | 13.8 | 14.0 | 18.0 | 20.7 | 23.7 | 19.4 | 27.1 |

Website: www.ge.com

GROWTH AND INCOME

# General Mills, Inc.

Ticker symbol: GIS (NYSE) ❑ Large Cap ❑ Value Line financial strength rating: A+ ❑ Current yield: 3.3% ❑ Dividend raises, past 10 years: 10

## Company Profile

Every year we take a hard look at General Mills—a staple of our *100 Best* list—because, frankly, we're concerned that its cereal may have become soggy as the market shifts toward new, more nutritious, more interesting, and varied food products. That market shift is indeed real, and General Mills has seen an erosion of sales in its important prepared cereal and traditional yogurt lines. But if you dig deeper, we see an approach to innovation that resonates well, some strong new product offerings, and strength in international markets that all work together to keep us on board. Sell when there's something better to buy, and after a close scan of the food-processing universe we found nothing that offered the equal prospects of defensiveness, profitability, strong cash returns, and innovation we were looking for. So welcome back, GIS, for another year at least.

General Mills is one of the world's largest producers of consumer branded foods sold in retail stores. Sales are broken out into three major segments, organized by channel: US Retail (60 percent of 2016 revenues), International (28 percent), and Convenience Stores and Foodservice (12 percent).

Major cereal brands, most of which bear the Big G label, include Cheerios, Wheaties, Lucky Charms, Total, and Chex (which is as much a snack base as a cereal). The company owns Pillsbury, which it acquired in 2001. Other consumer packaged food products include baking mixes (Betty Crocker and Bisquick); meals (Betty Crocker dry packaged dinner mixes), Progresso soups, Annie's, and Hamburger Helper; snacks (Pop Secret microwave popcorn, Fiber One, Gardetto's, Fruit by the Foot, and grain, fruit, and baked snack products); Pillsbury refrigerated and frozen dough products, including Pillsbury Doughboy, frozen breakfast products, and frozen pizza and snack products; Yoplait (which was acquired in 2011 along with Go-Gurt), and Colombo yogurt. On the natural/organic side of the ledger are Annie's (also previously mentioned under "meals"), the Nature Valley grain products, and Cascadian Farm organic packaged fruit and vegetable products. Other important brand names include Häagen-Dazs ice cream and an assortment of international brands such as Old El Paso Mexican foods. The company sold the North American Green Giant frozen food business in 2015.

The company is in a 50–50 joint venture with Nestlé known as Cereal Partners Worldwide. International accounts for about $4.6 billion in sales, or 28 percent of the total, with Europe holding the largest share (43 percent) followed by Canada (20 percent), Asia-Pacific at 22 percent, and Latin America at 15 percent of the International total. The company operates 30 plants in the US and 29 outside the US in key international markets.

The company offers a summarized breakdown of its US Retail business by type of product to better understand this relatively diverse food business:

- Meals, 24 percent
- Cereals, 23 percent
- Snacks, 21 percent
- Baking products, 19 percent
- Yogurt and other, 13 percent

As you can see, General Mills is part of most well-stocked pantries, and it has at least a moderate amount of healthy fare to go with the traditional offerings. Once again we kept this company on the list not just for good financial performance and a better-than-most percentage of healthful offerings, but also for the promise of innovation. The company plans to double its current sourcing of organically grown food; it is now the fourth-largest manufacturer of organic food products in the US. Prominent organic brands include Cascadian Farm, Annie's, and Muir Glen, now accounting for about 4 percent of total sales.

Innovation is one of the keys to staying abreast of today's changing markets, and frankly, if we didn't like the story here, we would have probably not finished this bowl of cereal and moved on to something else. New focus on organic, natural, and specialty products, along with speed to market, is evident in today's GIS. Peter Erickson, EVP of Innovation, Technology, and Quality, is pioneering a shift toward becoming "the best big small food company in the industry," embracing customer-centered innovation and reducing time to market from 24 months to less than 12 months. The new product portfolio includes many new products and concepts—prepackaged "Plenti" oatmeal with Greek yogurt mixed in; "carmelized banana nut" is one flavor variety. The company is investing in the important and relatively more profitable gluten-free food lines. The company has made most of the Cheerios line gluten-free and will soon eliminate artificial flavors in cereal. As the company develops new products, it places emphasis not just on the Millennial group, but also the 55-and-over age groups. We like that, too!

## Financial Highlights, Fiscal Year 2016

FY2016 was a complete mixed bag on the results front, as currency, struggling brands in the cereal sector and Yoplait, declining US retail volumes, food price deflation, and the Green Giant disposition combined with an improved product mix, new product introductions, and decent international volumes to bring a 6 percent overall revenue drop, which would have been 2 percent in constant currency. Cost containment and the better mix drove net profit margins significantly higher, from 10 percent to 10.8 percent, already among the best in this typically low-margin business—net profit actually *rose* just over 1 percent. The company sees more of the same going forward: declining sales, increasing profits. The company foresees a 5–6 percent sales decline in FY2017 followed by a 1–2 percent drop in FY2018, but a net earnings rise in the 2–3 percent range in FY2017 and 4–6 percent in FY2018. Moderate dividend increases and share buybacks should continue.

## Reasons to Buy

As stated earlier, we had mixed feelings about General Mills. We like its slow, steady trajectory, defensive characteristics, strong profitability and financials—now with a stronger, more strategic innovation "kicker" to help it transition to today's (and tomorrow's) changing markets. The company has a good mix of cash-cow businesses like flour and baking mixes to help finance the necessary advancements into the Millennial realm without depriving shareholders. We expect to see faster advancements into organic and other areas popular with Millennials (who, we believe, will continue to crave convenience), which should of course enhance revenue and especially profit growth through the decade.

The long-term policy aimed at share repurchases has recently brought the share count down from 758 million in 2004 to an expected 570 million in 2018. Finally—and once again—General Mills continues to be a safe and stable defensive play and "sleep at night" stock with a beta of 0.58.

## Reasons for Caution

The shift in consumer preferences is real and here to stay and is a scary thing to a company used to putting the same thing on the table day in and day out. Our long-term commitment to GIS is based on their long-term commitment to innovate. While commodity prices have moderated, the company can be affected by commodity prices and cycles.

SECTOR: **Consumer Staples** ◻ BETA COEFFICIENT: **0.58** ◻ 10-YEAR COMPOUND EARNINGS PER-SHARE GROWTH: **7.5%** ◻ 10-YEAR COMPOUND DIVIDENDS PER-SHARE GROWTH: **10.5%**

|  | 2009 | 2010 | 2011 | 2012 | 2013 | 2014 | 2015 | 2016 |
|---|---|---|---|---|---|---|---|---|
| Revenues (mil) | 14,691 | 14,796 | 14,880 | 16,658 | 17,774 | 17,910 | 17,630 | 16,593 |
| Net income (mil) | 1,367 | 1,571 | 1,652 | 1,707 | 1,789 | 1,824 | 1,765 | 1,787 |
| Earnings per share | 1.99 | 2.30 | 2.48 | 2.56 | 2.69 | 2.83 | 2.86 | 2.92 |
| Dividends per share | 0.86 | 0.96 | 1.12 | 1.22 | 1.32 | 1.55 | 1.67 | 1.78 |
| Cash flow per share | 2.78 | 3.09 | 3.29 | 3.47 | 3.71 | 3.94 | 3.93 | 4.01 |
| Price:   high | 36.0 | 39.0 | 40.8 | 41.9 | 53.1 | 55.6 | 59.9 | 72.9 |
| low | 23.2 | 33.1 | 34.5 | 36.6 | 40.4 | 46.7 | 47.4 | 53.5 |

Website: www.generalmills.com

## CONSERVATIVE GROWTH

# W.W. Grainger, Inc.

Ticker symbol: GWW (NYSE) ◻ Large Cap ◻ Value Line financial strength rating: A++ ◻ Current yield: 2.0% ◻ Dividend raises, past 10 years: 10

## Company Profile

W.W. Grainger is North America's largest supplier of maintenance, repair, and operating supply (MRO) products. It sells more than 1.9 million different products from more than 4,800 suppliers through a network of 668 branches (330 in the US), 33 distribution centers (19 in the US), and several websites, with a catalog containing some 570,000 items (a fascinating read if you like this sort of thing). Grainger also offers repair parts, specialized product sourcing, and inventory management supplies. Grainger sells principally to industrial and commercial maintenance departments, contractors, and government customers, but the range of both customers and products is quite broad (see the 2016 Fact Book referenced later in this entry). The company has nearly 2 million worldwide customers, 1.1 million in North America, achieves overnight delivery to approximately 95 percent of them, and processes about 111,000 transactions a day.

Its Canadian subsidiary is Canada's largest distributor of industrial, fleet, and safety products. It serves its customers through 165 branches and five distribution centers and offers bilingual websites and catalogs. Grainger, S.A. de C.V. is Mexico's leading facilities maintenance supplier, offering customers more than 84,000 products. The company also has important operations, through joint ventures, in Japan, China, and India and does business in 166 countries worldwide.

The top five product categories are Safety and Security (19 percent), Material Handling (12 percent), Metalworking (11 percent), Cleaning and Maintenance (9 percent), and Pumps, Plumbing, and Equipment (8 percent), with 15 categories in all. Although Grainger is the largest single player, the market remains quite fragmented, with Grainger itself claiming only about 6 percent of the total market in North America.

Many of Grainger's customers are corporate account customers, primarily *Fortune* 1000 companies that spend more than $5 million annually on facilities maintenance products. Corporate account customers typically sign multiyear contracts for facilities maintenance products or a specific category of products, such as lighting or safety equipment. The company also helps its customers, large and small, with inventory management, supplying a tool called "Keepstock" to help them manage their MRO inventories (sometimes with vending machine–like dispensing machines) and place orders automatically. The Grainger strategy is quintessentially multichannel and centered on being easy to do business with; they strive to "...build [their] business for how [their] customers think, buy, and act, even down to the individual buyer." Customers can interact with a direct sales force, with one of the 330 distribution outlets in the United States, or order online.

E-commerce is a major focus. The strategy is to expand online sales (currently 46 percent of the total) and automatic orders out of Keepstock (currently 20 percent) while decreasing reliance on phone and counter orders and downsizing branch count (49 branches were closed in 2015, 100 more in 2016, and 55 additional are planned for 2017). Online ordering is also possible through mobile apps and through an eProcurement (ePro) module, which connects directly to larger customers' procurement systems. EPro currently accounts for about a third of e-commerce revenue. Grainger has plans to grow e-commerce beyond 50 percent of the total—making it one of the stronger e-commerce success stories out there.

## Financial Highlights, Fiscal Year 2016

The strong dollar, soft domestic and international manufacturing markets, and softness in the energy industry particularly in Canada threw another wrench into Grainger's works in FY2016. Revenues increased a modest 2 percent, but net income fell about 10 percent as the net profit margin slipped a full point to 7 percent due to overcapacity, restructuring and facility closings, and an increase in smaller-volume shipments to smaller businesses. Share buybacks limited the drop in per-share earnings to about 3 percent.

Going forward, the strategy is to continue to grow e-commerce and centralized fulfillment, "rightsize" the distribution center network, and lower prices on certain key items to boost sales. Revenues are projected to grow about 3 percent in FY2017 and 4–5 percent in FY2018; these figures could be conservative if Trump administration policies favoring domestic manufacturing gain momentum. Per-share earnings should recover to 2015 levels in FY2017, then are projected to rise in the 8–10 percent range in FY2018. Grainger has reduced share counts from 84 million in 2006 to 58 million recently, a 31 percent drop. Notably, the company has raised its dividend 45 consecutive years and 10 percent dividend raises look likely going forward.

## Reasons to Buy

"For the Ones Who Get It Done" is the subtitle of the company's excellent 2016 Fact Book (available on its Investor Relations webpage), an appropriate title and an informative and fun read on the company. Grainger is far and away the biggest presence in the MRO world—and we think the story is still intact.

The only broadline competitor is one-quarter its size, and as noted earlier the rest of the market is highly fragmented. The company also has the deepest catalog by far. It's estimated that 40 percent of purchases in the MRO market are unplanned, so having the broadest inventory, fastest delivery, and friendliest service is a big advantage for Grainger. Likewise, the small market share across the globe offers a good growth opportunity. The business structure is changing rapidly due to e-commerce, forcing some closures and expenses and short-term pain, but its marketplace strength, positioning for a manufacturing rebound, solid customer interface strategies, and strong cash flow will keep us "maintained" through 2018.

## Reasons for Caution

Grainger will always be vulnerable to economic cycles and manufacturing displacement, especially so long as it remains concentrated on US soil. Grainger's international expansion should have helped alleviate this concern, but that sector has softened of late as well, leaving the company with some unused capacity in once-hot manufacturing regions. The company appears to be a little behind in its efforts to rightsize the footprint with e-commerce, but it will catch up eventually.

SECTOR: **Industrials** ❏ BETA COEFFICIENT: **0.76** ❏ 10-YEAR COMPOUND EARNINGS PER-SHARE
GROWTH: **13.0%** ❏ 10-YEAR COMPOUND DIVIDENDS PER-SHARE GROWTH: **17.0%**

|  | 2009 | 2010 | 2011 | 2012 | 2013 | 2014 | 2015 | 2016 |
|---|---|---|---|---|---|---|---|---|
| Revenues (mil) | 6,222 | 7,182 | 8,075 | 8,950 | 9,438 | 9,965 | 9,973 | 10,137 |
| Net income (mil) | 402 | 502 | 643 | 690 | 824 | 838 | 793 | 711 |
| Earnings per share | 5.25 | 6.81 | 9.04 | 9.52 | 11.52 | 12.26 | 11.94 | 11.58 |
| Dividends per share | 1.78 | 2.08 | 2.52 | 3.06 | 3.59 | 4.17 | 4.59 | 4.83 |
| Cash flow per share | 7.60 | 9.40 | 11.33 | 12.22 | 14.51 | 15.81 | 16.46 | 16.33 |
| Price:        high | 102.5 | 139.1 | 193.2 | 221.8 | 276.4 | 269.7 | 257.0 | 240.7 |
|               low | 59.9 | 96.1 | 124.3 | 172.5 | 201.5 | 223.9 | 189.8 | 176.9 |

Website: www.grainger.com

## CONSERVATIVE GROWTH
# Honeywell International

Ticker symbol: HON (NYSE) ❏ Large Cap ❏ Value Line financial strength rating: A++ ❏ Current
yield: 2.2% ❏ Dividend raises, past 10 years: 9

## Company Profile

Honeywell is a diversified international technology and manufacturing company engaged in the development, manufacturing, and marketing of aerospace products and services; control technologies for buildings, homes, and industry; and specialty and safety materials. The company groups these activities into four segments: Aerospace (38 percent of FY2016 sales), Home and Building Technologies (27 percent), Performance Materials and Technologies (24 percent) and Safety and Productivity (11 percent). This segmentation is new and reflects end markets (like Home and Building) rather than products; it also reflects the recent disposal of some, but not all, of the automotive businesses.

The Aerospace businesses produce and market products, software, and services including avionics, cockpit controls, power-generation equipment, satellite and space components, and wheels and brakes for commercial and military aircraft and for airports and ground operations. It also makes jet engines for regional and business jet manufacturers. Products include avionics, auxiliary power units (APUs), aircraft lighting, and landing systems. The remaining automotive business includes parts and supplies for the automotive, railroad, and other industries such as cooling system components and turbochargers. In 2014 the company sold its "friction materials" business (mainly brake components) and had previously sold its retail consumer automotive brands to focus on OEM components.

Honeywell's Home and Building Technologies segment (formerly called Automation and Control Solutions) is best known as a maker of home and office climate-control equipment. It also makes home automation systems; thermostats; sensing and combustion controls for heating, A/C, and other environmental controls; lighting controls; security systems and sensing products; metering and measuring products; and fire alarms. This segment produces most of the components of what is known in the trade and advertising lingo as a "smart building," along with devices that play well with the new "connected" homes, data analytics, and "Internet of Things" concepts. Indeed, the company is looking at itself as ever more a software company in all of its businesses and is investing management time, effort, and new hiring in improving the software development cycle. Honeywell estimates that its products are at work in some 150 million homes and 10 million commercial buildings worldwide. This part of the business also produces a number of factory automation products. The company estimates that it holds the number one market-share position in environmental and combustion controls, security and fire-protection systems, and industrial safety products and systems.

The Performance Materials and Technologies operation makes a wide assortment of specialty chemicals and fibers, plastics, coatings, and semiconductor and electronics materials, which are sold primarily to the food, pharmaceutical, petroleum-refining, and electronic packaging industries. Carbon fiber materials are among the more important and fastest-growing products in this segment. Safety and Productivity Solutions markets supply-chain and warehouse automation equipment, portable data collection devices, gas detection equipment, and an assortment of other solutions and components.

The company has a considerable international footprint, with technology and manufacturing centers located outside the US; five such centers are located in China along with a similar number in India. About 56 percent of its business comes from outside the US. US Government sales, mainly from the Aerospace segment, account for about 9 percent of total sales.

"Great positions in good industries" is one of its strategic slogans.

## Financial Highlights, Fiscal Year 2016

Foreign exchange, continued turmoil in the energy industry, and general economic softness all held FY2016 revenue growth to 2 percent—a figure that would have been (–3) percent without the effects of acquisitions and divestitures. However, operational and mix improvements led to another half-percent gain in operating margin to 20.4 percent (it was 16.0 percent as recently as 2012), driving another healthy income gain, this time 10 percent after an 8 percent gain last year on a 4 percent sales *decline*. With modest buybacks, per-share earnings advanced 9 percent. Going forward, the same limiting factors will hold revenues roughly flat in 2017, again, with a 5 percent earnings gain; revenues are projected to turn higher (3–5 percent) in FY2018 on strategic acquisitions and stronger economic conditions with an 8–10 percent hike in earnings as productivity and mix gains continue. The company has been increasing the dividend at a double-digit rate while also executing modest share buybacks; these trends look to continue. However, if the Trump administration enables repatriation of about $12 billion in cash held overseas, the company has said it will commit most of that to buybacks unless significant acquisition opportunities materialize.

## Reasons to Buy

A bet on Honeywell is a bet on a well-managed "best in class" producer of a wide variety of business and consumer products with an underlying technology theme—not really "high tech" but using advanced technologies to deliver a solution. The company shows many of the traditional signs of being well managed, with a strong and strategic focus on profitability, cash flow, and operational efficiency and a healthy respect for transparency, as evidenced by its informative annual reports, investor presentations, and other corporate materials. The company's profit margins are notably higher than others in this type of business—and growing—in this case, one doesn't care so much about anemic revenue growth. Buybacks could give a boost to shareholder returns beyond already healthy dividend raises.

Honeywell has outlined its key growth vectors as technology, innovation, globalization, and expanded presence in key markets like home and business energy management. It is now expanding its focus to complete solutions through "connectivity" and "adjacency" opportunities, many being software driven, within many of their platforms; software sales are expected to grow by a factor of four over the next five years. We like this diverse but timely set of focal points. Honeywell has a solid balance sheet and participates almost exclusively in high-margin businesses.

## Reasons for Caution

Many of the industries Honeywell sells to can be cyclical and/or low-growth businesses: e.g., aviation, construction, and even the well-regarded energy management businesses. Also it's easy to question the reliance on acquisitions to fuel growth. However, as we've seen, the focus on efficiency and profitability will make the most of cyclically sensitive businesses. The stock has been on a long run, more than doubling since 2011; new investors are advised to be patient.

SECTOR: **Industrials** ◻ BETA COEFFICIENT: **0.96** ◻ 10-YEAR COMPOUND EARNINGS PER-SHARE GROWTH: **11.5%** ◻ 10-YEAR COMPOUND DIVIDENDS PER-SHARE GROWTH: **10.5%**

|                     |      | 2009   | 2010   | 2011   | 2012   | 2013   | 2014   | 2015   | 2016   |
|---------------------|------|--------|--------|--------|--------|--------|--------|--------|--------|
| Revenues (mil)      |      | 30,908 | 33,370 | 36,500 | 37,665 | 39,055 | 40,306 | 38,581 | 39.302 |
| Net income (mil)    |      | 2,153  | 2,342  | 2,998  | 3,552  | 3,965  | 4,422  | 4,768  | 5,104  |
| Earnings per share  |      | 2.85   | 3.00   | 3.79   | 4.48   | 4.97   | 5.56   | 6.04   | 6.59   |
| Dividends per share |      | 1.21   | 1.21   | 1.37   | 1.53   | 1.68   | 1.87   | 2.15   | 2.45   |
| Cash flow per share |      | 4.07   | 4.27   | 5.11   | 5.72   | 6.32   | 6.83   | 7.34   | 8.06   |
| Price:              | high | 41.6   | 53.7   | 62.3   | 64.5   | 91.6   | 102.4  | 107.4  | 120.0  |
|                     | low  | 23.1   | 36.7   | 41.2   | 52.2   | 64.2   | 82.9   | 87.0   | 93.7   |

Website: www.honeywell.com

# Illinois Tool Works Inc.

Ticker symbol: ITW (NYSE) ◻ Large Cap ◻ Value Line financial strength rating: A++ ◻ Current yield: 2.0% ◻ Dividend raises, past 10 years: 10

## Company Profile

Illinois Tool Works is a longstanding multinational conglomerate involved in the manufacture of a diversified range of mostly industrial intermediary and end products. Customers include the automotive, machinery, construction, food and beverage, and general industrial markets. The company currently operates some 84 businesses in seven segments in 57 countries, employing approximately 48,000 people. Some of the products are branded and familiar, like Wolf and Hobart kitchen equipment and Paslode air power tools; most are obscure and only known to others in their industries. Sales outside North America account for 47 percent of the total.

The seven segments are presented below with approximate revenue percentages:

- Automotive OEM (18 percent) includes transportation-related components, fasteners, and polymers, as well as truck remanufacturing and related parts and service for the automotive manufacturer market. Important brands include Drawform ("high volume, highly toleranced deep drawn metal stampings"), and Deltar Interior Components, which makes things like interior door handles.

- Test & Measurement/Electronics (15 percent) supplies equipment and software for testing and measuring of materials and structures, solder, and other materials for PC board manufacturing and microelectronics assembly. Brands include Brooks Instrument, Buehler, Chemtronics, Instron, Magnaflux, and Speedline Technologies.
- Polymers & Fluids (15 percent) businesses produce adhesives, sealants, lubrication and cutting fluids, and hygiene products for an assortment of markets. Their primary brands include Futura, Krafft, Devcon, Rocol, and Permatex and such brands as Rain-X and Wynn's for the automotive aftermarket.
- Food Equipment (16 percent) produces commercial food equipment and related services, including professional kitchen ovens, refrigeration, mixers, and exhaust and ventilation systems. Major brands include Hobart, Traulsen, Vulcan, and Wolf.
- Construction Products (11 percent) concentrates on tools, fasteners, and other products for construction applications. Their major end markets are residential, commercial, and renovation construction. Brands include Ramset, Paslode, Buildex, Proline, and others.
- The Welding segment (13 percent of revenues) produces equipment and consumables associated with specialty power conversion, metallurgy, and electronics. Their primary products include arc-welding equipment and consumables, solder materials, equipment and services for electronics assembly, and airport ground support equipment. Primary brands include AXA Power, Hobart, and Weldcraft.
- Specialty Products (14 percent) is a hodgepodge of brands and businesses that includes Diagraph (industrial marking and coding systems), Fastex (engineered components for the appliance industry), and ZipPak reclosable plastic packaging.

In 2012, the company embarked on a five-year "Enterprise Strategy" program aimed at simplifying the business and applying sound customer-driven operating principles to fine-tune its base of customers, markets, products, facilities, and supply chains. Emphasis is placed on removing customer pain points, reducing complexity by applying the "80–20" rule (focusing on the 20 percent of customers, products, and processes that deliver 80 percent of the results), and by fine-tuning the relationships between headquarters and the operating entities. Growing organically (instead of by acquisition) and improving margins are the chief business objectives; the main strategy is to focus on businesses with strong sustainable differentiation. The company closely monitors operating margin improvements in each of its seven segments. We normally don't bring too many such strategic initiatives to light, but we will in this case because (1) it's working, as company-wide operating margins have improved from the 19–21 percent range to a projected 27 percent in FY2018; and (2) such focus is needed in a company with such size and operating complexity; otherwise, it quickly becomes an uncoordinated conglomerate jumble, as many others before it have.

These efficiency measures and "80-20" thinking have not only improved profitability of continuing operations but have also guided the company's thinking in terms of acquiring and selling businesses. The net result can be no better demonstrated than by the fact that in the five years since 2012, per-share earnings have increased 40 percent while revenues have *decreased* 20 percent in that time. Good management has had no finer hour, and we continue to appreciate ITW's efforts and look forward to the ongoing benefits of this initiative in 2018.

## Financial Highlights, Fiscal Year 2016

FY2016 continued the trend of improved profit performance on relatively stable sales volumes—a deliberate strategy for ITW. Earnings rose 7 percent on a mere 1.4 percent rise in revenues. The Automotive OEM and Food Equipment segments are showing the strongest growth, and thanks to larger per-vehicle content of ITW products, the Automotive OEM segment has been growing even though total automotive builds are relatively flat. Margin improvements have also been strongest in the Automotive segment, up more than 3 percent, with Test & Measurement/Electronics and Welding both up about 2 percent. Projections call for sales gains in the 2–4 percent range through FY2018, with per-share earnings rising in the 8–10 percent range due to margin improvements and steady aggressive 2–5 percent share buybacks each year. The company commits half its profits each year to shareholder returns through dividends and buybacks.

## Reasons to Buy

Buying shares of ITW continues to be like buying a fund of medium-sized manufacturing businesses you've probably never heard of but would definitely like to own. Indeed, think of it as the Berkshire Hathaway of manufacturing companies if you will—we do. The process of management is obviously effective, with headquarters prescribing strategies such as margin focus and the 80–20 mindset; managers of the subsidiary businesses have the autonomy to figure out how to deliver results. The model works. We enjoy doing this presentation every year; it's a good tour through how to run a modern conglomerate effectively, and they present themselves well to investors.

ITW is well diversified and serves many markets, some with end products, some with components, some in cyclical industries such as automotive and construction, some in steady-state industries like food processing. The company has solid models for making acquisitions and seems to do better than most conglomerates historically in choosing candidates and then managing them once they're in the fold. The new "Enterprise" initiative appears to be doing a good job of turning opportunity into cash flow and using that cash flow to enhance shareholder returns. The balance sheet is strong and net profit margins are projected to rise quite nicely for this type of business.

## Reasons for Caution

ITW is by nature tied to some of the more volatile elements of the business cycle, so it may not be the best pick for investors living in fear of the next downturn. In particular, we worry a bit about the Automotive segment going forward, although recently the unit has been gaining share in the automotive market. Conglomerates are notoriously difficult to manage (it's hard enough to manage one business, let alone 84 of them); that said, the company is putting fewer new acquisitions on its plate.

SECTOR: **Industrials** ◻ BETA COEFFICIENT: **1.00** ◻ 10-YEAR COMPOUND EARNINGS PER-SHARE GROWTH: **7.5%** ◻ 10-YEAR COMPOUND DIVIDENDS PER-SHARE GROWTH: **12.0%**

|  | 2009 | 2010 | 2011 | 2012 | 2013 | 2014 | 2015 | 2016 |
|---|---|---|---|---|---|---|---|---|
| Revenues (mil) | 13,876 | 15,870 | 17,787 | 17,924 | 14,135 | 14,484 | 13,405 | 13,599 |
| Net income (mil) | 969 | 1,527 | 1,852 | 1,921 | 1,629 | 1,890 | 1,886 | 2,036 |
| Earnings per share | 1.93 | 3.03 | 3.74 | 4.06 | 3.63 | 4.67 | 5.13 | 5.70 |
| Dividends per share | 1.24 | 1.27 | 1.38 | 1.46 | 1.60 | 1.75 | 2.07 | 2.40 |
| Cash flow per share | 3.27 | 4.17 | 5.06 | 5.55 | 5.20 | 6.25 | 7.17 | 7.22 |
| Price:          high | 51.2 | 52.7 | 59.3 | 63.3 | 84.3 | 97.8 | 100.1 | 128.0 |
| low | 25.6 | 40.3 | 39.1 | 47.4 | 59.7 | 76.3 | 78.8 | 79.1 |

**Website: www.itw.com**

AGGRESSIVE GROWTH

# International Flavors & Fragrances, Inc.

Ticker symbol: IFF (NYSE) ❑ Large Cap ❑ Value Line financial strength rating: A+ ❑ Current yield: 2.0% ❑ Dividend raises, past 10 years: 10

## Company Profile

"We are the catalyst for discoveries that spark the senses and transform the everyday" crows the well-crafted website for International Flavors & Fragrances—a company that continues to pass our smell tests after several years of indecision. IFF is a leading manufacturer of "sensorial experiences"— natural and artificial flavoring and fragrance chemicals for the food and beverage and consumer products industry, including cosmetics, perfumes, soap and detergents, hair care, pharmaceuticals, and a wide variety of other products. Fragrances accounted for about 54 percent of 2016 sales; flavorings the other 46 percent. Not surprisingly, the company's value proposition and strategy is to create a differentiated and high value add for its customers by providing critical, unique, and highly researched ingredients. For the food and beverage industry, the company estimates that its flavorings cost only 1–5 percent of the product's total cost, but generate 45 percent of the motivation to purchase it and to purchase it repeatedly.

IFF is truly "international," with 75 percent of sales originating outside North America; in fact, nearly 50 percent of sales originate in emerging markets. Recognizing that flavor and fragrance preferences are very local in nature, the company has established an operational presence in 32 countries and lab facilities in 13 of them, including the US. Still, it estimates only a 16 percent share of the global flavorings and fragrances market and holds the number two position behind Swiss flavorings maker Givaudan. For US investors, it is by far the largest pure play available in this niche.

Research and development—at 8.2 percent of sales—is a big part of what IFF does. The company does extensive research on consumer tastes and preferences, how flavors and aromas work and hold up in different environments, and how to manufacture their products and develop the best delivery system to make them work over the desired life cycle. Research includes things like study of the "psychophysics of sensory perception" and the genetic basis for preferences in flavor and fragrance. New products and concepts include a proprietary encapsulation technology, which coats individual fragrance droplets with a polymeric shell to enhance life-cycle performance, and a product called "PolyIFF"—a solid-fragrance technology embedding scent into molded plastic. Such new delivery systems are a high-growth opportunity, with growth rates in the 40–50 percent range for flavors and 30 percent for fragrances according to one recent company presentation.

## Financial Highlights, Fiscal Year 2016

IFF projects that the $20 billion market for flavors and fragrances will grow about 2–3 percent annually, with fully 75 percent of the growth coming from emerging markets, as taste and aroma become more important as product components in China, Latin America, Africa, and the Middle East. With its broad international footprint, the strong US dollar continues to be a negative. Net sales were up 3 percent for the year but up 5 percent on a constant currency basis. Net earnings marched to the same tune, also up 3 percent. Forecasts call for a 7 percent revenue growth in FY2017 and 8–9 percent in FY2018, as new technologies come to market, again with commensurate to slightly stronger earnings growth as cost reduction initiatives take hold. The company also has a stated acquisition goal to add $500 million to $1 billion to revenues by 2020. This and a weakening dollar could make some of these figures much larger. IFF has accelerated its dividend increases into the low double-digit range annually, and steady share buybacks should continue, propelling per-share earnings growth into the 10 percent range in 2018.

## Reasons to Buy

After years of indecision about IFF, we finally added it to our list only to have it stink things up with an off year mostly due to currency and softness in emerging markets. Things started smelling better in 2016, and we think we could come out of 2018 smelling like a rose, especially if current trends continue and the company gets a boost from currency, emerging markets, and new products. Current forecasts may prove conservative.

IFF has a strong niche and produces elements critical in differentiating products in the fairly undifferentiated food and consumer products businesses. That should play better over time as people's tastes become more trained and more demanding—both in the rich world and especially in developing nations, which is an important trend right now. Not only does the company produce many of the world's leading flavorings and fragrances, it also has the market research and know-how to give it a competitive advantage—a moat—both with its customer insights and knowing how to make and deliver the stuff. We also like the relatively recession-proof nature of this business; we doubt that they will take the flavoring out of your favorite foods anytime soon. Again, flavorings only account for 1–5 percent of the cost of your favorite beverage, and we Coke drinkers all know what happens when a company monkeys with that.

## Reasons for Caution

The cost and availability of key ingredients like vanilla (a large portion of which comes from unstable regions in West Africa) can affect IFF adversely. The strong overseas footprint is probably an advantage most of the time, but today's strong dollar and volatile emerging markets like China and Brazil attenuate that advantage; also, it's hard to keep up with changing consumer tastes in so many places. At 2–3 percent growth, the flavorings and fragrances business is low growth; growth has to come from market share gains and acquisitions, always a challenge. Intellectual property protection is also a challenge; many try and some succeed in reverse engineering key ingredients.

SECTOR: **Consumer Staples** ◻ BETA COEFFICIENT: **1.04** ◻ 10-YEAR COMPOUND EARNINGS PER-SHARE GROWTH: **9.0%** ◻ 10-YEAR COMPOUND DIVIDENDS PER-SHARE GROWTH: **10.0%**

|  |  | 2009 | 2010 | 2011 | 2012 | 2013 | 2014 | 2015 | 2016 |
|---|---|---|---|---|---|---|---|---|---|
| Revenues (mil) | | 2,326 | 2,623 | 2,788 | 2,821 | 2,953 | 3,089 | 3,023 | 3,116 |
| Net income (mil) | | 214 | 264 | 306 | 328 | 368 | 416 | 427 | 441 |
| Earnings per share | | 2.69 | 3.26 | 3.74 | 3.98 | 4.47 | 5.08 | 5.25 | 5.51 |
| Dividends per share | | 1.00 | 1.04 | 1.16 | 1.30 | 1.46 | 1.72 | 2.06 | 2.40 |
| Cash flow per share | | 3.70 | 4.27 | 4.71 | 4.95 | 5.54 | 6.25 | 6.45 | 6.70 |
| Price: | high | 42.6 | 56.1 | 66.3 | 67.8 | 90.3 | 105.8 | 123.1 | 143.6 |
| | low | 25.0 | 39.3 | 51.2 | 52.1 | 67.5 | 82.9 | 97.6 | 97.2 |

Website: www.iff.com

---

**AGGRESSIVE GROWTH**

# Itron, Inc.

Ticker symbol: ITRI (NASDAQ) ◻ Mid Cap ◻ Value Line financial strength rating: B+ ◻ Current yield: Nil ◻ Dividend raises, past 10 years: NA

## Company Profile

Finally!

After five years of writing about the virtue of patience in love, marriage, business, and investing, using the moribund Itron as a premier example (it was our worst pick in 2014), we now have a winner! Yes, new products, better sales of older ones as its smart metering products gain traction, and the advantages of higher volumes led to a tripling of earnings and a 45 percent stock price gain—and there's more to come. We've long liked the company and the business they're in, so we stuck with it through bad times, somewhat against our better judgment or so it seemed. Now, happily, we can finally say we were right.

"Creating a more resourceful world" is the main webpage slogan of Itron, the world's largest provider of standard and intelligent metering systems, mainly to utility companies, for residential and commercial gas, electric, and water usage. Intelligent meters, in addition to tracking raw usage over time, can also measure at the point of use operating parameters such as pressure, temperature, voltage, phase, etc. This information can be extremely valuable to the supplying utility but has in the past been difficult and expensive to obtain.

Itron supplies a range of products from basic meters that are read manually to meters that act as network devices and transmit their data in real time to the managing utility and/or to the consuming customer. Products and systems are produced and sold in three groupings:

- Standard metering—basic meters that measure electricity, gas, or water flow by electrical or mechanical means, with displays but no built-in remote reading or transmission capability.
- Advanced metering—these units, depending on the country and the communications technologies available, transmit usage data remotely through telephone, cellular, radio frequency (RF), Ethernet, or power line carrier paths. Among other value adds, these meters transmit usage data for billing, thereby eliminating the need for onsite meter reading—a big savings for utility companies.
- Smart metering—smart meters collect and store interval data and other detailed info, receive commands, and interface with other devices through assorted communication paths to thermostats, smart appliances, and home network and other advanced control systems.

Itron also sells a range of software platforms for utilities and building managers for the management of the installed base and the analysis and optimization of usage, and it is active in developing so-called "smart grid" solutions for utilities and utility networks. The company also markets advanced metering initiative (AMI) contracts to utilities, where it installs devices and monitors and optimizes power usage for a utility. At present, electric meters represent about 43 percent of the business, gas meters about 29 percent, and water meters the remaining 29 percent. The company has about 8,000 customers in 100 countries, and about 55 percent of the business comes from outside the US and Canada. Itron has become a major player in the emerging "Smart City" energy use concept, and sees long-term benefit from the growing electrification of transport. Itron products are also frequently mentioned in "Internet of Things" circles. The company has brought several new technologies to market, including an expansion "OpenWay Riva:" a new technology "ecosystem" where computing power is embedded in local electric and water meters and is capable of real-time data analysis and management of the overall grid.

Pretty smart stuff, don't you think? The question has always been, can they make money? Finally, the answer is "yes."

## Financial Highlights, Fiscal Year 2016

For years, Itron has struggled with soft demand and the lack of critical mass—that is, the lack of enough demand and throughput to keep its factories, offices, and labs running at full efficiency—also referred to as *operating leverage*. Now, new technologies and an increased adoption of the old ones as utilities see the virtues of, and budget for, these new technologies has led to several major deals for existing and new products.

As a consequence, FY2016 revenues gained 8 percent—not that exciting but good considering flat to negative performance in the previous five years. The real story was the operating margin expansion, led by a better factory usage and mix, up from 6.8 percent in FY2015 to 10 percent in FY2016, a huge jump by any standard. As a consequence, net profit and per-share earnings almost tripled. And is this simply a one-time energy spike? Not really—earnings are expected to triple again by FY2018 on continued improved margins and 3–4 percent sales growth.

*Whew.*

## Reasons to Buy

Can you picture a day when you might manage your energy consumption, device by device, in your home using your smartphone? Even if you're away from the home? And the day when utilities can monitor usage in real time to shift supply of a resource such as electricity that cannot be easily stored? A day when you (or your apps) work together with your utility to optimize energy use from all sources at all times of the day? A day when solar energy generated from one locale on a sunny day is moved to another with clouds and rain?

If you believe that the need for managed energy efficiency will continue to catch on, Itron is a good place to be. As utilities modernize, reduce costs, and replace infrastructure, Itron products and networks will be in the sweet spot. Internationally, utilities are adding infrastructure, as well as replacing it, and Itron is positioned well for that, too. Public policy will provide some tailwinds too. Recent droughts bode well for water conservation and smart metering. Worldwide, only about 15 percent of 2.5 billion meters are "smart" or "advanced," while in the US that figure is approaching 50 percent. Smarter, more advanced meters are where the puck is going, and Itron has a commanding share of this market.

Itron and its markets appear be "switched on" for a good run—the recent abundance of press releases announcing new sales deals and new products is evidence. Finally, while the company doesn't pay a dividend, it returns ample cash to shareholders through share buybacks.

## Reasons for Caution

Companies that sell good ideas don't always grow, particularly if the size of their markets is limited or they are particularly conservative about spending money. For these past few years, we thought we were a victim of this mantra, but held out hope and we were right. That said, an economic downturn or some other disruption to Itron's recent success in its marketplace could put us right back in the penalty box. The next few years will be a test of Itron's sustained ability to execute.

SECTOR: **Information Technology** ❑ BETA COEFFICIENT: **1.26** ❑ 10-YEAR COMPOUND EARNINGS PER-SHARE GROWTH: **1.5%** ❑ 10-YEAR COMPOUND DIVIDENDS PER-SHARE GROWTH: **NA**

|  |  | 2009 | 2010 | 2011 | 2012 | 2013 | 2014 | 2015 | 2016 |
|---|---|---|---|---|---|---|---|---|---|
| Revenues (mil) | | 1,687 | 2,259 | 2,434 | 2,178 | 1,949 | 1,971 | 1,883 | 2,040 |
| Net income (mil) | | 44.3 | 133.9 | 156.3 | 128.5 | 15.0 | 13.7 | 12.7 | 34.5 |
| Earnings per share | | 1.15 | 3.27 | 3.85 | 2.71 | 0.36 | 0.35 | 0.33 | 0.90 |
| Dividends per share | | — | — | — | — | — | — | — | — |
| Cash flow per share | | 2.53 | 4.85 | 5.56 | 4.84 | 2.60 | 2.93 | 2.34 | 2.75 |
| Price: | high | 69.5 | 81.9 | 64.4 | 50.3 | 48.4 | 43.7 | 42.7 | 66.1 |
| | low | 40.1 | 52.0 | 26.9 | 33.3 | 37.0 | 32.3 | 27.9 | 29.0 |

Website: www.itron.com

# The J.M. Smucker Company

Ticker symbol: SJM (NYSE) ◻ Large Cap ◻ Value Line financial strength rating: A++ ◻ Current yield: 2.4% ◻ Dividend raises, past 10 years: 10

## Company Profile

"With a name like Smucker's, it has to be good!" This ad copy says it all about this eastern Ohio–based firm, a leading manufacturer of jams, jellies, and other processed foods for years. Thanks in part to divestitures from the Procter & Gamble food division and other companies, it has grown itself into a premier player in the packaged food industry. The 2015 acquisition of Big Heart Pet Brands, a premier player in the pet food industry, signals further expansion into adjacent markets.

Smucker manufactures and markets products under its own name, as well as under a number of other household names such as Crisco, Folgers, Knudsen, Hungry Jack, Eagle, Carnation, Pillsbury, Jif (why not sell the peanut butter if they sell the jelly?), and naturally, Goober (a combination of peanut butter and jelly in a single jar), and Uncrustables (why not just sell the whole sandwich?). The company also produces and distributes Dunkin' Donuts coffee and produces an assortment of cooking oils, toppings, juices, and baking ingredients. The company has revitalized such brands as Folgers and Jif through improved marketing, channel relationships, and better focus on the packaging and delivery of these brands to the customer. In the coffee business, for example, Smucker now offers custom blends, K-cup offerings, etc., notably under the Dunkin' Donuts brand. A new Café Bustelo brand targets Hispanic and Millennial markets with edgy "experiential" marketing with pop-up cafes at music festivals and the like. "Coffee Served Your Way" is Smucker's motto, and there are new convenience packages for peanut butter, jelly, and other spreads as well—Jif To Go Dippers is but one example. Organic brands, most of which have been around for a while, include Santa Cruz Organic, Sahale Snacks, and truRoots brands, Smucker's Natural, Laura Scudder's, and a handful of others. New areas include fruit spreads, nut butters, and other organic baking materials, beverages, and snacks; they also produce a line of sugar-free, reduced sugar, and sugar alternative products. The Big Heart acquisition brought some top brands in the pet food business, including Meow Mix, 9Lives, Milk Bone, and others, and grew the total business by about a third. Overall, the company aims to sell the number one brand in the various markets it serves.

With the Big Heart acquisition the company is currently organized into four evenly split reporting segments: Retail Coffee (29 percent of revenues), Retail Consumer Foods (29 percent), Retail Pet Foods (29 percent), and International and Foodservice (13 percent). (The pet food segment had not seen a whole year's integration at the time of this narrative, so the figures here are estimates.) Operations are centered in the United States, Canada, and Europe, with about 10 percent of sales coming from outside the US with Canada representing more than 80 percent of that.

Smucker, like most other food companies these days, is emphasizing innovation, which includes not only new food products in new arenas like organic, but also new convenience packages to fit modern lifestyles. Examples of the latter include Smucker's Fruit Fulls blended fruit pouches and the aforementioned Jif To Go Dippers packaged peanut butter snacks.

Even as a nearly $7.5 billion-a-year enterprise (in 2016), the company still retains the feel of a family business, with brothers Tim and Richard Smucker sharing the CEO responsibilities as chairman and president respectively. Their annual report is the only one we've come across that has recipes in it. Last but not least, the Company Store and Café located just outside of Orrville, Ohio, is a national treasure and a classic case study in branding and brand image.

## Financial Highlights, Fiscal Year 2016

Competitive pressures in the coffee business and headwinds in the new pet food segment (specifically, pet snacks) led the way to a surprising 5 percent revenue decline for Smucker in FY2016. Competitors in these businesses have been aggressive with price cuts. The good news was on the bottom line, where cost efficiencies led to a 6.5 percent profit *gain*. Forecasts call for a slow recovery to 2015 sales levels by FY2018, but the good news is on the bottom line once again, where net profit margins will advance a full percentage point to about 10.5 percent (healthy for the food business) and net income will rise about 10 percent by the end of FY2018. The company issued nearly 20 million shares to finance the acquisition; the shares will likely be bought back gradually through the decade; they've retired about a quarter of them so far. Dividend growth should continue in the mid-single-digit range.

## Reasons to Buy

This is a very well-managed company with an excellent and lasting reputation in its markets. In recent years, it has a proven track record in buying and revitalizing key brands, the most prominent being former Procter & Gamble food brands, Sara Lee foodservice coffee and beverage brands, and a few International Multifoods brands. We expect this trend to continue. The company's aggressive moves into coffee and other beverages were well timed; it remains to be seen whether the pattern is repeated with the Big Heart acquisition, which was expected to bring a measure of stability, profitability, and growth to the table.

Overall growth and profitability figures are both among the best for the relatively staid food industry; the base for steady growth in cash flows and investor returns is well established over the long term. Steady and safe: Smucker is the ever-improving peanut butter and jelly sandwich of the investing landscape.

## Reasons for Caution

The prepared-food business is very sensitive in the short term to competition as well as commodity costs. Too, there is the ever-present transition of the customer base to the Millennial generation and tastes—do Millennials eat peanut butter and jelly sandwiches? Smucker seems to have plenty on the drawing board in case they don't.

We do wonder if the company has strayed just a bit outside of its traditional feel-good, relatively healthy or at least wholesome, peanut-butter-and-jelly base. While you can't grow a business much on peanut butter and jelly alone, ventures into donut-shop coffee, and now, pet food especially may not be such a good fit with what has made Smucker's taste so good up to now. Time will tell in the long run, but we still think that with a name like Smucker's, it has to be good.

SECTOR: **Consumer Staples** ▢ BETA COEFFICIENT: **0.59** ▢ 10-YEAR COMPOUND EARNINGS PER-SHARE GROWTH: **8.0%** ▢ 10-YEAR COMPOUND DIVIDENDS PER-SHARE GROWTH: **9.5%**

| | 2009 | 2010 | 2011 | 2012 | 2013 | 2014 | 2015 | 2016 |
|---|---|---|---|---|---|---|---|---|
| Revenues (mil) | 4,605 | 4,826 | 5,526 | 5,897 | 5,611 | 5,450 | 7,811 | 7,400 |
| Net income (mil) | 520.3 | 566.5 | 535.6 | 584 | 588 | 540 | 704 | 753 |
| Earnings per share | 4.15 | 4.79 | 4.73 | 5.37 | 5.64 | 5.30 | 5.89 | 6.45 |
| Dividends per share | 1.40 | 1.68 | 1.88 | 2.06 | 2.32 | 2.56 | 2.68 | 2.92 |
| Cash flow per share | 5.60 | 7.06 | 6.75 | 7.85 | 8.30 | 6.87 | 9.75 | 10.10 |
| Price:      high | 62.7 | 66.3 | 80.3 | 89.4 | 114.7 | 107.1 | 125.3 | 157.3 |
| low | 34.1 | 53.3 | 61.2 | 70.5 | 86.5 | 87.1 | 97.3 | 117.4 |

Website: **www.smuckers.com**

GROWTH AND INCOME

# Johnson & Johnson

Ticker symbol: JNJ (NYSE) ❑ Large Cap ❑ Value Line financial strength rating: A++ ❑ Current yield: 2.8 percent ❑ Dividend raises, past 10 years: 10

## Company Profile

"Caring for the world, one person at a time" is the slogan of Johnson & Johnson, one of the largest and most comprehensive healthcare "family of companies" in the world. JNJ offers a broad line of consumer products, over-the-counter drugs, prescription drugs, and various other medical devices and diagnostic equipment. It is—or at least has been—one of the most solid and steady names in an ever-changing medical and pharmaceutical field.

With total FY2016 sales of over $71 billion, the company has three reporting segments: Pharmaceuticals (about 44 percent of revenues), Medical Devices and Diagnostics (about 38 percent), and Consumer Healthcare (surprisingly, only about 19 percent). Across those segments, Johnson & Johnson has more than 250 operating companies in 60 countries, selling some 50,000 products in more than 175 countries. Among Johnson & Johnson's premier assets are its well-entrenched brand names, which are widely known in the United States as well as abroad. As a marketer, JNJ's reputation for quality has enabled it to build strong ties to commercial healthcare providers. About 64 percent of sales come from overseas.

In the Consumer segment, the company's vast portfolio of well-known trade names includes Band-Aid adhesive bandages; Tylenol; Stayfree, Carefree, and Sure & Natural feminine hygiene products; Mylanta; Pepcid AC; Motrin; Sudafed; Zyrtec; Neosporin; Neutrogena; Johnson's baby powder, shampoo, and oil; Listerine; and Reach toothbrushes. Names in the Pharmaceutical segment are less well-known but include major entries in the areas of antiseptics, antipsychotics, gastroenterology, immunology, neurology, hematology, contraceptives, oncology, pain management, metabolics, and many others distributed both through consumer and healthcare professional channels. Leading diseases addressed include rheumatoid arthritis, inflammatory bowel disease, Alzheimer's, schizophrenia, prostate cancer, diabetes, and many others.

Medical Devices and Diagnostics products include professionally used cardiovascular, orthopedic, diabetic, neurologic, and surgical products among others.

The company is typically fairly active with acquisitions, acquiring small niche players to strengthen its overall product offering. In January the company acquired the Swiss biotech company Actelion Ltd., a more significant acquisition $30 billion in size. Actelion's biggest line of drugs addresses pulmonary arterial hypertension; drugs in the pipeline also address rare diseases like multiple sclerosis. The acquisition points to a deeper commitment to higher-margined but also higher-risk research pharmaceuticals.

## Financial Highlights, Fiscal Year 2016

Johnson & Johnson continues to own a dominant and stable franchise in a secure and lucrative industry. The basic model is to have steady, recurring income from solid consumer brands such as Tylenol combined with more aggressive and lucrative ventures into pharmaceuticals and surgical products. Recently the company has become more aggressive in the pharma segment. FY2016 saw a modest 3 percent revenue rise, with results hemmed in by currency effects. Net income rose a stronger 7 percent aided by modest mix and operational improvements, which resulted in improved margins. The greater emphasis on pharma going forward will lift net profit margins into the 24–25 percent range (from 22.5 percent) into FY2018. Revenue is forecast to rise in the 3–4 percent range each year; the improved margins will drive earnings up 7–8 percent annually. Buybacks may attenuate as the company becomes a more aggressive acquirer, while dividend increases should continue at 5–7 percent annually. The company has raised its dividend for 54 straight years.

## Reasons to Buy

JNJ continues to be a conservatively run company whose growth prospects are on the lower end of this book's scale, but clearly the company has great appeal in the investment community especially in periods of market volatility. Even if it's more often unexciting for the growth and momentum investor, JNJ's slow steady business model mixing reliable, branded performers with more lucrative pharma and medical device products brings steady earnings and cash flow combined with healthy dividend growth, all leading to gratifying shareholder returns. The 23–25 percent *net* profit margins are enviable. It's a "sleep at night" stock with a decent track record for shareholder "raises."

## Reasons for Caution

While we still think JNJ is a good, steady horse for a relatively long race, it has picked up some speed of late through increased emphasis on pharma, the recent Actelion acquisition, and others that may be pending, increasing the chance of getting winded somewhere along the way. The P/E, a figure we don't rely on heavily but do look at, has expanded from 14–15 to the 17–18 range, adding a bit of downside risk to the mix. We wouldn't like to see JNJ take too much risk just to achieve growth; the company should be quite content with its market position and high profit margins—don't monkey with what works! Every year JNJ is an almost automatic inclusion on the *100 Best* list; this year we had to take a second look.

SECTOR: **Healthcare** □ BETA COEFFICIENT: **0.74** □ 10-YEAR COMPOUND EARNINGS PER-SHARE GROWTH: **6.0%** □ 10-YEAR COMPOUND DIVIDENDS PER-SHARE GROWTH: **9.5%**

|  | 2009 | 2010 | 2011 | 2012 | 2013 | 2014 | 2015 | 2016 |
|---|---|---|---|---|---|---|---|---|
| Revenues (mil) | 61,897 | 61,587 | 65,030 | 67,224 | 71,312 | 74,311 | 70,074 | 71,890 |
| Net income (mil) | 12,906 | 13,279 | 13,867 | 14,345 | 15,576 | 16,323 | 15,409 | 16,540 |
| Earnings per share | 4.63 | 4.76 | 5.00 | 5.10 | 5.52 | 5.70 | 5.50 | 5.93 |
| Dividends per share | 1.93 | 2.11 | 2.25 | 2.40 | 2.59 | 2.76 | 2.97 | 3.15 |
| Cash flow per share | 5.69 | 5.90 | 6.25 | 6.45 | 7.10 | 7.26 | 6.90 | 7.45 |
| Price: high | 65.9 | 66.2 | 66.3 | 72.7 | 96.0 | 109.5 | 106.5 | 126.1 |
| low | 61.9 | 56.9 | 64.3 | 61.7 | 70.3 | 86.1 | 81.8 | 94.3 |

Website: www.jnj.com

GROWTH AND INCOME
# Kimberly-Clark Corporation

Ticker symbol: KMB (NYSE) □ Large Cap □ Value Line financial strength rating: A++ □ Current yield: 2.9% □ Dividend raises, past 10 years: 10

## Company Profile

"Essentials for a better life," is the tagline of Kimberly-Clark, the classic manufacturer and marketer of a full line of personal care products, mostly based on paper and paper technologies. Well-known for its ubiquitous Kleenex brand tissues, KMB also is a strong player in consumer bath tissue, diapers, feminine and incontinence products—and in industrial and professional markets as well as all primarily paper-based cleaning and sanitation products. The company was founded in 1872 and is headquartered today near Dallas, TX, with a historical, technology, and manufacturing base in the Fox River Valley in Wisconsin. There are manufacturing facilities in 35 countries serving customers in 175 countries; about 48 percent of the company's sales originate outside North America.

After the 2015 major spin-off described shortly, the company now operates in three segments: Personal Care, Consumer Tissue, and K-C Professional & Other. The Personal Care segment (now 49 percent of FY2016 revenues, and fastest growing and highest margined of the K-C businesses) provides disposable diapers, training and youth pants, and swim pants; baby wipes; and feminine and incontinence care products, and related products. Brand names include Huggies, Pull-Ups, Little Swimmers, GoodNites, Kotex, Kotex Lightdays, Depend, and Poise. Baby care is the single largest business category with $6 billion in revenues—about 28 percent of the business—mostly sold under the Huggies brand. The diaper brands, including adult versions Poise and Depend, are among the faster-growing businesses.

The Consumer Tissue segment (32 percent) offers facial and bathroom tissue, paper towels, napkins, and related products for household use under the Kleenex, Scott, Cottonelle, Viva, Andrex, Scottex, Hakle, and Page brands. Ah (choo), there's Kleenex, a $2 billion business in itself, almost 10 percent of the total. But Scott is no softie either, accounting for another 10 percent.

The K-C Professional & Other segment (20 percent) provides paper products for the away-from-home, that is, commercial/institutional marketplace under Kimberly-Clark, Kleenex, Scott, WypAll, Kimtech, KleenGuard, Kimcare, and Jackson brand names.

On the innovation front, KMB is working on personalized "MyKleenex" tissue packaging (yes, you can create your own Kleenex boxes with your own name, pictures, and designs), fast-dissolving Scott toilet tissue, new Kleenex Balsam tissues to soothe sore noses, and new Huggies sun care lotions and dispensers for "little swimmers." Finally, there are new "premium tier" versions of Huggies, Pull-Ups, and certain incontinence items coming to market.

## Financial Highlights, Fiscal Year 2016

Once again, currency headwinds and special items made year-to-year comparison difficult. Reported FY2016 revenues dropped 2 percent but actually *grew* 2 percent before currency effects. Comparisons to previous years look weak but are affected by the 2015 healthcare products segment ("Halyard") spin-off. Earnings are higher, as large write-offs for Venezuelan operations and some pension accounting changes hit earnings, but more to the point, cost savings from the "FORCE" operational efficiency initiative are over $1 per share—higher than forecast—and have resulted in an almost 50 percent increase in operating and net margins. So the net profit reported for FY2016 is more than double FY2015.

New products, a better mix, and continued "FORCE" efficiencies will drive revenues about 1 percent higher for FY2017 (still some currency effects too) but the top-line growth will pick up into the 3–4 percent range in FY2018. Earnings should grow in the 2–3 percent range into FY2018; share buybacks will grow per-share earnings closer to 4–6 percent. Cash returns to investors should continue to grow into FY2017. Mid-single-digit dividend increases and measured share buybacks should continue. The share count is down 37 percent in the past fifteen years.

## Reasons to Buy

Despite recent numbers, the story hasn't changed. Kimberly-Clark has shown itself to be a steady and solid business and investment performer in all kinds of economic climates. Cost savings and efficiency measures have been very effective, more so than we see for most other companies. Much-improved margins have been achieved and look to stay in place for the future.

The decent yield and strong track record of raising dividends and buying back shares is a definite plus. Strong cash flow has financed strategic business investments, including international expansion in emerging markets, product innovations, and strategic marketing. The company continues to prioritize shareholder interests.

The company has stellar brands and should do well expanding them into overseas markets. Also, compared to some rivals, the company is less inclined to go for "glamour" markets such as cosmetics, choosing instead to add to margins through operating efficiencies and scale. Safety-oriented investors may find this approach preferable, and the company gets top ratings for financial strength and price stability.

## Reasons for Caution

While the paper products business is steady, it isn't easy to see where additional growth will come from, even with more innovation and brand-strengthening activity. The company, rightly so, is targeting international expansion, but competition and currency fluctuation make the results far from certain. The cost of pulp and paper raw materials will always be volatile. Companies like KMB have sometimes come to rely on acquisitions for growth; KMB has, so far, largely resisted this temptation but that could change. Finally, investors and the markets have recognized KMB's consistent excellence and have bid up the share price accordingly.

SECTOR: **Consumer Staples** ❑ BETA COEFFICIENT: **0.69** ❑ 10-YEAR COMPOUND EARNINGS PER-SHARE GROWTH: **1.0%** ❑ 10-YEAR COMPOUND DIVIDENDS PER-SHARE GROWTH: **7.0%**

|                    | 2009   | 2010   | 2011   | 2012   | 2013   | 2014   | 2015   | 2016   |
|--------------------|--------|--------|--------|--------|--------|--------|--------|--------|
| Revenues (mil)     | 19,115 | 19,746 | 20,846 | 21,063 | 21,182 | 19,724 | 18,591 | 18,202 |
| Net income (mil)   | 1,884  | 1,843  | 1,591  | 1,750  | 2,142  | 1,476  | 1,013  | 2,166  |
| Earnings per share | 4.52   | 4.45   | 3.99   | 4.42   | 5.53   | 3.91   | 2.77   | 5.99   |
| Dividends per share| 2.38   | 2.58   | 2.76   | 2.92   | 3.24   | 3.36   | 3.52   | 3.68   |
| Cash flow per share| 6.40   | 6.53   | 6.78   | 6.70   | 7.89   | 6.40   | 4.67   | 8.05   |
| Price:       high  | 67.0   | 67.2   | 74.1   | 88.3   | 111.7  | 118.8  | 125.0  | 138.9  |
|              low   | 43.1   | 58.3   | 61.0   | 70.5   | 83.9   | 102.8  | 103.0  | 111.3  |

Website: www.kimberly-clark.com

---

## CONSERVATIVE GROWTH

# The Kroger Company

Ticker symbol: KR (NYSE) ❑ Large Cap ❑ Value Line financial strength rating: A ❑ Current yield: 1.6% ❑ Dividend raises, past 10 years: 10

## Company Profile

Those of you who follow our fortunes year in and year out know that our fortunes declined a bit last year with Retail. Once-solid names like Target and Macy's, which had seemed to be making progress despite the advance of Amazon Prime and other Internet shopping strengths, pretty much bagged our chances of beating the S&P 500 for the year. And Kroger too seemed not immune to shifts in the shopping space, not just online but also to competitive shifts as Walmart and others continue to challenge the traditional grocery store with more warehouse-y discount formats. Was Kroger getting hit from all sides with these shifts? Should we be alarmed that net profit margins are starting to slide ever so slightly as price competition slices things up into ever thinner slices? The stock market seemed to think so, driving the share price down almost 30 percent from the high. We took a hard look and decided that operational excellence plus one marketplace shift that we think will work in Kroger's favor will carry the day—so after a careful review we kept Kroger on out *100 Best* list. We hope we've chosen the right checkout line with this one.

Kroger is the nation's largest retail grocery store operator, with about 2,796 supermarkets and multi-department stores, 784 convenience stores, and 319 specialty jewelry stores operated around the country. Supermarket operations account for about 94 percent of total revenue and are located in 35 states with a concentration in the Midwest (where it was founded) and in the South and West, where it grew mostly by acquisition. The company is dominant in the markets it serves, with a number one or two market share position in 42 of its 49 major markets. Kroger operates through a series of store brands many of you will be familiar with but probably did not associate with the Kroger name, including King Soopers, City Market, Fred Meyer, Fry's, Ralphs, Dillons, Smith's, Baker's, Food 4 Less, Harris Teeter, and an assortment of others totaling about two dozen business names. In late 2015 it acquired Roundy's, parent company of the urban upscale supermarket chain Mariano's which operates 34 stores in the Chicago area and 117 other stores mainly in Wisconsin. The Mariano's footprint is urban and somewhere between a traditional grocery and Whole Foods—an interesting new style of store that should play well with urban and Millennial consumers and naturally could be expanded elsewhere.

The typical Kroger supermarket is full service and well appointed with higher-margin specialty departments such as health foods, seafood, floral, and other perishables. The Fred Meyer stores carry a large assortment of general merchandise in addition to groceries, turning them into modern-era big-box department stores; the company has 132 stores in all that meet this format, mostly in the West. There are also 131 "price impact warehouse" stores under the Food 4 Less, Foods Co., and Ruler Foods brands and 117 "marketplace" stores— "Kroger Marketplace," "Fry's Marketplace," "King Soopers Marketplace," and so forth—with expanded offerings similar to Fred Meyer to complement the supermarkets. About 1,445 "supermarket fuel centers" and 1,950 pharmacies round out the supermarket picture. Finally, the company has a considerable presence in manufacturing its own store-branded food items, with 38 such plants located around the country and estimates that 26 percent of revenues and 40 percent of unit volumes come from in-house brands. On the innovation front, Kroger has applied technology in stores to enhance the shopping experience, an example being "QueVision," which prominently displays checkout line availability on large in-store monitors, reducing customer wait times an average of three-and-a-half minutes and reducing labor costs by driving more even capacity use. Like others in the business, a new online and mobile "Clicklist" tool allows customers to shop online and pick up at the store. Other initiatives focus on loyalty and data-driven promotion to valued customers.

## Financial Highlights, Fiscal Year 2016

Kroger boasts that same-store supermarket sales have grown for 45 consecutive quarters, and this is a good track record particularly in light of the Great Recession and more recently, heightened competition from the likes of Wal-Mart,

Target, and others. However, this streak came to an end in early 2017 on a combination of competition, food price deflation, and lower gas prices. For FY2016 same-store sales were up about 1 percent and total sales advanced about 5 percent, while net earnings were virtually unchanged as critically tight net margins decreased from 1.9 to 1.8 percent, again largely on price competition. One bit of good news: we can chuck the line "hurt by currency headwinds"—Kroger is 100 percent US based. Going forward, sales should advance 4–6 percent again in FY2017 as food inflation subsides and as the grocer cuts prices to compete more aggressively in some segments and locations. Another slight margin hit will keep profits virtually unchanged—although share buybacks will lead to a 3–4 percent per-share earnings gain. An improved mix by FY2018 should bring net earnings growth back to the 5 percent range. Kroger's own shares continue to top its own shopping list; they have now retired more than 40 percent of their float since 2005. The dividend, which commenced in 2006, should also continue to rise, perhaps a bit faster as strong cash flows continue.

## Reasons to Buy

Kroger continues to do a good job in a tough market. Major discount retailers such as Wal-Mart and Target have stepped into the grocery business with a fairly significant price advantage, yet so far Kroger has been able to fend them off by focusing on product breadth, the shopping experience, and strategic price reductions. Here's the kicker: While we see price competition taking away some share on typical mostly commoditized grocery products, we see full-line grocers like Kroger taking away share on higher-margined organic and natural products at the expense of Whole Foods, Sprouts, and other "natural" retailers. Kroger loses some share to Wal-Mart but gets some from this direction, which should help margins and overall results going forward.

We also like the Fred Meyer quality grocery-plus-department-store format, a more pleasant and balanced shopping experience than either Walmart or Target and a format that Kroger would do well to roll out nationwide. We also see the recently acquired Mariano's as a good expansion model.

All told, Kroger is a well-managed company that continues to dominate its niches, and its shares have been on the discount endcap of late.

## Reasons for Caution

You can't think "full-service grocer" without raising the fear of competition from discounters, and the Great Recession trained a lot of shoppers to look for the lowest possible prices, even if they had to go to two or three stores to complete a week's shopping. And now Amazon's acquisition of Whole Foods adds another competitive uncertainty. If the conventional grocery store format is condemned to the dustbin of retail history, Kroger could be vulnerable, but we feel it has the direction and wherewithal to adapt and upgrade both the shopping experience and the food basket to please today's choosier Millennial shoppers. But the razor-thin 1.8 percent profit margins characteristic of this industry leave little room for error. We continue to believe that differentiated bricks-and-mortar retail can still succeed in today's world, and we hope we're right that Kroger remains a category winner. But if we see them trying to compete broadly on price rather than selection, convenience, healthfulness, and so forth, it will be time to find another checkout line.

SECTOR: **Retail** ❏ BETA COEFFICIENT: **0.78** ❏ 10-YEAR COMPOUND EARNINGS PER-SHARE GROWTH: **12.0%** ❏ 10-YEAR COMPOUND DIVIDENDS PER-SHARE GROWTH: **12.0%**

|  | 2009 | 2010 | 2011 | 2012 | 2013 | 2014 | 2015 | 2016 |
|---|---|---|---|---|---|---|---|---|
| Revenues (bil) | 76.7 | 82.1 | 90.4 | 96.7 | 98.5 | 108.5 | 109.8 | 115.3 |
| Net income (mil) | 1,122 | 1,118 | 1,192 | 1,423 | 1,445 | 1,757 | 2,039 | 2,046 |
| Earnings per share | 0.87 | 0.87 | 1.00 | 1.32 | 1.43 | 1.76 | 2.06 | 2.12 |
| Dividends per share | 0.19 | 0.20 | 0.22 | 0.27 | 0.32 | 0.35 | 0.41 | 0.47 |
| Cash flow per share | 2.08 | 2.19 | 2.52 | 2.99 | 3.15 | 3.81 | 4.27 | 4.75 |
| Price: high | 13.5 | 12.1 | 12.9 | 13.5 | 21.9 | 32.5 | 42.8 | 35.0 |
| low | 9.7 | 9.5 | 10.5 | 10.5 | 12.6 | 17.8 | 27.3 | 28.3 |

Website: www.kroger.com

## CONSERVATIVE GROWTH

# McCormick & Company, Inc.

Ticker symbol: MKC (NYSE) ❏ Large Cap ❏ Value Line financial strength rating: A+ ❏ Current yield: 1.9% ❏ Dividend raises, past 10 years: 10

## Company Profile

"McCormick Brings Passion to Flavor" is their tasty slogan. The company manufactures, markets, and distributes spices, herbs, seasonings, flavors, and flavor enhancers to consumers and to the global food industry. It is the largest such supplier in the world. Customers range from retail outlets and food manufacturers to foodservice businesses.

McCormick's Consumer business (about 62 percent of sales), its oldest and largest, manufactures consumer spices, herbs, extracts, proprietary

seasoning blends, sauces, and marinades. Spices are sold under an assortment of recognizable brand names: McCormick, Lawry's, Zatarain's, Thai
Kitchen, Simply Asia, Club House, Billy Bee, Produce Partners, Golden
Dipt, Old Bay, and Mojave. The company estimates its retail market share
to be four times the nearest competitor.

Industrial customers include foodservice, food-processing businesses, and
retail outlets. The Industrial segment was responsible for 38 percent of sales.

Many of the spices and herbs purchased by the company, such as black
pepper, vanilla beans, cinnamon, and herbs and seeds, must be imported
from countries such as India, Indonesia, Malaysia, Brazil, and the Malagasy
Republic. Other ingredients such as paprika, dehydrated vegetables, onion,
garlic, and food ingredients other than spices and herbs originate in the
United States.

The company was founded in 1889 and has approximately 10,000
full-time employees in facilities located around the world. The company
has brands for sale in about 150 countries, and tapping into local tastes is
a priority—there are innovation centers in 14 countries. The biggest sales
components are Americas Consumer (41 percent), Americas Industrial (26
percent), EMEA Consumer (13 percent), EMEA Industrial (7 percent), and
Asia-Pacific Consumer (8 percent). McCormick has been innovating both
on the product and on web and media fronts, including more informative
print and web content with recipes and other information to spur cooking
with spices. Product innovations included the conversion of 75 percent of
their premium spice line to organic; the company is now number one in
the US for organic spices and seasonings and major US retail chains have
expanded the presence of these lines in response. New gluten-free and non-
GMO products and relabelings have entered the market. Overall, 9 percent
of 2016 sales came from products introduced in the past three years.

Too, for the past three years, the company has been ranked in the Top 5
out of 114 food brands in the US market for its "Digital IQ" index. The company has expanded the digital portion of its advertising budget from 11 percent
in 2011 to 46 percent last year. A new marketing campaign emphasized the
importance of flavor and quality of McCormick's spices and seasonings—the
company estimated a 2 percent rise in Millennial household penetration as a
result. More examples of innovative brand and Internet marketing include an
initiative to map your spice tastes by giving you a personalized "FlavorPrint"—
then emailing you weekly recipes with spice recommendations tailored to that
map. Flavor and flavor trend innovations include a new packaging initiative—
called Recipe Inspirations—to sell prepackaged spices set to cook a particular

meal. As well, they have a place on their website to enter in a singular spice, one that you might like and/or have an abundance of in your pantry; they shoot back recipes for that spice (something we amateur hash slingers have longed for in cookbooks; give me a selection of recipes that use allspice, for instance). All of these initiatives broaden the market to reach the millions of plain folks like us who weren't born with a wooden spoon in our mouths. For those who were born with such a spoon, or who acquired one through years of training and experience, there is also a "McCormick for Chefs" page. In short, we like this recipe: dominant brand, effective digital marketing to spice it up. McCormick continues to be one of the best examples we've seen.

## Financial Highlights, Fiscal Year 2016

Overall, business continues to respond nicely to new trends for more interesting foods and a stronger preponderance to stay at home for meals. Growth has slowed somewhat, but looks more attractive without currency effects; FY2016 revenues grew 3 percent but grew 6 percent (consumer) and 4 percent (industrial) on a constant dollar basis, mostly on brand marketing, new products, and distribution expansion. Margins rose slightly, and net earnings also increased about 6.5 percent and about 9 percent on a per-share basis.

A fine-tuning of the product mix toward higher-margined offerings and moderate productivity improvements should bring another 4–5 percent sales gain for FY2017 and a matching gain in earnings; top-line gains may slow to the 2–4 percent range for FY2018 while net income rises 9 percent on continuing margin improvement. Dividend increases, which have occurred for 31 straight years now, should continue, as should modest but steady share buybacks.

## Reasons to Buy

Simply put, McCormick dominates its food business niche and it's an important one—some 90 percent of food flavor is delivered with 10 percent of its cost, and flavor is the biggest determinant of choice. As a strong pure play in the seasonings business, McCormick is the largest branded producer of seasonings in North America and one of the largest in the world. McCormick is not just a producer, it is also an innovator and a marketer, and we feel they've done the right things to build interest in their products and in their brand. They also do well in specialized niche markets such as Mexico and China. We think they're in the right place as new, fresher, and more tailored, customized, interesting, and international food trends all emerge.

We also think they're in a pretty good place with Millennials, who want new, different, healthy, and customizable approaches to almost everything—including food—and who want to source their information about food and culinary excellence from the Internet.

On the consumer side, as amateur cooks ourselves we continue to feel that people would use more spices if they only knew how to use them. The website and its recipe offerings and the prepackaged Recipe Inspirations meal kits will get the less experienced cooks using spices more effectively in their own cooking. In our view, these initiatives, combined with continuing growth in the health-conscious segment by learning to replace fat flavoring with spice flavoring, will add to a solid business base for the company.

McCormick estimates the spice market to be growing at 6 percent annually, and with its 22 percent share of the global market, there is plenty of opportunity; market share expansion is a key strategy. That all mixes well with the profitability, stability, and defensive nature of the company; it's an attractive combination for investors.

## Reasons for Caution

Downsides include the rising cost of ingredients and the sourcing of many of these ingredients in geopolitically unstable regions. Top-line growth is likely to remain moderate except by acquisition; and projections seem muted in contrast to their view of global spice market growth (maybe they're just being conservative?). While earnings and share-price growth have been steady, the price of the stock has been spiced up a bit by its success. All that said, we don't see people's tastes in taste diminishing anytime soon.

SECTOR: **Consumer Staples** ▫ BETA COEFFICIENT: **0.48** ▫ 10-YEAR COMPOUND EARNINGS PER-SHARE GROWTH: **8.0%** ▫ 10-YEAR COMPOUND DIVIDENDS PER-SHARE GROWTH: **10.5%**

|  | 2009 | 2010 | 2011 | 2012 | 2013 | 2014 | 2015 | 2016 |
|---|---|---|---|---|---|---|---|---|
| Revenues (mil) | 3,192 | 3,339 | 3,650 | 4,014 | 4,123 | 4,243 | 4,396 | 4,411 |
| Net income (mil) | 311 | 356.3 | 380 | 408 | 418 | 442 | 450 | 479 |
| Earnings per share | 2.35 | 2.65 | 2.80 | 3.04 | 3.13 | 3.37 | 3.48 | 3.78 |
| Dividends per share | 0.96 | 1.04 | 1.12 | 1.24 | 1.36 | 1.48 | 1.60 | 1.72 |
| Cash flow per share | 3.08 | 3.39 | 3.55 | 3.85 | 4.00 | 4.24 | 4.36 | 4.64 |
| Price:        high | 36.8 | 47.8 | 51.3 | 66.4 | 75.3 | 77.1 | 87.5 | 107.8 |
|              low | 28.1 | 35.4 | 43.4 | 49.9 | 60.8 | 52.6 | 70.7 | 78.4 |

Website: www.mccormick.com

CONSERVATIVE GROWTH

# McKesson Corporation

Ticker symbol: MCK (NYSE) ❑ Large Cap ❑ Value Line financial strength rating: A++ ❑ Current yield: 0.8% ❑ Dividend raises, past 10 years: 7

## Company Profile

Sometimes even your surest bets—like our bets on healthcare—hit a rough patch. Such is the case with McKesson, one of our steadiest healthcare performers, and winners, over the years. We wrote about this last year, and to our surprise, it continues. The business hasn't changed much, but the valuation did, with a P/E ratio falling from the low 20s to—what, 11?—on some pricing weakness in generic and prescription lines, weakness in the international sector, and uncertainty about the Affordable Care Act. In emotional markets, often the business is just fine; the pricing of the stock gets out of whack. Once again we'll retain McKesson on the *100 Best* list, now as a top value pick, in the fundamentally solid healthcare industry.

McKesson Corporation is America's oldest and largest healthcare services company and engages in two distinct businesses to support the healthcare industry. Pharmaceutical and medical-surgical supply distribution is the first and by far the largest business: The company is the largest such distributor in North America, delivering about a third of all medications used daily to 50 percent of US hospitals and all but one of the top 25 health plans. The company delivers to approximately 40,000 pharmaceutical outlets as well as hospitals and clinics throughout North America from 28 domestic and 17 Canadian distribution facilities, and has just added a major distribution stronghold for Europe. The distribution business accounts for about 98 percent of sales.

Second, and not to be ignored, is a technology solutions business that provides clinical systems, analytics, clinical decision support, medical necessity and utilization management tools, electronic medical records, physical and financial supply-chain management, and connectivity solutions to hospitals, pharmacies, and an assortment of healthcare providers. "We build essential connections that make health care smarter" is their apt slogan. The strategically important information technology business is a $2.9 billion business all by itself. McKesson's software and hardware IT solutions are installed in some 76 percent of the nation's hospitals with more than 200 beds and 52 percent of hospitals overall.

The company offers products and services covering most aspects of pharmacy and drug distribution, including not only physical distribution and supply-chain services but also a line of proprietary generics and automated dispensing systems, record-keeping systems, and outsourcing services used in retail and hospital pharmacy operations. The central strategies are to provide a one-stop distribution solution for pharmaceuticals, generics, and surgical supplies, and to provide technology solutions to deliver higher-quality and more cost-effective care at the hospital and clinical levels.

In line with those strategies, McKesson continues along the path of acquiring significant healthcare businesses—large and small—to add to its core offering and to expand globally. In early 2014, the company completed the acquisition of German pharmaceutical distributor Celesio, gaining a strong entry into the international wholesale, retail, and generic distribution markets, particularly in Europe. In 2016 they acquired two more distributors in the UK and Ireland.

## Financial Highlights, Fiscal Year 2016

Once again you'd think that with a 30 percent drop in the share price, revenues and earnings would be marching backward at a rapid rate. FY2015 was indeed a bit soft on the earnings front, but revenues continue to advance and net earnings FY2016 through FY2018 are on a solid growth path. Revenues advanced about 5 percent in FY2016, with per-share earnings up a solid 29 percent from depressed 2015 levels and up 14 percent from the stronger FY2014. Forecasts call for 7–8 percent revenue growth annually through FY2018 and per-share earnings advances in the 10 percent range. The company will continue with moderate dividend increases and share buybacks (we'd like to see them buy back more at today's depressed share prices). MCK has also deployed significant cash—$4 billion—to pay off long-term debt from recent acquisitions.

## Reasons to Buy

Although price reductions do hurt in such a low-margin business, the distribution business continues to be solid and relatively recession-proof. Demographics and the addition of millions to the insured healthcare rolls have kept demand moving in the right direction, and acquisitions have strengthened that position in domestic and especially international markets. McKesson dominates its niches and is a go-to provider of much of what hospitals and clinics need to operate. It holds market leader position in several important market categories, including number one in pharmaceutical distribution in the United States and Canada, number one in generic pharmaceutical distribution, number one in medical management software and services to payers…you get the idea.

Additionally, hospitals and other healthcare providers are starting to get the memo that it is time to improve utilization and operational efficiency, and McKesson's technology solutions are hard to ignore, although many might do so at first glance, as they are only 2 percent of the business. As most distributors do, McKesson operates on very thin margins; the expansion of technology services and generic-equivalent drugs should eventually become a growth driver as efficiency measures continue to catch on.

The company has a strong track record of stability and operational excellence and is well managed; for long-term investors the recent share-price weakness would seem to signal a buying opportunity; a recent P/E of 11.5 seems too low for a company of this strength and track record, especially with solid earnings growth projected ahead.

## Reasons for Caution

McKesson does operate on thin margins and as such has a low tolerance for mistakes or major changes in the healthcare space, changes that could be brought on by legislation, regulation, or competition. Changes in the ACA could hurt some, as well as new efforts to reduce drug pricing, and other healthcare changes present more of a wild card than the company has faced in the past. We'd like to see a bit more return to shareholders in the form of cash dividends; that said, the company has quintupled the indicated dividend since 2007 and appears to be poised to continue on that path.

SECTOR: **Healthcare** ❑ BETA COEFFICIENT: **1.06** ❑ 10-YEAR COMPOUND EARNINGS PER-SHARE GROWTH: **16.0%** ❑ 10-YEAR COMPOUND DIVIDENDS PER-SHARE GROWTH: **15.0%**

|  |  | 2009 | 2010 | 2011 | 2012 | 2013 | 2014 | 2015 | 2016 |
|---|---|---|---|---|---|---|---|---|---|
| Revenues (bil) |  | 106.7 | 112.1 | 122.7 | 122.5 | 137.6 | 179.5 | 190.1 | 200.0 |
| Net income (mil) |  | 1,251 | 1,316 | 1,463 | 1,516 | 1,947 | 2,614 | 2,290 | 2,795 |
| Earnings per share |  | 4.58 | 5.00 | 6.05 | 6.33 | 8.35 | 11.11 | 9.84 | 12.70 |
| Dividends per share |  | 0.48 | 0.72 | 0.76 | 0.80 | 0.88 | 1.04 | 1.08 | 1.28 |
| Cash flow per share |  | 6.37 | 7.18 | 8.40 | 9.30 | 11.50 | 15.68 | 14.11 | 17.20 |
| Price: | high | 65.0 | 71.5 | 87.3 | 100.0 | 166.6 | 214.4 | 243.6 | 199.4 |
|  | low | 33.1 | 57.2 | 66.6 | 74.9 | 96.7 | 96.7 | 160.1 | 114.5 |

Website: www.mckesson.com

AGGRESSIVE GROWTH

# Medtronic, PLC

Ticker symbol: MDT (NYSE) ❑ Large Cap ❑ Value Line financial strength rating: A++ ❑ Current yield: 2.2% ❑ Dividend raises, past 10 years: 10

## Company Profile

Medtronic is the world's largest manufacturer of implantable medical devices and is a leading medical technology company, providing lifelong solutions to "alleviate pain, restore health, and extend life," primarily for people with chronic diseases. FY2015 was a year of major change for the company, as it completed a $50 billion acquisition of "rival" device maker Covidien, expanding sales by almost 40 percent mostly by gaining market share internationally and in three key segments: Surgical Solutions, Vascular Therapies, and Respiratory and Monitoring Solutions. Through the acquisition of Covidien, Medtronic also acquired an offshore headquarters in Dublin, Ireland, reducing tax rates and increasing net profit margins in the process.

Post-acquisition, Medtronic continues to operate mainly in the areas of cardiovascular, neurological, and other surgeries and therapies and in diabetes management. There are four business segments:

- Cardiac and Vascular Group (35 percent of FY2016 sales). Businesses include Cardiac Rhythm & Heart Failure, Coronary & Structural Heart, and Aortic & Peripheral Vascular. This group as a whole develops products that restore and regulate a patient's heart rhythm as well as improve the heart's pumping function. This segment markets implantable pacemakers, defibrillators, Internet and non-Internet–based monitoring and diagnostic devices, and cardiac resynchronization devices. Micra, a new implantable cardiac monitor about a third the size of an AAA battery and 80 percent smaller than competing products—about the size of a medicine capsule—exemplifies the company's R&D leadership in this industry, as do new efforts to automate remote monitoring and management of heart rhythm patients, a promising expansion of the "Internet of Things" concept into healthcare. Products also include therapies to treat coronary artery disease and hypertension, including balloon angioplasty catheters, guide catheters, diagnostic catheters, guidewires, and accessories. Another line of products and therapies treats heart valve disorders and repairs/replaces heart valves, some through catheters without chest incisions. The unit also markets tools to assist heart surgeons during surgery, including circulatory support systems, heart positioners and tissue stabilizers, ablation tools, stent graft, and angioplasty solutions.

- The Minimally Invasive Therapies Group (35 percent of sales) produces an assortment of products under its Surgical Solutions and Patient Monitoring and Recovery business units. The majority of Covidien's products fall into this group; hence the sales percentage rise from 12 percent to 29 percent between 2015 and 2016.

- The Restorative Therapies Group (24 percent of sales) includes Spine, Biologics, Neuromodulation, Surgical Technologies, and Neurovascular business units. The Spine unit develops and manufactures products that treat a variety of disorders of the cranium and spine, including traumatically induced conditions, deformities, herniated discs and other disc diseases, osteoporosis, and tumors. The Biologics business is the global leader in biologics regeneration and pain therapies across a variety of musculoskeletal applications including spine, orthopedic trauma, and dental. The Neuromodulation unit employs many technologies used in heart electrical stimulation to treat diseases of the central nervous system. It offers therapies for movement disorders; chronic pain; urological and gastroenterological disorders, including incontinence, benign prostatic hyperplasia (BPH), enlarged prostate, and gastroesophageal reflux disease (GERD); and psychological diseases. The Surgical Technologies unit develops and markets products and therapies for ear, nose, and throat–related diseases and certain neurological disorders; among them are precision image-guided surgical systems.

- The Diabetes Group (6 percent of sales) offers advanced diabetes management solutions, including insulin pump therapy, glucose monitoring systems, and treatment management software.

Overseas sales represent about 43 percent of the total; R&D is 7.7 percent of sales.

## Financial Highlights, Fiscal Year 2016

The Covidien acquisition, completed in early 2015, added about $8 billion in sales, 3 points to the net profit margin to the already-solid 22 percent due to tax savings and operational efficiencies, and about $3.3 billion to net profits. From 2015 to 2016, the first "apples to apples" measure post-acquisition, sales rose about 2.5 percent while net earnings rose only 1.5

THE 100 BEST STOCKS TO BUY IN 2018

percent. The weak performance was mostly due to currency, product launch delays, and some weakness in emerging markets. Figures perk up a bit for FY2017 and FY2018 with 3–4 percent top-line growth expected in 2017 and 4–5 percent expected for 2018. Earnings growth should be in a similar range. Steady dividend raises and share buybacks will continue to be part of the shareholder picture.

## Reasons to Buy

The name Medtronic continues to be synonymous with medical technology; the company remains one of the pure plays in the healthcare technology space. The company was already a "best in class" player in the markets and technologies it was engaged in, and over time its technologies have become more mainstream. Too, we are big supporters of its investments in remote medicine, its investments in emerging markets, and its involvement with new products and breakthroughs, especially in neuromodulation and diabetes management. The Covidien merger appears to be working both as a product line expansion and as an entry ticket into overseas markets. Finally, while the merger adds some acquisition risk and long-term debt, we expect the company to gradually retire the 400 million shares issued for the acquisition and to continue its steady track record of dividend increases.

## Reasons for Caution

Having an overseas headquarters in Ireland and a large manufacturing plant in Puerto Rico looked like a good idea until the Trump administration came to be; now there is some risk that strategy could backfire. Our previous concerns had to do with exposure to new trends in healthcare cost containment and utilization, particularly in the US—the new administration adds some uncertainty there, too. Adding Covidien's geographic and product line diversity tempers these concerns somewhat. Some might find the company's growth rates to be a little shy of the mark, which of course suggests more acquisitions may be forthcoming—another risk factor. Still, that all said, Medtronic continues to be a strong, entrenched leader in medical technology, and well positioned to get stronger still.

SECTOR: **Healthcare** ❑ BETA COEFFICIENT: **0.96** ❑ 10-YEAR COMPOUND EARNINGS PER-SHARE
GROWTH: **9.0%** ❑ 10-YEAR COMPOUND DIVIDENDS PER-SHARE GROWTH: **15.0%**

|  | | 2009 | 2010 | 2011 | 2012 | 2013 | 2014 | 2015 | 2016 |
|---|---|---|---|---|---|---|---|---|---|
| Revenues (mil) | | 15,817 | 15,933 | 16,184 | 16,590 | 17,005 | 20,261 | 26,833 | 29,500 |
| Net income (mil) | | 3,576 | 3,647 | 3,447 | 3,857 | 3,878 | 4,937 | 8,750 | 7,359 |
| Earnings per share | | 2.92 | 3.22 | 3.46 | 3.75 | 3.82 | 4.45 | 5.16 | 5.40 |
| Dividends per share | | 0.82 | 0.90 | 0.97 | 1.04 | 1.12 | 1.22 | 1.52 | 1.72 |
| Cash flow per share | | 3.96 | 4.16 | 4.13 | 4.60 | 4.73 | 5.15 | 7.28 | 7.55 |
| Price: | high | 44.9 | 46.7 | 43.3 | 44.6 | 58.8 | 75.7 | 79.5 | 89.3 |
| | low | 24.1 | 30.8 | 30.2 | 35.7 | 41.2 | 53.3 | 55.5 | 71.0 |

Website: www.medtronic.com

## AGGRESSIVE GROWTH

# Microchip Technology, Inc.

Ticker symbol: MCHP (NASDAQ) ❑ Large Cap ❑ Value Line financial strength rating: A ❑ Current
yield: 2.0% ❑ Dividend raises, past 10 years: 9

## Company Profile

Your washing machine senses the load, adjusts the wash time and temperature
accordingly, and tells you when it's done. Your refrigerator expands or contracts
its power cycle according to outside temperature and the time of day to save
on peak power costs. Your car shows you what it's about to back up into and
may even prevent such a collision in the first place. Your garage door opens at
the push of a button, allowing you to get the car out in the first place. Security
systems show you what's happening in all parts of your home—and in other
homes, such as that of your aging elders. Asset monitors keep track of inventory
and key business equipment. It's all connected, always on, all the time.

The "Internet of Things," this Star Wars world of all of our stuff connected to all our other stuff and doing our thinking for us, has arrived.
The possibilities are almost endless. But not every electronic product is connected to the Internet; many, many other products have intelligence and/
or ease-of-use features like touch sensitivity to make life easier; Microchip
Technology products provide the "distributed intelligence" for many of the
smart, feature-rich products we use every day.

Microchip Technology is a leading manufacturer and supplier of specialized semiconductor products primarily embedded as controllers, processors, or
memory into products, mostly products other than computers. The company's

devices, many of which are customizable, custom-made, or programmable, sense motion, temperature, touch, proximity, and other environmental conditions, process the information, and control the device accordingly. Applications number literally in the thousands but are concentrated in automotive, communications, consumer product, appliance, lighting, medical, safety and security, and power and energy management products. Microchip products are typically small in size (the smallest is 1.3 × 2.4 millimeters), low power, low cost, and capable of operating reliably in extreme conditions. The company offers a full suite of design assistance, tools, and consulting services to help customers, usually OEMs, develop the best applications. They position these services as "low-risk product development" resources for their customers.

Microchip owns most of its manufacturing capability in four plants: two in Arizona, one in Oregon, one in California, and one in Thailand, as part of a deliberate strategy to increase process yields and shorten cycle times (the list of facilities has grown somewhat at least short term with acquisitions, as we'll see). Most but not all products are shipped "off the shelf" with short cycle times or as a scheduled production. R&D accounts for about 17 percent of revenues. As the company sells primarily to other OEM electronic product manufacturers, about 84 percent of sales are to international customers; about 30 percent are to China. Technology licensing accounts for about 4 percent of revenues.

Microchip has more clearly aligned itself and its branding behind the concept of embedded control solutions and now calls itself "The Embedded Control Solutions Company"—a clear and well-defined business position. The company continues to be an active acquirer as the semiconductor industry consolidates; the latest in early 2016 is the $3.4 billion acquisition of microcontroller and touch technology supplier Atmel. Previous good-sized acquisitions in 2014–15 include communications device maker Micrel, Taiwan-based ISSC, a provider of semiconductors and solutions for the Bluetooth and wireless markets, Supertex, a medical and industrial lighting products company, and Belgian high-speed data and video transceiver maker EqcoLogic.

## Financial Highlights, Fiscal Year 2016

With all of the acquisitions it continues to be difficult to separate the "organic" growth from the total, which is quite impressive for FY2016. Beyond acquisitions, broad product acceptance, the expanding "IoT" (Internet of Things), and new products all led to a substantial 55 percent gain in revenues, and a corresponding gain in net profit. The company doesn't break out all the acquisitions but reports that Atmel accounted for about 10 percent of the 55 percent earnings gain. Still, Microchip is hitting on all cylinders. Revenue growth rates should return to a more steady 5–6 percent for FY2017 and FY2018, with per-share earnings growing in the 10–15 percent range annually. Share counts have risen somewhat with the acquisitions, but dividend growth may accelerate somewhat.

## Reasons to Buy

Distributed intelligence and the Internet of Things are upon us. One doesn't have to look hard to find "smart" products; they're almost everywhere. Not just your smartphone, but your appliances, car, climate-control system, alarm system, in elevators, airplanes, airports, hospitals—you name it. As their functionality improves, they will become a standard part of daily life, just as compact discs, Bluetooth, flat-screen TVs, smartphones—the Internet itself—have all become in the past few decades. Manufacturers will *have* to embrace these new technologies and build them in just to stay in the market.

We like companies that make the things that make things work, and Microchip seems well positioned as a leading supplier of all this intelligence as "smart" moves far beyond the "smartphone." We remain hesitant about semiconductor companies in general; development and manufacturing costs are high, especially if a company owns its own "fabs" (manufacturing facilities) and product cycles are short. There is plenty of competition everywhere for most products, much of it from lower-cost producers in Asia. Inventory cycles can also play havoc with semiconductor producers, who do best by producing in large quantities. Microchip, in our view, has overcome a lot of that by choosing high-value-add niches and by offering plenty of design and technical support "value add" to go along with the product—and now with its acquisitions, by becoming a more dominant player in its niche.

All that said—and for many of these reasons—it has also become a tradition for capital-intensive semiconductor companies to not pay dividends or much else in the way of cash returns to shareholders. Capital is gobbled up internally for what seems to be endless new investments in fab capacity, design tools, and ever more expensive materials and supplies. Microchip has bucked that trend—how many semiconductor firms have paid a dividend, let alone raised it, for nine consecutive years?

## Reasons for Caution

A tour through Microchip's website may convince you that this investment is not for the technologically faint-of-heart—the product assortment and applications are highly technical stuff, and unfortunately Microchip doesn't do much to make it easy to understand for the common person (or investor).

The growth-by-acquisition strategy makes us a little nervous, although we see the logic in niche dominance and in efficiency and scale.

It's a given that semiconductor makers will always endure the burdens of high capital requirements, short product cycles, inventory cycles of OEMs and distributors, and to no small degree the economy as a whole. Competition, especially from low-cost foreign suppliers, is keen in all semiconductor markets. To address all forms of competition, Microchip has worked hard to make its offering more "whole" with design assistance and short lead times, both of which have pleased its customers.

SECTOR: **Information Technology** ◻ BETA COEFFICIENT: **1.14** ◻ 10-YEAR COMPOUND EARNINGS PER-SHARE GROWTH: **11.0%** ◻ 10-YEAR COMPOUND DIVIDENDS PER-SHARE GROWTH: **4.0%**

|  | 2009 | 2010 | 2011 | 2012 | 2013 | 2014 | 2015 | 2016 |
|---|---|---|---|---|---|---|---|---|
| Revenues (mil) | 948 | 1,487 | 1,383 | 1,606 | 1,920 | 2,150 | 2,180 | 3,475 |
| Net income (mil) | 213 | 430 | 337 | 389 | 531 | 594 | 590 | 910 |
| Earnings per share | 1.14 | 2.21 | 1.65 | 1.89 | 2.45 | 2.65 | 2.65 | 3.90 |
| Dividends per share | 1.36 | 1.37 | 1.39 | 1.41 | 1.42 | 1.43 | 1.43 | 1.44 |
| Cash flow per share | 1.63 | 2.83 | 2.26 | 3.02 | 3.60 | 4.32 | 4.25 | 6.30 |
| Price:    high | 29.6 | 36.4 | 41.5 | 38.9 | 44.9 | 50.0 | 52.4 | 66.8 |
| low | 16.2 | 25.5 | 29.3 | 28.9 | 32.4 | 36.9 | 37.8 | 39.0 |

Website: www.microchip.com

AGGRESSIVE GROWTH

# The Mosaic Company

Ticker symbol: MOS (NYSE) ◻ Large Cap ◻ Value Line financial strength rating: A ◻ Current yield: 2.1% ◻ Dividend raises, past 10 years: 4

## Company Profile

Call us stubborn if you want. And sometimes we get stubborn about removing good companies experiencing bad times from our *100 Best* list.

As value-oriented investors, that stubbornness has often served us well, as it has with Itron, Otter Tail, Microchip Technologies, and many others on our current list. True, sometimes we hang on too long in the face of major strategic or market shifts, as we did perhaps last year with Macy's. And sometimes we don't hang on *long enough*, as happened with Tiffany's. In the case of Mosaic, which has been beaten up by the commodity bust and some competitive shifts inside the industry, we still think we see value—first, at a macro level, because of long-term trends and dependence on agriculture, and on a micro level because it's a well-run business and market leader. So we'll be stubborn and take the plunge—despite a plunge in sales, earnings, and the dividend—into Mosaic once again. Consider it a buying opportunity if you will. We hope we're right…and if not, we've just offered up another big bag of fertilizer.

"Helping the World Grow the Food it Needs" is the website headline for plant nutrient miner and producer Mosaic Company. Formed in 2004 through a merger of Cargill's fertilizer operations with IMC Global, Mosaic is the dominant world producer in the so-called "P+K" market—that's phosphorus and potassium, for those of you who shied away from high school chemistry. And in case you're not clear on why P and K are important, they are vital fertilizer ingredients and hence essential to most of the world's agriculture production. Plants require more potassium than any other nutrient besides nitrogen, and it is important to root-system development and many processes that form plant starch and proteins. Potassium is mined and sold in its oxide form known more popularly as potash. Phosphorus is a vital component of photosynthesis for plant metabolism and growth.

Mosaic is the largest combined—and among the most efficient—P+K producers in the world. About two-thirds of the business is phosphorus and a third potash. Both minerals are produced commercially in a limited number of places in the world. Mosaic has interests in the important locations in North and South America, notably Florida phosphorus mines and potash mines in Saskatchewan, Michigan, New Mexico, and Peru. Through a network of processing and packaging plants in several countries, the company sells its product in approximately 40 countries, and international sales account for about a third of the total.

## Financial Highlights, Fiscal Year 2016

As expected, a number of factors continued to plague the company in FY2016: weak agriculture prices, a resulting glut in channel inventories, weakness in Brazil, where Mosaic had made a significant investment in 2014, weakness in China, the stronger dollar, and a new resource tax levied by Canada affecting Saskatchewan potash mining. Commodity prices for P and K dipped another 25–33 percent. All together, revenues dropped 20 percent and earnings, hurt by low prices and poor operating leverage, were off about 70 percent. Many would justifiably close the book there, but channel inventories started to return to normal and prices strengthened a bit at the end of FY2016. A better supply/demand balance is now projected to bring sales growth in the 4–6 percent range annually through FY2018 with a stronger recovery after that. New efficiencies should bring better news to earnings to the tune of 15–25 percent gains annually, again accelerating after FY2018. We're betting that most of the bad news is in the rearview mirror now and that a stronger and more "resilient" Mosaic will capitalize strongly on the rebound. That said, the company cut its dividend almost in half; we were disappointed in this move but feel that a healthy dividend will soon return; in the meantime, buybacks continue at bargain prices.

## Reasons to Buy

Obviously, a lot depends on what happens from here, as the markets balance and prices and production recover. We're betting on Mosaic's long-term industry leadership in a long-term strategic industry. Demand for food will only increase over time—as much as 70 percent by 2050 according to company projections, and 90 percent of that will have to come from land already in production, which means it must be made more effective and efficient through induced nutrients—which of course are supplied by Mosaic, the largest of ten world producers of P+K. The combination of prime mining sites, size, and operational efficiency in its processing and distribution operations should lead to at least maintaining, if not expanding, market share. Cost savings are expected to reach $500 million annually by 2018, part of the "resiliency" strategy currently in play. While the recent dividend cut hurts, the company is wisely taking advantage of the low share price to buy back 10 million shares—3 percent annually—and expects to retire about a third of its shares in the ten-year period 2011–2020. In sum, we see good, "resilient" management, a leaner meaner emerging company, and continued emphasis on shareholder returns.

## Reasons for Caution

A lot of negatives have piled up for this company, and how they sort out over time will matter, although the company has enough financial strength and management savvy to deal with them in the best way possible. Commodity markets and commodity producers are inherently volatile, and any reduction in planting or backup in inventory, not to mention overall global economic weakness or short-term droughts, can drive prices down in a heartbeat. Low crop prices, while often driven by larger plantings (using more fertilizer) also strain farm budgets; this mixed effect is hard to predict and can cause short-term inventory disruptions. Commodity volume and price wars can be a race to the bottom, for if one company gains an advantage it doesn't usually last for long; we typically prefer companies that have paths other than cost and price to gain and sustain advantage. For Mosaic, we think the natural economics of world food demand and supply will take over; Mosaic continues to be a long-term story as well as a buying opportunity as market conditions begin to improve.

SECTOR: **Materials** ❑ BETA COEFFICIENT: **1.31** ❑ 10-YEAR COMPOUND EARNINGS PER-SHARE
GROWTH: **20.5%** ❑ 10-YEAR COMPOUND DIVIDENDS PER-SHARE GROWTH: **11.5**

|  | 2009 | 2010 | 2011 | 2012 | 2013 | 2014 | 2015 | 2016 |
|---|---|---|---|---|---|---|---|---|
| Revenues (mil) | 10,298 | 6,759 | 9,937 | 11,108 | 9,974 | 9,056 | 8,895 | 7,163 |
| Net income (mil) | 1,910 | 863 | 1,942 | 1,930 | 1,744 | 1,029 | 1,000 | 298 |
| Earnings per share | 4.28 | 1.93 | 4.34 | 4.42 | 4.09 | 2.68 | 2.78 | 0.85 |
| Dividends per share | 0.20 | 0.20 | 0.20 | 0.28 | 1.00 | 1.00 | 1.08 | 1.10 |
| Cash flow per share | 5.11 | 2.94 | 5.35 | 5.73 | 5.51 | 4.64 | 4.94 | 2.86 |
| Price:       high | 62.5 | 76.9 | 59.5 | 62.0 | 64.6 | 51.3 | 53.8 | 31.5 |
|             low | 31.2 | 37.7 | 44.9 | 44.4 | 39.8 | 40.3 | 27.0 | 22.0 |

Website: www.mosaic.com

## GROWTH AND INCOME

# NextEra Energy, Inc.

Ticker symbol: NEE (NYSE) ❑ Large Cap ❑ Value Line financial strength rating: A ❑ Current yield: 2.8% ❑ Dividend raises, past 10 years: 10

## Company Profile

NextEra is a full-service utility, power-generating unit, and utility services provider built around the utility stalwart Florida Power & Light, which formally changed its name to NextEra in 2010. NextEra not only represents an evolution in name but also a hint about how the company does business and expects to do business in the future as a leading user and innovator in clean and large-scale alternative energy sourcing for the power market.

Headquartered in Juno Beach, FL, FPL Group's principal operating subsidiaries are NextEra Energy Resources, LLC, and the original Florida Power & Light Company, the third-largest rate-regulated electric utility in the country. FP&L serves 8.9 million people and 4.8 million customer accounts in eastern and southern Florida. Through its subsidiaries, NextEra collectively operates the third-largest US nuclear power generation fleet and has a significant presence in solar and wind generation markets. NEE is the world's largest user of wind and sun resources to generate electricity. As proof that such leadership works, customer electricity rates in its operating territories are 30 percent below the national average.

As a nonregulated subsidiary, NextEra Energy Resources, LLC (or "NEER"), is a wholesale energy provider and is the world's largest generator of electricity from the wind and the sun. Unlike many other alternative-energy-driven businesses, it is a viable standalone business entity. About 95 percent of NEER's generation comes from clean or renewable fuels—wind (59 percent), natural gas (19 percent), nuclear (13 percent), solar (5 percent), and oil (4 percent).

NEER has 4,700 employees at 115 facilities in 25 states and Canada with solar and wind farms, nuclear energy facilities, and gas infrastructure operations in most of those locations. NEER's energy-producing portfolio includes 9,300 wind turbines on 110 farms in 19 states and four Canadian provinces which is estimated to comprise 17 percent of the entire wind power–generating capacity in the US, 14 percent of utility-scale solar power production, and 6 percent of total US nuclear power production. All told, the combined fuel mix of alternative energy and natural gas not only reduces NEE's overall fuel costs (30 percent of revenues, compared to 40s and 50s in much of the industry), but it also produces levels of sulfur dioxide (the cause of acid rain) some 97 percent below the average for the US electric industry, a nitrous oxide emission rate 79 percent below the industry, and a carbon dioxide ($CO_2$) emission rate 55 percent below industry averages—these numbers are still improving. The NEER subsidiary accounts for nearly a third of NextEra's total revenue—and nearly half of its profits—a healthy return for an alternative energy–based operation.

The company has a few small but promising nonregulated subsidiaries, offering design and consulting services for other alternative and conventional utility providers, and it also operates a fiber-optic network. NextEra is a regular winner of awards for most green, most ethical, and most admired companies—in fact, it made a Top 10 position on 2015 *Fortune*'s list of World's Most Admired Companies and was number one in the Utility industry category.

Finally, a planned acquisition of Hawaiian Electric fell through due to local opposition, but NEE is now acquiring Oncor, a distribution utility in east and north central Texas. Once again, the merger appears to be an attempt to lead the development of a "new era" for electric utilities integrating individual with centralized generation. NEE will likely set a path for optimized, integrated grids while also satisfying the state's desire to move to alternative energy platforms. Stay tuned—it should be another interesting show of NEE's global leadership in the electric industry.

## Financial Highlights, Fiscal Year 2016

Milder weather and Hurricane Matthew hurt both revenues and earnings—revenues dropped a surprising 7.5 percent while earnings dropped only 2.5 percent. Population growth plus continued expansion of the renewables and non-utility businesses should lead to annual top-line growth in the 4 percent range through FY2018, with earnings advancing in the 8 percent range, depending in part on regulatory cooperation—a pretty decent growth picture for a utility business. Notably, the dividend was raised 15 percent; similar raises are likely through 2018.

## Reasons to Buy

Every year we look forward to evaluating and writing about NextEra; they are leading so many initiatives in what's otherwise a pretty boring industry, and their website and presentation materials do a good job describing them.

For those who believe that alternative energy is the future for large-scale power generation, NextEra continues to be the best play available. The company continues to grow alternative energy capacity on all fronts, particularly wind and solar, and continues to make money on these efforts. All of this adds to the solid and traditional FP&L regulated utility base; this company has the steady feel of a traditional utility with a bit more interest in the form of alternative energy plays and leading-edge power utility technology. As previously mentioned, NEE will lead the way into figuring out the grid of the future, utilizing an optimized mix of centralized and distributed alternative and conventional generating resources. Cash flow is very strong and supports both hearty dividend increases and continued investments in alternative energy production but hasn't been used to reduce share counts.

## Reasons for Caution

The company's FP&L subsidiary is still a regulated utility and may not always receive the most accommodating treatment. Additionally, alternative energy tax credits may diminish over time. Alternative energy innovations and nuclear power carry some risk, and the merchant energy business has fallen on hard times of late. Too, the low price of natural gas makes some of the alternative energy offerings less attractive in the short run. Growth prospects lead to a relatively high share price and low yield for the industry—this is not your Grandma's utility stock—but NEE also is a clear leader in the industry, a trendsetter rather than a trend follower.

SECTOR: **Utilities** ❑ BETA COEFFICIENT: **0.23** ❑ 10-YEAR COMPOUND EARNINGS PER-SHARE GROWTH: **8.5%** ❑ 10-YEAR COMPOUND DIVIDENDS PER-SHARE GROWTH: **8.0%**

|                     |      | 2009   | 2010   | 2011   | 2012   | 2013   | 2014   | 2015   | 2016   |
|---------------------|------|--------|--------|--------|--------|--------|--------|--------|--------|
| Revenues (mil)      |      | 15,646 | 15,317 | 15,341 | 14,256 | 15,136 | 17,021 | 17,465 | 16,155 |
| Net income (mil)    |      | 1,615  | 1,957  | 2,021  | 1,911  | 2,062  | 2,469  | 2,761  | 2,687  |
| Earnings per share  |      | 3.97   | 4.74   | 4.82   | 4.56   | 4.83   | 5.60   | 6.06   | 5.78   |
| Dividends per share |      | 1.89   | 2.00   | 2.20   | 2.40   | 2.64   | 2.90   | 3.08   | 3.48   |
| Cash flow per share |      | 8.75   | 9.60   | 9.29   | 8.70   | 10.65  | 12.10  | 12.90  | 12.60  |
| Price:              | high | 60.6   | 56.3   | 61.2   | 72.2   | 89.8   | 110.8  | 112.6  | 132.0  |
|                     | low  | 41.5   | 45.3   | 49.0   | 58.6   | 69.8   | 84.0   | 93.7   | 102.2  |

Website: www.nexteraenergy.com

AGGRESSIVE GROWTH

# Nike, Inc.

Ticker symbol: NKE (NYSE) ❑ Large Cap ❑ Value Line financial strength rating: A++ ❑ Current yield: 1.3% ❑ Dividend raises, past 10 years: 10

## Company Profile

Nike is the world's largest designer, developer, and marketer of athletic foot-wear, apparel, and related equipment and accessory products. Products are sold through a mix of traditional and direct retail, including Nike-owned retail outlets (of which there are 362 in the US and 683 overseas), its web-site, and a mix of independent distributors and licensees in more than 190 countries around the world. Recently, the company has added specialized destination "Running Stores" and has expanded reach with more "Direct-to-Consumer," or DTC or "factory" outlets, carrying its traditionally strong product innovation to the channel and retail marketplace. DTC sales now account for 26 percent of Nike brand revenues.

Nike does no manufacturing—virtually all of its footwear and apparel items are fashioned by independent contractors outside the United States, while equipment products are produced both in the United States and abroad. In total, there are 142 footwear and 394 apparel factories in 39 countries, the largest of which accounted for 7 percent of total footwear production.

Nike's shoes are designed primarily for athletic use, although a large per-centage of them are worn for casual or leisure purposes. Shoes are designed for men, women, and children for running, training, basketball, and soccer use, although the company also carries brands for casual wear. The company has been very successful with its offerings for the women's market.

Nike sells apparel and accessories for most of the sports addressed by its shoe lines, as well as athletic bags and accessory items. Nike apparel and accessories are designed to complement its athletic footwear products, feature the same trademarks, and are sold through the same marketing and distribution channels. The new buzzword is "athleisure," and Nike is there front and center. All Nike-branded products are marketed with the familiar "swoosh" logo, one of the most recognized and successful branding images in history.

Nike has a number of wholly owned subsidiaries, or "affiliate brands," including Converse, Hurley, Jordan, and Nike Golf, which variously design, distribute, and license dress, athletic, and casual footwear, sports apparel, and accessories, some targeted to specific audiences like Hurley to a youth audience.

Nike-branded products account for about 94 percent of 2016 revenues. Of the total $30.5 billion in Nike-branded revenues (excluding subsidiaries), about 65 percent of it comes from footwear, 30 percent from apparel, and the remainder from equipment. Footwear remains the fastest-growing segment of the business at 8 percent; the much smaller Converse subsidiary accounts for the remaining 6 percent of the total business and was roughly flat for the year. Equipment declined 8 percent as Nike exited the golf equipment business (golf clothing will remain).

In total, 53 percent of FY2016 sales came from outside the US. Approximately 46 percent of sales come from North America, 18 percent from Western Europe, 11 percent from China, 4 percent from central and eastern Europe, 2.5 percent from Japan, and 11 percent from other emerging markets. FY2016 growth came from China (23 percent), Japan (15 percent), and North America (7 percent), while emerging markets were actually off 5 percent.

## Financial Highlights, Fiscal Year 2016

FY2016 revenues slowed to a fast jog but were up despite currency effects, disruptions in the retail channel, and soft emerging markets. Sales rose 6 percent—but 12 percent on a constant currency basis. While labor and material costs rose again, the company also leveraged newer, higher-margined products, firm pricing, DTC sales, and some operating efficiencies into another 0.3 percent increase in operating margins (to 15.9 percent) to cross the finish line with a winning 15 percent gain in net income. That and another 1.3 percent share buyback combined to strengthen per-share earnings by almost 17 percent.

Maturing markets are slowing growth somewhat, but the company remains well positioned for growth especially for its size. For the next two years, revenues are projected up 6–8 percent and net income up 5–8 percent annually over the two-year pull through 2018. Double-digit dividend increases and 1–3 percent share buybacks should continue through the period.

## Reasons to Buy

Why buy Nike? In a word, brand—and brand extension. The Nike brand and its corresponding swoosh continue to be one of the most recognized—and sought after—brands in the world. It is a lesson in simplicity and image congruence with the product behind it. Nike doesn't sit still with it; rather, the company is learning to leverage it into more products outside the traditional athletic wear circuit even to a new line of GPS watches and apps to find, say, a new route for your run and to track your performance right on your phone. The company continues to invest in innovation in all of its segments, including new fabrics, colors, uniform materials, and digital linkages to make active lifestyles more productive and fun—and it is now extending this innovation further into marketing and retail. Today's "fast fashion" context requires fast time-to-market, and the innovation cycle at Nike has been turned into more of a sprint in response. As well, Nike doesn't just limit the brand appeal to athletes: Slogans such as "Just Do It" and "If you have a body, you're an athlete" emphasize the appeal and lifestyle across all segments of the population. We continue to think this is drop-dead smart.

We also think it's drop-dead smart to be investing in the DTC channel now, as traditional retail struggles. Nike is in the front of the pack in this regard, a good thing as the retail shift accelerates. Improved manufacturing efficiencies, strong channel relationships, and international exposure all keep the company moving faster in the right direction. Despite its size, the company continues to deliver double-digit per-share earnings, cash flow, and dividend growth. We continue to like the combination of protected profitability through brand excellence, operational excellence, and a clean conservative balance sheet, all providing a good combination of safety and growth potential. Finally, the recent slowdown to a fast jog has enabled some of us looking for good entry points to finally get onto the track.

## Reasons for Caution

Our biggest source of caution this year, as sales growth slowed somewhat, was whether the Nike brand resonates as well with the upcoming Millennial generation as it did with us for so many years since the company's inception in the early eighties. In particular, we looked at some more "trendy" brands like Under Armour, and after seeing some of their struggles, decided that the slowdown was probably related more to an overall maturity of this market than a brand shift away from Nike. Nike is still the best pair of shoes in this race.

Other risks come from the rollout of the DTC channel in keeping the right balance between DTC and traditional wholesale and in avoiding channel conflicts. Risks also include higher labor and commodity input prices. Second, the company has occasionally been in the news—and the rumor mill—for unfair labor practices and child labor violations in some of its foreign manufacturing plants. The company doesn't actually own or operate these plants, but the rumors can stick nonetheless.

SECTOR: **Consumer Discretionary** ▫ BETA COEFFICIENT: **0.47** ▫ 10-YEAR COMPOUND EARNINGS PER-SHARE GROWTH: **12.5%** ▫ 10-YEAR COMPOUND DIVIDENDS PER-SHARE GROWTH: **16.0%**

|  |  | 2009 | 2010 | 2011 | 2012 | 2013 | 2014 | 2015 | 2016 |
|---|---|---|---|---|---|---|---|---|---|
| Revenues (mil) | | 19,176 | 19,014 | 20,862 | 24,128 | 25,313 | 27,799 | 30,601 | 32,376 |
| Net income (mil) | | 1,727 | 1,907 | 2,133 | 2,223 | 2,464 | 2,693 | 3,273 | 3,750 |
| Earnings per share | | 0.88 | 0.97 | 1.10 | 1.18 | 1.35 | 1.49 | 1.85 | 2.16 |
| Dividends per share | | 0.25 | 0.27 | 0.30 | 0.35 | 0.41 | 0.47 | 0.52 | 0.62 |
| Cash flow per share | | 1.06 | 1.15 | 1.30 | 1.42 | 1.62 | 1.85 | 2.26 | 2.62 |
| Price: | high | 16.7 | 23.1 | 24.6 | 28.7 | 40.1 | 49.9 | 68.2 | 65.4 |
| | low | 9.6 | 15.2 | 17.4 | 21.3 | 25.7 | 34.9 | 45.3 | 49.0 |

Website: www.nikeinc.com

CONSERVATIVE GROWTH

# Norfolk Southern Corporation

Ticker symbol: NSC (NYSE) ▫ Large Cap ▫ Value Line financial strength rating: A ▫ Current yield: 2.0% ▫ Dividend raises, past 10 years: 9

## Company Profile

Norfolk Southern Corporation was formed in 1982 as a holding company when the Norfolk & Western Railway merged with the Southern Railway. Including lines received in the split takeover (with CSX) of Conrail, the current railroad operates 21,000 route-miles of track in 22 eastern and southern states. It serves every major port on the East Coast of the United States and has the most extensive intermodal network in the east.

Company business in FY2016 was about 15 percent coal (down from the high teens and low 20s in previous years), 63 percent carload industrial, agricultural, chemical, automotive, and basic materials products, and 22 percent intermodal. Major gateways include ports in the eastern half of the US, Great Lakes ports, and major interchange points with the two major Western systems, Union Pacific (another *100 Best* stock) and Burlington Northern Santa Fe. The company estimates that its networks reach 65 percent of US manufacturing and 55 percent of US energy consumption. In the late 1990s, the company split the acquisition of northeastern rail heavyweight Conrail with rival CSX Corporation, so it has considerable operations in the Northeast and Midwest in addition to its traditional southern base. The heaviest traffic corridors are New York–Chicago; Chicago–Atlanta; and Cleveland–Kansas City. The company has a diverse base of large Midwestern factories and large and smaller southern factories and basic materials producers in the coal, chemical, automotive, and lumber industry, giving a well-diversified traffic base.

The company provides a number of logistics services and has substantial traffic to and from ports and overseas destinations. The opening of the widened Panama Canal is giving some lift to southern and East Coast ports, which NSC serves well. The company has an active program to attract lineside customers to build freight volumes.

## Financial Highlights, Fiscal Year 2016

Continued shifts in the energy market, which first reduced coal and now oil shipments, are still affecting NSC. Coal revenues were down another 19 percent in FY2016 on top of a 33 percent drop in FY2015. Coal is now 15 percent of revenues, down from 31 percent in 2011. Oil, which had made up some of the shortfall, is now in decline as well as the recent oversupply has cut into domestic production. Other commodities made up some of the gap, but overall FY2016 revenues declined just under 6 percent. However, lower fuel costs and an assortment of operational improvements led to a 7 percent increase in net earnings, and a solid 2.5 percent share buyback hit the whistle for a 10 percent per-share earnings rise. As the US industrial economy strengthens and higher oil prices bring resumed drilling activity, the company is now projecting revenue gains in the 4–6 percent range through FY2018, with continued productivity gains and share buybacks giving a green light to per-share earnings gains in the 10–12 percent range through the period. The key "operating ratio" measure—the ratio of variable to total costs—was back down to a healthy 68.9 after rising to 72.6 in 2015. It was 75.4 in 2011.

## Reasons to Buy

NSC and its competitors have all been hurt, first by the coal slowdown, then the slowdown in exports due to the dollar, and finally, by a slowdown in oil shipments and fracking supplies necessary to support oil production. But we appear to be at the end of the cycle—demand for these commodities should recover—and in the meantime, NSC, like other companies, became more efficient in the interim and is well positioned to perform even better as freight volumes recover. It remains to be seen how much the trade policies of the Trump administration will affect domestic business, but a renewed emphasis on US manufacturing will help NSC, as will the Panama Canal widening.

Additionally, NSC serves some of the more dynamic and up-and-coming manufacturing markets in the United States, namely, Asian and other foreign-owned manufacturing facilities found particularly in the Southeast. The company has created a Heartland Corridor time freight and double-stack container routing between Chicago and the East Coast, reducing distance by 250 miles and, more importantly, transit time is down from four to three days. Similar improvements have occurred on its Crescent Corridor between Louisiana and New Jersey. Such innovations will further assert the company's leadership. Additionally, we like the strength and diversity coming from serving the domestic and especially the foreign-owned auto industry—the company serves plants for (in alphabetical order) BMW, Chrysler, Ford, General Motors, Honda, Isuzu, Mazda, Mercedes-Benz, Mitsubishi, Nissan, Subaru, Suzuki, and Toyota.

Finally, cash flow continues to be strong. The company decided against a dividend raise due to soft business in 2016, but otherwise the track record of raises and share buybacks is excellent.

## Reasons for Caution

The decline in coal traffic, which mostly supports electric utilities, also exposes the company more to general economic downturns as the remaining mix is more economically sensitive. Oil-related traffic may take a while to come back if energy prices stay low and if pipeline building resumes at full speed ahead due to Trump administration policies. Too, oil shipments expose the company to headline risk and accidents.

Finally, in the railroad industry, as in other capital-intensive, high–fixed-cost industries, it's hard to have just the right amount of capacity. Too much volume can actually be a bad thing as it overtaxes physical plant and causes service disruptions, but we think NSC has made the right investments and has proven agile overall in managing business cycles. That said, major changes in traffic flows due to new trade policies could cause some short-term hiccups.

Finally, the stock price has risen sharply in view of the end of the down cycle; it would be wise to stop, look, and listen before investing.

SECTOR: **Transportation** □ BETA COEFFICIENT: **1.24** □ 10-YEAR COMPOUND EARNINGS PER-SHARE GROWTH: **10.5%** □ 10-YEAR COMPOUND DIVIDENDS PER-SHARE GROWTH: **19.0%**

|  | | 2009 | 2010 | 2011 | 2012 | 2013 | 2014 | 2015 | 2016 |
|---|---|---|---|---|---|---|---|---|---|
| Revenues (mil) | | 7,969 | 9,516 | 11,172 | 11,040 | 11,245 | 11,624 | 10,513 | 9,888 |
| Net income (mil) | | 1,034 | 1,498 | 1,853 | 1,749 | 1,850 | 2,000 | 1,556 | 1,668 |
| Earnings per share | | 2.76 | 4.00 | 5.27 | 5.37 | 5.85 | 6.39 | 5.11 | 5.62 |
| Dividends per share | | 1.36 | 1.40 | 1.68 | 1.94 | 2.04 | 2.22 | 2.36 | 2.36 |
| Cash flow per share | | 5.07 | 6.48 | 8.22 | 8.49 | 8.96 | 9.57 | 8.76 | 9.25 |
| Price: | high | 54.8 | 63.7 | 78.4 | 78.5 | 93.2 | 117.6 | 112.1. | 111.4 |
| | low | 26.7 | 46.2 | 57.6 | 56.1 | 62.7 | 87.1 | 72.1 | 64.5 |

Website: www.nscorp.com

**AGGRESSIVE GROWTH**

# Novo Nordisk A/S

Ticker symbol: NVO (NYSE) □ Large Cap □ Value Line financial strength rating: A++ □ Current yield: 2.7% □ Dividend raises, past 10 years: 9

## Company Profile

Unfortunately, diabetes is a huge and growing disease as more people around the world live to an older age and eat higher-calorie diets. Novo Nordisk, which started out in the early 1920s as two separate diabetes medicine producers, merged in 1989 and now garners almost 80 percent of its current $16 billion in revenues supplying diabetes medicine and care products. The company estimates that it owns 46 percent of the world market and 36 percent of the US market for insulin.

Although diabetes is a complex disease for which the many treatments aren't easy to understand, it does break down into two "types" (really, three, if you include the rarer gestational diabetes occurring only in pregnant women): Type 1, in which the pancreas fails to produce enough insulin (and regular insulin supplements are required), and Type 2, a condition whereby cells fail to absorb insulin properly, often called "adult onset" diabetes. NVO estimates that 415 million people (about 6 percent of the world population) have diabetes of one type or another—and that only about half of them have been diagnosed. On top of that, NVO estimates that 600 million live with obesity, which has a tendency to bring on diabetes. The company estimates that its products are used by about 25 million people worldwide today, and plans to grow this to 40 million by 2020.

Major products include traditional human-based insulin and protein-related products for Type 1 diabetes treatment, which are being replaced by higher-performance "modern" and "new generation" insulins. The company is now rolling out several new-generation insulins. One is *Tresiba*, which lasts 42 hours or more; as with many such rollouts the product became well established abroad before attaining US FDA approval. Another treatment called *Ryzodeg* for both Type 1 and Type 2 diabetes is manufactured artificially. It is absorbed faster and lasts longer than traditional human insulin and has recently launched in Japan. Another called *Xultophy* for Type 2 diabetes and hypoglycemia treatment, which has been rolled out in Europe, is gearing up for its US launch. Another product, with the rather nondescript moniker "NN218" delivers a faster-acting insulin for both diabetes types and is up for approval in both Europe and the US. Another recently approved new treatment called *Saxenda* addresses obesity and overweight adults with Type 2 diabetes or cardiovascular problems. And still another fast-acting insulin called *Fiasp* has been approved for marketing in Europe.

You can see the pattern and emphasis on new, more effective formulas and delivery systems (including new oral delivery systems) typically being approved and rolled out in non-FDA-controlled markets first. By the time they hit the US, they are both proven and more profitable. These new therapies now comprise over half of the overall diabetes care revenue stream, are growing at a 20–35 percent clip annually, and deliver both sales growth and higher margins.

We shouldn't ignore the 20 percent of Novo Nordisk devoted to diseases outside the diabetes space. The Biopharmaceuticals segment targets hemophilia and other bleeding disorders, hormone-replacement therapies, and human growth hormone markets. The model is similar—pioneering approvals outside the US, then migrating them into US markets. The company spends about 15 percent of revenues on R&D; about 51 percent of sales in total come from the US, which the company indicates is currently responsible for 37 percent of its top-line growth.

## Financial Highlights, Fiscal Year 2016

When you're particularly strong in a key segment of a key industry such as diabetes and healthcare, sometimes you attract the wrong kind of attention. So it was for Novo Nordisk in 2016, as diabetes became a focus area for reducing health costs by insurers and in the course of political rhetoric in the US and other nations. The "crackdown" led to a rapid slowing of growth in the key US market in mid-2016 and going forward into 2017, with a significant cut in both revenue and profit growth projections. FY2016 sales growth slowed to less than 1 percent, while earnings growth slowed to 5 percent. New products are expected to return growth to a 3–5 percent annual rate through FY2018—slower than earlier forecasts, while earnings are projected flat in FY2017 and resuming to a 5 percent growth rate in FY2018. This is well off the 15–20 percent sales and earnings gains experienced in the recent past. Meanwhile, NVO has plans to retire about 10 percent of its shares over the next few years and grow the dividend at something around 10 percent. Also worth noting: the company has zero long-term debt and, since domiciled outside the US, enjoys a tax rate in the low 20s versus low 30s for most US-based corporations.

## Reasons to Buy

Despite the recent hiccup—again reflecting its dominance in key healthcare areas—Novo Nordisk still appears to be an excellent long-term growth story. It is the closest thing to a "pure play" in the diabetes market, and it's an important player in obesity, growth disorder, coagulation (hemophilia), and hormone replacement markets as well. There is a lot of interest in new medications such as *Saxenda* that address obesity and diabetes simultaneously.

Steady revenues and profits from a traditional insulin treatment base fund new research and releases of more effective, more tailored, easier-to-use diabetes treatments. Despite the recent pricing pressures, we still feel very comfortable with this course, and the strong international footprint allows them to gain regulatory and market acceptance long before they enter the prized US market. Financials, too, continue to be excellent.

## Reasons for Caution

Once you're targeted as a "bad guy" in healthcare, it can take a long time to shake that notion. We don't think NVO has been a bad guy, nor do we hear reports of predatory pricing rampant in other parts of the drug industry. That said, the company is making 32–33 percent net profit margins, so some may see room for complaint, and a less aggressive stance on pricing and growth may rule for a while. Naturally, we are concerned about regulatory approvals, attempts to control prescription drug costs, and the potential aggressiveness of competitors, who could want their bigger slice of this lucrative market. Some regulatory bodies outside the US are holding prices to less-than-acceptable levels—the blockbuster Tresiba was taken off the market in Germany recently as a consequence because the price was held by regulators to the level of ordinary insulin, something the company refers to as an "extreme" case. Finally, even though Novo presents itself well, it is in a complex business on a complex international stage; it continues to push our "buy businesses you understand" mantra to its limits.

SECTOR: **Healthcare** ◻ BETA COEFFICIENT: **0.75** ◻ 10-YEAR COMPOUND EARNINGS PER-SHARE GROWTH: **21.0%** ◻ 10-YEAR COMPOUND DIVIDENDS PER-SHARE GROWTH: **26.5%**

|  |  | 2009 | 2010 | 2011 | 2012 | 2013 | 2014 | 2015 | 2016 |
|---|---|---|---|---|---|---|---|---|---|
| Revenues (mil) | | 9,842 | 10,814 | 11,559 | 13,384 | 15,435 | 14,511 | 15,779 | 15,832 |
| Net income (mil) | | 2,075 | 2,563 | 2,979 | 3,800 | 4,651 | 4,326 | 5,093 | 5,356 |
| Earnings per share | | 0.69 | 0.88 | 1.04 | 1.38 | 1.73 | 1.65 | 1.98 | 2.11 |
| Dividends per share | | 0.22 | 0.27 | 0.38 | 0.50 | 0.62 | 0.83 | 0.73 | 1.41 |
| Cash flow per share | | 0.87 | 1.05 | 1.24 | 1.58 | 1.95 | 1.88 | 2.19 | 2.32 |
| Price: | high | 14.0 | 22.8 | 26.6 | 34.1 | 38.9 | 49.1 | 60.3 | 58.2 |
| | low | 8.3 | 12.8 | 18.9 | 22.8 | 29.9 | 36.6 | 41.7 | 30.9 |

Website: www.novonordisk.com

## AGGRESSIVE GROWTH

# Oracle Corporation

Ticker symbol: ORCL (NYSE) ◻ Large Cap ◻ Value Line financial strength rating: A++ ◻ Current yield: 1.7% ◻ Dividend raises, past 10 years: 8

## Company Profile

Founded in 1978 as the rather blandly named Software Development Laboratories, Oracle Corporation has since grown to become the second-largest software company in the world (by revenue) only behind Microsoft. The company's early entry into the then-new relational database market eventually led to an extended period of dominance for that flagship product (the Oracle Database) in the enterprise market. The company successfully leveraged this position with associated software and hardware products through acquisitions and internal development and now has a strong presence in both the middleware and applications space.

Oracle was one of the early proponents of cloud architecture before the name "cloud" became a catchall for any remotely run and managed software. As a consequence, today some of the company's strongest growth vectors are in what are becoming widely adopted IaaS, PaaS, and SaaS architectures (Infrastructure/Platform/Software as a Service). In this space, the customer doesn't own the tool or application but rather pays a fee to use it on a remote server.

The company owes its current product breadth to both internal development and an aggressive acquisition strategy, most significantly with the purchases of applications software provider PeopleSoft in 2004, hardware supplier Sun Microsystems in 2010, and e-commerce software specialist NetSuite in 2016. Acquisitions continue to be a focus for Oracle, with over $70 billion spent since 2006 and $12 billion spent in 2016 alone, mostly on small firms in the tool, applications, and security spaces.

## Financial Highlights, Fiscal Year 2016

Revenues in FY2016 (ending June 1) were flat to slightly down for Oracle, though sales were actually up slightly on a constant-currency basis. Currency headwinds, however, reduced total revenue by 5 percent and operating margin by 7 percent. The bottom line for FY2016 came in slightly below expectations for Oracle, also affected by the transition to SaaS and PaaS in their customer base, which cut somewhat into the growth of the company's more profitable software service and licensing businesses. Margins in the licensing and service segment of the business grew slightly to 91 percent nonetheless.

Revenues and margins on hardware products (the old Sun business) continued to struggle, with a 13 percent decline in revenue and a drop in margins to just 2 percent of revenue. Cost cuts and restructuring are in order for that business. In total, Oracle is projecting revenues flat to ahead 1 percent in FY2017 and up 3–4 percent in FY2018, with similar figures for net earnings. The stronger earnings gains are expected in 2019 and beyond as the cloud-based models achieve scale. Annual share buybacks in the 2–3 percent range appear likely, with gradual dividend increases as well.

## Reasons to Buy

Oracle is one of those rare beasts: a mature technology company. There aren't many, and at the ripe old age of 40 years, Oracle is clearly in select company. The fact that they've been able to grow and remain at the head of the pack in an industry where it is commonplace for technological tidal shifts to eliminate entire classes of companies speaks to their robust market awareness, sound and aggressive acquisition strategy, and competent execution.

That said, this is a large company with a large presence in older, slow-growth businesses. For decades Oracle was a strong proponent of captive, in-house IT operations and sold software, hardware, and services into that segment quite successfully. As this model fades in favor of SaaS/PaaS and similar models that require less capital investment, Oracle is in the happy position of having a solid, high-margin revenue stream to fund the development of the replacement. Many of their competitors in this developing space are not as established or as well funded and so will need to be good, fast, and lucky, where Oracle really just has to be good. Displacing an existing Oracle "seat" (software installation) will require a long sales cycle and a compelling solution. Retaining an Oracle seat, however, simply requires a reasonable transition and a credible road map going forward. Oracle thus gains a helpful march on their competition during this critical period of transition to the new computing model.

The company's financials are in good shape, with impressive gains in cash flow funding both a new and growing dividend and solid, steady reductions in outstanding shares (down 27 percent in the last fifteen years). The yield is not great at 1.7 percent, but with a payout ratio (dividends to per-share earnings) of just 28 percent, there's certainly room for it to grow.

A quick glance at Oracle's share price history does not stir the blood. But looking at Oracle's revenues and share price over the past five years (which have been basically flat) does not really inform the reader. The bigger part of the story here is what the company has been doing to prepare for the current transitional period in their major business. Having platforms and strategies in place to cannibalize your own businesses is far preferable to having others eat it for you.

## Reasons for Caution

Oracle would never admit to overpaying for some of their acquisitions, but it's clear in retrospect that some of their purchases have been driven less by the numbers and perhaps more by exuberance. The Sun acquisition, which we actually defended previously as a move to sell a bundled software and platform solution, has not turned out as well as hoped. The numbers have not been a disaster, but Oracle has scaled back the scope of the Sun business more than most had expected.

In their cloud businesses, Oracle's IaaS infrastructure service will be going up against established IBM SoftLayer and Amazon Web Service offerings. IaaS is inherently a lower-margin model, and the marketplace challenges will be significantly greater than in SaaS/PaaS. More broadly, the company must not become too complacent or play fast and loose with its existing installed base, which today is one of its chief advantages and "moats" against its rivals.

SECTOR: **Information Technology** ❑ BETA COEFFICIENT: **1.05** ❑ 10-YEAR COMPOUND EARNINGS PER-SHARE GROWTH: **15.5%** ❑ 10-YEAR COMPOUND DIVIDENDS PER-SHARE GROWTH: **41.4%**

|  | 2009 | 2010 | 2011 | 2012 | 2013 | 2014 | 2015 | 2016 |
|---|---|---|---|---|---|---|---|---|
| Revenues (mil) | 23,495 | 27,034 | 35,850 | 37,221 | 37,253 | 38,305 | 38,253 | 37,056 |
| Net income (mil) | 7,393 | 6,494 | 11,385 | 12,520 | 12,958 | 13,214 | 12,489 | 11,236 |
| Earnings per share | 1.44 | 1.67 | 2.22 | 2.46 | 2.68 | 2.87 | 2.77 | 2.61 |
| Dividends per share | 0.05 | 0.20 | 0.20 | 0.24 | 0.30 | 0.48 | 0.51 | 0.60 |
| Cash flow per share | 1.53 | 1.75 | 2.32 | 2.65 | 2.91 | 3.10 | 3.04 | 2.93 |
| Price:      high | 25.1 | 32.3 | 36.5 | 34.3 | 38.3 | 46.7 | 45.3 | 42.0 |
|          low | 13.8 | 21.2 | 24.7 | 25.3 | 29.9 | 35.4 | 35.1 | 33.1 |

Website: www.oracle.com

## AGGRESSIVE GROWTH

# Ormat Technologies

Ticker symbol: ORA (NYSE) ❑ Mid Cap ❑ Value Line financial strength rating: C++ ❑ Current yield: 0.7% ❑ Dividend raises, past 10 years: 6

## Company Profile

Ormat Technologies, a developer and operator of geothermal plants and maker of thermal power recovery products, is the largest geothermal energy pure play in North America. A renewed interest in baseline "green" power, combined with a growing need for electrification far from traditional grid-based solutions puts Ormat in a unique position as a provider of clean, always-on baseline electricity at the lowest operating cost of any solution. "Green energy you can rely on" is their apt slogan.

The company operates in two business segments. The Electricity segment builds, owns, and operates geothermal power plants, selling the electricity mostly into the grid as a wholesale power generator. The Product segment sells power plant equipment utilizing their proprietary geothermal technology to geothermal operators and to industrial users for use in remote power generation and recovered energy applications.

Ormat's total worldwide installed capacity is 713 megawatts, concentrated in 19 sites mainly in the states of Nevada and California. Their geothermal plants (66 percent of 2016 revenue) top out at about 35MW each in the western United States, the Pacific Rim, and the Mediterranean and east Africa.

The Product segment has sold and built 150 power plants producing 2,200 megawatts in installations located around the world, including far-off locations such as Turkey, Ethiopia, and Indonesia as supported by the local geology. The power generation products are particularly attractive for harsh, remote locations as the technology requires very little in the way of management or maintenance. The company also produces "REGs"—Recovered Energy Generation units, which produce electricity from nearly any form of waste heat. The vast majority of these units are currently sold outside of the United States and are commonly used in gas pipeline compressor stations, but are suited to any process which generates significant waste heat, including oil refineries.

The company owns over 100 patents on its efficient "binary" geothermal energy conversion process and related technologies. Their products do not require exotic manufacturing processes or materials, and the company builds almost all of its own products at its plants in Nevada and Israel.

### Financial Highlights, Fiscal Year 2016

For FY2016, Electricity segment revenues rose 16 percent mainly due to three new plants coming online; most prices are fixed by purchased power agreements. Product segment revenues rose 3.5 percent, helped along by new revenue from a plant built by the unit. In total, revenues increased about 11 percent. Net income shows a modest decline from FY2015 but only because an exceptional tax benefit was recorded in that year. Orders and backlog remain strong in the Product segment. Forecasts call for high single-digit revenue gains through FY2018, with greater operating leverage, higher and more consistent profit margins, and low to mid-double-digit net income gains each year. Moderate dividend increases should continue and are well supported by the cash flow.

### Reasons to Buy

In our earlier book *The 100 Best Aggressive Stocks You Can Buy 2012* we recommended Ormat as a somewhat speculative play in the emerging green energy sector. Now for 2018 the company has transitioned from a good idea to a good business dominating a good niche. We're happy to see it has paid off for the brave souls who read our earlier book and bought in at $16.

Although Ormat is far less of a speculative play now, this sector still relies on governmental incentives for a significant chunk of its financial lifeblood, but those incentives are far broader now, taking the form of well-established long-term carbon credit swaps and carbon reduction mandates at both the state and federal level. Global incentives are also taking shape, following an agreement at the UN Climate Change Conference and several other Eurozone initiatives. The State of Nevada, long a friend of Ormat, may well lead the nation in clean energy implementation, recently passing legislation requiring the elimination of at least 800MW of coal-fired generating capacity by the end of 2019. Neighboring California has stringent renewable energy requirements as well. In short, compared to 2011, in 2018, the business opportunity is well established.

Incentives are important for geothermal installations. Geothermal plants are quite a bit more expensive to bring online than, say, a gas turbine plant. A geothermal plant will cost approximately $2,500 per kW of installed capacity versus $1,000 per kW for a gas turbine facility. Operating costs, however, are where the geothermal plant shines—generation costs are in the range of $0.01–$0.03 per kilowatt hour. Coal, the next cheapest alternative, yields costs of $0.02–$0.04 per kilowatt hour. Geothermal plants are also extremely reliable, with 24/7 availability (a big differentiator from solar and wind power) and near 98 percent uptime, with very little maintenance and near zero environmental impact. Coal plants, on the other hand, average about 75 percent availability and come saddled with massive environmental costs that are rarely subsidized directly by ratepayers (for now). These geothermal plants are very good solutions for particular needs in particular locations, but cannot be plopped down just anywhere as they require a source of geothermal heat. Fortunately, the Department of Energy estimates a large number of potential sites in the western United States, and developing nations without access to coal or oil can create baseline electrical capacity with extremely low rates with appropriate levels of investment.

All taken together, Ormat has turned this unique and important niche into a viable and growing business.

## Reasons for Caution

The company occupies a space somewhat at the fringes of the rapidly growing renewable energy market. Because its installations are only possible in certain geographies, geothermal production may not be front-of-mind when renewable legislation is penned unless actively lobbied. (Indeed, Congress forgot to include geothermal energy in the latest energy investment tax credit bill—oops!) We're not sure how Trump administration energy policies will play out, but even if they result in greater use of cheaper hydrocarbon fuels, geothermal energy is still cheaper particularly once the plant is built.

Also, some of the areas in which the company operates are politically unstable, and the company's installations may be the largest outside investment for hundreds of miles around. There have been few problems to date, but the highly detailed annual report is worth reading on this topic and on the business and technology in general. Finally, as of mid-2017 the stock had built up a lot of steam—choose entry points carefully.

SECTOR: **Energy** ◻ BETA COEFFICIENT: **1.06** ◻ 10-YEAR COMPOUND EARNINGS-PER-SHARE GROWTH: **10.0%** ◻ 10-YEAR COMPOUND DIVIDENDS PER-SHARE GROWTH: **NA**

|  |  | 2009 | 2010 | 2011 | 2012 | 2013 | 2014 | 2015 | 2016 |
|---|---|---|---|---|---|---|---|---|---|
| Revenues (mil) | | 415.2 | 373.2 | 437.0 | 514.4 | 533.2 | 559.5 | 594.4 | 662.6 |
| Net income (mil) | | 68.9 | 10.4 | (43.1) | (51.1) | 37.3 | 54.2 | 119.6 | 93.9 |
| Earnings per share | | 1.51 | 0.22 | (0.95) | (1.12) | 0.81 | 1.18 | 2.43 | 1.88 |
| Dividends per share | | 0.25 | 0.27 | 0.13 | 0.08 | 0.08 | 0.21 | 0.26 | 0.52 |
| Cash flow per share | | 2.93 | 2.14 | 1.17 | 1.13 | 2.87 | 3.40 | 4.62 | 4.02 |
| Price: | high | 44.1 | 38.8 | 31.2 | 22.2 | 28.2 | 30.5 | 40.9 | 53.9 |
| | low | 22.8 | 25.8 | 14.1 | 16.0 | 18.8 | 24.0 | 25.9 | 32.3 |

Website: www.ormat.com

## GROWTH AND INCOME

# Otter Tail Corporation

Ticker symbol: OTTR (NASDAQ) ◻ Mid Cap ◻ Value Line financial strength rating: A ◻ Current yield: 3.6% ◻ Dividend raises, past 10 years: 4

## Company Profile

Otter Tail Corporation is a holding company and a mini-conglomerate operating primarily in the upper Midwest. The conglomerate is centered on and stabilized by the Otter Tail Power Company, a regulated utility serving about 130,000 customers in rural western Minnesota, the eastern half of North Dakota, and the eastern quarter of South Dakota. (In case you're wondering about the geography, these areas just miss the vast energy exploration territories of western North Dakota, but they do include a lot of areas involved in recently approved pipeline construction.) About 53 percent of electric revenues come from Minnesota, 38 percent from North Dakota, and 9 percent from South Dakota. The utility accounted for about 53 percent of the total revenues in FY2016 (and 76 percent of operating profits), while the Manufacturing & Infrastructure unit, a group of four businesses engaged in metal parts, plastic pipe, and infrastructure products manufacturing make up the other 47 percent (24 percent of profits); these non-utility businesses are further described (following).

Extensive use of wind generation and hydro power, and lower grades of coal available in the region, have driven fuel costs down to a rock-bottom 14.7 percent of revenues (from 15.5 percent in 2015 and 16.6 percent in 2014), a very low figure for the industry. (By comparison, Xcel Energy, which supplies electricity to surrounding areas in North Dakota and Minnesota as well as other Great Plains locations, Colorado, and Texas, spends 43 percent of revenues on fuel, and most conventional utilities run in the 35–50 percent range.)

Approximately 18.4 percent of power generation came from wind and hydro sources in 2016. A plan to decommission a coal plant by 2021 combined with the acquisition and buildout of a 150-megawatt wind farm to be completed in 2019 will increase the approximate percentage of energy generated by wind from 19 to 28 percent. Too, the company has made its first investments in solar to meet a Minnesota state requirement by 2020. Regulatory recovery of this investment, and another investment in two new high-voltage transmission lines, which also broadened the service area, should help earnings going forward.

Beyond the utility, the company continues to own and operate four businesses within its Manufacturing & Infrastructure segment:

- BTD Manufacturing is a metal-stamping, fabricating, and laser-cutting shop supplying custom parts for agriculture, lawn care, health and fitness, and the RV industry.
- T.O. Plastics supplies thermoformed packaging and handling products for the horticultural, medical, food, electronics, and other consumer industries, including medical device packaging, plastic trays, housings and enclosures, and food and plant containers.
- Northern Pipe Products produces PVC water and sewer pipes up to 24 inches in diameter for pressurized applications and drainage.
- VinylTech, a producer of a similar line of utility-grade PVC products in Arizona, serves customers mostly in the Southwest.

The non-utility activities are split into two groups: Manufacturing (BTD), which generated $221 million in revenues in FY2016 and $11.8 million in operating profits; and the Plastics group, which includes the other three businesses and generated $18.1 million in income on $155 million in revenues.

The company takes a very hands-off approach to managing its Manufacturing & Infrastructure subsidiaries; in fact, each has its own unique website with links within the Otter Tail Corporation site. In total, the company has 2,054 employees, and most operations are centered in the upper Midwest, VinylTech being the exception.

## Financial Highlights, Fiscal Year 2016

FY2016 results were helped along by higher electric volumes due to pipeline construction, moderate rate increases, and lower fuel costs in the electric business, with the manufacturing businesses remaining largely unchanged. Within manufacturing, greater efficiencies from a new plant were offset by volume declines in some key markets, while in plastics higher volumes were offset by lower selling prices; all worked together to create little change for FY2016 from the non-utility businesses. Revenues rose 3.1 percent, while earnings rose 5.8 percent. (Note that per-share earnings rose at a far lesser rate as share count increased 5 percent in keeping with recent industry trends to "deleverage"—that is, reduce debt.) For FY2017–18, the company projects earnings and revenue gains in the mid-single digits. While Otter Tail intends to retain and improve the non-utility businesses, it has stated that it will focus capital investment on the utility operations for the time being.

## Reasons to Buy

Despite the low growth rates and recent stock price gains (a good thing for last year's readers!) we retain OTTR on the *100 Best* list as a conservative play. We have a hard time turning away from a steady utility with such best-in-class low fuel costs. And, when we first added Otter Tail to the 2012 *100 Best Stocks* list, we were admittedly taken by its Berkshire Hathaway–like construct of a basic business around a steady core, the electric utility. Some of the other businesses may have been a bit too far-flung to manage effectively—so the company retrenched, trimmed the branches, so to speak, in 2014–15, first with windmill construction and transportation, then with other businesses that didn't fit so well. After the pruning, the company is still more or less constructed around this diversified and well-anchored model. The non-utility core is managed much in the Berkshire Hathaway style of hands-off, autonomous, you-supply-the-management-not-us style, which we also like.

Although the returns have been a bit below our standards, we like the steady yield, safety, and diversification inherent in this issue. Based on cash flows, we think dividend growth could accelerate. The manufacturing and plastics businesses offer a potential upside "kicker" as the energy and manufacturing cycle recovers, and the Trump agenda of infrastructure and domestic manufacturing should provide a tailwind. Otter Tail remains a "small town" company in contrast to "big city" corporate America.

## Reasons for Caution

The utility is stable but not likely to be helped along by population growth, and the manufacturing and construction businesses are cyclical. The company is on much more solid operating and financial footing than it was a few years ago, but it still doesn't have the reserve strength of larger companies. We compare Otter Tail to Berkshire Hathaway but should note that Berkshire is more diversified and has much larger anchor businesses.

SECTOR: **Energy** ❑ BETA COEFFICIENT: **0.78** ❑ 10-YEAR COMPOUND EARNINGS PER-SHARE GROWTH: **4.0%** ❑ 10-YEAR COMPOUND DIVIDENDS PER-SHARE GROWTH: **1.0%**

|  |  | 2009 | 2010 | 2011 | 2012 | 2013 | 2014 | 2015 | 2016 |
|---|---|---|---|---|---|---|---|---|---|
| Revenues (mil) |  | 1,040 | 1,118 | 1,078 | 859 | 893 | 799 | 780 | 804 |
| Net income (mil) |  | 26.0 | 13.6 | 16.4 | 39.0 | 50.2 | 56.9 | 58.6 | 62.0 |
| Earnings per share |  | 0.71 | 0.38 | 0.45 | 1.05 | 1.37 | 1.55 | 1.56 | 1.60 |
| Dividends per share |  | 1.19 | 1.19 | 1.19 | 1.19 | 1.19 | 1.21 | 1.23 | 1.25 |
| Cash flow per share |  | 2.76 | 2.82 | 2.39 | 2.71 | 3.03 | 3.09 | 3.14 | 3.44 |
| Price: | high | 25.4 | 25.4 | 23.5 | 25.3 | 31.9 | 32.7 | 33.4 | 42.6 |
|  | low | 18.5 | 18.2 | 17.5 | 20.7 | 25.2 | 26.5 | 24.8 | 25.8 |

Website: www.ottertail.com

---

### AGGRESSIVE GROWTH

# Paychex, Inc.

Ticker symbol: PAYX (NASDAQ) ❑ Large Cap ❑ Value Line financial strength rating: A ❑ Current yield: 3.2% ❑ Dividend raises, past 10 years: 8

## Company Profile

Paychex, Inc., provides payroll, human resources, and benefits outsourcing solutions for small- to medium-sized businesses with 10–200 employees. Founded in 1971, the company has more than 100 offices and serves over 605,000 clients in the United States as well as about 2,000 clients in Germany and a new base through a partnership in Brazil. Some 85 percent of its customers are the small- to medium-sized businesses previously mentioned; the company estimates that it pays one out of every 12 employees nationwide. The company has two sources of revenue: service revenue, paid by clients for services, and interest income on the funds held by Paychex for clients.

Paychex offers a one-stop shop portfolio of services and products:

- Payroll processing
- Payroll tax administration services
- Employee payment services, including expense reporting, reimbursements, etc.
- Regulatory compliance services (new-hire reporting and garnishment processing)
- Retirement services administration
- Workers' compensation insurance services
- Health and benefits services
- Time and attendance solutions
- Medical deduction, state unemployment, and other HR services and products

About 60 percent of Paychex's revenue originates from payroll (service revenue plus interest income); the remaining 40 percent comes from its human resource services offerings. In addition to its website and direct sales force, the company uses its relationships with existing clients, CPAs, and banks for new client referrals and to grow the base of services used by existing clients. Approximately half of its new clients come via these referral sources.

Larger clients can choose to outsource their payroll and HR functions or to run them in-house using a Paychex platform. For those clients, the company offers what it calls "Paychex Flex," which can be run locally or on a web-hosted, SaaS environment.

In addition to traditional payroll services, Paychex offers full-service HR outsourcing solutions; custom-built solutions including payroll, compliance, HR, and employee benefits sourcing and administration; outsourcing management; and even professionally trained onsite HR representatives. The company also manages retirement plans and other benefits, including pretax "cafeteria" plans, and has a subsidiary insurance agency offering property and casualty, workers' comp, health, and auto policies to an employer's employee base.

The company is the nation's number one provider of payroll services to small businesses (1–50 employees) and number two for midsized businesses (50–500 employees). About 35,000 of the 605,000 Payroll clients use the full Human Resource Services offering, with a total employee count of about one million. The company has recently implemented web-based and mobile versions of its key products, adding to convenience and reducing paperwork for its clients, and has also added a suite of analytics to its HR offerings. Through the Retirement Services Group, the company administers 74,000 retirement plans, achieving the number one spot nationwide by number of plans.

## Financial Highlights, Fiscal Year 2016

The economy appears healthy, and it appears that many of the policies of the Trump administration will help domestic businesses, and this will help Paychex. The company should (1) add new clients, (2) sell more services to new and existing clients, (3) sell more to each client as the employee base rises. This combination led to an 8 percent top-line gain and a 12 percent bottom-line gain in FY2016 as the mix and scale of the business improved. Favorable margin and mix trends should continue into FY2017 and beyond, with revenues up 7 percent and net profit up in the 9–10 percent range. Interest income ("Interest on Funds Held for Clients" in company vernacular) is starting to become a factor as the Fed has finally started raising rates; this could give a nice upside lift in FY2018.

## Reasons to Buy

A bet on Paychex is a bet on three things: (1) continued improvement in the economy, (2) continued adoption of broader "one stop" platform services, and (3) an increase in interest rates (so they can make money on the float). In the meantime, you get a decent yield, steady gains, and little downside risk if you own the stock.

Paychex's primary market is companies with fewer than 100 employees. The all-important small business segment has been strong since the Great Recession and is likely to get stronger with Trump's domestic business–friendly approach. Beyond that, the cost of switching and good client relationships have made for a loyal client base. We continue to think the trend to outsource payroll and HR activities will not only continue but accelerate as easier Internet-based solutions come more into favor.

The company is conservatively run, well managed, and well financed. It isn't just a "service" company, it is an IT company with a lot of innovation in its DNA. Margins are significantly higher than its closest competitor, Automated Data Processing (ADP). It carries no long-term debt—zero—and should have little difficulty funding the generous dividend, even at its current payout level of 80 percent of earnings. Fragmentation in the market and Paychex's extremely strong financial position will allow the company to continue to grow market share through acquisition. Finally, as short-term interest rates tick upward the company will once again be able to profit from the float (the company has $3–$4 billion of its customers' money held for payroll at any given time). This is one of the few stocks on our list that can tangibly benefit from *moderate* interest rate increases. We like that defensive characteristic.

## Reasons for Caution

This company will always be vulnerable to economic swings, such as those brought on by *large* interest rate increases. The company's acquisitions of small payroll processors and human resource service providers make sense, as those acquisitions increase market share, but they do come with costs and risks.

SECTOR: **Information Technology** ❑ BETA COEFFICIENT: **0.86** ❑ 10-YEAR COMPOUND EARNINGS PER-SHARE GROWTH: **7.5%** ❑ 10-YEAR COMPOUND DIVIDENDS PER-SHARE GROWTH: **12.5%**

|  |  | 2009 | 2010 | 2011 | 2012 | 2013 | 2014 | 2015 | 2016 |
|---|---|---|---|---|---|---|---|---|---|
| Revenues (mil) | | 2,083 | 2,001 | 2,084 | 2,230 | 2,326 | 2,519 | 2,739 | 2,952 |
| Net income (mil) | | 534 | 477 | 516 | 548 | 569 | 627 | 675 | 757 |
| Earnings per share | | 1.48 | 1.32 | 1.42 | 1.51 | 1.56 | 1.71 | 1.85 | 2.09 |
| Dividends per share | | 1.24 | 1.24 | 1.24 | 1.27 | 1.31 | 1.40 | 1.52 | 1.68 |
| Cash flow per share | | 1.72 | 1.56 | 1.67 | 1.78 | 1.83 | 2.02 | 2.16 | 2.42 |
| Price: | high | 32.9 | 32.8 | 33.9 | 34.7 | 45.9 | 48.2 | 54.8 | 62.2 |
| | low | 20.3 | 24.7 | 25.1 | 29.1 | 31.5 | 39.8 | 41.6 | 45.8 |

Website: www.paychex.com

AGGRESSIVE GROWTH

# Perrigo Company

Ticker symbol: PRGO (NASDAQ) ❑ Large Cap ❑ Value Line financial strength rating: A ❑ Current yield: 0.9% ❑ Dividend raises, past 10 years: 10

## Company Profile

Unfortunately—and much to our surprise—Perrigo was the number one "excuse stock" and loser for the 2017 *100 Best Stocks* list, losing some 47 percent in our measurement period. Ouch. But what business could be better than supplying the billions of generic over-the-counter pills branded for the likes of Target, Wal-Mart, and CVS? We expect that more people have these generics in their medicine cabinets than have Campbell's Soup cans in their pantry—and that's a lot. We thought this business was as safe as one could get…and we were wrong. But that doesn't mean it isn't a good business. They have some things to sort out, but we think it is now a good business at a good price. So we're hanging on (and keeping a few store-branded acetaminophen tablets handy just in case).

Perrigo is the world's largest manufacturer of over-the-counter pharmaceutical products for the store-brand market. They also manufacture generic prescription pharmaceuticals, nutritional products, and active pharmaceutical ingredients (APIs) for other drug makers.

Consolidation is the name of the game in the pharmaceutical business and especially in the lucrative generics segment. In 2014, Perrigo acquired Elan, an Irish maker of mostly prescription pharmaceuticals, broadening their offering in this subsegment and acquiring an Irish headquarters base for tax advantages. The company also added another generic marketer to its portfolio—Omega Pharma—mostly to build the generics business in European markets and 35 countries in all.

Both acquisitions added considerably to the size and profitability of the company. They also added to long-term debt, which tripled in 2015. All seemed well when the company received a bid from rival Mylan at $205 per share, but then the acquisition failed, and the shares dropped 40 percent in 2015. The company has now sold the royalty stream to its best in-house–developed Rx pharmaceutical *TYSABRI* (for multiple sclerosis) for $2.85 billion to pay off some debt due, but in so doing it has jettisoned its most profitable revenue stream, thus hurting margins and per-share earnings. This in turn triggered *another* 47 percent decline in the stock. The company is working to turn itself into a more focused and cost-efficient store-brand product producer while readjusting its Rx pharmaceuticals portfolio.

Perrigo operates in three main segments: Consumer Healthcare, Rx Pharmaceuticals, and API. Consumer Healthcare, which includes generics and nutritionals such as baby formula and vitamins, is by far the largest segment, generating about 75 percent of Perrigo's projected FY2017 revenue. About two-thirds of this segment is based in the US, Canada, and Latin America. Rx Pharma produces about 18 percent, and APIs and other specialty businesses, about 7 percent.

The company's success depends on its ability to manufacture and quickly market generic equivalents to branded products. It employs internal R&D resources—which run 4 percent of sales—to develop product formulations and manufacture in quantity for its customers. It also develops retail packaging specific to the customers' needs. The company expects a greater percentage of medicines to become available over the counter (versus Rx); this has been the case with Allegra and similar medications in recent years. The company estimates that 72 percent of educated consumers choose store brands, and 91 percent of them stay with them once chosen. They also estimate that they save consumers $7.5 billion a year with more favorably priced generics.

If you have bought a store-branded over-the-counter medication such as ibuprofen, acetaminophen, skin remedies, or cough medicine at a store like Target or Walmart in the past year, there's a good chance (a 75 percent chance, in fact) that it was made by Perrigo. The company's Consumer Healthcare business produces and markets over 2,700 store-brand products in 26,000 individual SKUs of 11,000 formulations (the difference between the two is mainly different package sizes) to approximately 1,000 customers, including Wal-Mart, CVS, Walgreens, Kroger, Target, Safeway, Dollar General, Costco, and other national and regional drugstores, supermarkets, and mass merchandisers. Wal-Mart is its single largest customer and accounts for 15 percent of Perrigo's net sales (down from 19 percent a few years ago). It's a good deal, because it's a steady cash stream, and Perrigo doesn't really have to invest in marketing. The company estimates that population demographics, new store-branded products, and transitions of certain drugs from prescription to over-the-counter sales all contribute about equally to growth.

The Nutritionals business, part of Consumer Healthcare, distributes 900 store-brand products in 3,400 SKUs to more than 150 customers.

Enlarged by the Elan acquisition, the Rx Pharma operations produce generic prescription drugs (in contrast to the over-the-counter drugs produced in the Consumer Healthcare segment), obviously benefitting when key patented drugs run past their patent protection. Rx Pharma markets approximately 800 generic prescription products, many of them topicals and creams, with more than 1,300 SKUs, to approximately 350 customers, while the API division markets an assortment of active ingredients to other drug manufacturers as well as for the company's own products, including a number of active ingredients that we'd have trouble spelling correctly, so we won't even try.

## Financial Highlights, Fiscal Year 2016

Financial performance flattened in FY2016, with revenues up but only due to acquisitions and net profits advancing less than 2 percent. The sale of the *TYSABRI* royalty stream is expected to take almost a third out of per-share earnings and about 12 percent out of revenues, while also dropping net profit margins from the 18–20 percent range down to 13–15 percent. Debt reduction has also taken priority over share buybacks for the moment.

## Reasons to Buy

Perrigo has been a story of solid niche dominance (store-branded medications) with a couple of high-growth, high-margin businesses mixed in. While we don't like the margin deterioration, a stronger focus on over-the-counter and generic medicines seems to make sense, and the niche dominance should keep it moving forward. We like the slogan "Quality Affordable Healthcare Products." People are becoming more sensitive to their own healthcare costs and spending in general and are opting more often for the store brand; after all, 200 mg of ibuprofen is 200 mg of ibuprofen. This all sits on top of the demographic tailwind of the aging population and the institutional tailwind of doing what's necessary to rein in costs.

While the Mylan merger failed, and while the company forecasts a 37 percent hit to per-share earnings due to the *TYSABRI* sale, the stock as of this writing has lost more than two-thirds of its value and is priced at less than 15 times earnings. We think it's a good value at a time when good values are particularly hard to find.

## Reasons for Caution

Perrigo broke most of our rules in making a major acquisition of a complex business, then moving to another country where accounting standards make business evaluation more difficult. Normally we would have dropped the company right then and there, but again, we like its track record and niche dominance. And now—losing its most profitable product and all of this restructuring—not necessarily a good pill to swallow. True, it was probably overvalued two years ago; takeover fever will do that. And naturally, we're not too thrilled with the company's cash returns to investors and increasing share counts. There's a lot not to like here. But behind all this fog sits a pretty good business in our opinion, one that has become more fairly valued to boot—albeit not without risk. Keep those medications handy.

SECTOR: **Healthcare** ◻ BETA COEFFICIENT: **0.60** ◻ 10-YEAR COMPOUND EARNINGS PER-SHARE GROWTH: **24.0%** ◻ 10-YEAR COMPOUND DIVIDENDS PER-SHARE GROWTH: **13.5%**

|  | 2009 | 2010 | 2011 | 2012 | 2013 | 2014 | 2015 | 2016 |
|---|---|---|---|---|---|---|---|---|
| Revenues (mil) | 2,007 | 2,269 | 2,765 | 3,173 | 3,540 | 4,061 | 4,604 | 5,521 |
| Net income (mil) | 176 | 263 | 341 | 411 | 442 | 739.5 | 1,001 | 1,020 |
| Earnings per share | 1.87 | 2.83 | 3.64 | 4.37 | 4.68 | 6.39 | 7.24 | 7.10 |
| Dividends per share | 0.22 | 0.25 | 0.27 | 0.32 | 0.35 | 0.39 | 0.46 | 0.58 |
| Cash flow per share | 2.67 | 3.69 | 4.78 | 5.84 | 6.41 | 8.21 | 10.60 | 12.20 |
| Price: high | 61.4 | 67.5 | 104.7 | 120.8 | 157.5 | 171.6 | 215.7 | 152.4 |
| low | 18.5 | 37.5 | 62.3 | 90.2 | 98.6 | 125.4 | 140.4 | 79.7 |

Website: www.perrigo.com

CONSERVATIVE GROWTH

# Praxair, Inc.

**Ticker symbol: PX (NYSE) ❑ Large Cap ❑ Value Line financial strength rating: A ❑ Current yield: 2.7% ❑ Dividend raises, past 10 years: 10**

## Company Profile

Praxair, Inc., is the second-largest supplier of industrial gases in the world. The company, which was spun off to Union Carbide shareholders in June 1992, supplies a broad range of atmospheric, process, and specialty gases; high-performance coatings; and related services and technologies.

Praxair has long been a staple on the *100 Best* list, but this could be its last year in its current form. In late 2016 the company agreed to a 50-50 merger with German-based gas supplier Linde. Ordinarily we remove companies from the list upon merger or acquisition at least until we get a better handle on the combined entity. In this case, the business will stay much the same as Linde is in much the same business—although the combined company (to be called Linde) will be three times the size ($30 billion in sales annually) with $1 billion in cost synergies. We think the combined entity will qualify for the *100 Best* list ongoing, and the merger has not been approved, so we will retain Praxair for the 2018 list; this narrative is for Praxair as a standalone business.

Praxair's primary products are atmospheric gases—oxygen, nitrogen, argon, and rare gases (produced when atmospheric air is purified, compressed, cooled, distilled, and condensed) and process and specialty gases—carbon dioxide, helium, hydrogen, and acetylene (produced as by-products of chemical production or recovered from natural gas). Customers include makers of primary metals, metal fabricators, petroleum refiners, and producers of chemicals, healthcare products, pharmaceuticals, biotech, food and beverage, electronics, glass, pulp and paper, and environmental products. By end market, manufacturing, metals, and energy producers account for 51 percent of 2016 sales (energy alone is 11 percent, down from 13 percent in 2015); chemicals, electronics, and aerospace another 21 percent; and healthcare and food/beverage the next 17 percent, with the remaining 11 percent to "other" industries.

The gas products are sold into the packaged-gas market and the merchant market. In the packaged-gas market, bulk gases are packaged into high-pressure cylinders and either delivered to the customer or to distributors. In the merchant market, bulk gases are liquefied and transported by tanker truck to the customer's facility.

The company also designs, engineers, and constructs cryogenic and non-cryogenic gas supply systems for customers who choose to produce their own atmospheric gases onsite. This is obviously a capital-intensive delivery solution for Praxair but results in lower delivered cost to the customer and higher returns for Praxair, as all operational costs are paid by the customer. Contracts for these installations can run to 20 years. About 28 percent of volume is packaged, 35 percent is "merchant," and 29 percent is generated onsite (8 percent is "other").

Praxair Surface Technologies is a subsidiary that applies wear-, corrosion-, and thermal-resistant metallic and ceramic coatings and powders to metal surfaces in order to resist wear, high temperatures, and corrosion. Aircraft engines are a primary market, but it serves others, including the printing, textile, chemical, and primary metals markets, and provides aircraft engine and airframe component overhaul services. About 47 percent of Praxair's sales come from outside North America.

## Financial Highlights, Fiscal Year 2016

Softness in energy, basic materials manufacturing such as steel, coal gasification, and select other vertical markets, weakness in emerging markets, and continued dollar headwinds blended with strength in food, beverage, and healthcare industries to produce mixed and mostly flat to lower results once again for FY2016, although results started to turn positive at the end of the year. Total FY2016 sales fell another 2 percent after a 13 percent dip in FY2015; net and per-share earnings fell about the same amount. While the merger will change all of this, current projections, on the back of some volume recovery, selective price increases, and small acquisitions, are for a rise in revenues of 4–6 percent per year through 2018. Higher volumes, higher prices, and operating leverage will propel earnings forward about 10 percent. The company specifically aims to return about half of its cash flow to shareholders while investing the other half in the business.

## Reasons to Buy

The big story is the Linde merger, and the outcome should be in place as 2018 commences. We don't know a lot, but we do know that the combined company will be much larger, more diversified, and more cost efficient.

Until recently Praxair has had a steady history of high margins, growth, and few to no surprises. The "perfect storm" of energy and manufacturing weakness, emerging market problems, and a strong dollar had interrupted this steady flow. However, we didn't feel that the fundamental business had changed, and like so many others, Praxair, either as a combined or a separate entity, will again flourish as we come out of the cycle and new efficiencies take effect. Praxair is the largest gas provider in the emerging markets of China, India, Brazil, Mexico, and Korea and continues to invest heavily in plants in these regions. The company is a big player in the re-emergence of US manufacturing, and that could be important as new Trump administration policies take hold.

## Reasons for Caution

As hydrocarbon energy products are feedstock for many of Praxair's products, the company has enjoyed recent trends but could take a minor hit as energy prices recover. The strong international presence means that results are sensitive to currency headwinds. And, of course, the merger, which we think is likely, could produce some disruptions should it come to pass.

SECTOR: **Materials** ❑ BETA COEFFICIENT: **0.98** ❑ 10-YEAR COMPOUND EARNINGS PER-SHARE GROWTH: **10.5%** ❑ 10-YEAR COMPOUND DIVIDENDS PER-SHARE GROWTH: **16.0%**

|                     |      | 2009  | 2010   | 2011   | 2012   | 2013   | 2014   | 2015   | 2016   |
|---------------------|------|-------|--------|--------|--------|--------|--------|--------|--------|
| Revenues (mil)      |      | 8,956 | 10,118 | 11,252 | 11,224 | 11,925 | 12,273 | 10,776 | 10,534 |
| Net income (mil)    |      | 1,254 | 1,195  | 1,672  | 1,692  | 1,755  | 1,694  | 1,547  | 1,500  |
| Earnings per share  |      | 4.01  | 3.84   | 5.45   | 5.61   | 5.87   | 5.73   | 5.35   | 5.21   |
| Dividends per share |      | 1.60  | 1.80   | 2.00   | 2.20   | 2.40   | 2.60   | 2.86   | 3.00   |
| Cash flow per share |      | 6.85  | 6.95   | 8.95   | 9.10   | 9.70   | 9.90   | 9.45   | 9.30   |
| Price:              | high | 86.1  | 96.3   | 111.7  | 116.9  | 130.5  | 135.2  | 130.4  | 125.0  |
|                     | low  | 53.3  | 72.7   | 88.6   | 100.0  | 107.7  | 117.3  | 98.6   | 95.6   |

Website: www.praxair.com

CONSERVATIVE GROWTH

# The Procter & Gamble Company

Ticker symbol: PG (NYSE) ❑ Large Cap ❑ Value Line financial strength rating: A++ ❑ Current yield: 2.9% ❑ Dividend raises, past 10 years: 10

## Company Profile

Procter & Gamble dates back to 1837, when William Procter and James Gamble began making soap and candles from surplus animal fat from the stockyards in Cincinnati, OH. The company's first major product introduction took place in 1879 when it launched Ivory soap. Since then, P&G has continually created a host of blockbuster products, added some key acquisitions, exited the food business and a few others, and, in total, has some of the strongest, most recognizable consumer brands in the world.

P&G is a uniquely diversified consumer products company with a strong global presence. P&G markets its broad line of products to nearly 5 billion consumers in more than 180 countries.

The company is a recognized leader in the development, manufacturing, and marketing of quality laundry, cleaning, paper, personal care, and healthcare products.

To understand Procter, it's worth a look at how the company is organized:

- *Beauty* (18 percent of FY2016 sales, 20 percent of net profits) includes shampoo, skin care, deodorant, hair care and color, and bar soap products, including such traditional brands as Head & Shoulders, Ivory soap, Safeguard, Secret, Pantene, Vidal Sassoon, Cover Girl, and Old Spice, and some newer and edgier brands like Olay, Hugo Boss, SK-II, James Bond 007 men's fragrances, Gucci, and Dolce & Gabbana, and a handful of professional brands. The mid-2016 Coty divestiture (further described following) cut 43 beauty brands, mostly in hair color and styling, fine fragrance, and cosmetics.

- *Grooming* (11 percent, 15 percent) includes razors, blades, pre- and post-shave products, and other shaving products, including Braun, Gillette, Fusion, Mach3, and Prestobarba brands.

- *Health Care* (11 percent, 12 percent) is made up of two subunits, Personal Health Care and Oral Care. Personal Health Care in turn includes gastrointestinal, respiratory, rapid diagnostics, and vitamins/minerals/supplements, and includes such brands as Vicks, Metamucil, Prilosec, and Pepto-Bismol. Oral Care includes the familiar Crest, Scope, Fixodent, and Oral-B brands among others.

- *Fabric and Home Care* (32 percent, 27 percent) covers many of the familiar laundry and cleaning brands—Tide, Cheer, Dawn, Febreze, Downy, Bounce, Era, Mr. Clean, and a handful created for international markets.

- *Baby, Feminine, and Family Care* (28 percent, 26 percent) markets mostly paper products like Puffs, Charmin, Pampers, Luvs, Bounty, Always, and Tampax into baby care, feminine care, adult incontinence, and family care markets.

Procter has always been a hallmark example of brand management and building intrinsic brand strength—that is, strength not from the company name but through the brand's own name and reputation. It is described as a "house of brands," not a "branded house," although we're starting to see the "P&G" name more prominently in its marketing and advertising. The company tells us that its 50 "Leadership Brands" are some of the world's most well-known household names, that 90 percent of its business comes from these 50 brands, and that 25 of them are billion-dollar businesses.

The company has a strong and growing international presence, with 56 percent of sales originating outside the US and Canada. The company also manufactures locally in its largest international markets, with on-the-ground operations in approximately 70 countries.

In an effort to become a "much simpler company," Procter has nearly completed a process of brand realignment, which entailed shrinking the portfolio from 166 brands down to just 65 by the end of 2017. Additional savings will result from everything from reducing manufacturing sites to organizational units to the number of legal entities and invoices produced. The remaining brands account for approximately 85 percent of earlier FY2015 sales and 95 percent of pre-tax profit. In 2016 the company completed its sale of its Duracell batteries business to Berkshire Hathaway for $2.9 billion and reached an agreement to sell 43 of its Beauty brands to Coty for $12.5 billion. Other professional grooming and Pet Care brands will be gone by the 2018 year, achieving 100-brand divestiture goal. The number of country/category combinations will drop from 140 to 50, with new focus on everything from innovation to a reconfigured supply chain. In beauty parlance, it's a total makeover.

## Financial Highlights, Fiscal Year 2016

FY2016 is a difficult compare to FY2015 on a sustained revenue and profit basis due to the disposition of Duracell and several other unprofitable product lines. These moves along with continued currency headwinds rang up a 15 percent decline in revenues but only a 9 percent decrease in net profit and a 6 percent decrease in per-share cash flows all while the net profit margin advanced from 15 to 16 percent—all solid evidence of a successful "rightsizing" and trimming of dead branches. Currency effects accounted for a 6 percent hit to revenues and a 9 percent hit to net earnings as well.

Continued product portfolio adjustments, currency effects, and "rightsizing" will keep revenues flat in FY2017 even with a 2.5 percent volume growth; modest revenue growth in the 2–3 percent range should resume in FY2018. Net earnings will stay relatively flat through the period, then resume a growth trajectory in FY2019 and beyond. The company reduced share count by 5 percent in 2017 in part by converting P&G shares to Coty shares in the spin-off transaction. Cash flows will be used for an equal mix of steady dividend increases, share buybacks, and debt reduction after that.

## Reasons to Buy

Regardless of developments in the world economy, people will continue to shave, bathe, do laundry, and care for their babies, and P&G is the global leader in baby care, feminine care, fabric care, and shaving products. Everyone should consider at least one defensive play in their portfolio, and P&G continues to deserve a spot at the top of the list.

We like the company's new position on brand proliferation. More is not always better, particularly when each brand carries with it a not-insignificant SG&A and Marketing overhead. Also, does a company like P&G bring anything special to the battery business? We didn't think so, and we're glad they agreed. As the company continues to evolve its organizational structure, it has departed from its traditional model of managing brands as wholly separate businesses with brand-specific advertising budgets, product research labs, and so forth. Synergies from combining ads and ad strategies alone should reduce total costs across the company's many portfolios (to that point, they estimate a 50 percent reduction in advertising, PR, and other agencies). While we will miss some of the brands they are likely to cut, the business won't miss them all that much; focus, critical mass, simplicity, and profitability appear to be their strategic mainstays moving forward.

In short, we continue to like the brand, marketplace, and financial strength; sure and steady dividend growth (the company has raised its dividend 61 straight years); and short- and long-term prospects.

## Reasons for Caution

So much change so fast can be disruptive, and at least one buzzard has started to circle as shareholder activist Nelson Peltz and his Trian Partners have bought a $3.5 billion stake. Competition is fierce in P&G's markets, and operational and marketing missteps can be painful.

Revenue growth remains a key challenge. P&G will be spending a lot of money on innovation in its core markets, but the company has stated that gains in top-line growth won't be immediate and will likely be quite irregular. The recent recession made consumers much more price conscious, and many switched to generics. That switch has reversed to a degree, but not everyone is coming back on board. While commodity prices are favorable today, rising commodity costs can negatively affect P&G as it is hard to pass them on through price increases.

SECTOR: **Consumer Staples** ❑ BETA COEFFICIENT: **0.62** ❑ 10-YEAR COMPOUND EARNINGS PER-SHARE GROWTH: **4.5%** ❑ 10-YEAR COMPOUND DIVIDENDS PER-SHARE GROWTH: **9.5%**

|  | 2009 | 2010 | 2011 | 2012 | 2013 | 2014 | 2015 | 2016 |
|---|---|---|---|---|---|---|---|---|
| Revenues (mil) | 79,029 | 78,938 | 82,559 | 83,680 | 85,500 | 83,062 | 76,279 | 65,299 |
| Net income (mil) | 11,293 | 10,946 | 11,797 | 11,344 | 11,869 | 12,220 | 11,535 | 10,441 |
| Earnings per share | 3.58 | 3.53 | 3.93 | 3.85 | 4.05 | 4.22 | 4.02 | 3.67 |
| Dividends per share | 1.64 | 1.80 | 1.97 | 2.14 | 2.29 | 2.45 | 2.59 | 2.66 |
| Cash flow per share | 4.65 | 4.87 | 5.21 | 5.20 | 5.33 | 5.57 | 5.31 | 4.97 |
| Price:　high | 63.5 | 65.3 | 67.7 | 71.0 | 85.8 | 93.9 | 91.8 | 90.3 |
| low | 43.9 | 39.4 | 57.6 | 59.1 | 68.4 | 75.3 | 65.0 | 74.5 |

Website: www.pg.com

---

## GROWTH AND INCOME

# Prologis, Inc.

Ticker symbol: PLD (NYSE) ❑ Large Cap ❑ Value Line financial strength rating: B+ ❑ Current yield: 3.6% ❑ Dividend raises, past 10 years: 3

## Company Profile

In most of life, when you try something and it works, you try it again. We're strong believers in this principle when it comes to investing, especially when there's some logic—not just sheer luck—behind the success.

And so it goes with REITs. Real Estate Investment Trusts. Specialized investments that allow you to become a landlord and to collect (usually rising) rents. Doesn't that sound enticing? Especially when you get a share of a diversified portfolio with professional management built in? And especially when you get a good business on top of the core real estate?

Long averse to investment "products," we first dipped our toes into this pool by adding Welltower to the *100 Best* list four years ago. Good business (senior living) on top of a strong real estate asset core (high-end senior living properties). It worked and has been one of our better performers since added, especially on a "risk adjusted" basis. Then we added Public Storage three years ago, which had an off year last year but has also been one of our better performers. Then we added the cream-of-the-office-space crop, Empire State Realty Trust, two years ago. Good pick, and we think this skyscraper will reach new heights again this year. So last year we went to the well one more time with a logistics business and real estate core called Prologis. Pretty good results once again—and plenty more to come we think.

Prologis is the global leader in industrial logistics real estate across the Americas, Europe, and Asia. "Industrial logistics real estate" is mainly distribution warehouses and specialized facilities that store goods and prepare them for shipment, sometimes with some final assembly or value add, and are an integral component of the supply chain for many types of organizations. Major clients include third-party logistics providers, transportation companies, retail (including online), and manufacturers.

Prologis operates 3,136 properties in all across 20 countries on four continents, with 2,058 in the US, 240 in three countries in the "Other Americas," 736 in 13 countries in Europe, 102 in three countries in Asia. The company owns and operates most of these properties mainly as standard warehouses in industrial parks or near port or airport facilities, leasing them to large and small companies either in whole or in sections according to need. Prologis also develops custom partner solutions through their "Global Customer Solutions" business which designs, builds, and operates custom distribution facilities for major accounts like Amazon, DHL, and others. In fact, their top ten customers accounted for 12.6 percent of the business; Amazon is the largest customer at 5.0 percent of "net effective rent" (up from 4.5 percent last year); Home Depot is second at 1.8 percent; and FedEx is third at 1.3 percent. Overall, however, the customer base is quite diverse with 5,200 customers in all.

## Financial Highlights, Fiscal Year 2016

FY2016 was another very good year for the business, with demand exceeding supply for such kinds of facilities—a statement borne out in the numbers. Occupancy rates rose to a record 97.1 percent. Same-store net operating income was up 5.6 percent on a 13.8 percent average rent increase on property rollovers (rentals to new tenants). Rollover rent increases were 21.5 percent in the US, which accounts for 73 percent of total income, and they are projected at 17 percent going forward. Core Funds From Operations (FFO—a standard measure of true income for REITs) was up 15 percent on a similar 15.3 percent increase in revenues.

Revenues should advance 4–6 percent per year through 2018; per-share FFO is expected to rise 3–4 percent in 2017 and a stronger 5–6 percent in 2018.

## Reasons to Buy

The value proposition of modern, flexible logistics sites for today's organizations is strong, and particularly strong for e-commerce businesses—such as Amazon, as previously noted. More generally, the state of the art in supply-chain management has advanced significantly in just a few years, driven by e-commerce and just-in-time production management. As supply chains become more global, and as products become more customized and have shorter life cycles, as shipments get smaller, more numerous, and more likely to have an assembly and a "reverse" component, flexible logistics solutions become far more important. Too, e-commerce, because of its high shipment "granularity," requires about three times the space per dollar of revenue as bricks-and-mortar warehouse operations. And the company projects a 162 percent increase in e-commerce volumes over the five-year period 2015–2020.

Equally important is today's current business climate, with companies relying on back-end productivity rather than top-line growth to increase profits. Prologis sits right in the middle of this trend, with a solid base of real estate, skills to manage it, and skills to partner with major clients to deliver the right and often customized solution.

All major financial metrics are on a strong upward advance, occupancy levels are at an all-time high, pricing power is apparent, and steady dividend increases appear likely. We think, given the favorable supply/demand picture in this business, that Prologis's financial forecasts could be too conservative going forward; there is more upside than downside assuming continuing strong global e-commerce growth. Consistent with much of the REIT industry, share counts are on the rise as Prologis replaces depth with equity or uses equity to finance acquisitions. The current debt-to-equity ratio of 38 percent is very healthy for the industry and getting healthier.

## Reasons for Caution

We've picked four REITs now—in senior living, self-storage, New York real estate—and now, logistics and warehousing—Prologis. Guess which one is most vulnerable to economic downturns. Prologis? Right. A protracted economic downturn would hurt this business more than many REITs (we have avoided shopping center and hospitality REITs altogether because in our view they're even more vulnerable). We should also note that e-commerce, the strongest growth vector, currently accounts for only about 13 percent of the business. As Millennials shift their focus from goods to experiences, and as most sought-after goods get smaller (such as smartphones), the future global economy could simply require less physical space to operate.

SECTOR: **Real Estate** ❑ BETA COEFFICIENT: **1.02** ❑ 10-YEAR COMPOUND EARNINGS PER-SHARE
GROWTH: **NM** ❑ 10-YEAR COMPOUND DIVIDENDS PER-SHARE GROWTH: **NM**

| | 2009 | 2010 | 2011 | 2012 | 2013 | 2014 | 2015 | 2016 |
|---|---|---|---|---|---|---|---|---|
| Revenues (mil) | — | — | 1,533 | 2,006 | 1,750 | 1,761 | 2,197 | 2,533 |
| Net income (mil) | — | — | (153.4) | (102.4) | 219.4 | 636.2 | 869.4 | 1,210 |
| Funds from operations per share | — | — | 1.10 | 1.19 | 1.65 | 1.88 | 2.23 | 2.57 |
| Real estate owned per share | — | — | 57.25 | 55.74 | 45.67 | 47.63 | 52.47 | 51.30 |
| Dividends per share | — | — | 1.12 | 1.12 | 1.12 | 1.32 | 1.52 | 1.68 |
| Price:        high | — | — | 37.5 | 37.6 | 45.5 | 44.1 | 47.6 | 54.9 |
|                low | — | — | 21.7 | 28.2 | 34.6 | 36.3 | 36.3 | 35.3 |

Website: www.prologis.com

---

**GROWTH AND INCOME**

NEW FOR
2018

# Prudential Financial

Ticker symbol: PRU (NYSE) ❑ Large Cap ❑ Value Line financial strength rating: B++ ❑ Current
yield: 2.8% ❑ Dividend raises, past 10 years: 9

## Company Profile

"Own a Piece of the Rock" is one of the classic slogans of corporate America.
We've all heard it so many times it's like a song you can't get out of your head;
yet it's so familiar that you might well have forgotten the company it stands
for. Oh yeah. Prudential. The Rock of Gibraltar in the picture. A trademarked
symbol. Does it ring a bell? In choosing stocks for our *100 Best* list, we look for
stability and safety, yes, we look for a piece of the rock in every choice we make.
But we also look for innovation and the sort of market leadership that leads to
profitable growth. We usually do not look for financial stocks, as they are hard to
understand and can be fickle as we all learned in 2008. But due to a rock-solid
base plus an innovative growth vector we'll share in a moment, we're adding
Prudential to our list as a replacement for the tarnished Wells Fargo.

Prudential began selling life insurance 141 years ago, and has evolved
this rather unsexy business into an insurance, asset management, and retirement powerhouse well positioned not only to handle your retirement planning needs but also those of major corporations—that's where the innovation
we hinted at previously comes in. The company operates in three Divisions of
highly divergent profit contribution:

■   United States Retirement Solutions and Investment Management (50 percent of 2016 operating income) has within it three segments: Individual Annuities, Retirement, and Asset Management. The Individual Annuities segment (25 percent of operating income) "manufactures" and distributes individual variable, fixed, and fixed indexed annuities primarily to the "mass affluent" market for retirement income stabilization and supplement. The Retirement segment (14 percent) provides administrative services and products, including group annuities, structured investment products, and the pension risk transfer products (the "innovation") cited several times in this narrative. The Asset Management segment (11 percent) provides portfolio management and specific investment products such as mutual funds, which are both publicly and privately available.

■   US Individual Life and Group Insurance (4 percent of income) creates and markets individual term, variable, and universal life insurance products to all markets through individual agents and a full range of group life and disability insurance products to employers.

■   International Insurance (45 percent of income) creates, modifies, and distributes life insurance, retirement, and related products outside the US through various channels. Important developed markets include Japan and Korea while emerging markets include Brazil and Chile.

The company has $1.3 trillion in assets under management, and currently operates in 47 countries. Unlike many such companies, international expansion is a major strategy; individuals and workers outside the US have significant needs for financial services as well.

The innovation we're really excited about is a new initiative to sell packaged corporate pension plans to employers of all types. When a company takes on a pension obligation, either willfully or as a consequence of a union negotiation or some such, it takes on a risk. The pension is a promise to pay a defined amount (hence "defined benefit"), and it's up to the company to pay this amount come whatever happens to its own resources and investments. Bottom line: the employer company takes on a lot of risk when it creates a pension program. Here's where Prudential comes in: Companies can transfer this risk to Prudential by paying Prudential a fee to take over, essentially buying an annuity to cover future pension obligations. Prudential takes on the risk of the employer for a fee. That's what insurers do, and Prudential is leading in this new niche; United Technologies (another *100 Best* stock) just paid PRU $1.8 billion to take over their pension program. This is new business that Prudential knows how to do, and will realize economies from as it takes over in larger volumes from employer customers.

## Financial Highlights, Fiscal Year 2016

Lower fees, foreign exchange, continued low interest rates, and certain changes to assumptions primarily in the Annuities segment contributed to a soft net profit performance in FY2016 (off 13 percent) despite good gains in premium revenues (10 percent higher) and total investment income (up 8 percent). The year ended on a strong note with favorable sales volumes, underwriting income, higher fees in some businesses, and investment income as interest rates finally started to move higher. Going forward, favorable regulatory rulings (including the postponement of the new "fiduciary" rule), higher interest rates, and strength in annuities and the pension risk transfer product (the "innovation") are projected to lead to an 11 percent net profit gain on a 1 percent revenue gain in FY2017 followed by another 3 percent profit gain on 4 percent higher revenues for FY2018. We feel this could be conservative with the new business opportunity and growth in the individual retirement planning market. Shareholder returns continue to be strong with 11 percent of shares retired since 2011 and a new $1.25 billion authorization for FY2017; 2–3 percent annual share reductions are likely along with high-single-digit dividend increases.

## Reasons to Buy

Prudential, long a stalwart of the sleepy life insurance business, has witnessed an accelerating transition toward the ever-greater need for retirement planning solutions both on the part of individuals and employer organizations. Annuities, long another fairly sleepy part of the business, are enjoying a resurgence as corporate and public pensions evolve away from full-coverage defined benefit plans; annuities are also becoming more acceptable and more easily used by financial advisors to round out financial plans as their roles and features are better tailored and better understood. The new pension risk transfer product "innovation" offers an exciting path to growth as more employers with traditional pension obligations come on board; Prudential is the market leader in this new growth opportunity. The international expansion also bodes well particularly if the dollar stabilizes. All of the businesses should fare well in a higher interest rate and less regulated environment. Finally, investor cash returns have been on the rise for years and should continue along that path.

## Reasons for Caution

Hats off to you if you can understand this business! We found this company's investor materials profoundly difficult to understand. Like most financials it is hard to sort through the terminology and nuances of each business; too, it seems as if managers of a financial business speak in financial terms—it took quite a bit of research to understand exactly what products Prudential supplies to what markets! And we're still not sure we got it.

There are some other risks here too: longevity (people living longer makes annuities less profitable) and general risks associated with the financial industry, mostly risks of complexity and greed we fell into back in 2008 and regulatory actions that can result from such events. We're breaking the "invest in things you understand" rule a bit here, but we do understand the idea of pension risk transfer and of annuities becoming a more important and more trusted retirement planning vehicle as pensions continue to go away and people become more responsible for their own retirement destinies.

SECTOR: **Financials** ❑ BETA COEFFICIENT: **1.68** ❑ 10-YEAR COMPOUND EARNINGS PER-SHARE GROWTH: **8.0%** ❑ 10-YEAR COMPOUND DIVIDENDS PER-SHARE GROWTH: **12.0%**

|  | | 2009 | 2010 | 2011 | 2012 | 2013 | 2014 | 2015 | 2016 |
|---|---|---|---|---|---|---|---|---|---|
| Premium income (bil) | | 13.3 | 15.3 | 21.4 | 62.1 | 23.1 | 25.1 | 25.5 | 28.0 |
| Total income (bil) | | 27.7 | 31.0 | 39.4 | 81.1 | 45.3 | 49.8 | 48.6 | 51.6 |
| Net profit (bil) | | 2.5 | 3.0 | 3.1 | 3.0 | 4.8 | 4.2 | 4.5 | 3.9 |
| Earnings per share | | 5.58 | 6.27 | 6.41 | 6.27 | 9.67 | 9.21 | 10.04 | 9.13 |
| Dividends per share | | 0.70 | 1.15 | 1.45 | 1.60 | 1.73 | 2.17 | 2.44 | 2.80 |
| Price: | high | 56.0 | 66.8 | 67.5 | 65.2 | 92.7 | 94.3 | 92.6 | 108.3 |
| | low | 10.6 | 46.3 | 42.4 | 44.5 | 53.4 | 75.9 | 73.2 | 57.2 |

Website: www.prudential.com

# Public Storage

Ticker symbol: PSA (NYSE) ❑ Large Cap ❑ Value Line financial strength rating: A+ ❑ Current yield: 3.5% ❑ Dividend raises, past 10 years: 8

## Company Profile

You have stuff. We have stuff. We all have stuff. Stuff to store somewhere. Stuff from our families, stuff from our kids, stuff from our past. Boats, RVs, and extra vehicles. Boxes, boxes, and more boxes. And we all need to store that stuff somewhere. But where? As more of us live in houses with smaller yards and devoid of basements, where? As more of us choose to rent rather than buy, where? As more of us, especially the younger "Millennials" among us, choose to live closer to the centers of larger cities, where? As the retirees among us downsize, where? As the elderly give up their primary residences, where?

You get the idea. There is more personal stuff for most of us to store, and less space to do it. That's where Public Storage becomes a pretty good investment idea.

Public Storage is a real estate investment trust (REIT) owning and operating 2,348 self-storage properties (2,277 in 2015) in 38 states and another 219 facilities in seven countries in Europe. The company has a 49 percent interest in Europe's "Shurgard," and also owns a 42 percent interest in another trust called PS Business Parks, which owns 103 rentable properties in six states. The company points out that, based on the number of tenants, it is one of the world's largest landlords. The slogan "We're in your neighborhood" also tells you something.

Most are probably familiar with the format—small, unfinished, generally not-climate-controlled lockers rentable on a month-to-month basis for personal and business use. They range in size from 25–400 square feet, and there are typically 350–750 storage spaces in each facility. Some include covered parking for vehicle, boat, and RV storage. On average the company nets a little over $1 per square foot per month—a rather handsome sum considering these units do not come with any of the finish or comfort of an apartment or even a home, which may rent for something similar per square foot depending on the market.

Not surprisingly, the largest concentrations are in California, Texas, and Florida (since these are centers for retirees and homes with no basements), and most are near a major US or European city. The three largest markets are New York, San Francisco, and Los Angeles. Branding in the US is "Public Storage"; in Europe it is "Shurgard." US self-storage revenues account for about 75 percent of the total; European self-storage accounts for about 7 percent, and the commercial business park business accounts for about 12 percent. The remaining "ancillary businesses" include selling supplies like locks for storage units and storage unit insurance.

The key strategies continue to be revenue and cost optimization, market-share growth in major markets, and building brand recognition. The company has a centralized call center and a website to help market its product and facilitate transactions. Acquisitions are also an important part of the strategy; the current market is fragmented with PSA only owning 10–20 percent of the market at most, and good properties come up regularly. The company expects to grow its property base a steady 1–2 percent annually.

Our principle in owning REITs remains the same; we're not looking for just real estate, we want to own a good business that *just happens* to own a lot of real estate. REITs are typically good income producers, as they are required by law to pay a substantial portion of their cash flow to investors. The accounting rules are different, and REIT investors should focus on Funds From Operations (FFO), which is analogous to operating income; net income figures have depreciation expenses deducted, which can vary in timing and not always be realistic. FFO supports the dividends paid to investors.

## Financial Highlights, Fiscal Year 2016

High occupancy rates, higher rents, and the stronger margins that came as a result drove moderate revenue and FFO gains for FY2016. Occupancy rates ended 2016 at 94.5 percent, same as 2015 but a record level and very strong given the relatively high turnover in this type of business. Realized rents rose 5.6 percent, a little worse than 2015's 6 percent but better than 2014's 5 percent. As a consequence, revenues grew about 7.5 percent and per-share FFO grew more than 10 percent with a record 46.2 percent net profit margin. Forecasts call largely for more of the same, with revenues advancing 7–12 percent and per-share FFO advancing 7–10 percent annually through 2018. The company has been adding a few more shares following an industry-wide trend toward deleveraging its balance sheet (more equity, less debt)—but current long-term debt is already at a ridiculously low 5 percent of total capital.

## Reasons to Buy

With REITs, our emphasis continues to be more on the business and less on real estate, and with Public Storage, we feel we've found a good business that happens to be based on real estate. PSA has the best brand and highest operating efficiency in the business, and the core business model and need for its product is sustained and growing. No matter how easy it is to sell stuff on Craigslist, it's also too easy to acquire stuff, and although Millennials are more about "experiences" than "things," we still don't see people getting out of that habit anytime soon. At the same time, real estate is trending away from large suburban McMansions with extra space and more toward city digs, patio homes, cluster homes, and the like. All point to strong, steady business prospects for providers of flexible storage solutions, and as PSA strengthens its brand and market-share foothold, more of that business will go its way. The rising rents and occupancy rates are good evidence that this is already happening. The dividend has risen at a substantial and accelerating rate in recent years and is well funded; too, there is *far* less debt than typically found in a real estate investment business. Finally, the stock took a breather last year as we had suggested might happen; recent prices have looked to be more attractive entry points than in earlier years.

## Reasons for Caution

Any profitable business will attract competitors, and there is some evidence of overbuilding and competition in markets like Houston, Chicago, DC, and Denver. That said, PSA has a pretty good lock on the tighter, more lucrative markets like Los Angeles, San Francisco, Seattle, and Portland with three to ten times the market share of the next competitor. Longer term, one must watch the "collective" habits of Millennials; today they collect "experiences," but as they get older, will they ultimately collect as much "stuff" over time as Mom and Dad did? It remains to be seen.

SECTOR: **Real Estate** ◻ BETA COEFFICIENT: **0.51** ◻ 10-YEAR COMPOUND FFO PER-SHARE
GROWTH: **8.0%** ◻ 10-YEAR COMPOUND DIVIDENDS PER-SHARE GROWTH: **14.0%**

| | 2009 | 2010 | 2011 | 2012 | 2013 | 2014 | 2015 | 2016 |
|---|---|---|---|---|---|---|---|---|
| Revenues (mil) | 1,628 | 1,647 | 1,752 | 1,826 | 1,982 | 2,195 | 2,382 | 2,561 |
| Net income (mil) | 835 | 672 | 824 | 670 | 845 | 908 | 1,053 | 1,184 |
| Funds from operations per share | 5.03 | 5.22 | 5.93 | 6.31 | 7.53 | 7.98 | 8.79 | 9.70 |
| Real estate owned per share | 46.48 | 44.51 | 43.35 | 42.71 | 47.97 | 49.20 | 49.49 | 51.49 |
| Dividends per share | 2.20 | 3.05 | 3.65 | 4.40 | 5.15 | 5.60 | 6.50 | 7.30 |
| Price:         high | 85.1 | 106.1 | 136.7 | 152.7 | 176.7 | 190.2 | 253.9 | 277.6 |
|                low | 45.3 | 74.7 | 100.0 | 129.0 | 144.4 | 148.0 | 192.1 | 200.9 |

**Website: www.publicstorage.com**

**AGGRESSIVE GROWTH**

# Qualcomm, Inc.

Ticker symbol: QCOM (NASDAQ) ❑ Large Cap ❑ Value Line financial strength rating: A++ ❑ Current yield: 3.6% ❑ Dividend raises, past 10 years: 10

## Company Profile

Qualcomm, based in surf-friendly San Diego, is responsible for producing the hardware and related software at the heart of most of the high-end mobile web-surfing devices in use today. These are mainly integrated circuits and system software used in voice and data communications, networking, GPS, and other technologies. It also licenses most of the key technologies used in today's cell phone networks, including CDMA and LTE. Their Snapdragon processors are used in most of the "flagship" smartphones on the market, as well as many tablets. In addition to processors, the company also makes many of the modems and "front-end" hardware used at both ends of a cellular connection, as well as peripheral devices for Wi-Fi and Bluetooth transmission for personal computers.

Integrated circuits, software, and other tangible products account for about 65 percent of Qualcomm's revenue—most of the rest is derived from the company IP (intellectual property) licensing activity. Qualcomm, founded in 1985, has been at the forefront of the development of much of the fundamental technology of cellular communications. Their CDMA, LTE, and GSM patents are at the core of the world's cellular industry and form the foundation for the bulk of the company's business, both in hardware and licensing.

Not surprisingly, the licensing arm generates the bulk of the earnings (85 percent in 2015), while the cost-heavy chip development and production arm generates most of the remaining 15 percent. Qualcomm began as a "front-end" and licensing business and later got into the general-purpose processor business with the advent of smartphones. The company is still investing heavily in their relatively new Snapdragon CPU development, as well as preparing 5G chipsets, while the existing fundamental IP continues to garner licensing fees.

Qualcomm also continues to invest heavily in the "Internet of Things." Their apt slogan: "We started by connecting the phone to the Internet; now we're connecting the Internet to everything else." In late 2016 the company announced the acquisition of the large IoT chipmaker NXP after buying CSR, an IoT chipmaker mainly in the automotive market, in 2015. Expect Qualcomm to become a major player in hooking everything from cars to homes to medical devices up to the Internet.

## Financial Highlights, Fiscal Year 2016

Following a six-year run over which revenues grew 205 percent, Qualcomm's FY2015 brought a 5 percent downturn. That was followed by a 7 percent revenue decline in FY2016. Net earnings declined 13 percent, while per-share earnings and cash flows fared better due to a 3 percent share buyback. What's going on? Mainly there is more competition at the high end of the market, some from Intel, that shifted both the volume and the mix downward. Soft shipments from Apple and Samsung also didn't help—these two players accounted for 45 percent of revenue in FY2015, although there was a pickup in the fourth quarter 2016 as Apple recorded record shipments with the iPhone 7 and as Qualcomm gained share in the Chinese wireless market. All together, the results were not a surprise but were disappointing nonetheless.

Acquisitions and a resumption of competitive gains both in the hardware/software and licensing markets should right the ship in 2017 and 2018, with modest 2–3 percent gains in revenues and net earnings. Healthy dividend increases and share buybacks should continue to provide decent shareholder returns even through this lull in the core business.

## Reasons to Buy

If there's a word to describe Qualcomm's presence in the mobile market, it's "ubiquitous." Qualcomm's platform, voice, and data communications devices are used in the mobile products of over 90 manufacturers. In some cases, only the front-end parts are used. In many cases, however, the manufacturer will simply copy Qualcomm's whole product reference designs for particular price points and use them without modification. This minimizes the manufacturer's development cost and time-to-market, while absolutely maximizing Qualcomm's product content and revenue.

As the developer (or co-developer) of many of the technologies used in modern wireless communications, Qualcomm is a major beneficiary of all licensing activity associated with cellular communication. Every cell phone produced in at least the past ten years has come with Qualcomm IP, for which the manufacturer has been (or should have been) paying Qualcomm on a per-unit basis. We mention the licensing collections issue only because there has been a growing level of attention on a number of licensees who are under-reporting device sales in order to avoid payment of fees. Recent litigation has addressed this issue for the most part.

Qualcomm is a major presence in the growing mobile automotive market. In-car communication and data services have become extremely popular with consumers, to the point where manufacturers are offering a range of those services either as standard equipment or options, even on their entry-level cars. Qualcomm's GPS and sensor technologies are already in wide use here, but plans for extended functionality in these applications hold promise for significant growth. We expect the growth of Apple's CarPlay, Android Auto, and other in-car data services to leverage strongly on Qualcomm's existing technology while, again, providing for licensing revenue regardless of the hardware employed.

Qualcomm is investing heavily in IoT. All of these interconnected devices use Bluetooth, near-field communication, or simple Wi-Fi to provide wireless, always-on connectivity, and all of these technologies are already in place and under further development at Qualcomm. The company's product line here includes technology for wearables, smart homes, healthcare, and other markets.

Lastly, as often happens with companies that we like, Qualcomm is using the period of slow sales to address costs company wide. The company expects to eliminate $1.1 billion in costs from a FY2015 basis of $7.3 billion over a period of two years.

Finally, a dividend north of 3 percent and growing rings loudly in our ears, especially for a growing tech company.

## Reasons for Caution

Competitive losses and signs of saturation in the upper-tier markets still plague QCOM, although licensing fees are still collected when competitors get design wins (at least in theory). The biggest issue facing the company currently is a lawsuit by Apple contesting QCOM's "unreasonable and costly" royalty rates, and now Apple and South Korean antitrust regulators are in together on this action. The FTC seems to agree, and previous actions in both Korea and China have led to legal losses. The company feels it will be able to resolve these disputes, but the headlines bear watching. If you believe in QCOM's lead role in new markets like IoT plus its ability to garner profitable revenue from traditional communications markets, such news would seem to present a buying opportunity.

SECTOR: **Information Technology** ❑ BETA COEFFICIENT: **1.21** ❑ 10-YEAR COMPOUND EARNINGS PER-SHARE GROWTH: **14.5%** ❑ 10-YEAR COMPOUND DIVIDENDS PER-SHARE GROWTH: **19.0%**

|  |  | 2009 | 2010 | 2011 | 2012 | 2013 | 2014 | 2015 | 2016 |
|---|---|---|---|---|---|---|---|---|---|
| Revenues (mil) | | 10,387 | 10,982 | 14,957 | 19,121 | 24,866 | 26,487 | 25,277 | 23,507 |
| Net income (mil) | | 3,169 | 4,071 | 5,407 | 6,463 | 7,911 | 9,032 | 7,641 | 6,653 |
| Earnings per share | | 1.90 | 2.46 | 3.20 | 3.71 | 4.51 | 5.27 | 4.66 | 4.44 |
| Dividends per share | | 0.66 | 0.72 | 0.81 | 0.93 | 1.20 | 1.54 | 1.80 | 2.02 |
| Cash flow per share | | 2.28 | 2.94 | 3.85 | 4.31 | 5.30 | 6.10 | 5.81 | 5.48 |
| Price: | high | 48.7 | 50.3 | 59.8 | 68.9 | 74.3 | 82.0 | 75.3 | 71.6 |
| | low | 32.6 | 31.6 | 46.0 | 53.1 | 59.0 | 67.7 | 45.9 | 42.2 |

Website: www.qualcomm.com

---

**AGGRESSIVE GROWTH**

# Quest Diagnostics Inc.

Ticker symbol: DGX (NYSE) ❑ Large Cap ❑ Value Line financial strength rating: B++ ❑ Current yield: 2.3% ❑ Dividend raises, past 10 years: 6

## Company Profile

If you have gone for any kind of medical test, either at the recommendation of a doctor or as required by an employer or insurance company, chances are you got that test in a lab operated by Quest Diagnostics. Quest is the world's leading provider of diagnostic testing, information, and services to support doctors, hospitals, and the care-giving process.

The company operates more than 2,200 labs and patient service centers including about 150 smaller "rapid-response" labs in the US and has facilities in India, Mexico, the UK, Ireland, and Sweden. It provides about 150 million lab test results a year and serves physicians, hospitals, employers, life and healthcare insurers, and other health facilities. The company has a logistics network including 3,700 courier vehicles and 23 aircraft, and has some 20 *billion* test results from the past decade in its databases, a rich source for medical research data. Quest estimates that it serves more than half the hospitals and physicians in the United States and estimates that it "touches the lives" of 30 percent of all US adults each year.

The company offers diagnostic testing services covering pretty much the gamut of medical necessity in its testing facilities. It also offers a line of diagnostic kits, reagents, and devices to support its own labs, home and remote testing, and other labs. Employer drug testing is a big business. The company offers a series of "wellness and risk management services," including tests, exams, and record services for the insurance industry. The company also does tests and provides other support for clinical research and trials, and finally, through its information technology segment, it offers a Care360 platform to help physicians maintain charts and access data through its network, which has about 200,000 physicians enrolled. Mobile technology is another innovation front; the company has developed a mobile solution within Care360 known as "MyQuest" to help patients keep track of test results, schedule appointments and medications, and share information with physicians and other care providers.

The company has also been a leader in developing so-called "moderate complexity" direct molecular testing procedures, where more complex diagnostic tests can be performed in "moderate complexity" environments—i.e., a "retail" lab format such as Quest operates. The company is a leader in "gene-based" and "esoteric" testing and has launched an assortment of molecular genetics tests supporting new trends in the health industry toward individualized medicine— medicine based on a patient's own unique gene makeup and characteristics. Finally, a new package of tests called "Blueprint for Athletes," which examines a wide range of sports-related attributes like blood sugar, blood cell counts, food sensitivities, and other allergies, costs $150 to $400 and illustrates the kind of package and brand marketing Quest is capable of—and is starting to deploy.

## Financial Highlights, Fiscal Year 2016

Despite new patients from the Affordable Care Act and some of the new tests just described, volumes haven't increased much—only 1 percent for FY2016—while earnings backed by a better mix and margin performance rose a healthier 6 percent for the year. A 4 percent share buyback led to an 8 percent per-share earnings gain, not bad on flatlined revenues. New, more esoteric tests and "package deals" like the Blueprint for Athletes may finally move the revenue needle some 2–3 percent in FY2017 and FY2018, while per-share earnings should continue to rise in the 6–8 percent range on relatively steady share counts. We think these forecasts could be conservative as new tests and test packages become mainstream.

## Reasons to Buy

People are becoming more health conscious, and an ever-greater emphasis on wellness and preventative care is likely to send more people for routine checkups, particularly if insurance carriers offer benefits (like free tests or lower coinsurance) to motivate such preventative care.

Even more, we're excited about the innovative new tests performed at the retail lab level for molecular-level and gene-based diagnostics, which bode well for the future; the company is advancing to higher, more profitable levels of the diagnostic food chain.

We're also fans of the "package" tests and of Quest's ancillary businesses—clinical trials, insurance qualifications, employer testing, and IT services—which all should do well in an environment favoring greater cost control and outsourcing of distinct services such as Quest provides. The company is a leader in its industry and has a beta of 0.71 indicating relative safety. Finally, Quest has retired 30 percent of its shares in the past ten years.

## Reasons for Caution

Continued pressure to contain healthcare costs may bring some additional malaise over the next few years. Offsetting that is the placement of more emphasis on preventative care, a Quest sweet spot. The path to sustained revenue growth seems to be the big question, and the company continues to work on answers.

Quest may face more competition as large-group physician practices get larger and bring some of their lab operations in-house—although that trend may be countered by hospitals and other large organizations getting *out* of this relatively easily outsourced business. In all, it's a complex and ever-changing environment with a lot of moving parts.

SECTOR: **Healthcare** ❑ BETA COEFFICIENT: **0.71** ❑ 10-YEAR COMPOUND EARNINGS PER-SHARE GROWTH: **5.5%** ❑ 10-YEAR COMPOUND DIVIDENDS PER-SHARE GROWTH: **15.5%**

|  |  | 2009 | 2010 | 2011 | 2012 | 2013 | 2014 | 2015 | 2016 |
|---|---|---|---|---|---|---|---|---|---|
| Revenues (mil) | | 7,455 | 7,400 | 7,511 | 7,468 | 7,146 | 7,435 | 7,493 | 7,515 |
| Net income (mil) | | 730 | 720 | 728 | 700 | 612 | 587 | 695 | 737 |
| Earnings per share | | 3.88 | 4.05 | 4.53 | 4.43 | 4.00 | 4.10 | 4.77 | 5.15 |
| Dividends per share | | 0.40 | 0.40 | 0.47 | 0.81 | 1.20 | 1.29 | 1.52 | 1.65 |
| Cash flow per share | | 5.52 | 5.00 | 6.42 | 6.23 | 6.22 | 6.21 | 6.99 | 7.19 |
| Price: | high | 62.8 | 61.7 | 61.2 | 64.9 | 64.1 | 68.5 | 89.0 | 93.6 |
| | low | 42.4 | 40.8 | 45.1 | 53.3 | 52.5 | 50.5 | 60.1 | 59.7 |

Website: www.questdiagnostics.com

AGGRESSIVE GROWTH

# ResMed, Inc.

Ticker symbol: RMD (NYSE) ❑ Large Cap ❑ Value Line financial strength rating: A ❑ Current yield: 1.8% ❑ Dividend raises, past 10 years: 4

## Company Profile

Sleep disorders are a big deal among adult populations. Reading the clinical description of sleep disorders and their myriad causes could for some be a cure for such disorders, but suffice it to say (as ResMed does in its market analysis) that 26 percent of US adults age 30–70, or about 46 million people, have some form of sleep apnea. That's where the story of ResMed begins, and it continues around the world: A recent study estimated that one in four adults worldwide has some form of sleep apnea.

Perhaps you know someone using a "CPAP" (continuous positive airway pressure) machine to alleviate "SDB" (sleep-disordered breathing) or "OSA" (obstructive sleep apnea). As we age and tend to gain weight, these devices are becoming a more mainstream way for folks (and their partners) to get some much-needed sleep.

Formed in 1989, ResMed develops, manufactures, and distributes medical equipment for treating, diagnosing, and managing sleep-disordered breathing and other respiratory disorders. Products include diagnostic products, airflow generators, headgear, and other accessories. The original and still largest product line of CPAP machines delivers pressurized air through a mask during sleep, to prevent collapse of tissue in the upper airway, a condition common in people with narrow upper airways and poor muscle tone—in many cases, people who are older and overweight. A great many of the estimated 46 million with sleep apnea, who exhibit the typical symptoms of daytime sleepiness, snoring, hypertension, and irritability, have yet to be diagnosed.

CPAP machines and their cousins VPAP (variable positive airway pressure) and others were at one time massive, clunky machines restricting movement and very difficult to travel with. No more: The new machines are smaller, lighter, cheaper, and easier to use. We don't like solutions that are worse than the problem, and ResMed has turned the corner on that with the new machines; they're becoming more acceptable, less expensive, and more mainstream. We think the company's four-pronged strategy is a good one: Make the machines easier to deal with (and afford), increase clinical awareness and the rate of diagnosis, expand into new applications including stroke and congestive heart failure treatment, and expand internationally. The company has executed effectively on all fronts.

The company markets its products in 100 countries, makes them in five countries outside the US, and invests about 6.5 percent of revenues in R&D.

ResMed continues to develop a holistic sleep management offering; a new "S+" non-contact sleep tracker is one new product example. A new line of airflow diagnostic machines known as AirFit is a good example and is expected to give a good boost to the business. The "AirMini" line of traveling CPAP machines is another new entry. The company continues to make small acquisitions to broaden its product line particularly into disease treatment and into new international markets. The 2016 acquisition of cloud software provider Brightree entered the company into the teleconnected post-acute home sleep disorder care market. A new cloud-connected platform known as AirView now has over 4 million cloud-connected diagnostic and monitoring devices with more than 2 million of those receiving home monitoring. Predictive analytics are now making diagnostic use of the one billion nights of sleep data gathered by these cloud tools. Finally, consumables—mainly sleep masks—add a strong repeatable sales base and today comprise about 37 percent of sales.

## Financial Highlights, Fiscal Year 2016

FY2016 sales rose 10 percent on robust sales of both devices and software. Earnings were flat, dragged down mostly by one-time costs from the Brightree acquisition, a trend that will continue for most of FY2017. Sales should continue to grow in the 10 percent range in FY2018, while, with one-time costs behind it, earnings should grow at a similar rate. Dividends should grow steadily through the period; buybacks have been curtailed as the Brightree acquisition is absorbed.

## Reasons to Buy

We believe that the company's four-pronged strategy, previously outlined, is right on. As these machines, and the diagnosis of the condition they're designed for, become more mainstream, we expect more people in the market, lower prices, and reduced inconvenience. All these things should open up larger and larger slices of the market for the company. And we like the robust application of teleconnected medicine; it really makes sense in this space and can go a long way to reduce hospital admissions and overall healthcare costs.

Demographics are a plus, too—as people get older and heavier, these machines will find more potential users. It's a niche business, and ResMed dominates the niche and is the only company solely focused on this market. While we tend not to rely on this in our selections, we feel the company has the earmarks of a good acquisition candidate for a larger provider of health-care technology products.

## Reasons for Caution

One of the bigger issues facing CPAP and related technologies is the eligibility for reimbursement or coverage through Medicare/Medicaid and through private insurers. The current landscape is a mixed bag: Many non-Medicare health insurance plans do not cover the machines (which range from about $600–$1,900 in price), and Medicare has driven payment rates down through competitive bidding and across-the-board cuts.

Too, the market is becoming more competitive, and there have been a few legal contests on intellectual property—most of which have gone ResMed's way so far. We feel that ResMed's technology leadership, full-line offering, and experience in this market will prevail.

SECTOR: **Healthcare** ▫ BETA COEFFICIENT: **0.82** ▫ 10-YEAR COMPOUND EARNINGS PER-SHARE GROWTH: **17.5%** ▫ 10-YEAR COMPOUND DIVIDENDS PER-SHARE GROWTH: **NM**

|  | 2009 | 2010 | 2011 | 2012 | 2013 | 2014 | 2015 | 2016 |
|---|---|---|---|---|---|---|---|---|
| Revenues (mil) | 921 | 1,092 | 1,243 | 1,368 | 1,514 | 1,555 | 1,679 | 1,839 |
| Net income (mil) | 146.4 | 190.1 | 227.0 | 254.9 | 307.1 | 345.4 | 352.9 | 352.4 |
| Earnings per share | 0.95 | 1.23 | 1.44 | 1.71 | 2.10 | 2.39 | 2.47 | 2.49 |
| Dividends per share | — | — | — | — | 0.68 | 1.00 | 1.12 | 1.20 |
| Cash flow per share | 1.33 | 1.66 | 1.96 | 2.40 | 2.71 | 2.99 | 3.03 | 3.12 |
| Price:     high | 26.7 | 35.9 | 35.4 | 42.9 | 57.3 | 57.6 | 75.3 | 70.9 |
| low | 15.7 | 25.0 | 23.4 | 24.4 | 42.0 | 41.5 | 49.0 | 50.8 |

Website: www.resmed.com

---

AGGRESSIVE GROWTH

# C.H. Robinson Worldwide, Inc.

Ticker symbol: CHRW (NASDAQ) ▫ Large Cap ▫ Value Line financial strength rating: A ▫ Current yield: 2.3% ▫ Dividend raises, past 10 years: 9

## Company Profile

C.H. Robinson Worldwide, Inc., is one of the largest third-party logistics ("3PL") providers in North America. The company provides bundled and "turnkey" freight transportation services and logistics solutions to companies of all sizes, in a variety of industries. The company is a non-asset–based provider, meaning it contracts with a network of 71,000 transportation carriers (mostly trucking firms but also railroads, intermodal operators, ship and air lines) and a network of warehousing, customs clearance operations, and other supply-chain components to provide a complete, flexible, and tailored solution to customers across and around the world. In addition to transportation, the company has a division called Robinson Fresh that provides sourcing services in the perishable food industry buying, selling, and marketing fresh fruits, vegetables, and other perishable items and transporting them to market—120 million cases annually for 2,000 growers. The fresh produce division accounts for about 10 percent of revenues, while "Transportation" accounts for the other 90 percent (and about 72 percent of that comes from trucking services).

In 2016, C.H. Robinson handled approximately 16.9 million shipments and worked with over 113,000 active customers. The customer base is diverse—manufacturing, food and beverage, retail, chemical, and automotive are the largest customer segments. The company has 285 offices across North and South America, Europe, and Asia.

The company has invested heavily in technology; its "Navisphere" single global technology "ecosystem" connects 150,000 customers, carriers, and suppliers and covers the entire "life cycle" of a shipment from notification to scheduling to delivery. Customers can track their shipments down to a single item; about 70 percent of Robinson's customer contacts come through this platform. The 2015 acquisition of electronic freight broker Freightquote added significant revenues and customer convenience especially in the LTL ("less than truckload") shipping market for smaller customers.

## Financial Highlights, Fiscal Year 2016

Driven (no pun intended) by an oversupply-related weakness in truck freight pricing, truckload and intermodal revenues lost ground in FY2016 and dragged total revenues down about 2.5 percent; net income stayed roughly flat. The pricing softness in trucking is thought to be due to industry fleet expansion in advance of next year's new rules requiring electronic time-logging devices to regulate hours of service; that extra capacity will put pressure through most of 2017. Revenues should return to a 2–3 percent growth trajectory in FY2017 and a more robust 3–4 percent rate in FY2018 with similar gains in net profit. Operating margins should improve from 6.0 to about 7.0 percent in part due to new efficiencies and revenue streams garnered through technology, i.e., Freightquote. The company reiterated a stated goal to return 90 percent of net income to shareholders annually, foreshadowing continued dividend increases and capturing the fact that the company has bought back about 20 percent of its shares since 2011.

## Reasons to Buy

"Connecting the World—One Supply Chain at a Time" is Robinson's apt slogan. The main idea behind C.H. Robinson is to provide businesses, large and small, with a flexible and scalable way to outsource their logistics operations, thus reducing poorly matched capacities and risks (Do you, as operator of a private trucking fleet, ever have the right number of trucks? Nope—always too few or too many!).

A 3PL firm can also achieve efficiencies by combining loads for different customers. The company's value proposition for customers, in fact, is to "drive costs down," "improve efficiency," "mitigate risk," and "manage change." In today's fast-moving business world, products and supply chains change quickly, and companies have an increasing mandate to find ways to control costs and create supply-chain advantages. ("Accelerate your Advantage" is another apt slogan.) As top-line improvements are hard to come by, services such as those offered by C.H. Robinson continue to make sense for an ever-increasing customer base. And we like the way they do this with a minimal asset base—no trucks, ships, or trains of their own!

Traditionally, the company operated as a procurement, or forwarding, service for transportation services for its customers; today as much as anything else, it is a technology company deploying technology solutions to not only procure but manage and optimize the network. We like companies that deploy technology to create an advantage, particularly when it's an advantage for their customers. The strategy seems to be to become a fully integrated, technology-connected solution for firms shipping big stuff, just as FedEx and UPS have for firms shipping small stuff. The strong commitment to shareholder returns and the steady price related to the market (beta = 0.39) add to the list of attractions.

## Reasons for Caution

Shipping and transportation services are always cyclical; in addition, large changes in fuel costs can be difficult to adjust to. Changes in transportation economics—such as those caused by fuel prices, shortages of truck drivers, environmental regulations, and the like—can disrupt supply-chain networks and be costly to comply with. Competition in the industry is fierce, but C.H. Robinson has a pretty strong lead in integrating its suppliers and customers, and even the 68,000 transportation suppliers stand to gain from the Robinson intermediary even if it crimps their own margins. The company is a "win-win" in the transportation and logistics market.

SECTOR: **Transportation** ❑ BETA COEFFICIENT: **0.39** ❑ 10-YEAR COMPOUND EARNINGS PER-SHARE GROWTH: **13.5%** ❑ 10-YEAR COMPOUND DIVIDENDS PER-SHARE GROWTH: **19.0%**

|  | | 2009 | 2010 | 2011 | 2012 | 2013 | 2014 | 2015 | 2016 |
|---|---|---|---|---|---|---|---|---|---|
| Revenues (mil) | | 7,577 | 9,274 | 10,336 | 11,369 | 12,752 | 13,470 | 13,476 | 13,144 |
| Net income (mil) | | 361 | 387 | 432 | 594 | 416 | 450 | 510 | 515 |
| Earnings per share | | 2.13 | 2.33 | 2.82 | 3.67 | 2.65 | 3.05 | 3.51 | 3.59 |
| Dividends per share | | 0.97 | 1.04 | 1.20 | 1.67 | 1.40 | 1.43 | 1.57 | 1.74 |
| Cash flow per share | | 2.34 | 2.51 | 2.62 | 3.92 | 3.18 | 3.46 | 4.00 | 4.15 |
| Price: | high | 61.7 | 81.0 | 82.8 | 71.8 | 67.9 | 77.5 | 76.2 | 77.9 |
| | low | 37.4 | 51.2 | 62.3 | 50.8 | 53.7 | 50.2 | 59.7 | 60.3 |

Website: www.chrobinson.com

**AGGRESSIVE GROWTH**

# Ross Stores, Inc.

Ticker symbol: ROST (NASDAQ) ❑ Large Cap ❑ Value Line financial strength rating: A ❑ Current yield: 1.0% ❑ Dividend raises, past 10 years: 10

## Company Profile

The current retail transition to more of an online, "from the couch" approach has claimed a lot of victims recently. In fact, the turmoil has caused us to eliminate two retail stocks—Macy's and Target—and has forced us to evaluate whether the others have sufficient defenses against the Amazon Prime threat to continue to exist. We examined Ross carefully, and once again it passes the test; it is unique enough and its stores are enough of a destination for its current loyal shopper base that we think it can keep people coming to its bargain bins and largely fend off the change. So we will keep Ross on our shopping list for at least another year.

"There's Always a Bargain in Store" is the apt and timely motto of Ross Stores, the second-largest off-price retailer in the United States. Ross and its subsidiaries operate two chains of apparel and home accessories stores. As of 2016 the company operated a total of 1,553 stores, up from 1,446 in 2015, 1,362 in 2014, and 1,125 in 2011. Of that total, 1,340 were Ross

Dress for Less locations in 36 states, DC, and Guam and 193 were dd's DISCOUNTS stores in 15 states. Just under half the company's stores are located in three states—California, Florida, and Texas—although the bulk of 2016 new store additions were in the Midwest.

Both chains target value-conscious women and men between the ages of 18 and 54. Ross's target customers are primarily from middle-income households, while dd's DISCOUNTS target customers are typically from lower- to middle-income households. Merchandising, purchasing, pricing, and the locations of the stores are all aimed at these customer bases. Ross and dd's DISCOUNTS both offer first-quality, in-season, name-brand and designer apparel, accessories, and footwear for the family at savings typically in the 20–60 percent range off department store prices (at Ross) or 20–70 percent off (at dd's DISCOUNTS). The stores also offer discounted home fashions and housewares, educational toys and games, furniture and furniture accents, luggage, cookware, and at some stores jewelry.

Sales break down by category roughly as follows: 28 percent Ladies', 25 percent Home Accents, Bed, and Bath, 13 percent each for Men's and for Accessories, Lingerie, Jewelry, and Fragrances, 13 percent for Shoes, and 8 percent Children's. The shopping demographic is 75–80 percent female, shopping for herself or other family members; the core customer averages about three store visits a month. Their market research also suggests that the average customer "wants"—not "needs"—a bargain; there are a number of frugal but fairly well-heeled customers looking for a brand at a price.

Ross's strategy is to offer competitive values to target customers by offering a well-managed mix of inventory with a strong percentage of department store name brands and items of local and seasonal interest at attractive prices. The company plans to add 70 more Ross stores and 20 dd's DISCOUNTS stores for 2017 while closing or relocating about 10 stores, and it plans to grow to about 2,000 Ross and 500 dd's DISCOUNTS stores by the end of the decade.

## Financial Highlights, Fiscal Year 2016

The main growth vector continues to be store base expansions, which continue at a healthy clip; Ross added 87 new stores again in FY2017 onto a 1,446-store base. A 4 percent increase in same-store sales, same as last year, drove a 7.8 percent revenue increase, somewhat ahead of the 6 percent increase in the store base. Both pricing and average size of sale in turn drove the comp increase. Operating margins grew sequentially about 0.5 percent (significant for a retailer) mostly on supply-chain efficiencies to 16.4 percent; net income rang up a nice 9.5 percent gain. A 2.5 percent share buyback rounded out the picture, helping per-share earnings to a 12 percent gain for the year—fairly familiar figures to you regular readers.

FY2017 forecasts call for roughly 6 percent revenue gains annually through FY2018 as comparable store sales growth slows somewhat. Margin expansion should likewise slow as wages rise and expansion expenses continue; net earnings gains of 6–7 percent annually make up the current projections, although healthy share buybacks should continue, keeping per-share earnings growth humming along in the 10 percent range.

## Reasons to Buy

We had become a little tired of this story, which really got a boost from the now-fading Great Recession years. We saw revenue growth being driven mainly by store expansion, and profit growth attenuating. Did we also see that, with more disposable income, consumers may wander away? Did we see signs of too many stores? All might be warning signs of future trouble, and gives us a bit of fright every year. But we've stayed on this horse year after year for one big reason: profitability. Net profit margins—after taxes and everything else—run in the 8–9 percent range. And they've been steadily improving over the years. Where else can you find that in the retail world? It's not easy.

The recession apparently helped Ross gain mainstream appeal across a wider set of customers. While some of those customers defected back to full-price retail stores as things improved, a greater number have shown that they will continue to shop at the stores. At the same time, the company was successful with operational changes begun years ago to improve merchandising and inventory management, which led to better stocking of a more favorable mix of goods and better inventory turnover. The higher store count has increased operating leverage as well—more volume through the same infrastructure and cost base. Nothing is mentioned about international expansion, but we wonder if there too lies an opportunity.

Strong, defensible niche, moderate expansion, operational excellence, sustained shareholder returns; it's an attractive formula and the results speak for themselves as well as pointing to good management. And one more thing: We like how they present all of this to shareholders; their Investor Relations materials are better than average.

## Reasons for Caution

E-commerce doesn't seem to have taken a bite out of Ross yet, but there's always that possibility, particularly with the advance of online promotional and coupon portals like Groupon. We still think the typical Ross shopper actually likes the "hunt" and is less likely to transition to couch-based shopping than most other shoppers. Another concern is that the company is dependent on the actions of others—mainly first-line apparel retailers—for its success. The availability of surplus inventories is high now as first-line retailers struggle… but who knows what lies ahead? We also remain concerned that the company still depends to a degree on store expansion, which carries its own risks, and could make supply bubbles and constraints hurt even more.

SECTOR: **Retail** ❑ BETA COEFFICIENT: **0.92** ❑ 10-YEAR COMPOUND EARNINGS PER-SHARE GROWTH: **21.0%** ❑ 10-YEAR COMPOUND DIVIDENDS PER-SHARE GROWTH: **25.0%**

|  | 2009 | 2010 | 2011 | 2012 | 2013 | 2014 | 2015 | 2016 |
|---|---|---|---|---|---|---|---|---|
| Revenues (mil) | 7,184 | 7,866 | 8,608 | 9,721 | 10,230 | 11,042 | 11,940 | 12,867 |
| Net income (mil) | 443 | 555 | 657 | 787 | 837 | 925 | 1,021 | 1,118 |
| Earnings per share | 0.89 | 1.16 | 1.43 | 1.77 | 1.94 | 2.21 | 2.51 | 2.83 |
| Dividends per share | 0.12 | 0.18 | 0.24 | 0.30 | 0.36 | 0.40 | 0.47 | 0.54 |
| Cash flow per share | 1.22 | 1.52 | 1.81 | 2.21 | 2.44 | 2.79 | 3.22 | 3.62 |
| Price:      high | 12.6 | 16.8 | 24.6 | 35.4 | 41.0 | 48.1 | 56.7 | 69.6 |
|      low | 7.0 | 10.6 | 15.0 | 23.5 | 26.5 | 30.9 | 43.5 | 50.4 |

Website: www.rossstores.com

## AGGRESSIVE GROWTH
# RPM International Inc.

Ticker symbol: RPM (NYSE) ❑ Large Cap ❑ Value Line financial strength rating: B+ ❑ Current yield: 2.2% ❑ Dividend raises, past 10 years: 10

### Company Profile
Have you ever finished a piece of furniture or a wood floor with Varathane? Stained it with Watco? Caulked a bathtub or sink with DAP? Spray-painted a rusty gate with Rust-Oleum? Primed bathroom walls with Zinsser primers before painting it? Glued a model airplane together with Testors? We have—and it seems like every time we do those little weekend warrior tasks around the house, we're using one of these products.

So we wondered, who makes and markets this stuff? Where do these well-established brands that seem to show up in every hardware store and home improvement center we go into come from? How did they become household names, even category-defining names like Kleenex? After a little digging, we came up with a company we'd never heard of. Sometimes, that's a really good sign. A "house of brands," each with its own strength, image, and loyal following, can have more staying and growing power than a "branded house." Just ask anyone on the marketing team at Procter & Gamble.

Anyway, the company we found is in all likelihood one you've never heard of, based in Medina, OH—a town you've probably never heard of, either. "The Brands You Know and Trust" is their slogan, and the company is RPM International. RPM International makes and markets an assortment of specialty chemicals and coatings, targeted mostly to repair, maintenance, and replacement, for consumer and industrial markets.

Industrial markets? Indeed, only about a third (34 percent, actually) of RPM's sales come from the aforementioned "consumer" brands found in Home Depot and the like. The company also makes and markets a vast line of brands for industrial and construction use—sealants, chemicals, roofing systems, corrosion control coatings, marine paints and coatings, fluorescent pigments (you've probably heard of DayGlo, their line of fluorescent paints), powder coatings, fire coatings, and concrete waterproofing and repair products.

There are now 37 "Industrial" brands in all including brands such as Increte Systems, a maker of textured stamped concrete systems, or USL bridge-care solutions, or Carboline corrosion control coatings; you get the idea. The Industrial segment makes many products aimed at the preservation and corrosion protection of existing structures, which makes the company a strong play in the infrastructure reinvestment market. About 85 percent of the company's business comes from repair and maintenance, and about 15 percent comes from new construction. The Industrial segment accounts for 51 percent of the business, and many of its brands are made and sold in foreign markets. In fact, about 50 percent of Industrial business is overseas, while 85 percent of the consumer business originates in North America.

The "Specialty" segment produces DayGlo as well as other specialty coatings for specialty powder and marine coatings, edible coatings, insulation, and concrete repair, with 18 brands and about 15 percent of RPM's business.

Not to beat the brand thing to death, but Rust-Oleum, Varathane, DAP, and Zinsser on the consumer side own number one positions in their respective markets, while eight industrial and specialty brands, including DayGlo of course, own number one positions in their markets.

## Financial Highlights, Fiscal Year 2016

We like the products and the brand strength, but we also continue to like the improving financials of this company. Competitive strength in most of its markets and lower input costs overcame a 5 percent currency headwind to give a 5 percent revenue gain (after currency). That translates to a 10 percent gain before currency effects, a strong performance. Net income rose 10 percent, another smooth finish after a 9 percent gain last year. Net revenue gains should continue in the 3–5 percent range through FY2017 and FY2018 as some new acquisitions come into play. Higher advertising costs and costs associated with a few small acquisitions will keep earnings flat in FY2017 with a stronger "pop" in the 10–12 percent range expected in FY2018 as margins continue to grow. RPM states a goal of growing 45 percent by 2020. Steady high-single-digit dividend increases should continue; the company has increased its dividend for 43 consecutive years.

## Reasons to Buy

We always like premier brands in relatively simple, well-managed businesses, and RPM International seems to fit the model. The company presents itself well—its website is one of the best and most informative we've encountered (maybe this goes hand in hand with a relatively straightforward business; anyway, kudos to management and to the web designer). These factors alone wouldn't be enough to land RPM on our *100 Best* list; however, we also take notice when financials improve at a steady pace. We also take notice of a company that has raised its dividend 43 straight years, and we like the defensive nature of its repeat-purchase, mainly maintenance and repair, product lines. Finally, RPM should do well as new Trump administration infrastructure improvements take hold—this factor is not included in our forecasts.

## Reasons for Caution

While we were impressed with the breadth of the RPM brand universe and the depth and strength of a few of them, we wonder if the business is stretched a bit too thin and if consolidating some of those brands to make stronger brands might make sense. That said, the way these brands are presented on the website leads us to believe that a Berkshire Hathaway model is in effect here: Let the business leaders of those business units do things as they see fit without undue influence from headquarters. RPM would also be somewhat exposed to price recovery in petrochemical inputs.

RPM is also not on as solid a financial footing as other companies on our *100 Best* list, with a debt-to-total-capital ratio exceeding 50 percent. The company is addressing that issue with plans to pay down about 25 percent of the debt, but that plan largely eliminates share buybacks.

SECTOR: Materials ❏ BETA COEFFICIENT: 1.38 ❏ 10-YEAR COMPOUND EARNINGS PER-SHARE
GROWTH: 6.5% ❏ 10-YEAR COMPOUND DIVIDENDS PER-SHARE GROWTH: 5.5%

|  | 2009 | 2010 | 2011 | 2012 | 2013 | 2014 | 2015 | 2016 |
|---|---|---|---|---|---|---|---|---|
| Revenues (mil) | 3,368 | 3,413 | 3,382 | 3,777 | 4,081 | 4,376 | 4,595 | 4,814 |
| Net income (mil) | 135 | 188 | 189 | 215 | 241 | 292 | 323 | 355 |
| Earnings per share | 1.05 | 1.45 | 1.45 | 1.65 | 1.83 | 2.18 | 2.38 | 2.63 |
| Dividends per share | 0.79 | 0.82 | 0.84 | 0.86 | 0.89 | 0.95 | 1.02 | 1.09 |
| Cash flow per share | 1.71 | 2.10 | 2.01 | 2.20 | 2.45 | 2.86 | 3.17 | 3.50 |
| Price:          high | 21.0 | 22.9 | 26.0 | 29.6 | 41.6 | 52.0 | 51.4 | 55.9 |
|                  low | 9.1 | 16.1 | 17.2 | 23.0 | 29.1 | 37.6 | 40.1 | 36.8 |

Website: www.rpminc.com

---

## AGGRESSIVE GROWTH

# Schlumberger Limited

Ticker symbol: SLB (NYSE) ❏ Large Cap ❏ Value Line financial strength rating: A++ ❏ Current yield: 2.8% ❏ Dividend raises, past 10 years: 8

## Company Profile

Patience pays off. At least we hope so. That's a major investing thesis every year in our construct of *The 100 Best Stocks to Buy*. And in few places is that thesis tested more than recently in the energy industry. Even more so for a key supplier to the energy industry, itself in a crowded field: oil field services leader Schlumberger (is that really pronounced "Slumber – ger?"). Yes, in the midst of a sharp industry downturn, and in the midst of a 40 percent decline in revenues and an 80 percent decline in earnings, just how patient can we be? Are we in a cycle? Or has this business changed forever, perhaps a victim of its own past success in delivering efficient, high-volume energy production, now responsible for a lasting market glut? We took another close look as usual and decided that there's a good chance that, yes, patience will pay off once again.

Schlumberger Limited is the world's leading oil field services company. It provides technology, information solutions, and integrated project management services with the goal of optimizing reservoir performance for its customers in the oil and gas industry. Founded in 1926, today the company has a large international footprint, employing 100,000 people in 85 countries, with 75 percent of revenue generated outside of North America. The company currently operates in four primary business segments:

- The Reservoir Characterization Group (24 percent of FY2016 revenues, 36 percent of pretax income) is mostly a consulting service, applying many digital and other technologies toward finding, defining, and characterizing hydrocarbon deposits. Interestingly, the company compares the electronic characterization of a hydrocarbon-producing zone to the imaging of a human body, using an assortment of technologies (for example, a technology referred to as a "Saturn 3D radial fluid sampling probe") to identify what you can't see directly.
- Not surprisingly, the Drilling Group (30 percent of revenues, 29 percent of pretax income) does the actual drilling and creation of wells for production, both in onshore and offshore environments. Again, a number of new drilling, drill bit, and drilling fluid technologies are in play, and naturally, so-called "fracking" is an important part of the product offering.
- The Reservoir Production Group (31 percent of revenues, 16 percent of pretax income) completes and services the well for production, maintaining and enhancing productivity through its life.
- The Cameron Group (15 percent of revenues, 19 percent of pretax income) is newly formed with last year's acquisition; Cameron specializes in pressure and flow control systems of onshore and offshore wellhead management.

Throughout the petroleum production process, the company not only provides physical onsite services but also substantial consulting, modeling, information management, total cost, yield, and general project management around these activities. In short, SLB offers a fully outsourced supply chain for oil and gas field development and production.

Schlumberger manages its business through 28 GeoMarket regions, which are grouped into four geographic areas: North America (25 percent); Latin America (15 percent); Europe, Commonwealth of Independent States, and Africa (26 percent); and Middle East and Asia (34 percent). You might have expected that such an oil field services company, dependent on the now-attenuated production plans of oil "E&P" producers worldwide, who are suffering from the 40 percent drop in oil prices in 2014 and 20 percent in 2015 and only a small recovery in 2016, might have been cut from our *100 Best* list. Obviously, we didn't drop it. The question, of course and as always, is whether the market changes represented a fundamental and irreversible negative shift in the business. In the end, we determined that the changed markets present a challenge to the company, but not an irreversible one. The company continues to position itself as a technology leader in the industry. As an example, the recent partnership with Weatherford called

"OneStim" announced in March 2017 targets "unconventional resource development"—high-tech fracking, essentially. We also think the slump will both shake out weak competitors and drive down the cost of acquiring others (the purchase of Cameron International in 2016 is an example), and lead to efficiency measures within the company, both of which bode well during an eventual recovery. Being the biggest and best in the business helps a lot in these situations.

Bottom line, as the company itself suggests: US producers will have to lower costs, and thus apply SLB technologies and know-how to producing shale oil and gas at a cost economical to a $50 or $60 oil price. In the company's view, the shakeout, the need to produce more cheaply, and a strong financial base to weather a continued price downturn and the inevitable long-term growth in world oil consumption, will get them by and position them well for recovery, which should be under way by 2018 if not before.

We continue to agree—but it's worth watching carefully.

## Financial Highlights, Fiscal Year 2016

"Better decrementals than the competition" boasted one company slide presentation last year—and it's a classic. We've never seen such a statement in a corporate pitch before. It's a good example of "thinking positive"—but as you look at SLB revenue and margin declines they aren't as bad as the competition, many of whom have slipped into the red. Not SLB. While revenues did drop about 22 percent again in FY2016 (after a 25 percent drop in FY2015) and net earnings by another 25 percent, some of that was asset write-downs, as evidenced by per-share cash flow checking in only 17 percent lower. The year was highlighted by a 46 percent drop in North American land-based rig count and "slow growth" mode most everywhere else.

As 2017 unfolds, the company is experiencing an uptick in North American land-based exploration driven by higher prices and recent OPEC production restraint. Chairman and CEO Paal Kibsgaard also observes that depletion rates are now far outpacing reserve replacement, which in the long term bodes well for Schlumberger as eventually E&P producers will be forced to catch up. Mr. Kibsgaard suggests that SLB will be in good position to capture this cyclical upswing when it happens with its recent investments and "performance trailblazer" mentality. Forecasts call for a 6–10 percent revenue recovery in FY2017 followed by a 15–20 percent uptick in FY2018, with a rapid escalation in net income in the 40 percent range in FY2017 and as much as 75 percent in FY2018. Share buybacks and dividend increases will resume if this scenario plays out.

The company projects a return to full health—and likely beyond as the E&P cycle progresses and weaker hands in the industry decline—in the 2020–2022 time frame.

## Reasons to Buy

The cycle of supply and demand is the key here. It isn't lost on us—nor on SLB—that major producers *still* have to replace depleted reserves, and that world oil demand will continue to grow, albeit slowly, in the longer term. The most efficient producers in the US and abroad will prosper, and SLB is well positioned, with its size, present geography, and expertise, to move with them. The company is applying its competitive advantages in technology and size strategically.

In the long term, we agree that SLB could come out of this shift stronger than ever as the oil service industry and the US producer landscape both consolidate. But as an investor, you'll have to be patient, and view current events as a buying opportunity. Remember too, that most stocks recover in advance of the actual business recovery; we expect that the stock price recovery, if not the business recovery, will be well under way by 2018.

## Reasons for Caution

The shifts and uncertainties caused by the oil market disruption could get larger, and that plus cutthroat competition could put a bigger dent in the oil service industry. The fortunes of SLB are inevitably tied to the price of oil, and nobody is predicting with any great certainty where that price will end up by 2018—although most agree that it will be well north of the low-$30s low experienced in January 2016. The company will always face the traditional risks of oil drilling—particularly offshore drilling—that culminated in the BP disaster of 2010.

SECTOR: **Energy** ❑ BETA COEFFICIENT: **1.11** ❑ 10-YEAR COMPOUND EARNINGS PER-SHARE GROWTH: **2.0%** ❑ 10-YEAR COMPOUND DIVIDENDS PER-SHARE GROWTH: **16.0%**

|                    | 2009   | 2010   | 2011   | 2012   | 2013   | 2014   | 2015   | 2016   |
|--------------------|--------|--------|--------|--------|--------|--------|--------|--------|
| Revenues (mil)     | 22,702 | 27,447 | 39,540 | 42,149 | 45,266 | 48,580 | 35,475 | 27,810 |
| Net income (mil)   | 3,142  | 3,408  | 3,954  | 5,439  | 6,210  | 5,643  | 2,072  | 1,550  |
| Earnings per share | 2.61   | 2.70   | 3.51   | 4.06   | 4.70   | 4.32   | 1.63   | 1.14   |
| Dividends per share| 0.84   | 0.84   | 0.96   | 1.06   | 1.25   | 1.60   | 2.00   | 2.00   |
| Cash flow per share| 4.70   | 4.55   | 6.05   | 6.73   | 7.55   | 7.64   | 4.90   | 4.06   |
| Price:     high    | 71.1   | 84.1   | 95.6   | 80.8   | 94.9   | 118.8  | 92.1   | 87.0   |
|            low     | 35.1   | 54.7   | 54.8   | 59.1   | 69.1   | 78.5   | 66.6   | 59.8   |

Website: www.slb.com

**AGGRESSIVE GROWTH**

# Schnitzer Steel Industries, Inc.

Ticker symbol: SCHN (NASDAQ) ❑ Small Cap ❑ Value Line financial strength rating: B ❑ Current yield: 3.6% ❑ Dividend raises, past 10 years: 2

## Company Profile

One more year. We've stuck with you through the thick and thin (mostly thin) for the past four years, Schnitzer Steel. We know you've been caught in the crosshairs of the commodity bust and slack emerging market demand (translation: China) and the strong dollar. We know you've seen the legs knocked out from under the prices of your primary products: scrap metals and finished steel.

But we know that the commodity bust is—albeit somewhat erratically—coming to an end. We know that you've taken advantage of the opportunity, as many well-managed companies like you, to make your processes more efficient and cost effective. We know you've done the best you could, Schnitzer Steel, with the hand you were dealt. And now that we see signs of recovery, we'll hang on. Finally, we like having at least one "small cap" stock on our list. So, one more year, Schnitzer Steel.

Founded in 1946, Schnitzer Steel is mainly a collector and recycler of ferrous and nonferrous scrap, with smaller operations that collect, dismantle, and market auto and truck parts and a steel mill "mini mill" finished steel product business. There are two business segments: Auto and Metals Recycling (AMR) and the Steel Manufacturing Business (SMB).

The "AMR" business, which accounts for about 87 percent of Schnitzer's revenues, includes the Metals Recycling business (about 89 percent of AMR) which collects, recycles, processes, and brokers scrap steel and nonferrous metals to domestic and foreign markets—3.3 million tons of ferrous scrap metal and 510 million pounds of nonferrous metal in all. By revenues, 68 percent of 2016 revenues were ferrous (iron and steel) and 32 percent were nonferrous (dominated by copper and aluminum, but also including stainless steel, nickel, brass, titanium, and lead among others).

Larger scrap mills are located in Oregon; Washington; Oakland, CA; and Massachusetts, with smaller mills in Rhode Island, Puerto Rico, Hawaii, and Alaska, all with adjacent deep-water ports, correctly suggesting an orientation toward international export of scrap metal for foreign mills. Indeed, that is true—some 50 percent of ferrous shipments go to Asia, 25 percent to Europe/Africa/Middle East, and 25 percent to US steel mills (this means that it doesn't much matter who wins the current trade wars in steel). The company operates 60 metals recycling facilities ("scrapyards," in popular vernacular) in 23 states, mostly on the coasts and in the south, seven in Canada, and five in Puerto Rico. The operation adds value in part by sorting and shredding input scrap into homogenous materials well suited to the needs of downstream customers.

The Auto Parts business portion of the AMR segment operates 52 self-serve locations and remarketing centers, some co-located with Metals Recycling facilities, in 16 states with a concentration in California under the "Pick-n-Pull" name. This operation processes about 350,000 cars per year. Inventories of scrapped autos and common parts from those autos are posted online and updated as new inventory is received.

The Steel Manufacturing business (13 percent of revenues) operates an electric arc furnace mini mill in McMinnville, OR, producing rebar, wire rod, merchant bar, and other specialty products, of course from scrap steel available from the company's own Metals Recycling facilities.

## Financial Highlights, Fiscal Year 2016

The FY2015 story of lower prices and somewhat lower volumes continued into FY2016. The late-2014 commodity price and oil price collapse, shrinking China end-user demand, soft Europe, continued production and a supply glut of iron ore and certain other metals, and the strong dollar continued to plague the business through the year. Modest volume declines and a 28 percent drop in average realized ferrous prices and 21 percent nonferrous resulted in a 29 percent overall revenue drop. The good news is that ferrous and nonferrous prices firmed at the end of the year as worldwide inventories dropped and as Trump administration prospects for infrastructure replacement and domestic manufacturing began to take center stage. Average ferrous selling prices recovered to $196 per ton Q4 FY2016 from $179 Q4 FY2015—a step in the right direction, and volumes were up 5 percent to boot. Margins improved with greater volumes and with significant productivity improvements started earlier, trimming losses substantially. The company's "average inventory cost" accounting policy means that costs declines lag sales and selling price declines which hurt profits further, but can help on a rebound. Forecasts call for a recovery to $1.6 billion in sales and 40 cents in per-share earnings for FY2017, with cash flows well north of $3.00 per share, and a far more robust $1.10 per-share earnings ($4.25 cash flow) in FY2018. These figures, if realized, should keep the dividend safe as the company indicates it would like to do.

## Reasons to Buy

Clearly we're still betting on a turnaround in steel and especially steel scrap prices as demand improves and competing iron ore supplies dwindle due mainly to mine closures. Scrap as a source of supply is much more flexible and environmentally sound and should lead the way in a metals-industry recovery. We don't believe the fundamental recycling-based business model is by any means broken. Too, and perhaps most importantly, today's modern electric-arc furnace mills such as those operated by Nucor are more cost-effective and flexible than traditional blast furnaces and tend to use scrap as the main input resource. Scrap is easier to source, more flexible, and more local than traditional iron ore inputs for these modern mills.

There are a lot of mom-and-pop scrap dealers around the world, but few have the size, operating leverage, and remarketing abilities of Schnitzer. The company is a strong and recognized brand in a fragmented and unbranded industry, offering advantages both on the sales and operational side. When prices and markets are soft, the company loses, but as we saw particularly in 2008, when markets are strong, the company does really, really well. And, whether steel is made domestically or imported, Schnitzer wins as a universal supplier. Schnitzer is well managed, adds a lot of value in a relatively non-value-add industry, and keeps its shareholders in mind. Much better numbers are expected in 2018 and going forward; we feel these will continue to be reflected in the stock price. The risk/reward profile still feels favorable.

## Reasons for Caution

There is risk here—more than we embrace with most other *100 Best* stocks. Schnitzer is very sensitive to global steel and nonferrous metals markets and the ups and downs of pricing. While its size and marketing advantages serve it well in tough times, inventory is inventory, and the company can get caught with a lot of it purchased at higher prices if the markets don't move to its advantage. It does okay in bad economic climates, but the company is really a bet on recycling value add and on good times in global manufacturing. If you buy in, you'll want to watch global steel and other metals prices. Too, while the company has a good track record, there are always some environmental risks and costs in this sort of business. The high beta of 1.63

reflects some of this risk and the volatility inherent in the relatively low share count of 26 million shares outstanding.

SECTOR: **Industrials** ❑ BETA COEFFICIENT: **1.63** ❑ 10-YEAR COMPOUND EARNINGS PER-SHARE GROWTH: **NM** ❑ 10-YEAR COMPOUND DIVIDENDS PER-SHARE GROWTH: **27.0%**

|  |  | 2009 | 2010 | 2011 | 2012 | 2013 | 2014 | 2015 | 2016 |
|---|---|---|---|---|---|---|---|---|---|
| Revenues (mil) | | 1,900 | 2,301 | 3,459 | 3,341 | 2,621 | 2,544 | 1,915 | 1,352 |
| Net income (mil) | | (32.2) | 67 | 119 | 30 | (2.0) | 5.1 | (58.8) | (19.4) |
| Earnings per share | | (1.14) | 2.86 | 4.24 | 1.10 | (0.07) | 0.19 | (2.25) | (0.66) |
| Dividends per share | | 0.20 | 0.20 | 0.20 | 0.41 | 0.75 | 0.75 | 0.75 | 0.75 |
| Cash flow per share | | 1.03 | 4.75 | 7.08 | 4.28 | 3.05 | 3.19 | 0.23 | 1.32 |
| Price: | high | 64.0 | 66.9 | 69.4 | 47.4 | 33.0 | 33.3 | 22.8 | 22.8 |
|  | low | 23.3 | 37.0 | 32.8 | 22.8 | 23.1 | 21.4 | 12.6 | 11.7 |

Website: www.schnitzersteel.com

# The Scotts Miracle-Gro Company

Ticker symbol: SMG (NYSE) ❑ Mid Cap ❑ Value Line financial strength rating: B++ ❑ Current yield: 2.2% ❑ Dividend raises, past 10 years: 7

## Company Profile

Scotts Miracle-Gro, formerly Scotts Co., formerly O.M. Scott & Sons, is a 148-year-old provider of mostly packaged lawn- and garden-care products for consumer markets. Originally a seed company, today its lawn-care products include packaged, pre-mixed fertilizers and combination fertilizer and weed/pest-control products marketed mainly under the Scotts and Turf Builder brand names. The company also markets packaged grass seed and a line of individually packaged pest/disease-control products mainly under the Ortho brand, acquired in 1997, and a line of specialty garden fertilizers and pest-control products under the Miracle-Gro name, acquired in 1995. The company also markets a line of home protection pest-control products, and acts as the exclusive worldwide distributor for the consumer Roundup brand (from Monsanto, a former *100 Best* stock recently acquired by Bayer AG). Through a series of small acquisitions, the company has entered the lawn service business, which now operates out of 88 company-operated and

94 franchised locations. Consumer businesses account for about 90 percent of revenues, Lawn Service another 9 percent.

Scotts is a study in branding in an otherwise highly fragmented market. The attractive core brands of Scotts, Turf Builder, Miracle-Gro, and Ortho and Roundup take center stage in this business and in their respective markets. The company measures brand strength and awareness closely and puts out the following stats: Scotts market share 66 percent, brand awareness 95 percent; Miracle-Gro market share 57 percent, brand awareness 88 percent; Ortho market share 53 percent, brand awareness 83 percent; and Roundup market share 70 percent and brand awareness 89 percent. Smaller but significant brands are Hyponex (bagged potting soil and manure), Weedol weed killers, Osmocote professional plant nutrients, and Fertiligene, Substral, and EverGreen fertilizers and chemicals in Europe.

The vision is interesting: "To help people of all ages express themselves on their own piece of the earth." While this sounds pretty groovy, it also connotes the possibilities to expand markets. Further trendy elements in this business include an ongoing demographic shift—more returning to cities—different styles of gardening, more specialty products—a shift that may prove positive but will take some work. To that end, in 2015 the company completed the purchase of two leading producers of equipment and consumables for hydroponic gardening. It isn't mentioned anywhere on their websites or in their financial reports, but this equipment also supports the rapidly legitimizing marijuana industry—a high-growth area (no pun intended).

People are also seeking organic gardening products in consumer packages; Scotts new line of organic Miracle-Gro products have begun to address this trend. Innovations also include new packaging to simplify the measurement and application and improve the safety of key products.

Somewhat to our surprise, the company divested its lawn service businesses, which were good case studies in adjacent branding, i.e., Ortho lawn service. Scotts is still acquiring smaller adjacent companies in organics, hydroponics, live goods (live plants), and in Europe.

## Financial Highlights, Fiscal Year 2016

Mainly due to the lawn service divestiture, FY2016 revenues dropped 9 percent. But the decision apparently made sense; thanks to that, in addition to efficiency measures and an improved product mix (hydroponics and organics products are profitable!), net income grew like a weed, up 53 percent to a record $258 million. Sales growth going forward looks to be in the 6–8 percent range (and this might be conservative) while earnings growth will be modest, up zero to 5 percent as acquisition and restructuring costs are recognized. Fertilized by 3–4 percent annual buybacks, per-share earnings should increase in the high single digits (and again this might be conservative). After 2019, the grass gets much greener as the mix of brands and subsidiaries settles and as operating leverage is achieved.

## Reasons to Buy

Scotts Miracle-Gro is increasingly leveraging its brand strength both in the US and abroad, although there are rumors of a sale of its European business. Beyond focus and increased prominence of core brands, there continue to be several tailwinds that should help the company. First on the list is the economy and renewed strength in the housing market; new homes come with new lawns and gardens, and an increase in home value should mean people will be spending more on their homes. We see more emphasis on quality landscapes over quantity and size of lawn, which should help Scotts. The younger crowd is taking an interest in specialized urban, suburban, and organic gardening, which are sweet spots for Scotts. And then, of course, there's marijuana. Scotts could well become the first major US corporation to have a defined business devoted to the growth of marijuana products. This will certainly be interesting to watch.

## Reasons for Caution

While big retailers have increasingly joined the Scotts bandwagon, they aren't the only brand in town, and the company does face some competition from less expensive house brands such as those sold at Ace Hardware, Home Depot, Lowe's, and elsewhere. Scotts' aggressive marketing, while clever ("Feed your lawn. Feed it!") and apparently effective, is not cheap. Lawn and garden spend is naturally sensitive to sluggish economies, but we do think that there is a baseline level people will drop to and remain at; they want to maintain their lawns and provide pleasant stay-at-home environments if they can't do much else. Finally, the past decade of demographic shifts away from the suburbs, including downsizing and increases in renting versus owning, will continue to put pressure on the traditional bagged fertilizer and lawn goods business; Scotts' new products and services in new niches like hydroponics will keep the spreader moving forward here.

SECTOR: **Materials** ▫ BETA COEFFICIENT: **0.64** ▫ 10-YEAR COMPOUND EARNINGS PER-SHARE
GROWTH: **6.5%** ▫ 10-YEAR COMPOUND DIVIDENDS PER-SHARE GROWTH: **24.5%**

|  | 2009 | 2010 | 2011 | 2012 | 2013 | 2014 | 2015 | 2016 |
|---|---|---|---|---|---|---|---|---|
| Revenues (mil) | 3,141 | 3,139 | 2,835 | 2,826 | 2,819 | 2,841 | 3,017 | 2,836 |
| Net income (mil) | 153.3 | 212.4 | 121.9 | 113.2 | 161.2 | 165.4 | 158.7 | 253.8 |
| Earnings per share | 2.32 | 3.14 | 1.84 | 1.62 | 2.58 | 2.64 | 2.57 | 4.09 |
| Dividends per share | 0.50 | 0.63 | 0.05 | 1.23 | 1.41 | 1.76 | 1.82 | 1.91 |
| Cash flow per share | 3.23 | 4.07 | 3.00 | 2.86 | 3.67 | 3.74 | 3.64 | 5.36 |
| Price:     high | 44.3 | 55.0 | 60.8 | 55.9 | 62.6 | 64.0 | 72.3 | 98.8 |
| low | 24.9 | 37.5 | 40.0 | 35.5 | 42.0 | 52.4 | 58.1 | 62.2 |

Website: www.scottsmiraclegro.com

**AGGRESSIVE GROWTH**

# Southwest Airlines Co.

Ticker symbol: LUV (NYSE) ▫ Large Cap ▫ Value Line financial strength rating: A ▫ Current yield: 0.7% ▫ Dividend raises, past 10 years: 5

## Company Profile

Loyal *100 Best Stocks* readers will recall that for years we were critical of the airline industry for its inability to control prices because of intense competition and costs that largely are comprised of fuel, airport, and unionized labor. Lack of profitability and inability to control these factors made airlines into poster children for the kinds of stocks we tend to avoid.

That's hardly the case any longer. Fuel costs have gone down and look to stay there for a while. Most airlines have, by design or by default, rationalized their route structures and capacity, necessitated by once-high fuel costs, airport constraints, and the Great Recession. With this rationalized capacity, they are better able to control both prices and costs, and their outlooks are much brighter.

We're happy to report that we boarded Southwest in 2012 just as it was taxiing for takeoff, and we're glad we did. Look at a five- or ten-year chart— it's a thing of beauty!

Southwest Airlines provides passenger air transport mainly in the United States, all within North America. In early 2016, the company served 101 cities in 40 states, and with the acquisition of AirTran it also serves Mexico and seven other countries in Central America, and the Caribbean (now including Cuba) with point-to-point, rather than hub-and-spoke, service. The company serves these markets almost exclusively with 723 Boeing

737 aircraft. Southwest continues to be the largest domestic air carrier in the United States, as measured by the number of domestic originating passengers boarded. At 3,300 peak-season departures per day, the airline also originates the most flights. This should give an idea of their business model—low cost, shorter flights, and maximum passenger loads.

The business model is one of simplicity—no-frills aircraft, no first-class passenger cabin, limited interchange with other carriers, no onboard meals, simple boarding and seat assignment practices, direct sales over the Internet (over 79 percent of sales processed online), no baggage fees—all designed to provide steady and reliable transportation, with one of the best on-time performances in the industry, and to maximize asset utilization with minimal downtime, crew disruptions, and other upward influences on operating costs. The company has long used secondary airports—such as Providence, RI, and Manchester, NH, to serve Boston and the New England area; Allentown, PA, and East Islip, NY, to serve the New York/New Jersey area (though it now serves LaGuardia, too, if you want that choice); and Chicago Midway to reduce delays and costs. This strategy has worked well.

Southwest has successfully implemented a few initiatives to squeeze out some extra revenue without alienating the core passenger group, mostly business travelers. One such initiative is Business Select, which offers priority boarding, priority security, bonus frequent flyer credit, and a free beverage for an upgrade fee. The company also sells early boarding as a standalone for a modest $15 fee. They're also tinkering with baggage fees, raising fees for overweight or excess bags, though leaving the basic two-bag limit free for now (we continue to applaud that move). Southwest also produces more than $600 million in revenue annually from its Rapid Rewards loyalty point program through partnerships and sales of points. The program routinely wins "best of" rewards in the industry.

New initiatives include a transition to newer Boeing 737 aircraft, including the Boeing 737-MAX, which can fly 500 miles farther than existing models opening up more international markets, and more 143-seat 747-700s and 175-seat 737-800s (typical older 737 models range from 117 to 132 seats). Well over half the fleet is comprised of one of these newer models, and the company currently has 200 new aircraft on order, all Boeing 737 models.

## Financial Highlights, Fiscal Year 2016

Southwest had already been taxiing into position with operational improvements, capacity rationalization, the AirTran acquisition, and other market and efficiency gains. The 50 percent drop in oil prices cleared Southwest for takeoff, and take off it did. Fuel costs as a percent of revenue dropped to

21.9 percent from the low to mid-30s a few years ago reflecting three favorable trends—higher revenues, lower fuel prices, and greater fuel efficiency.

In a leveling-off year, net earnings climbed 2.3 percent on a 3.1 percent revenue gain. Decent-sized share buybacks led to a 9 percent per-share earnings gain, however. Not only did fuel prices help, but so did strong gains in revenue seat miles. The load factor hit a record 84.0 from around 80 a few years ago (percentage of seats paid for and occupied—*that's* why their planes have been so crowded lately!), and that combined with more available seat miles, higher fares, and longer average trips really helped the top line; the aforementioned fuel cost declines and more efficient aircraft, not to mention a stronger economy, all contributed to solid results.

The altitude gain continues in FY2017 and FY2018 with 5 percent revenue gains projected each year but relatively flat earnings growth projected as labor and fuel costs increase modestly. These forecasts could be conservative, especially for the fuel. Annual share buybacks in the 2–4 percent range add to the story, as does (finally) a modernization of the dividend policy; while the yield is still very modest, it's getting better.

## Reasons to Buy

The story remains much the same: Southwest continues to be the best player in an industry whose fundamentals have dramatically improved. The company continues to be the "envy" value proposition of the industry, and we continue to be surprised that no one else has been able to emulate it successfully—but at this point, even if they do, Southwest has a decades-long first mover advantage.

The airline "gets it" that what customers want is no-hassle transportation at best-possible prices—and yes, no bag fees—and has been able to do that better than anyone else for years, and is now extending its value proposition further for business travelers, who increasingly book their own fares and respond well to $15 priority boarding upgrades and other offers. Good management, efficient operation, and excellent marketing make it all possible. With merit, the company refers to its customers as "fans." Financially, the company has earned a profit for 44 consecutive years—in the volatile airline industry we know no greater testimonial to good marketing and good management.

## Reasons for Caution

Fuel prices are a big part of the recent success but are still—and will always be—a wild card. The company has shown in the past that it can use hedges to manage fuel price shocks, and we're guessing they're putting their hedges in place now.

We hope the company doesn't become complacent with its recent success, assume low fuel prices will last forever, and start flying 747s to London or some such nonsense. The recession forced all airlines, even Southwest, to "fly smart," and we hope this continues.

Generally we fear anything that would move Southwest away from its core competencies—complacency in the short run, acquisitions in the longer term. The AirTran acquisition story appears to have a happy ending but was also a challenge—different practices, processes, and cultures. The longer Southwest can stay Southwest, and avoid looking like other airlines, the better.

Finally, much of the good news may have already been priced into the stock's steep ascent; once again it may be due for a leveling off.

SECTOR: **Transportation** ◻ BETA COEFFICIENT: **0.68** ◻ 10-YEAR COMPOUND EARNINGS PER-SHARE GROWTH: **16.5%** ◻ 10-YEAR COMPOUND DIVIDENDS PER-SHARE GROWTH: **28.0%**

|  |  | 2009 | 2010 | 2011 | 2012 | 2013 | 2014 | 2015 | 2016 |
|---|---|---|---|---|---|---|---|---|---|
| Revenues (mil) |  | 10,350 | 12,104 | 15,658 | 17,088 | 17,699 | 18,605 | 19,820 | 20,425 |
| Net income (mil) |  | 140 | 550 | 330 | 421 | 754 | 1,136 | 2,161 | 2,244 |
| Earnings per share |  | 0.19 | 0.73 | 0.42 | 0.58 | 1.05 | 1.64 | 3.27 | 3.55 |
| Dividends per share |  | 0.02 | 0.02 | 0.03 | 0.04 | 0.10 | 0.22 | 0.29 | 0.38 |
| Cash flow per share |  | 1.21 | 1.02 | 1.35 | 1.73 | 2.35 | 3.07 | 4.94 | 5.45 |
| Price: | high | 11.8 | 14.3 | 13.9 | 10.6 | 19.0 | 43.2 | 51.3 | 51.3 |
|  | low | 4.0 | 10.4 | 7.1 | 7.8 | 10.4 | 18.8 | 31.4 | 34.0 |

Website: www.southwest.com

**AGGRESSIVE GROWTH**

NEW FOR 2018

# Siemens AG (ADR)

Ticker symbol: SIEGY ◻ Large Cap ◻ Value Line financial strength rating: A ◻ Current yield: 2.7% ◻ Dividend raises, past 10 years: 8

## Company Profile

"Ingenuity for Life" is the clever and constructive slogan of the $90 billion diversified industrial conglomerate known worldwide as Siemens. Siemens touches many industries and sectors of interest to us: infrastructure, healthcare, urban transportation, industrial automation, and alternative energy with an assortment of mostly technology-enhanced products and services. The company was founded in the late nineteenth century by Werner von Siemens, an early electrical engineering pioneer and inventor of the electric elevator.

Siemens operates in eight product segments:

- Power and Gas (20 percent of FY2016 revenues) supplies an assortment of products to the oil and gas, power, and industrial markets: gas and steam turbines and other "heavy" power plant hardware of varying sizes.
- "Healthineers" (Healthcare—17 percent) is a leader in medical imaging, laboratory diagnostics, therapy systems, hearing instruments, and clinical IT.
- Energy Management (15 percent) is a leading global supplier of electrical grid hardware, solutions, and services "for the economical, reliable, and intelligent transmission and distribution of electric power," including high- and low-voltage and smart-grid solutions.
- Digital Factory (13 percent) offers a portfolio of integrated hardware and software solutions to support product design processes worldwide and to reduce their time to market.
- Process Industries and Drives (11 percent) is the manufacturing and factory automation complement to the Digital Factory group; the emphasis here is on creating, analyzing, and managing integrated, state-of-the-art manufacturing processes.
- Mobility (10 percent) makes and sells various urban transportation infrastructure products, most notably so-called "light rail" transit cars; a large factory in Sacramento, California, produces these vehicles for the US and certain global markets.
- Building Technologies (8 percent) is the "world market leader" for building automation technologies, HVAC controls, security, fire protection, and energy management products and services.
- Wind Power (7 percent) provides hardware, software, and services toward the creation of efficient onshore and offshore wind power generation facilities. The relative size and importance of this segment will increase with the 2017 acquisition of Gamesa, described more fully (following). Too, the group has been awarded the world's largest onshore order to date from MidAmerica Energy (a Warren Buffett/Berkshire Hathaway company) in Iowa.

By region, revenues break down as follows: Americas (29 percent), EMEA (ex Germany—39 percent), Asia/Australia (19 percent), and Germany (13 percent).

Not surprisingly, as an industrial conglomerate, Siemens is fairly active on the acquisition front, adding (and sometimes divesting) smaller companies active in the industrial technology and other spaces. As part of the development of what the company calls its "digital enterprise suite," the company acquired electronic design software maker Mentor Graphics for $4.5 billion in early 2017. Prior acquisitions include CD-adapco, a maker of physics simulation software in 2016; LMS, a 3D test and simulation software provider in 2012; and UGS, a design and factory automation software provider in 2007. Overall, the company intends to become a leader in digital product life-cycle management, including design, simulation, testing, and manufacturing. The 2017 acquisition of Spanish wind turbine manufacturer Gamesa will add 11 billion euros in annual orders and about 21 billion euros in backlog to the revenue mix.

## Financial Highlights, Fiscal Year 2016

Currency translation effects are a major driver of the numbers you see below; the recent euro/US dollar conversion rate of 1.10 and below pales in comparison to the 1.46 rate back in 2009, hence results (and dividend payouts) look more choppy than they really are. That said, soft global markets and divestitures led to a 14 percent revenue decline in FY2016, although on an organic volume basis, orders and revenue were up 5 percent. Efficiency measures and growth in the higher-margined Digital Factory and related groups actually led to a 4 percent increase in net profit on a continuing operations basis. Going forward, and aided by acquisitions, revenues are forecast to rise about 10 percent in FY2017 and another 6–8 percent in FY2018. Margin improvements could lead to net income gains in as much as the 20–25 percent range in FY2017, stabilizing to a 3–5 percent range in FY2018. Gradual share buybacks and dividend increases are likely.

## Reasons to Buy

"Digitalization, Globalization, and Urbanization" are the three stated marketplace themes of this progressive leader in the world of industrial design and infrastructure. Despite recent political events, we believe as Siemens does that the world will be a more integrated industrial and distribution arena, more connected, more processes will be created and managed digitally, and that new and modern urban infrastructure will become increasingly important as urban populations grow. To those trends, the company brings new focus on added value in "digitalization, automation, and electrification" of the industrial and infrastructure space worldwide. We think this is a solid and very progressive—not to mention more profitable—position in comparison to most of today's industrial and infrastructure suppliers. The strategy seems right, and we think Siemens has already achieved world leadership in these areas. In fact, we classified the company under "Industrials" as a sector, but could have easily justified classifying it as a "Technology" company. The world's factories, energy grids, transportation, and other infrastructure are all ripe for a major refresh, and Siemens will be right in the middle of it.

The company has made great progress to build and optimize its product portfolio going forward with these markets and principles in mind. Although Siemens is notably global in its business footprint, a nascent but growing recovery in Europe should help. A more profitable business mix and cost-efficiency measures are projected to increase gross and net margins significantly; as this occurs we expect moderately increasing shareholder returns over time.

## Reasons for Caution

As the numbers below show, performance has been (and can be) choppy, not just because of currency but also exposure to economic cycles and slowdowns. Siemens makes capital equipment, and capital equipment is one of the first things to be cut out of customer budgets when the going gets tough. That said, recent Trump administration policies, cash repatriation, and a general sense that manufacturing and public infrastructure needs to be modernized should all help Siemens out. Finally—the usual warning about foreign-based companies— Siemens is harder to understand than a lot of US equivalents; it is complex, it operates differently, and it presents itself differently. That said, the company does a better-than-average job of explaining itself to potential investors on its website.

SECTOR: **Industrials** ▫ BETA COEFFICIENT: **1.21** ▫ 10-YEAR COMPOUND EARNINGS PER-SHARE GROWTH: **7.5%** ▫ 10-YEAR COMPOUND DIVIDENDS PER-SHARE GROWTH: **9.5%**

|  | 2009 | 2010 | 2011 | 2012 | 2013 | 2014 | 2015 | 2016 |
|---|---|---|---|---|---|---|---|---|
| Revenues (bil) | 112.1 | 103.3 | 98.8 | 100.7 | 102.7 | 91.0 | 84.8 | 89.2 |
| Net income (bil) | 3.3 | 5.4 | 9.1 | 6.5 | 5.5 | 6.7 | 6.0 | 6.3 |
| Earnings per share | 1.89 | 3.09 | 5.19 | 3.67 | 3.26 | 3.91 | 3.53 | 3.80 |
| Dividends per share | 1.05 | 1.12 | 1.84 | 1.93 | 2.01 | 2.05 | 1.88 | 1.90 |
| Cash flow per share | 4.37 | 6.30 | 7.28 | 5.85 | 5.60 | 5.76 | 5.48 | 5.78 |
| Price:      high | 51.5 | 62.6 | 73.4 | 55.4 | 69.6 | 69.0 | 57.5 | 62.1 |
| low | 23.8 | 41.4 | 42.4 | 38.9 | 49.3 | 51.6 | 43.9 | 43.3 |

**Website: www.siemens.com**

# Starbucks Corporation

Ticker symbol: SBUX (NASDAQ) ❑ Large Cap ❑ Value Line financial strength rating: A++ ❑ Current yield: 1.7% ❑ Dividend raises, past 10 years: 6

## Company Profile

Starbucks Corporation, formed in 1985, is the leading retailer, roaster, and brand of specialty coffee in the world. The company sells whole-bean coffees through its retailers, its specialty sales group, and supermarkets. The Starbucks store footprint continues to expand. In the Americas there are now 9,019 company-owned stores (8,752 at the end of 2015) and 6,518 licensed stores. In "CAP" (China Asia-Pacific) there are 2,811 company-owned and 3,632 licensee stores; in EMEA (Europe, Middle East, and Africa) there are 523 and 2,119 stores respectively; in "Other" there are 358 company-owned stores and 35 licensees. In all it's a rich brew of 12,711 company-owned and 12,374 licensee stores worldwide. Retail coffee shop sales constitute about 89 percent of its revenue, unchanged from last year. About 79 percent of revenue originates in company-operated stores. Unlike many in the Restaurant sector, the company does not franchise its stores—all are either company owned or operated by licensees in special venues such as airports, college campuses, and other places where access is restricted, and in foreign markets where it is necessary or advantageous.

The company continues to expand overseas, usually at first through partnerships and joint ventures; sometimes it buys out the partner as it did in China in 2011. The FY2016 sales breakdown: 69 percent Americas, 5 percent Europe/Middle East/Africa, 14 percent China/Asia-Pacific, and 12 percent other segments and "channel development," which is largely made up of branded product sales through non-Starbucks retailers. The company now operates in 62 countries in total; India is one of the fastest-growing countries, followed by Vietnam.

The company is gradually expanding beyond its traditional coffee base, opening a new Teavana Fine Teas Bar in New York and adding Teavana and Tazo tea–related items into its traditional store offering. Evolution Fresh juices are now widely available, and the company has done well with its food menu, including its "La Boulange" line of pastries and Ethos water products. Specialty packaging, including "Via" and Keurig-compatible single-serve packages have done well also. Finally, Starbucks has joint ventures with PepsiCo and Dreyer's to develop bottled coffee drinks and coffee-flavored ice creams.

In 2016 as in 2015, the sum total revenue mix was 58 percent beverages, 16 percent food, 14 percent packaged and single-serve coffees and teas, and 12 percent "other" including the aforementioned joint venture–produced drinks and ice creams.

Starbucks continues to invest and expand its leadership in the deployment of technology. Always a leader in providing Wi-Fi connectivity to users in its stores, the company's "Mobile Order and Pay" app and platform, where users can order and pay for their drinks using smartphones, then subsequently arrive at locations to pick up their drinks, is doing quite well. Not only is this convenient for the customer, it effectively increases capacity and reduces wait time in the stores, and provides a platform to offer more items for sale.

The company's retail goal continues to be the unique Starbucks experience, which the company defines as a third place beyond home and work. The "experience" is built upon superior customer service and a clean, well-maintained retail store that reflects the personality of the community in which it operates—all aimed at building loyalty and frequent repeat visits.

The company also gets high marks for citizenship, continuing to offer health coverage, equity participation, and even college assistance for its 254,000 employees ("partners"). Commitments to hire veterans, military spouses, and more recently, Syrian refugees, are notable among a list of other commitments to community service and social issues of the day.

Finally, founder and chairman Howard Schultz left his role as CEO to work on his "Reserve" high-end coffee bar concept. Both his departure and the new adventure bear watching.

## Financial Highlights, Fiscal Year 2016

Technology, brand, optimized store locations, expansion, favorable coffee prices, and operating leverage led to a 5 percent same-store sales gain worldwide and an 11 percent increase in total revenues. The same-store sales gain was comprised of a 1 percent gain in transactions and a 4 percent gain in the average sales ticket. An operating margin increase of 0.8 percent to 19.6 percent led to a robust 14 percent gain in net income; a 2 percent reduction in the share count led to a 20 percent gain in per-share earnings. Estimates call for a 7 percent top-line growth in 2017 widening to 10 percent in 2018. Continued operational improvements and improved international profitability will gradually widen margins and bring earnings growth in the high single digits to mid-teens. "Room for cream" comes in the form of dividend increases in the low double digits with a moderate amount of share buyback activity added in for good measure.

## Reasons to Buy

Starbucks is still a great story. The company's stores continue to be more than coffee shops and are really that "third place" where professionals, students, moms, and other prosperous folks will meet and dole out a few bucks for quality drinks. The "third place" aura creates a lot of brand strength and, in our view, represents the company's *true* strength—well beyond the quality of the coffee itself and related products. The company has a steadily (and profitably) growing presence on the world stage and has learned how not to overbuild and cannibalize its business in the US. New packaging and food products are broadening appeal to larger customer segments and the single-cup market is going strong. And we believe the technology improvements will be big both for customers and operations.

The company is well managed, has an extremely strong brand, has solid financials, and, once again, a steady growth track record, and it is carving out an ever-stronger international footprint. Cash returns to investors are on the rise, and safety (as proxied by beta) has improved sharply from years ago. Starbucks offers both growth and, increasingly, cash and safety—a very nice brew for investors indeed. The recent flattening of the growth trajectory would appear to suggest that this is the time to start a grande half-caf caramel latte of your own.

## Reasons for Caution

The biggest risk used to be overexpansion and competition—both of which they've encountered and dealt with well in recent years but could reemerge as trouble spots down the road. Perhaps our biggest fear now remains the temptation to expand the foodservice business, which could reduce margins, dilute the experience, and make the stores smell like a sandwich shop, far less appealing for most than the aroma of coffee. Too, it brings operational complexities. So we score the experience with food so far as mostly a success but continue to keep our eyes (and noses) open for signs of stress.

Coffee prices are volatile, but as experienced before, they don't really affect this story much since coffee is a small part of the company's total cost picture. Finally, despite the recent lag in the stock price, it is still high relative to peer at 27 times earnings; any strategic or operational missteps could burn your tongue.

SECTOR: **Restaurant** □ BETA COEFFICIENT: **0.80** □ 10-YEAR COMPOUND EARNINGS PER-SHARE GROWTH: **19.0%** □ 10-YEAR COMPOUND DIVIDENDS PER-SHARE GROWTH: **NM**

| | 2009 | 2010 | 2011 | 2012 | 2013 | 2014 | 2015 | 2016 |
|---|---|---|---|---|---|---|---|---|
| Revenues (mil) | 9,774 | 10,707 | 11,701 | 13,299 | 14,892 | 16,448 | 19,163 | 21,316 |
| Net income (mil) | 598 | 982 | 1,174 | 1,385 | 1,721 | 2,068 | 2,394 | 2,635 |
| Earnings per share | 0.40 | 0.64 | 0.76 | 0.90 | 1.13 | 1.36 | 1.58 | 1.62 |
| Dividends per share | — | 0.12 | 0.26 | 0.34 | 0.42 | 0.52 | 0.64 | 0.80 |
| Cash Flow per share | 0.76 | 1.01 | 1.14 | 1.29 | 1.58 | 1.85 | 2.21 | 2.61 |
| Price:        high | 12.0 | 16.6 | 23.3 | 31.0 | 41.3 | 42.1 | 64.0 | 81.8 |
|               low | 4.1 | 10.6 | 15.4 | 21.5 | 26.3 | 34.0 | 39.3 | 50.8 |

Website: www.starbucks.com

## CONSERVATIVE GROWTH

# State Street Corporation

Ticker symbol: STT (NYSE) □ Large Cap □ Value Line financial strength rating: B++ □ Current yield: 2.0% □ Dividend raises, past 10 years: 8

## Company Profile

Are you afraid of SPDRs? Not the eight-legged kind, but the original and one of three leading brands of exchange-traded funds (ETFs) out there rapidly gaining ground on the "traditional" fund industry? If you aren't afraid of SPDRs, and you aren't too afraid of financial stocks in general, you might think about investing in State Street. State Street continues to be, in our opinion, more than most, a safe and sane way to play the Financials sector, which, despite a more favorable regulatory and interest rate environment, we continue to hold generally out of favor—if nothing else because it is very hard to understand financial companies and to analyze their stocks.

Their slogan is simple: "We are the engine that powers the world's investments." State Street is a financial powerhouse like many others. But unlike many, its core products are concentrated on offering services to other financial services firms and on offering the relatively new and growing ETF investment package to individual and institutional investors. It is often analyzed as a bank, but it acts more like a company providing services to other financial institutions and the public, receiving a steady and growing stream of fees for those services. Only about 20 percent of their net income comes as interest income; the other 80 percent is "non-interest income"—mainly fees for investment services. Run a mutual fund, hedge fund, or private equity fund? You might well come to State Street for the "picks and shovels" you need to run the fund—and many have.

The company operates with two main lines of business:

- Investment Servicing (53 percent of revenues) provides fee-based administrative, custodial, analytic, and other value-add functions to investment companies—mainly mutual funds, hedge funds, and pension funds, including settlement and payment services, transaction management, foreign exchange trading and brokerage, and setting the NAV (net asset value, or price) of about 40 percent of US-based mutual funds on a daily basis. The company has $28.8 *trillion* in assets under its custody.
- Investment Management (about 27 percent of revenues) provides investment vehicles and products through its State Street Global Advisors, or SSGA, subsidiary, including the well-known SPDR ETFs and some of the analytic tools and indexes supporting these products.

With these two fee-based business units accounting for 80 percent of total revenues, you might wonder where the rest of its $10.2 billion in revenues come from. The answer lies in interest income—as mentioned previously, 20 percent of revenues comes from the net interest generated on asset holdings.

State Street has operations in 29 countries, and about 64 percent of revenues come from assets managed in the US, 23 percent from the EMEA region, and 13 percent from Asia-Pacific.

## Financial Highlights, Fiscal Year 2016

Currency effects, low interest rates, and limited growth in the mutual fund sector held revenues flat for a second year in a row. A massive IT improvement project known as "Beacon," a small interest rate rise, and some tax benefits led to an 8 percent gain in net income for FY2016. An aggressive 4 percent share buyback resulted in an 11 percent rise in per-share earnings. For FY2017 and FY2018, interest rate rises, a stabilizing currency, and a continued favorable investment climate are projected to get the revenue train moving again with 7 percent growth; net and per-share earnings should roughly follow suit. By 2016, the company will have bought back 32 percent of its float issued to bolster finances during the Great Recession.

## Reasons to Buy

When there's a gold rush, the people who sell picks, shovels, and maps usually win. That's the case with State Street. It makes a lot of steady money selling services to other financial services firms. It's a steadier income stream absent some (but not all) of the risks facing its other financial brethren. We think that State Street has a steady business with an innovative growth path in the ETF business, and we like the SPDR brand. We also like the fact that, unlike most financial firms, the company's income is more driven by fees for services than interest margins and investment gains. That said, the prospect for increased interest rates would bode well for interest income. The company continues to focus on operational efficiency through the Beacon program, and should be well positioned to respond to a more favorable economic environment. State Street also continues to focus on investor returns, aggressively retiring shares and raising the dividend regularly.

## Reasons for Caution

Despite the fact that State Street sells picks and shovels to other investment funds, many of its fees are based on asset valuations—which are in turn vulnerable to market downturns. The company estimates that every 10 percent drop in the markets reduces total equity-based revenues about 2 percent and total fixed income revenues about 1 percent. If the investment markets turn sour that would hurt results.

Like other financial firms, State Street is enormously complex and hard to understand—we almost gave up when we introduced this issue for 2014. If you insist on fully understanding how a business works, what it sells, how it delivers, and so forth, this one might not be for you. Although the business is different than most financials, it could be swept up in another financial crisis. That said, we think the risk of such a crisis has diminished, and today's operating environment provides more tailwinds than headwinds.

SECTOR: Financials ❑ BETA COEFFICIENT: 1.40 ❑ 10-YEAR COMPOUND EARNINGS PER-SHARE GROWTH: 6.0% ❑ 10-YEAR COMPOUND DIVIDENDS PER-SHARE GROWTH: 6.0%

|  | | 2009 | 2010 | 2011 | 2012 | 2013 | 2014 | 2015 | 2016 |
|---|---|---|---|---|---|---|---|---|---|
| Assets (bil) | | 157.9 | 160.5 | 216.8 | 222.6 | 243.3 | 274.9 | 245.2 | 242.7 |
| Revenues (mil) | | 8,640 | 8,953 | 9,594 | 9,649 | 9,881 | 10,235 | 10,350 | 10,207 |
| Net income (mil) | | 1,803 | 1,559 | 1,920 | 2,061 | 2,136 | 2,037 | 1,980 | 2,142 |
| Earnings per share | | 3.46 | 3.09 | 3.79 | 4.20 | 4.62 | 4.57 | 4.47 | 4.97 |
| Dividends per share | | 0.04 | 0.04 | 0.72 | 0.96 | 1.04 | 1.16 | 1.32 | 1.44 |
| Price: | high | 55.9 | 48.8 | 50.3 | 47.3 | 73.6 | 80.9 | 81.3 | 81.9 |
| | low | 14.4 | 32.5 | 29.9 | 38.2 | 47.7 | 62.7 | 64.0 | 50.6 |

Website: www.statestreet.com

# Steelcase, Inc.

Ticker symbol: SCS (NYSE) ❑ Mid Cap ❑ Value Line financial strength rating: B+ ❑ Current yield: 3.0% ❑ Dividend raises, past 10 years: 7

## Company Profile

Steelcase is the world's leading producer of office furniture, and more importantly, office systems. The company makes several lines of more traditional modular walls, chairs, desks, files, and other kinds of cabinets, etc. But in addition, in part through emerging subbrands such as Coalesse, Nurture, Workspring, and Turnstone, Steelcase is bringing to market new ideas and office concepts that we'd probably all like to see and work in. Call it office *architecture* if you will.

Imagine arriving at the office, heading to a small visible conference area with two glass walls, a floor-to-ceiling whiteboard, and devices that connect immediately and wirelessly to your mobile device to display your work or your multimedia presentation. Imagine sitting (or standing) in small, comfortable work areas, again with a display, possibly built into the table in front of you, to work alone or with others. Impersonal, boring, paper-ridden, PC-based, space-consuming cubicle—be gone! And most cubicles in today's offices are empty anyway—so they might as well be gone. Steelcase continues to really be a bet on the demise of today's traditional office space. Why is that space going away? Several factors. One, today's new mobile worker, who doesn't spend so much time in the office. When she or he does, it's to get together, to collaborate, often on a ceramic or glass whiteboard, with other workers and to demonstrate their work. Most don't have traditional PCs. Less paper moves around, so workers don't need as much storage. What they need is a workbench, places to stash their backpacks, areas to meet, ways to connect and display what they're working on and work together, places to rest and contemplate in ergonomic comfort, possibly with an adjustable standup desk, all the while connected to the business and to each other.

Another factor in the death of the cube is the desire to reduce office space—and cost. Cubes, especially empty ones, take a lot of space. Just as the traditional four-walled, sometimes-windowed office went out in favor of the cubicle and cube farm when PCs took over and nobody needed a secretary pool any more, we think the office is ready for another transition. Steelcase has been studying and innovating in that space for quite some time, and it appears in our view to be ready to bring it to market, as a market leader. We think it could be big.

Steelcase doesn't just produce broad lines of office furnishings. It has conducted deep, customer-based studies of workplace activity, especially innovation, teamwork, leadership, and worker disengagement and it has studied and marketed to key vertical markets like healthcare, education, and hotels and hospitality—a case study for market-driven innovation. They offer design resources, tools, and consulting to current and potential customers. As if that all wasn't enough to drive home the point, the company added Tim Brown, the "design thinking" guru and CEO of consulting firm IDEO, to its board of directors, and announced a collaboration with Microsoft to design "solutions that enhance creativity."

## Financial Highlights, Fiscal Year 2016

A persistent slowdown in capital spending both in the US and abroad has continued to diminish the demand acceleration we had expected to materialize. FY2016 revenues fell about 2 percent but would have been up about 3 percent with constant currency. Modest restructuring costs led to a similar decline in net income. The company expects a recovery in capital spending and strength on the international front to return to growth in the 2–3 percent range through FY2018. (We think this could be conservative if Trump administration policies stimulate capital spending.) As efficiency measures and volume build, earnings gains should be in a more robust 8–15 percent range. A paced dividend growth and share count reduction looks likely.

## Reasons to Buy

We still think we are in the early stages of an accelerating trend—a couple of trends, really. First, traditional organizations are looking for new ways to meet the needs and reduce the stress of today's mobile worker. They are also looking to optimize floor space, which the new designs tend to use less of. Second, new companies (and there are a lot of them) cater to the new "Millennial" worker and aspire to create the perfect workspace for mobile collaboration, creativity, and innovation. This trend is spreading around the world; currently, only 29 percent of sales are overseas, but the company's concepts are picking up particularly in the space-constrained Asia-Pacific region. In short, we think the update of today's traditional cube farm, born in the 1980s, is well under way. Steelcase gets this and has been investing in it for years. We like the designs and its approach to key vertical markets like healthcare, hospitality, and education, which have their own special needs. As these trends accelerate, we expect stronger sales, an improved sales mix, higher profitability, and more brand recognition moving forward. The decent dividend yield gives something to count on while you wait.

## Reasons for Caution

Quite simply, the evolution we've been anticipating has taken longer than we thought to materialize. The office furniture business is subject to wide swings, and renovations can be one of the first things cancelled or delayed when business conditions shift. We are also concerned that a glut of office space may be forming (which, ironically, could result from the adoption of Steelcase's more space-efficient designs!). Too, while margins are improving, 10–12 percent operating margins and 3–5 percent net profit margins are nothing to write home about.

SECTOR: **Industrials** ❑ BETA COEFFICIENT: **1.13** ❑ 10-YEAR COMPOUND EARNINGS PER-SHARE GROWTH: **21.5%** ❑ 10-YEAR COMPOUND DIVIDENDS PER-SHARE GROWTH: **4.5%**

|  |  | 2009 | 2010 | 2011 | 2012 | 2013 | 2014 | 2015 | 2016 |
|---|---|---|---|---|---|---|---|---|---|
| Revenues (mil) | | 2,292 | 2,437 | 2,749 | 2,669 | 2,990 | 3,060 | 3,060 | 3,010 |
| Net income (mil) | | (12.2) | 51 | 76 | 101 | 106 | 112 | 130 | 125 |
| Earnings per share | | (0.09) | 0.38 | 0.58 | 0.79 | 0.84 | 0.89 | 1.03 | 1.04 |
| Dividends per share | | 0.24 | 0.16 | 0.24 | 0.36 | 0.36 | 0.42 | 0.44 | 0.48 |
| Cash flow per share | | 0.47 | 0.87 | 1.05 | 1.27 | 1.36 | 1.42 | 1.64 | 1.65 |
| Price: | high | 7.7 | 10.9 | 12.1 | 13.3 | 17.0 | 18.8 | 20.5 | 18.1 |
| | low | 3.0 | 6.2 | 5.4 | 7.3 | 12.2 | 13.6 | 14.1 | 11.7 |

Website: www.steelcase.com

---

**AGGRESSIVE GROWTH**

# Stryker Corporation

Ticker symbol: SYK (NYSE) ❑ Large Cap ❑ Value Line financial strength rating: A++ ❑ Current yield: 1.4% ❑ Dividend increases, past 10 years: 9

## Company Profile

Stryker Corporation was founded as the Orthopedic Frame Company in 1941 by Dr. Homer H. Stryker, a leading orthopedic surgeon and the inventor of several orthopedic products. The company now ranks as a dominant player in the global orthopedics industry with more than 59,000 products in its catalog and a strong innovation track record, with more than 6 percent of sales invested in R&D.

The Orthopaedics segment (that's how the company spells it) accounts for about 39 percent of 2016 sales and has a significant market share in such "spare parts" as artificial hips, prosthetic knees, implant products for other extremities, and trauma and recovery products. Within that group, knees are 34 percent, hips are 29 percent, and "Trauma & Extremities" are another 31 percent of sales.

The MedSurg unit, about 43 percent of sales, develops, manufactures, and markets worldwide powered and computer-assisted and robotic surgical instruments, endoscopic surgical systems, hospital beds, and other patient care and handling equipment. Instruments (32 percent of this group), endoscopy (30 percent), and medical devices, including emergency devices (33 percent) are the largest contributors, and a new group called "Sustainability," which reprocesses and remanufactures certain medical devices, now contributes 5 percent to the MedSurg unit.

The Neurotechnology & Spine segment, a large part of which was acquired from Boston Scientific in 2010, accounts for 18 percent of sales and sells spinal reconstructive and surgical equipment, neurovascular surgery equipment, and craniomaxillofacial products. Stryker's revenue is split roughly 72/28 percent domestic and international. Stryker has been active on the acquisition front. The early 2016 medium-sized complementary acquisition of Sage Products, a provider of disposable intensive-care products in the MedSurg segment, will add $400 to $500 million in mostly recurring revenues by FY2017. Another acquisition, Physio-Control International brings portable defibrillators and monitors into the Emergency Medical Services business, part of the MedSurg group. Still another brings Synergetics USA into the Neuro group (products too technical to describe) in 2016. As noted above, recovering and rebuilding surgical products is a new initiative and product group; a new launch of "Neptune 3" surgical suction and waste disposal systems is another 2016 add to this mix.

## Financial Highlights, Fiscal Year 2016

FY2016 sales rose 13.4 percent; 6.4 percent without acquisitions. Net earnings grew about 14.5 percent even with higher costs and lower margins due to acquisitions. Going forward, Stryker projects (with continuing effects from acquisitions) a 6–7 percent gain and possibly more in the top line for FY2017, and another 6–7 percent gain in FY2018. Acquisitions and a moderate to strong margin growth and operating leverage should bring earnings forward about 14 percent in FY2017 and another 10–11 percent in FY2018. Share buybacks have stopped for now due to acquisitions, but dividends should rise in the 8–12 percent range over the next few years.

## Reasons to Buy

We continue to see Stryker as an innovative healthcare products company with relatively less-entrenched competition than many others and a strong presence in the orthopedic market and a growing presence in surgical and neurological markets. This should allow it to capitalize on aging trends and a general economic recovery which will induce more elective surgeries. Emerging markets, particularly China, present a good opportunity, and recent acquisitions should strengthen the portfolio and brand worldwide. We also see steady dividend growth.

## Reasons for Caution

Ongoing scrutiny of healthcare costs and a continuation of small acquisitions bring some risks to the company, but we don't think they are excessive. The future of the Affordable Care Act and its replacement is another unknown and concern. The company makes fairly high-tech medical products and as such is exposed to legal, regulatory, manufacturing risks, and product recalls. While the dividend is increasing at a good pace, the yield could still be higher given the company's strong cash flow—obviously they think they can invest your cash (in acquisitions) better than you can—and they may be right for now given projected earnings increases.

SECTOR: **Healthcare** ❑ BETA COEFFICIENT: **0.80** ❑ 10-YEAR COMPOUND EARNINGS PER-SHARE GROWTH: **7.5%** ❑ 10-YEAR COMPOUND DIVIDENDS PER-SHARE GROWTH: **30.0%**

|  | 2009 | 2010 | 2011 | 2012 | 2013 | 2014 | 2015 | 2016 |
|---|---|---|---|---|---|---|---|---|
| Revenues (mil) | 6,723 | 7,320 | 8,307 | 8,656 | 9,021 | 9,675 | 9,946 | 11,325 |
| Net income (mil) | 1,107 | 1,330 | 1,448 | 1,298 | 1,006 | 960 | 1,439 | 1,647 |
| Earnings per share | 2.77 | 3.30 | 3.72 | 3.39 | 2.63 | 2.36 | 3.78 | 4.35 |
| Dividends per share | 0.50 | 0.63 | 0.72 | 0.85 | 1.10 | 1.26 | 1.42 | 1.52 |
| Cash flow per share | 3.75 | 4.40 | 5.08 | 4.69 | 4.01 | 3.94 | 5.44 | 6.15 |
| Price:    high | 52.7 | 59.7 | 65.2 | 64.1 | 75.8 | 96.2 | 105.3 | 123.6 |
| low | 30.8 | 42.7 | 43.7 | 49.4 | 55.2 | 74.0 | 89.8 | 86.7 |

**Website: www.stryker.com**

## CONSERVATIVE GROWTH

# Sysco Corporation

Ticker symbol: SYY (NYSE) ❑ Large Cap ❑ Value Line financial strength rating: A+ ❑ Current yield: 2.5% ❑ Dividend raises, past 10 years: 10

## Company Profile

Sysco is the leading marketer and distributor of food, food products, and related equipment and supplies to the US foodservice industry. The company distributes fresh and frozen meats, prepared entrées, vegetables, canned and dried foods, dairy products, beverages, and produce, as well as paper products, restaurant equipment and supplies, and cleaning supplies. The company might be familiar for its "institutional" number-ten-sized cans of food found in many high-volume kitchens, but the product line and customer base is much larger, including many specialty and chain restaurants, lodges, hotels, hospitals, schools, and other distribution centers across the country. Restaurants account for about 63 percent of the 2016 business; healthcare (mainly hospitals and nursing homes), education (schools and colleges), and government about 17 percent, travel and leisure (hotels and motels) and retail about 8 percent, and "other" categories make up the rest—about 12 percent. You see their lift-gated "bobtail" delivery trucks continuously, but you may not notice them delivering and unloading a pallet or two of goods at a time for a broad assortment of foodservice venues in your area. If you eat out at all, you've most likely consumed Sysco-distributed products.

Sysco has more than 425,000 customers and distributes over 400,000 products, including 41,000 under its own label. The company operates 199 distribution facilities and conducts business in more than 90 countries through company-owned facilities and joint ventures. From these centers, Sysco distributes 1.4 billion cases of food annually using a fleet of 10,200 delivery vehicles. The facilities include its 95 "Broadline" facilities, which supply independent and chain restaurants and other food-preparation facilities with a wide variety of food and nonfood products. It has 11 hotel supply locations, 25 specialty produce facilities, 17 SYGMA distribution centers (specialized, high-volume centers supplying to chain restaurants), 27 custom-cutting meat locations, and two distributors specializing in the niche Asian foodservice market. The company has recently been adding healthier, non-GMO, sustainably sourced, and other such items into its menu, which should play well with foodservice customers expanding their menus in this direction.

The company also supplies the hotel industry with guest amenities, equipment, housekeeping supplies, room accessories, and textiles. By product type, the top five products are: 20 percent meat and frozen meals, 17 percent canned/dry, 13 percent frozen, 11 percent dairy, and 11 percent poultry, with produce, paper goods, seafood, beverages, janitorial products, and others making up the rest.

Sysco is by far the largest company in the domestic foodservice distribution industry. It has grown mainly through small "bolt-on" acquisitions in specialty food companies (such as seafood) or new geographies. In mid-2016 Sysco acquired UK-based Brakes Group to become a leading foodservice provider in England, France, and Sweden. This move added about 10 percent to the top line and established a solid beachhead for growth in Europe.

## Financial Highlights, Fiscal Year 2016

Revenues on a comparable basis grew about 3.5 percent owing to an improving product mix and some effect from the Brakes acquisition; the improved mix plus cost deflation and good expense control led to a 10 percent increase in earnings as net margins ticked up to 2.4 percent from 2.3 percent last year and 2.0 percent in 2014. With Brakes included, revenues should rise in the 9–10 percent range in FY2017 and another 3–4 percent in FY2018, while earnings should climb 10 percent in FY2017 and 6–8 percent in the year following. Healthy share buybacks will keep per-share earnings rising at a higher rate; per-share earnings are forecast 28–30 percent higher by the end of FY2018. Dividend raises should continue at a steady pace.

## Reasons to Buy

Sysco continues to be a dominant player in a niche that won't go away anytime soon. The current foodservice environment is improving, and the company still has plenty to work on in the form of operational efficiencies, and now international expansion is added to the mix as a growth driver.

Sysco's recent investments in technology continue to bear fruit, and we like to see innovation in an industry not known for it. New analytics, routing optimization, and recycling initiatives are being applied to realize savings in people, fuel, and other costs; the effects are manifest in the profit margin improvement noted previously and should continue. New supply-chain tools—even a "My Sysco Truck" app—allow customers to view the location and status of the deliveries and more generally will expand efficiencies and extend the customer relationship. In sum, this is a steady and safe company with a pretty good track record for steady business, decent cash flow, and decent shareholder payouts.

## Reasons for Caution

Although the trend is slowly reversing, the recession got many folks away from the habit of eating out, and many restaurants disappeared altogether during this period. Volatility in food and ingredient prices, and fuel costs too, can pressure margins; this is always a cause for concern. Today, deflation is a concern too—lower selling prices make it difficult to keep revenues and profits going even with lower input prices. We also now worry that new dining trends and tastes of the Millennials and others will require more specialization in the restaurant market, something Sysco will need to adapt to at least to a degree (and has begun to).

As described previously, this is a low-margin business with not a lot of room for error. That said, Sysco, more than most, continues to be a "sleep at night" kind of investment.

SECTOR: **Consumer Staples** □ BETA COEFFICIENT: **0.55** □ 10-YEAR COMPOUND EARNINGS PER-SHARE GROWTH: **3.0%** □ 10-YEAR COMPOUND DIVIDENDS PER-SHARE GROWTH: **7.5%**

|  | 2009 | 2010 | 2011 | 2012 | 2013 | 2014 | 2015 | 2016 |
|---|---|---|---|---|---|---|---|---|
| Revenues (mil) | 36,853 | 37,243 | 39,323 | 42,381 | 44,411 | 46,517 | 48,681 | 50,367 |
| Net income (mil) | 1,056 | 1,181 | 1,153 | 1,122 | 992 | 931 | 1,100 | 1,214 |
| Earnings per share | 1.77 | 1.99 | 1.96 | 1.90 | 1.67 | 1.58 | 1.84 | 2.10 |
| Dividends per share | 0.93 | 0.99 | 1.03 | 1.07 | 1.11 | 1.16 | 1.19 | 1.23 |
| Cash flow per share | 2.44 | 2.67 | 2.62 | 2.63 | 2.57 | 2.54 | 2.78 | 3.22 |
| Price: high | 29.5 | 32.6 | 32.6 | 32.4 | 43.4 | 41.2 | 42.0 | 57.1 |
| low | 19.4 | 27.0 | 25.1 | 27.0 | 30.5 | 34.1 | 35.4 | 38.8 |

Website: www.sysco.com

AGGRESSIVE GROWTH

# The Timken Company

Ticker symbol: TKR (NYSE) □ Mid Cap □ Value Line financial strength rating: B++ □ Current yield: 2.3% □ Dividend raises, past 10 years: 8

## Company Profile

When you operate a 140-ton loaded railroad car, a giant windmill, or a rolling mill in a steel-fabricating plant, you have tremendous frictional forces to overcome, often in harsh environments, for long periods of operating time and with 100 percent reliability required. Without a dependable and efficient friction solution to these moving parts, they can overheat, fail, get out of alignment, and otherwise wreak havoc on your mobile system or stationary machine—not to mention make it cost more to operate. That's where premium-engineered, replaceable bearing assemblies come into play.

On rail cars, for instance, roller bearings—small, tapered, hardened steel bearings "rolling" between the rotating axle and the wheel housing—solved years of headaches (and fires and accidents) caused by oiled brass bearings. Years ago roller bearings became mandatory for US railroad operation. Similar gains in performance, reliability, reduced friction, and cost came to other businesses and technologies—much the same sort of bearings are used in aircraft wheels, for instance. These specialized, high-value-add bearings—and now application-specific bearing assemblies and housings that hold them—are a critical manufactured and serviced component of most of today's mobile and many of today's stationary systems.

"Keeping the World in Motion" is one apt slogan for Timken, the world's oldest, most established and focused, and largest producer of bearings and bearing products. Over time, they have evolved the product line from relatively simple tapered and ball bearings to a greater number of protected bearing assemblies, or "housed units" which enable solutions in harsher operating environments and create maintenance cost savings for the customer.

The company, after spinning off its steelmaking business in 2014, is made up of two business segments:

- *Mobile Industries* (54 percent of 2016 sales) offers bearings, bearing systems, seals, lubrication devices, and power transmission systems mainly to OEMs and operators of trucks, automobiles, rail cars and locomotives, rotor and fixed-wing aircraft, construction and mining machinery, and certain military items. There had been a separate Aerospace segment; it is now part of Mobile.
- *Process Industries* (46 percent of sales) supplies industrial bearings, bearing systems and assemblies, and power transmission components to OEMs and operators in metals, mining, cement, aggregates production, food processing, wind energy, turbine and oil drilling equipment, material handling equipment, and certain marine applications among many applications. These are stationary machines without wheels, whereas Mobile mainly supports things *with* wheels (or rotors or wings).

The company is still adding to its portfolio of adjacent machinery and mechanical power transmission parts, including chains, belts, gear drives, couplings, brakes, sprockets, clutches, including sales but also service and reconditioning businesses. Like bearings, these are relatively mission-critical, high-value–add components with serviceable lives requiring replacement, and Timken would like to expand its position as a single-source, branded, full-service vendor for such components. The top five end-user markets are Industrial Machinery (20 percent), Automotive (14 percent), Rail (11 percent), Energy (10 percent), and Heavy Truck (8 percent). About 62 percent of Timken's business originates in North America; EMEA (18 percent), Asia (11 percent), and Latin America (9 percent) make up the rest.

The product sales mix is about 75 percent bearings and related products, 18 percent power transmission products, and the remainder services. About half of total sales come from OEMs (manufacturers of new products) while the other half come from the Distribution and End User channel (mainly replacement and maintenance uses)—suggesting a steady revenue stream after the initial sale.

## Financial Highlights, Fiscal Year 2016
Currency, general malaise in the US and China industrial sectors, and segment-specific slowdowns in energy, rail, and other transportation businesses were offset by strong automotive sales and small acquisition-related gains to net out at a flat revenue year for FY2016. Earnings dropped 17 percent due to an unfavorable mix and reduced operating leverage due to lower volumes, although lower material costs helped somewhat. Per-share earnings dropped only 11 percent thanks to a 3 percent share buyback.

FY2017 looks to end up similar to 2016, with the same factors driving flat revenues. The company projects about a 5 percent decline in the Mobile segment and a 5 percent rise in the Process segment particularly as the energy industry recovers. Earnings are projected to rise 5–6 percent. FY2018 looks much better, with an 18 percent earnings advance on 5 percent revenue increase as the Mobile segment recovers and the Process segment strengthens. Moderate buybacks look to continue, and the company has been paying dividends since its IPO in 1922 and has been raising dividends albeit more moderately lately.

## Reasons to Buy
We like companies with strong brands and legacies that also happen to supply very key high-value–add components to a value chain. Timken offers such key components in several important value chains, and these components wear out and must be replaced periodically—they aren't just depending on new capital investment for business. Timken's presentations drive

this home—one highlights the rail car example (although the rail business has slowed recently), where a given rail car has a 35-year life and requires bearing replacement every five years bringing $800,000 in lifetime revenue to Timken for a 100-car train (or $8,000 per rail car for life for the million-and-a-half-plus of them out there if you'd prefer to look at it that way). Lifetime value calculations like this, spread across many industries, really bring Timken's value proposition home. The net profit margin of roughly 6–7 percent indicates a differentiated industry (not a commodity) and a strong market position.

## Reasons for Caution

Economic cycles, of course, will affect Timken's fortunes, as will competition from foreign manufacturers mainly in China and other parts of Asia. Despite the recognized brand and market leadership position, the company still has only 5 percent of the overall bearing and 30 percent of the tapered bearing market; competitors are out there. Some of the company's products go into the depressed energy extraction and mining industries—maintenance and replacement volume will depend on these industries, and now the rail industry too. Finally, the stock price has risen most likely in sympathy to Trump administration policies which could benefit the company on many fronts; new buyers should take this into consideration.

SECTOR: **Industrials** ◻ BETA COEFFICIENT: **1.36** ◻ 10-YEAR COMPOUND EARNINGS PER-SHARE GROWTH: **5.0%** ◻ 10-YEAR COMPOUND DIVIDENDS PER-SHARE GROWTH: **6.0%**

|  | 2009 | 2010 | 2011 | 2012 | 2013 | 2014 | 2015 | 2016 |
|---|---|---|---|---|---|---|---|---|
| Revenues (mil) | 3,142 | 4,056 | 5,170 | 4,987 | 4,341 | 3,076 | 2,872 | 2,670 |
| Net income (mil) | 51 | 289 | 457 | 456 | 263 | 234 | 189 | 156 |
| Earnings per share | 0.53 | 2.95 | 4.59 | 4.66 | 2.74 | 2.55 | 2.21 | 1.97 |
| Dividends per share | 0.45 | 0.53 | 0.78 | 0.92 | 0.92 | 1.00 | 1.03 | 1.04 |
| Cash flow per share | 2.61 | 4.89 | 6.65 | 6.81 | 4.93 | 4.19 | 3.98 | 3.70 |
| Price:   high | 26.1 | 49.3 | 57.8 | 57.9 | 64.4 | 69.5 | 43.6 | 41.2 |
| low | 9.9 | 22.0 | 30.2 | 32.6 | 47.7 | 37.6 | 26.4 | 22.2 |

**Website: www.timken.com**

# Total S.A. (ADR)

Ticker symbol: TOT (NYSE) ❑ Large Cap ❑ Value Line financial strength rating: A++ ❑ Current yield: 5.4% ❑ Dividend raises, past 10 years: 7

## Company Profile

Total S.A. (S.A. is short for Société Anonyme, which is the French equivalent of "incorporated") is one of the largest publicly traded oil and gas companies in the world. Headquartered in France and primarily traded on the French CAC stock exchange, the company has operations in more than 130 countries. Total is vertically integrated with upstream operations engaged in oil and gas exploration and downstream operations engaged in refining and distribution of petroleum products; the company also has a chemicals and a solar subsidiary.

Upstream activities are geographically well diversified, with exploration occurring in 50 countries and production happening in 30 of them. As a deliberate strategy to spread risk, many of the E&P projects are done through partnerships—if you examine their major productive assets, in most cases they own a 20–50 percent share—not the whole operation.

The largest production regions are (in production-volume sequence) in Africa (29 percent of 2015 production); the Middle East (21 percent); and the North Sea (17 percent), with smaller operations in Russia, Azerbaijan, Southeast Asia, and North and South America. Liquids (oil) account for about 61 percent of production, while natural gas is 39 percent. The company is a leader in the emerging liquefied natural gas (LNG) market for export, and recently strengthened an agreement to supply LNG to the China National Offshore Oil Corporation (CNOOC). In early 2017 it signed a major deal with Brazil's Petrobras.

Downstream operations are also worldwide and centered in Europe. Operations include interests in 20 refineries worldwide, with 8 refineries and 76 percent of total refining capacity in Europe. There are also 20 petrochemical plants. Total also operates 16,000 service stations in 65 countries, mainly under the Total, Elf, and Elan names, again weighted toward Europe and North Africa. The downstream presence is also growing in Asia-Pacific (including China), Latin America, and the Caribbean. The company now has a leading market presence in those regions.

Total also has ventures in alternative energy, notably solar. It owns a 65 percent interest in global solar leader SunPower, making it the number two solar operator in the world. What is thought to be the world's largest solar plant, the Solar Star project, was brought online in the US in 2015; another large plant was brought on in Abu Dhabi in 2013. The company started an initiative known as Awango to sell solar-powered lamps in remote regions of Indonesia and Africa along with traditional energy products. Long term, Total projects non-hydrocarbon energy sources to comprise 40 percent of total energy demand by the year 2035; the company is managing its energy portfolio accordingly.

## Financial Highlights, Fiscal Year 2016

World energy price declines and slack emerging market demand led to a very challenging year again in FY2016. Among the world's major oil companies, Total has taken one of the most aggressive approaches to dealing with it, including about $10 billion in non-strategic asset sales and a host of cost reduction measures, with a goal of reducing its breakeven oil price to about $40 per barrel. One stated strategy is to "take advantage of today's low cost environment" to develop new fields. The company estimates that it has completed about 80 percent of these adjustments; while that weighed on FY2016 performance it speaks well for the future, especially as demand strengthens and OPEC producers hold supply off the market.

Revenues dipped another 11 percent after a 26 percent decline in FY2015. As prices improved, the cost structure lowered, and write-downs slowed, however, net earnings rose almost 20 percent though still 60 percent lower than their heyday five years ago. With the aforementioned strategies and modestly stronger oil prices, the company predicts a 25 percent revenue gain for FY2017 and another 10 percent for FY2018 with a much stronger 50 percent and 20 percent earnings gain for the two years respectively. Meaningful dividend increases should resume while share buybacks remain on hold for now.

## Reasons to Buy

We think that good management and geographic positioning has led to the beginning of a sharp recovery in Total's fortunes; we anticipate the recovery to be sooner and stronger than most. We like their branding and dominance in the key worldwide markets they serve. Total has done better than most "big oils" in reserve replacement. Though the lowest share prices may be behind us, Total remains an opportunity for those who can stomach the ups and downs; we think long-term prospects are bright for a solid recovery and persistent and growing cash returns beyond that.

## Reasons for Caution

The downsides are pretty much still the same. Risks still come from (1) oil prices, (2) dollar versus euro fluctuations, and (3) international tensions. More aggression on Russia's part, both militarily and economically would add risk to a situation already destabilized by the usual Middle East tensions, European economic softness, and European Central Bank adventures. Finally, the company has taken on more long-term debt to get it through the down cycle.

More generally, we remain cautious on investing in foreign companies because of differences in management style and accounting rules; they aren't necessarily bad but are difficult to understand and follow. Company information is hard to sift through; the website is mainly a collection of PR pieces and offers less in accessible concrete facts and information than most. Antiquated European pension rules and other labor practices could also be a disadvantage, as could recent isolationist movements. Total may not qualify as one of our "sleep at night" stocks; however, we still think the rewards outweigh the risks.

SECTOR: Energy □ BETA COEFFICIENT: **0.85** □ 10-YEAR COMPOUND EARNINGS PER-SHARE GROWTH: **NM** □ 10-YEAR COMPOUND DIVIDENDS PER-SHARE GROWTH: **5.5%**

| | 2009 | 2010 | 2011 | 2012 | 2013 | 2014 | 2015 | 2016 |
|---|---|---|---|---|---|---|---|---|
| Revenues (bil) | 157 | 186 | 216 | 234 | 228 | 212 | 143 | 128 |
| Net income (bil) | 11.6 | 14.0 | 15.9 | 15.9 | 14.2 | 12.8 | 5.1 | 6.1 |
| Earnings per share | 5.31 | 6.24 | 7.05 | 7.01 | 6.28 | 5.63 | 2.19 | 2.52 |
| Dividends per share | 3.28 | 2.93 | 3.12 | 2.98 | 3.10 | 3.21 | 2.73 | 2.70 |
| Cash flow per share | 9.49 | 11.25 | 11.37 | 12.46 | 11.57 | 10.90 | 9.76 | 8.07 |
| Price: high | 66.0 | 67.5 | 64.4 | 57.1 | 62.4 | 74.2 | 55.9 | 51.4 |
| low | 42.9 | 43.1 | 40.0 | 41.8 | 45.9 | 48.4 | 40.9 | 39.1 |

Website: www.total.com

AGGRESSIVE GROWTH

NEW FOR 2018

# Tupperware Brands, Inc.

Ticker symbol: TUP (NASDAQ) □ Mid Cap □ Value Line financial strength rating: A □ Current yield: 4.4% □ Dividend raises, past 10 years: 6

## Company Profile

We review our portfolio every year to pick out the 100 best quality stocks with the best possibilities for gain for the amount of risk taken—put simply, the biggest bang for the buck. For 2018 we decided that meant doing a little housecleaning in the household products portion of the *100 Best* portfolio. For years we've carried the staid Kimberly-Clark, Procter & Gamble, and

Clorox, and more recently we picked up the more dynamic mid-cap WD-40 Corporation. As the traditional staples have achieved record highs recently, we became concerned that these horses—particularly Clorox—would run out of gas as they approached the 2018 finish line (or perhaps sooner). So we ventured not too far from home to pick another well-known household products name. One that has reinvented itself and seems on track for more dynamic growth and shareholder returns, another mid cap: Tupperware.

Sell when there's something better to buy. So we did.

We're all familiar with Tupperware. The famous lids that snap on with a solid click. The famous lids that, inevitably, somehow get separated from the rest of the container, giving us a drawer full of mismatched lids and containers. Tupperware kind of disappeared for a while as their direct sale "Tupperware Party" model languished in favor of the big-box discount shopping model. They went and hid overseas, in fact, and have done quite well there. But we think their brand and product quality are poised to reemerge in the domestic market—and you can't order Tupperware on Amazon Prime, or anywhere else for that matter. As bricks-and-mortar retail suffers, we think Tupperware and its sales model can prosper.

Tupperware Brands Corporation makes the familiar high-quality plastic household containers as regular products and distributes them almost exclusively through their vast direct-to-consumer model—a.k.a. Tupperware parties. They branched into the home-sale cosmetics business with the acquisition of Sara Lee beauty products in 2005; hence the recent renaming of the company to "Tupperware Brands," not just Tupperware. They have added several brands since, giving a total of five cosmetics brands including Avroy Schlain, Fuller Cosmetics, NatureCare, Nutrimetics, and Nuvo. These aren't exactly household brands (to us, anyway) but they come in nice packages, are relatively high end, and fit the Tupperware sales model well.

What's most interesting about Tupperware is its international presence. The FY2016 breakdown of sales and profits (in order) is telling: Asia-Pacific (34 percent of sales, 47 percent of profits), Europe (25 percent, 16 percent), South America (16 percent, 20 percent), North America Tupperware (16 percent, 18 percent), and North America Cosmetics (8 percent, nil). The company estimates that 66 percent of sales come from emerging markets, China and Brazil being the largest. Realizing that "North America" includes Mexico and Canada, the company in total has realized 90–92 percent of its total revenues from international markets over the past five years. Unfortunately we don't get a clear breakout of the cosmetics business in the international sector but can see that it is still an emerging opportunity based on the North America figures.

In total, Tupperware is distributed in 100 countries worldwide by some 3.1 million Tupperware party hosts (dealers).

## Financial Highlights, Fiscal Year 2016

The extremely high portion of overseas sales has kept the lid on revenues and profits through the past few years. Net sales actually dropped just over 3 percent for FY2016, but would have been up about 6 percent in the absence of currency effects. Margins improved as a 3 percent price increase, marketing, and efficiency measures took effect, rising 20 percent after an easy compare year in FY2015. Through FY2018 currency will continue to provide a headwind, but strong sales momentum especially in emerging markets and critical mass and efficiencies in Europe and in the cosmetics business should gradually build earnings momentum. Sales are projected zero to 1 percent ahead for FY2017 and 3–4 percent ahead for FY2018; net earnings should follow a similar trajectory but accelerate in the years beyond. With only 50 million shares outstanding and a 2 percent annual buyback, per-share earnings will rise 2 percent in FY2017 and a more robust 6–8 percent in FY2018. The dividend has stayed in place of late, but one must notice the high yield and the near doubling in 2013; too, dividend raises are expected to resume in 2018.

## Reasons to Buy

Tupperware is a play on (1) international business, (2) a strong brand, and (3) a sales model relatively immune to the shift to online buying. We like the rapid growth and acceptance in emerging markets, particularly the "BRIC"—Brazil, Russia, India, China—markets, an investing theme long out of favor but we feel ripe for recovery by 2018. We also think a domestic resurgence is likely. Put simply, the growth prospects exceed those of our replaced Clorox by a wide margin. The business is well run and profitable with healthy cash flows and a focus on shareholder returns.

## Reasons for Caution

With Tupperware's preponderance in international markets, obviously currency can keep a lid snapped down tight on things, as would isolationist policies that may emerge from the Trump administration. Although the administration's policies (so far) have favored exporters, the backlash against a more isolationist US—and its companies—could hurt, especially in emerging markets. As relatively frugal consumers, we find (and have always found) the plastic products to be a bit pricey, but they are appealing to rising emerging market middle classes.

And we'll admit that we don't really understand the cosmetics business; if you do, please write us at the email provided in the introduction.

SECTOR: **Consumer Staples** ❑ BETA COEFFICIENT: **1.65** ❑ 10-YEAR COMPOUND EARNINGS PER-SHARE GROWTH: **10.5%** ❑ 10-YEAR COMPOUND DIVIDENDS PER-SHARE GROWTH: **12.0%**

|  | | 2009 | 2010 | 2011 | 2012 | 2013 | 2014 | 2015 | 2016 |
|---|---|---|---|---|---|---|---|---|---|
| Revenues (mil) | | 2,127 | 2,300 | 2,585 | 2,584 | 2,672 | 2,606 | 2,834 | 2,213 |
| Net income (mil) | | 175 | 226 | 218 | 193 | 274 | 214 | 186 | 224 |
| Earnings per share | | 2.75 | 3.53 | 3.55 | 3.42 | 5.17 | 4.20 | 3.69 | 4.41 |
| Dividends per share | | 0.91 | 1.00 | 1.20 | 1.44 | 2.48 | 2.72 | 2.72 | 2.72 |
| Cash flow per share | | 3.60 | 4.39 | 4.74 | 4.49 | 6.54 | 5.60 | 4.92 | 5.55 |
| Price: | high | 50.2 | 54.2 | 72.0 | 67.8 | 97.1 | 94.6 | 72.9 | 66.9 |
| | low | 10.9 | 36.1 | 45.2 | 50.9 | 63.6 | 58.2 | 47.8 | 42.6 |

Website: www.tupperwarebrands.com

## CONSERVATIVE GROWTH
# Union Pacific Corporation

Ticker symbol: UNP (NYSE) ❑ Large Cap ❑ Value Line financial strength rating: A++ ❑ Current yield: 2.3% ❑ Dividend raises, past 10 years: 10

## Company Profile

Although slow-ordered through most of FY2016 by the commodity bust, a shift from coal to other utility fuels, reduced exports and a glut of inventory reducing import shipments from West Coast ports, we feel that Union Pacific is another excellent business on track to prosper—even better than before—for investors with patience. All aboard!

Union Pacific has been a familiar name and logo in the railroad business since its inception during the Civil War. With about 32,000 miles of track covering 23 states in the western two-thirds of the United States, today's Union Pacific Railroad, the primary subsidiary of the Union Pacific Corporation, describes itself as "America's Premier Railroad Franchise." The route system is anchored by Gulf Coast and West Coast ports and areas in between and has coordinated schedules and gateways with other lines in the eastern US, Canada, and Mexico.

With 10,000 customers, a large number in today's era of trainload-sized shipments, UNP has a more diversified customer and revenue mix than the other rail companies, including the other three of the "big four" railroads: Burlington Northern Santa Fe, Norfolk Southern, and CSX. Energy (mainly Powder River Basin and Colorado) accounts for 13 percent of revenues (down from 16 percent in 2015 and 18 percent in 2014); Intermodal (trucks or containers on flatcars), 20 percent; Agricultural, 18 percent; Industrial, 18 percent; Chemicals, 19 percent; and Automotive, 11 percent of FY2016 revenues. As coal declines the company is putting more emphasis on diversifying the traffic base and recapturing smaller single-car shipments once given up to truckers. New trucking rules requiring time-of-service logging for trucks in 2017 will put a tailwind behind this shift. Increased grain shipments have also helped fill the gap. Union Pacific has long been an innovator in railroad technology, including motive power, communications and technology automation, physical plant, community relations, and marketing. Although lower volumes caused a slight worsening in 2016, the all-important operating ratio of 63.5 percent (meaning that operating costs are 63.5 percent of revenue) is still the best in the industry. The ratio had reached an all-time low in FY2015 of 63.1 percent; it was 63.5 percent in FY2014, 65.0 percent in FY2013, 67.8 percent in FY2012, 70.6 percent in FY2011—you can see the long-term trend. This allows a solid contribution to the substantial fixed costs of owning and running a railroad. This success has translated to continued strong operating margins, which of course have helped earnings and cash flows and in turn have funded physical plant improvements and shareholder returns over time.

The company also invests a lot in marketing and community relations. One example is the steam-powered "Heritage Fleet" excursion train program, through which the company operates excursions with vintage equipment on selected lines. Literally thousands of people (and current and prospective customers) gather trackside in every town along the way as these beautiful trains roll through. The company recently began a five-year program to restore a "Big Boy" steam locomotive, the largest ever used in regular service (of course, for the UP originally) for a Golden Spike sesquicentennial rollout in 2019. Such public relations efforts show an extraordinary measure of pride and an appreciation for heritage and community. We continue to applaud this effort.

## Financial Highlights, Fiscal Year 2016

The company was already dealing pretty well with the shift away from coal. However, one major coal replacement was oil, and those shipments have fallen off too, although there is some sign of resurgence as oil prices firm and exploration resumes. The strong dollar and high supply-chain inventory levels ate away at intermodal shipments and the automotive cycle has peaked. All of this led to a 7 percent volume decrease and a 9 percent decrease in FY2016 revenue—a tough pill to swallow and hard especially for a business with a lot of fixed costs to cover. Not surprisingly, net earnings dropped 10 percent, although a substantial 4 percent share buyback (wise, as the stock price dipped considerably) slowed the per-share earnings decline to just over 6 percent.

Traffic is starting to rebound, and operational efficiencies put in place both in the recent slow year and back in the Great Recession will continue to pay off, as will the likely shift of some traffic from trucks. Revenues will recover more slowly at first, up 4–5 percent in FY2017 and more rapid 6–7 percent in FY2018. Earnings are forecasted to be out in front of the revenue train, up 7–8 percent in FY2017 and 11–12 percent in FY2018 as volumes recover. Cash flows remain strong and should support persistent buybacks; the company has retired 20 percent of its shares since 2009 and has plans to retire 15 percent more by 2020. The dividend continues to rise even in the flat year 2016.

## Reasons to Buy

Put simply—whether or not you enjoy watching trains, this company has performed well even in bad times and has also returned plenty of cash to shareholders. Now it hits another soft spot—but will it emerge stronger than ever? We think so.

UNP is an extraordinarily well-managed company and has become more efficient and at the same time more user friendly to its customers and to the general public. The company continues to make gains at the expense of the trucking industry, and new short- and long-distance intermodal services move higher-valued goods more quickly and cost-effectively; we see a steady shift toward this business especially as the new rules take effect. A recovery in the energy and other commodity and basic materials industries will also help. The company has a solid and diverse traffic base and continues to have a good brand and reputation in the industry. The company got an early start expanding and modernizing its physical plant and technology base; that has paid off well and will continue to do so.

## Reasons for Caution

No doubt, some of their traffic, like coal, has shifted away forever. Railroads are chiefly a commodity-hauling business, and when commodities are down, they suffer. The company will have to execute well both in marketing and operations to backfill this lost volume; traffic once lost is hard to get back.

Railroads are and will always be economically sensitive because of commodity revenue and their high fixed-cost structure. They also have significant headline risk—a single event like a derailment or spill can put them in a bad public eye or worse, tangle them up in regulation, lawsuits, and unplanned costs. Regulation and mandates for Positive Train Control and other safety features can be expensive. Longer-term factors also include effects from new Trump administration trade policies which could hurt import traffic, and the widening of the Panama Canal, which may shift some Asian import/export traffic to southern and eastern ports and away from the West Coast. These effects all bear watching.

Railroads will always struggle to put the right amount of capacity on the ground—too little causes service problems and delays; too much eats into profits. Right now, UNP is dealing with "too much," but, while capital budgets have been trimmed about 10 percent, capital improvements are still going in for the long term.

SECTOR: **Transportation** ❑ BETA COEFFICIENT: **0.71** ❑ 10-YEAR COMPOUND EARNINGS PER-SHARE GROWTH: **18.0%** ❑ 10-YEAR COMPOUND DIVIDENDS PER-SHARE GROWTH: **21.5%**

|  |  | 2009 | 2010 | 2011 | 2012 | 2013 | 2014 | 2015 | 2016 |
|---|---|---|---|---|---|---|---|---|---|
| Revenues (mil) | | 14,143 | 16,965 | 19,557 | 20,926 | 21,953 | 23,988 | 21,813 | 19,941 |
| Net income (mil) | | 1,826 | 2,780 | 3,292 | 3,943 | 4,388 | 5,180 | 4,702 | 4,233 |
| Earnings per share | | 1.81 | 2.77 | 3.36 | 4.14 | 4.71 | 5.75 | 5.41 | 5.07 |
| Dividends per share | | 0.54 | 0.66 | 0.97 | 1.25 | 1.48 | 1.91 | 2.20 | 2.26 |
| Cash flow per share | | 3.24 | 4.34 | 5.11 | 6.07 | 6.76 | 8.02 | 7.91 | 7.69 |
| Price: | high | 33.4 | 47.9 | 53.9 | 64.6 | 84.1 | 123.6 | 124.5 | 106.6 |
| | low | 16.6 | 30.2 | 38.9 | 52.0 | 63.7 | 82.5 | 74.8 | 67.1 |

Website: www.up.com

AGGRESSIVE GROWTH

# UnitedHealth Group, Inc.

Ticker symbol: UNH (NYSE) ❑ Large Cap ❑ Value Line financial strength rating: A++ ❑ Current yield: 1.5% ❑ Dividend raises, past 10 years: 7

## Company Profile

UnitedHealth Group is the parent company of a number of health insurers and service organizations. It is the largest publicly traded health insurance company in the United States, with almost $165 billion in revenue reported in 2016 and a Number 6 US company ranking on the *Fortune* 500 list.

The company operates in two major business segments: UnitedHealthcare (health insurance and benefits) and Optum (health services), which, combined, touch about 78 million people worldwide in 50 US states and 125 countries globally.

UnitedHealthcare provides traditional and Medicare-based health benefit and insurance plans for individuals and employers, covering approximately 30 million individuals, with about 400 national employer accounts and 200,000 other smaller employer accounts. The company estimates that it serves more than half of the *Fortune* 100 companies list. The company, mainly through this unit, has been an active acquirer of other familiar healthcare and insurance brands over the years. The UnitedHealthcare insurance business in total accounts for 64 percent of FY2016 revenues and 57 percent of profits.

The UnitedHealthcare business unit actively markets traditional individual and employee health plans ("Employer & Individual"), which account for about 36 percent of the UnitedHealthcare branded insurance products. Even larger at 38 percent today is the senior and military market ("Medicare & Retirement"), with a growing assortment of Medicare Advantage, Medicare Part D, and Medicare supplement plans. The recently added TRICARE insurance program for active and retired military is a large contributor to this subsegment: $3 billion today and growing. The rest of the insurance unit is made up by Community & State (22 percent) and Global (4 percent).

Beyond the insurance business lies the large and rapidly growing health services businesses, marketed under the Optum brand umbrella. This segment is far and away big enough to be a separate company and is a rapidly growing and increasingly important part of the overall UNH business offering.

Optum delivers service through three separate businesses. OptumHealth is an operating "information and technology–based health population management solution," deploying mostly remote telesupport for well care, mental health, ongoing disease management, and substance abuse programs to 83 million individuals. The OptumRx business is a pharmacy benefits provider serving 65 million customers and a network of 67,000 pharmacies and other outlets with about 600 million prescriptions annually, while OptumInsight is a management information, analytics, and process-improvement arm providing an assortment of services for health plans, physicians, hospitals, and life science research, formerly marketed under the Ingenix brand. Of the total Optum-branded business of $83 billion (36 percent of total company revenue and 24 percent ahead of FY2015), Rx accounts for the lion's share at $60 billion, while OptumHealth, which grew 22 percent in FY2016, weighs in at $17 billion, and OptumInsight at $7.3 billion with 18 percent annual growth. Although these numbers may seem small in the context of UNH's total $184 billion annual revenue footprint, they are sizeable businesses when looked at individually; all would be sizeable and significant standalone businesses. The Optum umbrella brand is gaining in prominence, and even has its own web presence at www.optum.com.

UnitedHealth Group has been a leader in process, delivery, and cost improvement and a recognized innovator in the industry. The company has moved aggressively to offer tools to manage and contain costs in the healthcare system, mostly through the Optum business. The company sits on top of a mountain of healthcare data and is putting it to good use, and has emerged as a leader in developing remote and preventative care models.

UNH's experience and participation in the Affordable Care Act has been curtailed substantially—from 34 to three states in 2017—citing costs and mounting losses. It remains to be seen how the company participates in future similar programs.

## Financial Highlights, Fiscal Year 2016

Price increases, market share gains, the incorporation of TRICARE, a few small acquisitions, and the growth of the Optum business all contributed to a healthy 17 percent top-line increase in FY2016. Net earnings rose a dizzying 34 percent as some of its marketable Optum cost reduction offerings helped inside their own four walls. Revenues are forecast ahead 8–10 percent through FY2018, while earnings gains should continue rising in the 12–16 percent range as margins improve and volumes expand across all business fronts. Dividend growth prospects are equally healthy, and share repurchase, while slowing some, should chip in as well.

## Reasons to Buy

This bellwether company is one of the most solid, diverse, and innovative enterprises in the health insurance industry. Health insurers such as Aetna, included on our *100 Best* list, seem to be getting past many of the fears of reform and other contrary public opinion; these companies by design simply pass costs through but are doing more to control and reduce costs through utilization management and other initiatives, and these efforts are paying off. Too, the scale of UNH's operation gives it tremendous leverage when negotiating for the services of healthcare providers. Too, the threat posed by the mergers among the four largest competitors (Aetna, Humana, Anthem, and Cigna) has gone away.

Meanwhile, like Aetna, UNH brings a fair amount of innovation to the marketplace, primarily through its Optum offerings. We like its initiatives to make use of its own "big data" with analytics; the size of its database and the tools it possesses can deliver efficiency improvements, and even slight efficiency improvements can help the bottom line substantially. If price competition eventually dictates lower premiums, UNH will be in good position with cost-side improvements.

## Reasons for Caution

The Affordable Care Act possible replacement and other regulatory changes present a wild card difficult to predict. The company is vulnerable to shifts in public opinion and to new regulation (and pulling in $8 billion in annual profit doesn't help), as well as economic downturns, which can hurt employer participation. The company also has demonstrated a fairly aggressive acquisition strategy in the past.

SECTOR: **Healthcare** ❑ BETA COEFFICIENT: **0.65** ❑ 10-YEAR COMPOUND EARNINGS PER-SHARE GROWTH: **10.5%** ❑ 10-YEAR COMPOUND DIVIDENDS PER-SHARE GROWTH: **54.0%**

|  | | 2009 | 2010 | 2011 | 2012 | 2013 | 2014 | 2015 | 2016 |
|---|---|---|---|---|---|---|---|---|---|
| Revenues (bil) | | 87.1 | 94.1 | 101.9 | 110.6 | 122.5 | 130.5 | 157.1 | 184.8 |
| Net income (mil) | | 3,660 | 4,633 | 5,142 | 5,526 | 5,625 | 5,619 | 5,947 | 7,792 |
| Earnings per share | | 3.24 | 4.10 | 4.73 | 5.28 | 5.50 | 5.70 | 6.15 | 8.05 |
| Dividends per share | | 0.03 | 0.41 | 0.61 | 0.80 | 1.05 | 1.41 | 1.88 | 2.38 |
| Cash flow per share | | 4.20 | 5.25 | 5.86 | 6.67 | 7.09 | 7.44 | 7.88 | 10.34 |
| Price: | high | 33.3 | 38.1 | 53.5 | 60.8 | 75.9 | 104.0 | 126.2 | 164.0 |
| | low | 16.2 | 27.1 | 36.4 | 49.8 | 51.4 | 69.6 | 95.0 | 107.5 |

Website: www.unitedhealthgroup.com

<hr>

CONSERVATIVE GROWTH

# United Parcel Service, Inc.

Ticker symbol: UPS (NYSE) ❑ Large Cap ❑ Value Line financial strength rating: A ❑ Current yield: 3.2% ❑ Dividend raises, past 10 years: 10

## Company Profile

UPS is the world's largest integrated ground and air package delivery carrier. Over the years, UPS and rival FedEx have converged on the same business from different directions—FedEx being an air company getting ever more into the ground business; UPS being a ground business taking to the air. That convergence is now nearly complete. Both companies continue to build international capabilities, invest in technology to track shipments, and provide logistics services beyond basic assortments of transportation services. UPS derives just over 63 percent of revenues from US package operations, 20 percent from international package operations, and 16 percent from Supply Chain & Freight, an assortment of bundled logistics and supply-chain services and solutions. Of the 63 percent US package operations, about 72 percent of that is ground, 18 percent is next-day air and the rest "deferred" (two days or longer) air.

The company operates 657 aircraft and 110,000 ground vehicles ("package cars"), most of the familiar brown variety. They serve more than 10 million customers in 220 countries with an assortment of priority to deferred services, with 154,000 domestic and international entry points including 39,000 drop boxes, 1,600 customer service centers, and 4,800 independently owned "UPS Store" (formerly "Mailboxes Etc.") storefronts. The company delivered 19.1 million packages per day worldwide in 2016, up 4.1 percent from 2015.

Once thought to be old-fashioned and averse to innovation, the company has invested in sophisticated package-tracking systems and links for customers to tie into them. An example is My Choice, which allows a customer to control the timing of deliveries mid-service—by smartphone if they choose—so no more waiting half a day at home for a delivery that might come anytime (hallelujah!). The service, which is now used by over 22 million customers, is a nice perk for a consumer waiting for an e-commerce shipment as well as a savings for the company, avoiding multiple delivery attempts and possible door-front theft. The company is also creating specialized logistics services for vertical markets, such as the auto industry "Autogistics" and the healthcare industry, retail, high tech, and more.

The company has embarked on numerous revenue and cost-optimization campaigns, among them a detailed analysis of the cost drivers for their businesses. As an example, they report that one mile saved in their Small Package Pickup & Delivery business across all delivery routes saves $50 million per year; one minute saved would save $14.6 million per year, and one minute of idle time reduced would save $515K. From this point, the company is working to improve these metrics one step at a time through technologies and analytics designed to predict and optimize route selection and other aspects of the delivery network. One such project, called "Orion" is dubbed as the "world's largest operations research project." These initiatives will be crucial to maintaining margins as the industry evolves to a higher percentage of single-package to single-address shipments with the e-commerce surge.

## Financial Highlights, Fiscal Year 2016

Despite the persistent shift toward e-commerce, which presents challenges to margins and thus profits, UPS had a pretty good 2016. Lower fuel costs and operational improvements kept revenue growth on track at just over 4 percent for the year, with net income at nearly 4.5 percent ahead. Looking forward, the shift to e-commerce foretells lower margins as sales grow. Revenues are projected to grow in the 5–6 percent range annually through FY2018. Lower-margined e-commerce shipments and the addition of some facilities for e-commerce will moderate profit increases to the 1 percent range, but anticipated price increases and operational improvements could lead to a 9 percent earnings gain in FY2018. Note that price increases are no sure thing in this highly competitive industry, but that said, a mix improvement driven by increased adoption of Amazon Prime's two-day air offering could also help. Gradual share buybacks should continue, and the dividend has been raised 46 consecutive years—notable in the up-and-down transportation industry.

## Reasons to Buy

The "fastest ship in the shipping business" continues to also be one of the most stable; UPS continues to position itself as the standard logistics provider of the world. The mainstay businesses are cyclical but sound; the emerging e-commerce business is gaining critical mass (volumes rising to the point of optimal efficiency) and will lead to better capacity utilization overall. E-commerce will become a bread-and-butter business as more Millennials take to the Internet as a first choice in shopping. UPS is well positioned to be a key "picks and shovels" provider for this trend—no matter who in the e-commerce business strikes gold, UPS will sell the delivery.

In general, we applaud the use of technology to get "details" right on the operational front.

We are also fans of its logistics and supply-chain management businesses and the many innovations in that space, as the push for many customers to optimize this part of their business will lead them to UPS's front door.

## Reasons for Caution

Competition in this industry is fierce. The Postal Service is getting more aggressive in marketing its small-package and logistics services as it sees the writing on the wall for traditional mail services, and rival FedEx has made gains on UPS's traditional turf with their SmartPost program (see FedEx, another *100 Best Stock*). Also of note is Amazon's saber rattling to get into the freight business itself—apparently they have started acquiring aircraft and assets in the ocean freight business. We think they would have a long way to go to displace the well-established supply-chain network of a UPS or a FedEx, but their actions (or threat) could force price concessions, and Amazon has been known to be surprisingly successful when attacking adjacent markets (like cloud computing). Labor relations and pension funding both bear watching. Of course, fuel prices are a wild card, and can turn back upward at any time.

SECTOR: **Transportation** ◻ BETA COEFFICIENT: **0.91** ◻ 10-YEAR COMPOUND EARNINGS PER-SHARE GROWTH: **5.5%** ◻ 10-YEAR COMPOUND DIVIDENDS PER-SHARE GROWTH: **9.0%**

|  | 2009 | 2010 | 2011 | 2012 | 2013 | 2014 | 2015 | 2016 |
|---|---|---|---|---|---|---|---|---|
| Revenues (mil) | 45,297 | 49,545 | 53,105 | 54,127 | 55,438 | 58,232 | 58,363 | 60,906 |
| Net income (mil) | 2,318 | 3,570 | 4,213 | 4,389 | 4,372 | 4,389 | 4,923 | 5,104 |
| Earnings per share | 2.31 | 3.56 | 4.25 | 4.53 | 4.61 | 4.75 | 5.43 | 5.75 |
| Dividends per share | 1.80 | 1.88 | 2.08 | 2.28 | 2.48 | 2.68 | 2.92 | 3.12 |
| Cash flow per share | 4.09 | 5.43 | 6.60 | 6.90 | 6.75 | 6.97 | 7.81 | 8.36 |
| Price:        high | 59.5 | 73.9 | 77.0 | 84.9 | 105.4 | 113.1 | 114.4 | 120.4 |
|               low | 38.0 | 55.6 | 60.7 | 75.0 | 75.0 | 93.2 | 93.6 | 87.3 |

Website: www.ups.com

---

**CONSERVATIVE GROWTH**

# United Technologies Corporation

Ticker symbol: UTX (NYSE) ◻ Large Cap ◻ Value Line financial strength rating: A++ ◻ Current yield: 2.3% ◻ Dividend raises, past 10 years: 10

## Company Profile

United Technologies is a large and diversified provider of mostly high-technology products to the aerospace and building systems industries throughout the world, selling to an assortment of mostly commercial and public sector customers. To many, it is an aerospace company, to others it is a producer of key pieces, parts, and systems for the building industry; to most investors it is a broadly diversified industrial conglomerate.

In 2015, the organizational sands shifted at UTX, with a management shakeup and the long-awaited sale of the Sikorsky helicopter unit. That turned out to be a good move as helicopter demand had crash-landed with the decline in offshore drilling and the necessary logistical support in the oil industry. That was followed by a fairly vast restructuring, reorganizing, and streamlining of existing assets, which has mostly concluded. Then Honeywell (another *100 Best* stock) made a $90 billion merger offer for the company, which was turned down mostly citing "regulatory concerns." This offer underscored the underlying value of the company and stimulated management to continue its streamlining—and it may not be finished. That sets the stage; now we'll describe the company and its four current business units:

- UTC Aerospace Systems (23 percent of FY2016 revenues) produces aircraft electrical power generation and distribution systems; engine and flight controls; propulsion systems; environmental controls for aircraft, spacecraft, and submarines; auxiliary power units; space life-support systems; and industrial products including mechanical power transmissions, compressors, metering devices, and fluid handling equipment. It also provides product support and maintenance and offers repair services.

- Pratt & Whitney (26 percent) produces large and small commercial and military jet engines, spare parts, rocket engines, and space propulsion systems, and industrial gas turbines, and it performs product support, specialized engine maintenance and overhaul, and repair services for airlines, air forces, and corporate fleets. P&W's commercial engines power about 25 percent of the world's passenger air fleet, and its military engines power fighters and transport aircraft for 29 world armed forces.

- UTC Climate, Controls & Security (30 percent) produces heating, ventilating, and air conditioning (HVAC) equipment for commercial, industrial, and residential buildings; HVAC replacement parts and services; building controls; and commercial, industrial, and transport refrigeration equipment, much of it under the "Carrier" brand name. The group also includes the old UTC Fire and Security business, which provides security and fire protection systems; integration, installation, and servicing of intruder alarms, access control, and video surveillance and monitoring; response and security personnel services; and installation and servicing of fire detection and suppression systems.

- Otis (21 percent) is one of UTX's most recognizable brands. It designs and manufactures elevators, escalators, moving walkways, and shuttle systems, and performs related installation, maintenance, and repair services; it also provides modernization products and service for elevators and escalators, maintaining some 1.9 million elevators, escalators, and moving walkways worldwide.

The company continues to provide useful breakdowns of their end markets to help understand its businesses:

- Commercial & Industrial: 50 percent
- Commercial Aerospace: 38 percent
- Military Aerospace & Space: 12 percent

These figures reflect the sale of Sikorsky and other changes, and reveal that UTX is not as tied to military and government contracts as many think. About 62 percent of sales are outside the US, and about 46 percent of sales are for aftermarket purposes (rough translation: maintenance and repair).

## Financial Highlights, Fiscal Year 2016

Continuing effects of the restructuring, currency effects, and emerging market softness led to a mixed FY2016 performance—once again difficult to compare to previous years. FY2016 revenues advanced about 4 percent, while cost headwinds for new product ramp-ups mainly in aerospace led to a 2 percent drop in net earnings; however, a substantial 4 percent buyback funded by recent business sales led to a 5 percent per-share earnings *gain*. UTX has bought back some 100 million shares, or 11 percent of its float, in the past two years, although that looks to cool off for now. Forward projections call for a continued moderate net profit drop (and per-share earnings drop in FY2017) as the ramp-up cost bulge continues into FY2017 on an 8–9 percent revenue gain; both top and bottom lines improve (5 percent each) in FY2018. Cash returns to shareholders will be led by mid-single-digit dividend increases over the period.

## Reasons to Buy

UTX has been a question mark for the past couple of years (especially with peers Honeywell and GE already on our *100 Best* list) and with the relatively tumultuous management and soft earnings performance. These problems have been mainly corrected as we move forward; UTX is a much more efficient and focused company than it was just a few years ago.

UTX is a classic conglomerate play and is becoming more focused on good commercial (and nonmilitary) businesses. The recent surge in the airline industry will help the business going forward. The company's brands, particularly Otis, are well-known and well supported worldwide, and a return of strength in global construction should help its two largest businesses.

Like many similar businesses, the prospect of acquisition speeds up necessary transformations—and the company was already well on its way to a more efficient form, a pattern commenced in the dark days of the Great Recession. Cash flow is solid; cash returns have been strong and are likely to be stronger if overseas cash ($6 billion) is repatriated.

## Reasons for Caution

Instability is good because it fosters necessary change, and it is bad because it distracts management from what it really should be doing. There had been a little of both going on here, and there's still some "newness" in today's business structure. The company is still sensitive to construction, and construction may not be out of the woods yet; there is plenty of competition in most of its construction businesses. If the recent airline boom falters, that too could bring UTX back to earth. Like all conglomerates, UTX is a complex business to manage. It can also be vulnerable to headline risk, such as aviation accidents resulting from failure of its jet engines.

SECTOR: **Industrials** ❑ BETA COEFFICIENT: **1.09** ❑ 10-YEAR COMPOUND EARNINGS PER-SHARE GROWTH: **7.5%** ❑ 10-YEAR COMPOUND DIVIDENDS PER-SHARE GROWTH: **11.5%**

|  |  | 2009 | 2010 | 2011 | 2012 | 2013 | 2014 | 2015 | 2016 |
|---|---|---|---|---|---|---|---|---|---|
| Revenues (mil) | | 52,920 | 54,326 | 58,190 | 57,708 | 62,626 | 65,100 | 56,098 | 57,244 |
| Net income (mil) | | 3,829 | 4,373 | 4,979 | 4,840 | 5,685 | 6,220 | 5,563 | 5,462 |
| Earnings per share | | 4.12 | 4.74 | 5.49 | 5.34 | 6.21 | 6.82 | 6.29 | 6.61 |
| Dividends per share | | 1.54 | 1.70 | 1.87 | 2.03 | 2.20 | 2.36 | 2.56 | 2.62 |
| Cash flow per share | | 5.43 | 6.22 | 6.97 | 6.93 | 8.19 | 8.94 | 8.86 | 9.18 |
| Price: | high | 70.9 | 79.7 | 91.8 | 87.5 | 113.9 | 120.7 | 124.4 | 111.7 |
| | low | 37.4 | 62.9 | 66.9 | 70.7 | 92.1 | 97.2 | 85.5 | 83.4 |

Website: www.utc.com

---

**AGGRESSIVE GROWTH**

# Valero Energy Corporation

Ticker symbol: VLO (NYSE) ❑ Large Cap ❑ Value Line financial strength rating: A+ ❑ Current yield: 4.2% ❑ Dividend raises, past 10 years: 9

## Company Profile

Valero Energy is the world's largest independent oil refiner. The company owns 15 refineries and distributes primarily through a network of 7,400 retail combined gasoline stations and convenience stores throughout the United States, the UK and Ireland, and Canada, most of it under the Valero, Ultramar, Shamrock, Diamond Shamrock, and Texaco brands. In 2013 the company spun off the Valero-branded retail operations, mostly US based, to shareholders in the form of an independent public company called CST Brands but still maintains distribution to most of these outlets, which total 1,900 in number in all but four US states and the eastern half of Canada. Aside from unlocking capital and increasing focus on refining, the separation of these businesses allowed more refining sales to other channels, and allows the retailers to source from their lowest-cost supplier—improving the performance of both.

Most of the 15 Valero refineries are located in the United States, centered in the South and on the Texas Gulf Coast (70 percent of total capacity) with others in Memphis, Oklahoma, and on the West Coast. Others are located in Quebec and Wales in the UK. The refining operations produce the full gamut of hydrocarbon products: gasoline, jet fuel, diesel, asphalt, propane, base oils, solvents, aromatics, natural gas liquids, sulfur, hydrogen, middle distillates, and special fuel blends to meet California Air Resources Board requirements. The company markets these products where the refineries are located, plus in the Caribbean and in Ireland.

Valero is strictly focused on downstream operations—now just the refining portion, not retail—and owns no oil wells or production facilities. Instead, they purchase a variety of feedstocks on the open market and can adjust those purchases to market conditions while using contracts and hedging tools to manage input prices to a degree—and rail transport along with existing pipelines to get it to the refinery. About half of feedstocks are purchased under contracts, with the other half on the spot market. Most of these refineries are legacy operations and have been in place for many years, as far back as 1908. The company has invested heavily in upgrading these refineries to improve capacity, efficiency, and environmental compliance and in recent years has grown its utilization rates to a strong 87 percent. The company has also added capacity in two plants to produce high-quality distillates from low-quality feedstocks and natural gas.

The company has increased its activities in transportation and logistics, where it already owns key pipelines—by adding approximately 4,100 rail cars to its fleet as part of a 5,300-car expansion, all using the new accident-resistant designs. While oversupply, relatively higher-cost "fracked" crude, and a lifting of a 40-year-old US export ban have disrupted logistics patterns recently, this logistics flexibility represents a key strategy toward optimizing input costs. The company now imports about half the amount of crude that it did back in 2006.

Bulk sales to other retail outlets, commercial distributors, and large-end customers like airlines and railroads are also important. The company also owns and operates 11 ethanol plants in the US Midwest, producing and shipping 1.4 billion gallons per year and a 50 percent interest in a 10,500 barrels-per-day renewable diesel plant.

## Financial Highlights, Fiscal Year 2016

Lower fuel prices and high inventory stockpiles highlighted another relatively weak year for Valero in FY2016; revenues dropped another 14 percent, while recovering crude prices dented the profit barrel by a stiff 43 percent. Oil and gasoline prices have since stabilized although inventories remain high in 2017; for the year the company expects sales gains in the 7–8 percent range and net earnings gains in the 5–6 percent range; FY2018 brightens to an 18–20 percent earnings gain on a 10 percent gain in revenues.

As oil and gasoline prices will always fluctuate, what's really important in this type of business is profits—the difference between revenue and costs. Lower oil prices led to a dramatic increase in net margins in FY2016 (from 2.8 percent to 4.5 percent)—small numbers but huge impact, especially considering the 1.5–1.7 percent "run rate" for several years before that. The 2014–2015 "crash" in oil prices led to a lot of that, but the company, through strategic sourcing and efficiency measures, plans for the net margin to remain in the 3–4 percent range through FY2018 and beyond—a level which throws off significant cash flows. As such, the dividend was raised 40 percent in 2016 and appears headed upward at a double-digit pace going forward. Valero has stated a goal to pay out 75 percent of net profits as dividends; today it's about 50 percent. You can do the math, but the message is: cash returns will rise rapidly. Valero is one of our strongest dividend aggressors.

## Reasons to Buy

The profitability of this business, like other refining businesses, depends on the supply and cost of feedstocks and the wholesale and retail prices of finished products. In addition, the availability of refining capacity is also a factor; when markets get tight, it is extremely difficult to put another refinery on the ground to handle demand. These two factors can work together very favorably for Valero—lower input costs, no new competition—it's an oligopolistic dream and should bode well for profits for years to come, especially in today's new world of crude oil (over)abundance.

Flexibility is the key, and is a key part of Valero's strategy. Rail transport provides excellent flexibility, and some say flexible methods, not fixed pipelines, are the optimal way to distribute crude from multiple sources in the future. Valero's investments in rail cars will help to capitalize on this trend. While the rail capacity is important, new pipelines recently greenlighted by the Trump administration to serve the Gulf Coast will also eventually add to the supply of relatively inexpensive crude.

We like Valero's leading position in the refining business, and having 15 well-distributed, efficient, and largely successful operating refineries on the ground already is a good thing. We also like the branding, abundance, look, and feel of the retail presence—even though the company no longer owns the stations outright.

Finally, one cannot overlook the commitment to cash returns to shareholders in the form of dividends.

## Reasons for Caution

The refining business in particular is inherently volatile and complex, and what may appear today as an advantageous input and output pricing profile might disappear in a minute. Indeed, refined products are in a glut too, making future prices uncertain, and the recent allowance of crude exports makes less oil available in Valero's own back yard.

Gross, operating, and net margins can become very thin, typically in the 1–2 percent range—although much of Valero's recent success is due to breaking out of that range. Refiners also endure the headline risk of refinery mishaps, a few of which have already come Valero's way in recent years. And now we incur more risks in rail transport of crude and saw what can happen in recent mishaps (neither of which affected Valero directly).

SECTOR: **Energy** ◻ BETA COEFFICIENT: **1.39** ◻ 10-YEAR COMPOUND EARNINGS PER-SHARE
GROWTH: **5.5%** ◻ 10-YEAR COMPOUND DIVIDENDS PER-SHARE GROWTH: **23.5%**

|                      |      | 2009   | 2010  | 2011  | 2012  | 2013  | 2014  | 2015  | 2016  |
|----------------------|------|--------|-------|-------|-------|-------|-------|-------|-------|
| Revenues (bil)       |      | 87.3   | 81.3  | 125.1 | 138.3 | 138.1 | 130.8 | 87.8  | 75.7  |
| Net income (mil)     |      | (352)  | 923   | 2,097 | 2,083 | 2,395 | 3,630 | 3,990 | 2,289 |
| Earnings per share   |      | (0.65) | 1.62  | 3.69  | 3.75  | 4.37  | 6.85  | 7.99  | 4.94  |
| Dividends per share  |      | 0.60   | 0.20  | 0.30  | 0.65  | 0.85  | 1.05  | 1.70  | 2.40  |
| Cash flow per share  |      | 1.91   | 4.10  | 6.52  | 6.60  | 7.65  | 10.47 | 12.25 | 9.25  |
| Price:               | high | 26.2   | 23.7  | 31.1  | 34.5  | 50.5  | 59.7  | 73.9  | 72.5  |
|                      | low  | 16.3   | 15.5  | 16.4  | 16.1  | 33.0  | 42.5  | 43.4  | 45.9  |

Website: www.valero.com

AGGRESSIVE GROWTH

# Valmont Industries, Inc.

Ticker symbol: VMI (NYSE) ❑ Mid Cap ❑ Value Line financial strength rating: A ❑ Current yield: 1.0% ❑ Dividend raises, past 10 years: 9

## Company Profile

If you read our work last year and read about Valmont, you may recall that we "called the company onto the carpet" for a careful review following a very poor year in 2015—we wanted to be sure that Valmont was suffering from "continued cyclical weakness" and not from a fundamental change in its business or its markets. We decided all was good for the core business. As this narrative will show, 2016 wasn't a great year either, but the company made a remarkable recovery on the bottom line despite declining sales, and stands in good position going forward due to "mega" trends in the agriculture, infrastructure, and government spending spaces. What lies ahead appears to be well worth the wait, and we're keeping Valmont around for at least another year.

Valmont Industries was founded in 1946 as a supplier of irrigation products and became one of the classic postwar industrial success stories, growing along with the need for increased farm output. It was an early pioneer of the center-pivot irrigation system, which enabled much of that growth and now dominates the high-yield agricultural business. These machines remain a mainstay of this most profitable product line. But the company has expanded on that core expertise in galvanized metal to make such familiar infrastructure items as light poles, cell phone towers, and those familiar high-tension electric towers that crisscross the landscape, and to provide such galvanizing services to other product manufacturers.

From the following product line summary you'll get a good idea how Valmont plays in important areas of infrastructure and agriculture:

- Engineered Support Structure products (30 percent of FY2016 revenues, 25 percent of operating income)—Lighting poles, including decorative lighting poles, guard rails, towers, and other metal structures used in lighting, communications, traffic management, wireless phone carriers, and other applications. Products are available as standard designs and engineered for custom applications as needed for industrial, commercial, and residential applications. If you've ever sat at a stoplight and wondered how a single cantilevered arm could support four 400-pound traffic signals, these are the folks to ask.

■ Utility Support Structures (25 percent, 21 percent)—This segment produces the very large concrete and steel substations and electric transmission support towers used by electric utilities. We like this unit's prospects as utility infrastructure is replaced and modernized in the interest of grid efficiency, and now, aesthetic and environmental sensibility.

■ Irrigation (23 percent, 31 percent)—Under the Valley brand name, Valmont produces a wide range of equipment, including gravity and drip products, as well as its center-pivot designs, which can service up to 500 acres from a single machine. Valmont also sells its irrigation controllers to other manufacturers.

■ Energy and Mining (12 percent, 5 percent)—Produces a series of products once mostly found in the Engineered Infrastructure Products segment but includes tubing and piping products, conveyance systems, grinding products, grates and screens for separation, windmill towers, and parts and products for human access like walkways and stair structures.

■ Coatings (10 percent, 17 percent)—Developed as an adjunct to its other metal products businesses, the coatings business now provides services such as galvanizing, electroplating, powder coating, and anodizing to industrial customers throughout the company's operating areas.

The company is a market leader in a number of segments including irrigation, power transmission poles, highway infrastructure, and certain coated products.

## Financial Highlights, Fiscal Year 2016

Cyclical recovery started to occur in FY2016, particularly in the larger and more profitable Engineered Support Structures and Utility segments. Energy & Mining, Irrigation, and Coatings continued weak. Sales in total sagged another 3-plus percent after a 17 percent decline in FY2015. Lower input prices and higher volumes, however, along with a one-time 2016 tax benefit and 2015 restructuring charges all combined to a quadrupling of net profit back to levels comparable to other good years. What had been a perfect storm of poor demand across all five businesses now appears to be a "perfect storm" to the good, with all five businesses expected to advance giving rise to 4–5 percent revenue gains annually across the board through FY2018. We think this could be conservative if proposed Trump administration infrastructure and manufacturing policies really gain traction. Earnings will stay roughly flat from FY2016's healthy number in 2017, then advance gradually into FY2018. Dividend and buyback activity will probably be steady state until the recovery takes hold.

## Reasons to Buy

We remain attracted to—and loyal to—the fundamental strengths of Valmont and its core businesses, and in particular their strategic importance to the interests of agriculture, water conservation, and infrastructure.

As much as anything we continue to view Valmont as a key infrastructure play. America's infrastructure needs to be replaced, as does infrastructure in much of the developed world. As for the less-developed world, that infrastructure needs to be built in the first place. We think, long term, that Valmont is in the right place to capture a decent share of this replacement business, including electric utility infrastructure—which in particular may be moving away from the traditional wooden telephone pole (as it has in most of the rest of the world) and as more aesthetic high-tension power poles come into favor. The original irrigation business should also do well in the long term as global food consumption increases and as agriculture, farmland, and farm commodity prices eventually strengthen—and as droughts in key "ag" markets persist. The company's continued emphasis on growth into new geographies should pay dividends as India and China begin to build infrastructure and adopt more modern agricultural methods. We also like the relatively simple, straightforward nature of this business and the way the company presents itself online and in shareholder documents.

## Reasons for Caution

Of course, we could be wrong about the "cyclical perfect storm" call and the long-term fundamentals of Valmont's businesses. The relatively small size and deep, large-scale manufacturing infrastructure of a company like Valmont makes it more vulnerable to cyclical weakness—although steadier public sector demand mitigates that somewhat. Valmont presents plenty of long-term opportunity in our view, but that doesn't come without some risk. Too, the stock price has rebounded sharply in anticipation of the positive cycle and probably, to some extent, in anticipation of boosted federal infrastructure funding.

SECTOR: **Industrials** ❑ BETA COEFFICIENT: **0.99** ❑ 10-YEAR COMPOUND EARNINGS PER-SHARE GROWTH: **12.5%** ❑ 10-YEAR COMPOUND DIVIDENDS PER-SHARE GROWTH: **15.5%**

| | 2009 | 2010 | 2011 | 2012 | 2013 | 2014 | 2015 | 2016 |
|---|---|---|---|---|---|---|---|---|
| Revenues (mil) | 1,787 | 1,975 | 2,661 | 3,029 | 3,304 | 3,123 | 2,619 | 2,523 |
| Net income (mil) | 155.0 | 109.7 | 158.0 | 234.1 | 278.5 | 184.0 | 40.0 | 173.2 |
| Earnings per share | 5.70 | 4.15 | 5.97 | 8.75 | 10.35 | 7.09 | 1.71 | 7.63 |
| Cash flow per share | 7.43 | 6.46 | 8.80 | 11.40 | 13.27 | 11.39 | 5.74 | 11.35 |
| Dividends per share | 0.58 | 0.65 | 0.72 | 0.88 | 0.98 | 1.38 | 1.50 | 1.50 |
| Price:      high | 89.3 | 90.3 | 116.0 | 141.2 | 164.9 | 163.2 | 129.1 | 156.0 |
| low | 37.5 | 65.3 | 73.0 | 90.2 | 129.0 | 116.7 | 92.3 | 96.5 |

Website: www.valmont.com

## AGGRESSIVE GROWTH

# Visa Inc.

Ticker symbol: V (NYSE) ❑ Large Cap ❑ Value Line financial strength rating: A++ ❑ Current yield: 0.8% ❑ Dividend raises, past 10 years: 8

## Company Profile

If we wrote about a company with a 40 percent *net* profit margin and a global brand that was in the business of collecting small fees on every one of the billions of transactions worldwide (worth about $8.2 *trillion* in 2016); a company that required almost no capital expenditures, plant, equipment, or inventory; a company that brought in almost 1.1 *billion* dollars per employee in revenue and more than $700,000 per employee in net profit (the company refers to this as "people light and technology heavy"); a company growing earnings 10–30 percent a year; a company with a time-tested business model and absolutely zero long-term debt until recently (to fund the acquisition of its European counterpart)—would you believe that it existed? No. it must be a dream. Though the meteoric rise has slowed a bit, Visa continues to be many an investor's dream.

But it's all true, in fact. Founded in 1958 but not taken public until 2008, the Visa emblem has traditionally appeared on a majority of the world's credit cards—and now debit cards. In fact, there are about 3.1 *billion* such cards dispersed through 200 countries worldwide. According to BrandZ's 2016 Top 100 Most Valuable Global Brands Study, Visa is the number six brand worldwide.

Visa operates the world's largest retail electronic payment network, providing processing services; payment platforms; and fraud-detection services for credit, debit, and commercial payments. The company also operates one of the largest global ATM networks with its PLUS and Interlink brands. In total, the company processes 109 billion transactions per year (which works out to about 3,500 transactions *per second*) and estimates that it can process about 18 times that amount in a peak scenario—65,000 transactions per second—while being operational 99.999999 percent of the time!

For years, Visa has been synonymous with credit and credit cards, but in recent years it has become more of a digital currency company, stitching together consumers, retailers, banks, and other businesses in a giant global network. Really, Visa is a global payments technology business that not only develops and supplies the technology but also collects fees upon its use.

The shift from traditional cash and check forms of payment to debit cards and other digital forms has been growing at about a 12 percent annual rate, driven by the security and convenience of these transactions as well as a shift away from consumer debt to more "paid for today" debit transactions. Debit transactions now account for more than half the company's overall business volume, albeit at a small penalty, as average transaction sizes are smaller.

The company is an active innovator, with several initiatives in what it calls an "evolving payments ecosystem" and in network security. Mobile payment and mobile wallet innovations include "V.me" and "payWave" licensed products, and, not surprisingly in light of recent news events, the company is also working on new payment and card security initiatives. A new platform called Visa Checkout makes it easier for merchants to integrate Visa payment into websites and mobile platforms, now for 15 million consumer accounts, and the company has partnered with Apple to create new connections with Apple Pay. A new mobile app allowing swipe-free payment at gas stations is but one example. The company is also very active in fraud prevention and into mining data to help merchants grow their businesses. Visa has hired some 1,700 new IT professionals in the past two years—a 20 percent bump in the workforce—to work on these initiatives. This all shows how Visa thinks of itself as a data and IT company, not merely a financial services firm.

The business continues to grow rapidly overseas; with the 2016 consolidation of Visa Europe Limited some 62 percent of its revenue now comes from outside the US, far more than its rivals and providing the company's strongest growth driver at present.

## Financial Highlights, Fiscal Year 2016

Despite some international and currency headwinds, growth continued on track in FY2016. Revenues rose a healthy 9 percent. Reported net earnings dropped 5 percent to about $6 billion, but this includes a $1.9 billion charge related to the Visa Europe acquisition; without that net earnings would have risen about 25 percent. Current projections call for revenue growth in the 15–17 percent range through FY2018 with commensurate gains in net earnings. The company continues to repurchase shares at about a 3 percent annual rate and has already retired about a third of its float since going public in 2008.

## Reasons to Buy

"The Power of Digital Currency" continues as Visa's apt corporate mantra. Simply, it's hard to come up with a better business model—a company that develops and sells the network and collects fees every time it's used. It would be like Microsoft collecting fees every time a file is created and saved or an e-mail platform charging fees for every message. Visa is in a great position to not only capitalize on overall world economic growth, as most companies should be, but also to capitalize on a shift in this growth toward electronic and mobile payments. Even as debt-conscious consumers pull back on using credit cards, debit card usage continues to advance. This reinforces one of Visa's big strengths—unlike most other financial services businesses, Visa is relatively immune to downturns, as it makes its money by processing payments, not by extending credit. On the growth side, the company is expanding its footprint in emerging markets, and there is plenty of innovation opportunity in this business. Overall, while Visa has competitors (MasterCard, American Express, and Discover), it continues to have the strongest franchise, technology leadership, and pricing power at its back. Its volumes are double its nearest competitor—MasterCard.

## Reasons for Caution

The company has pricing power, but as with many companies that do, that power has come under government, merchant, and public scrutiny; the company must tread lightly or face possible consequences. Recent litigation and regulatory actions have presented some headline and profit risk and may be construed as a threat to the franchise—perhaps if it sounds too good to be true, it may be. But even after some legal and regulatory bumps, Visa has emerged rock solid.

With the steady success, entry points have been hard to find.

SECTOR: **Financials** ❑ BETA COEFFICIENT: **1.01** ❑ 10-YEAR COMPOUND EARNINGS PER-SHARE
GROWTH: **NM** ❑ 10-YEAR COMPOUND DIVIDENDS PER-SHARE GROWTH: **NM**

|  |  | 2009 | 2010 | 2011 | 2012 | 2013 | 2014 | 2015 | 2016 |
|---|---|---|---|---|---|---|---|---|---|
| Revenues (mil) | | 6,911 | 8,065 | 9,188 | 10,421 | 11,776 | 12,702 | 13,880 | 15,082 |
| Net income (mil) | | 2,213 | 2,966 | 3,650 | 4,203 | 4,980 | 5,438 | 6,238 | 5,991 |
| Earnings per share | | 0.73 | 0.98 | 1.25 | 1.55 | 1.90 | 2.27 | 2.62 | 2.84 |
| Dividends per share | | 0.11 | 0.13 | 0.15 | 0.22 | 0.33 | 0.42 | 0.50 | 0.59 |
| Cash flow per share | | 0.80 | 1.09 | 1.39 | 1.67 | 2.05 | 2.44 | 2.82 | 3.07 |
| Price: | high | 22.4 | 24.3 | 25.9 | 38.1 | 55.7 | 67.3 | 81.0 | 84.0 |
| | low | 10.4 | 16.2 | 16.9 | 24.6 | 38.5 | 48.7 | 60.0 | 65.1 |

Website: www.usa.visa.com

## AGGRESSIVE GROWTH

NEW FOR 2018

# Vodafone Group

Ticker symbol: VOD (NASDAQ) ❑ Large Cap ❑ Value Line financial strength rating: B++ ❑ Current yield: 6.4% ❑ Dividend raises, past 10 years: 2

## Company Profile

Headquartered in the UK, Vodafone Group Plc. provides wired and wireless telecommunications services for Europe, the Middle East, Africa, and the Asia-Pacific region. Founded in 1991 as a divestiture from Racal Electronics, Vodafone has since grown organically and through acquisitions to be the second-largest mobile operator in the world, behind only China Mobile. The company maintains majority-owned operations in more than 30 countries with network partnerships in over 80 others. Their top five markets (Germany, UK, Italy, India, Spain) generate 65 percent of sales.

The Vodafone name is not well known in the US as a communications provider, but prior to a 2013 sale, the company owned 45 percent of Verizon Wireless (although the Vodafone branding was never used in the US). The $130 billion sale of those assets to Verizon was one of the biggest deals in the history of the deal-happy telecommunications industry.

The company has over the past few years concentrated on acquiring strategic cable assets in order to provide bundled services to their consumer markets. In that light, VOD recently completed a 50/50 joint venture arrangement with London-based Liberty Global, the largest international cable provider; see the following description.

## Financial Highlights, Fiscal Year 2016

Following the sale of its US-based assets to Verizon, Vodafone has been on a cost-control and infrastructure investment binge over the past few years. FY2016 results showed many positive effects from these efforts, with margin improvements in both Europe and AMAP (Africa, Middle East, Asia-Pacific), accompanying positive top-line trends. The company partially exited the hyper-competitive Indian market which, though showing great promise, has not produced the expected returns. The company retains a number two position in India with an 18 percent market share and 200 million subscribers as of March 2017.

Service revenues, excluding currency impacts, were up 2 percent year over year. After adjusting for certain restructuring and M&A costs, operating profits grew 12 percent. All in all, these are very encouraging results for an operation in the heart of a restructuring and in a tough operating environment. Revenue gains are projected in the 6–7 percent range annually through FY2018; earnings gains should roughly follow suit, with mid-single-digit dividend increases on top of an already generous payout.

## Reasons to Buy

From its Verizon deal "windfall," Vodafone set aside $84 billion to pay down debt and return value to shareholders. A large chunk of the rest was committed to "Project Spring," a program to increase capital spending $9 billion per year for three years. One goal was to improve network quality in Europe and emerging markets, gaining market share and pressuring their competitors to match their spending if possible. Funds were also committed to furthering the reach of its high-speed broadband, enhancing business services such as cloud computing, and improving its customer support and storefronts. The availability of funds came along just at the right time for VOD, as the EU regulatory commission soon after released a plan encouraging investment in telecom infrastructure with the goal of matching 4G development in the US and Asia.

A few years into the project, additional funding was needed to address customer support issues, and the company tapped into cash again. At the close of the project, Vodafone had met nearly all goals, falling short only on their commitment to achieve 90 percent 4G coverage in designated major markets, missing by 2 percent.

So what's important about this now three-year-old project? It's what Vodafone *didn't* do with the $130 billion—what nearly everyone in the industry expected them to do, which was to go out and buy up a bunch of small fish, paying what certainly would have been a premium for someone else's problems. Instead they addressed underlying needs in their finances and operations, creating a foundation for future growth in developed and developing markets, while still rewarding investors with a well-funded dividend stream.

It's not often you find a company in the telecom market that you could almost describe as a conservative play. Most are scrambling for market share and looking for acquisitions and/or partnership deals wherever they can find them. Vodafone has certainly been active in M&A (including the biggest deal in M&A history, their $181 billion acquisition of Mannesmann in 2000), but their only acquisition of real size post-Verizon was ONO, the largest cable operator in Spain. The deal with Liberty Global established a very strong "bundle" play in the Netherlands, with Liberty providing broadband and television services and Vodafone providing wireless. Bundled services are very popular with European customers and this deal also provides for significant cost savings as the deal matures.

We replaced Verizon with Vodafone on our *100 Best* list because we liked their growth profile (organic, not through acquisition) and their relative strength in their diverse international markets. They have more growth potential than Verizon, which is saddled with an intensely competitive business with price wars and little in the way of a growth path other than acquisitions—which so far we are not applauding in their takeovers of Yahoo! and AOL. We also like smart debt management and a well-funded dividend, and decided to make this switch to the stronger horse.

## Reasons for Caution

Vodafone is moving into developing markets in Africa and Asia, where there may be little in the way of existing communications infrastructure, making the benefits of wireless a natural fit. As they found in India, however, some of these markets *are* also fiercely competitive, both from multinationals and local interests. Partnerships are likely the way to proceed quickly in these areas, but can cut into margins significantly.

SECTOR: **Telecommunications Services** ❑ BETA COEFFICIENT: **1.10** ❑ 10-YEAR COMPOUND EARNINGS PER-SHARE GROWTH: **NA** ❑ 10-YEAR COMPOUND DIVIDENDS PER-SHARE GROWTH: **8.0%**

|  | 2009 | 2010 | 2011 | 2012 | 2013 | 2014 | 2015 | 2016 |
|---|---|---|---|---|---|---|---|---|
| Revenues (mil) | 67,597 | 73,414 | 74,267 | 67,112 | 63,654 | 62,496 | 59,001 | 60,000 |
| Net income (mil) | 12,876 | 14,042 | 12,080 | 11,621 | 7,706 | 2,261 | 1,935 | 1,995 |
| Earnings per ADR | 4.49 | 4.87 | 4.34 | 4.31 | 2.89 | 0.85 | 0.73 | 0.75 |
| Dividends per ADR | 2.35 | 2.39 | 3.81 | 2.80 | 3.02 | 1.82 | 1.71 | 1.53 |
| Cash flow per ADR | 8.72 | 9.37 | 9.10 | 8.58 | 7.66 | 6.19 | 5.88 | 6.00 |
| Price:     high | 44.1 | 52.3 | 59.9 | 55.1 | 72.3 | 72.5 | 39.5 | 34.7 |
|            low | 28.3 | 33.4 | 44.6 | 45.7 | 44.8 | 28.6 | 30.6 | 24.2 |

Website: www.vodafone.com

## GROWTH AND INCOME

# Waste Management, Inc.

Ticker symbol: WM (NYSE) ❑ Large Cap ❑ Value Line financial strength rating: A ❑ Current yield: 2.2% ❑ Dividend raises, past 10 years: 10

## Company Profile

You may refer to it as a "garbage company" if you want—we won't take offense. Waste Management is the largest and steadiest hand in the North American solid waste disposal industry. In their own words, "North America's leading provider of comprehensive waste management environmental services"; supporting this claim, they serve some 21 million municipal, commercial, and industrial customers in the US and Canada. Like most large waste firms, WM has grown over time by assembling smaller, more local companies into a nationally branded and highly scaled operation with a notable amount of innovation on several fronts in the core business and especially in material recovery—translation, recycling.

The business is divided into three segments:

- Collection, which accounts for 55 percent of the business, includes the standard dumpster and garbage truck operations. The company has about 600 collection operations, many of which have long-term contracts with municipalities and businesses. About 40 percent of the collection business is commercial, 30 percent residential, 26 percent industrial, and 4 percent other. For the industry, WM is considered an innovator even in its traditional collection operations; examples include the Bagster small-scale disposal units now sold through retail home-improvement outlets and 3,700 collection trucks converted to natural gas (some of which the company produces from waste). The company perceives itself as a world-class logistics company (and why not?) and has equipped its trucks with the latest in onboard computers, centralized dispatching, and routing processes, reducing collection costs an additional 1 percent during FY2015.

- Landfill (19 percent of revenues). The company operates 249 landfills across North America, servicing its own collection operations and other collection service providers. Among these sites, there are 136 landfill-gas-to-energy conversion projects producing fuel for electricity generation. There are also five active hazardous waste landfills and one underground hazardous waste facility.

- Transfer, Recycling, and Other (26 percent). These operations perform specialized material recovery and processing into useful commodities. There are 297 transfer stations set up for the collection of various forms of waste, including medical, recyclables, compact fluorescent (CFL), and e-waste. The company has also pioneered single-stream recycling, where physical and optical sorting technologies sort out unseparated recyclable materials. Single-streaming has greatly increased recycling rates in municipalities where it is used and provides a steady revenue stream in recovered paper, glass, metals, etc., for the company. WM also further refines these materials into industrial inputs, e.g., glass or plastic feedstocks in certain colors. In total there are 61 traditional and 43 "single-stream" operations, recycling some 14 million tons of commodities annually today, a figure expected to grow to 20 million by 2020 (a 2015 "rationalization" of some weaker recycling operations actually brought a slight dip in recycling tonnage from 15.3 million tons in 2014; the company still retains the 20 million–ton goal). "Capture Value from Waste" is a popular company slogan.

In 2014, the company sold its Wheelabrator Technologies subsidiary, which operated a network of waste-to-energy gasification plants at landfills. This operation had accounted for about 8 percent of total revenues and likely succumbed to low natural gas prices. Today's recycling operations are state of the art and a strategic part of WM's total offering, but are not big profit producers with today's soft commodity prices and diminished China demand.

## Financial Highlights, Fiscal Year 2016

Price increases, a strong late-year recovery in prices, and small acquisitions led to a 5 percent revenue gain in FY2016, making up for about two-thirds of the revenue lost in the Wheelabrator sale. Operational improvements and improved recycling business led to a strong uptick in margins and a 12 percent net earnings gain; buybacks led to a 15 percent per-share earnings gain. Forward projections call for 7–8 percent per-share earnings growth through FY2018 on revenue growth in the 3–4 percent bracket. Margin expansion should continue especially if recycled material price gains persist. Mid-single-digit dividend increases and modest buybacks should continue coming down the conveyor belt.

## Reasons to Buy

WM is the strongest and most entrenched player in a business that isn't going away anytime soon. "Strategic" waste collection, particularly with the high-value-add material recovery operations that have become a key part of WM's business, is not only here to stay but also will only become more important to residential, industrial, and municipal customers as time goes on. Despite recent low energy and material prices, we feel the "sweet spot" in this trend is yet to come; signs are rampant that the recovery (no pun intended) has begun.

WM exhibits a lot of innovation in an industry not particularly known for it. WM's performance has indeed improved as operational improvements and lower fuel costs have taken effect and material prices have increased.

Regulation and regulatory compliance has always been a big deal for WM, but relaxed regulation likely in the Trump administration may reduce this burden. In all, WM is a slow, steady, safe, well-managed investment with decent cash returns to shareholders.

## Reasons for Caution

WM does rely on acquisitions for a lot of its growth. In this business, that might not be so bad, for existing companies have captive markets and disposal facilities and can likely benefit from proven management processes and reduced overhead costs. The recycling operations, while cool and sexy, aren't always profitable as we've seen, especially when competing material prices, like natural gas these days, are soft. The right combination of factors to drive improved recycling profitability may be close at hand—but recycled materials prices could dip yet again especially if international demand softens—which in turn may be dependent on Trump administration trade policies. Additionally, any waste company runs the risk of going afoul of environmental regulations; WM has largely steered clear of trouble thus far (and has indeed been voted in as a "world's most ethical company" for the past nine years by the Ethisphere Institute—the only entry in the "environmental services" category), but there are no guarantees.

SECTOR: **Business Services** ❑ BETA COEFFICIENT: **0.70** ❑ 10-YEAR COMPOUND EARNINGS PER-SHARE GROWTH: **5.5%** ❑ 10-YEAR COMPOUND DIVIDENDS PER-SHARE GROWTH: **11.0%**

|  | | **2009** | **2010** | **2011** | **2012** | **2013** | **2014** | **2015** | **2016** |
|---|---|---|---|---|---|---|---|---|---|
| Revenues (mil) | | 11,791 | 12,515 | 13,375 | 13,649 | 13,983 | 13,996 | 12,961 | 13,609 |
| Net income (mil) | | 988 | 1,011 | 1,007 | 968 | 1,008 | 1,155 | 1,153 | 1,295 |
| Earnings per share | | 2.00 | 2.10 | 2.14 | 2.08 | 2.15 | 2.48 | 2.53 | 2.91 |
| Dividends per share | | 1.16 | 1.28 | 1.36 | 1.42 | 1.46 | 1.50 | 1.54 | 1.64 |
| Cash flow per share | | 4.43 | 4.64 | 4.85 | 4.88 | 5.04 | 5.34 | 5.36 | 5.90 |
| Price: | high | 34.2 | 37.3 | 36.7 | 36.3 | 46.4 | 51.9 | 55.9 | 71.8 |
| | low | 22.1 | 31.1 | 27.8 | 30.8 | 33.7 | 40.3 | 45.9 | 50.4 |

Website: www.wm.com

---

**AGGRESSIVE GROWTH**

# WD-40 Company

Ticker symbol: WDFC (NASDAQ) ❑ Mid Cap ❑ Value Line financial strength rating: A ❑ Current yield: 1.8% ❑ Dividend raises, past 10 years: 6

## Company Profile

Want to keep squirrels from climbing the poles to your bird feeders? We did, and we always have. And we found the solution through WD-40's website—spray the pole with WD-40.

Turns out, people have been spraying WD-40 on plenty of other things over the years to get them to work right, stop squeaking, dry out properly, or to be just plain in good repair. In fact, they've been spraying WD-40 for 62 years—only a few years after the Rocket Chemical Company first invented the stuff for the aerospace industry in 1953 to protect the outer skin of the SM-65 Atlas missile. And what is "WD-40"? It was the fortieth attempt to develop a good Water Displacement formula. It was so good, and had so many uses in unsticking stuck things, that employees started sneaking it out of the factory in lunch buckets. Shortly thereafter, in 1958, the product made its first appearance on store shelves as a spray.

Fast-forward to now: the professional and now-consumerized WD-40 remains a product of a thousand uses—2,000 in fact, according to the company's website—and a lesson in building a very effective brand around a fairly plain consumer product for distribution into what the company estimates to be four out of five US households and into 176 countries worldwide.

The base WD-40 product, in its familiar blue and yellow spray can of various sizes, is still the brand cornerstone, even though the company doesn't make a drop of it. They do the research and lab work but outsource production to other specialty chemical companies. In fact, the company in total has only 445 employees, probably the fewest on our *100 Best Stocks* list. In the late 1990s, they sought to extend their presence in the maintenance and repair market by acquiring canned light oil maker 3-IN-ONE, then went further into this market to acquire the maker and distributor of Lava soap and Solvol heavy-duty hand cleaner. After initial successes with these acquisitions, and as their products were adopted in greater quantities as consumer products for use in the home, not just the repair shop, they started adding cleaning products, including "X-14" stain removers and "2000 Flushes" bath cleaners, Carpet Fresh and Spot Shot carpet cleaners, and a handful of other products, some with only international distribution. "Multipurpose Maintenance Products" (the lubricants) make up 90 percent of sales and are the strategic focus; the company now admits the cleaning products "are not core strategic focus" and as such, we expect a sale of these lines sooner or later.

WD-40's strategy centers on two ideas: first, finding other adjacent uses and extensions of their core product and second, marketing to multiple channels and end users. (In contrast, they explain that many other manufacturers market many products in one or a few channels, which can be a more difficult proposition.)

In 2003 they added a "3-IN-ONE Professional" line, and in 2011 they sought to extend the WD-40 name itself beyond the namesake light oil spray with the addition of a "WD-40 Specialist" line for especially challenging jobs in maintenance and repair operations for the trade professional and the "doer enthusiast" like rust removal, engine degreasing, corrosion prevention, and electrical contact cleaning. They also introduced specialty lines for motorcycle maintenance, home maintenance, and a "WD-40 Bike" line specifically produced and packaged for bicycle maintenance. In 2017 the company will introduce a new line of products targeted to the RV market. New packages, spray tubes, and injectors help users get the product into difficult spaces—and into different marketing channels.

In short, WD-40 is a classic case study in *brand extension*, with new ways to package and position its core WD-40 and 3-IN-ONE lubricants for new and existing markets, and *business model extension*, where they leverage their operating and marketing model into other useful product lines sold through other channels, such as the WD-40 Specialist product lines.

## Financial Highlights, Fiscal Year 2016

More than half of WD-40's revenue comes from overseas, and as such, currency translation was the "primary culprit" for a relatively sluggish year on the revenue front, with FY2016 revenues up less than 1 percent. They would have risen 4 percent without currency effects. Operational efficiencies and a onetime foreign currency exchange gain drove margins up a full 2 percentage points, and thus net income up a full 17 percent, and with a modest buyback of its mere 14.4 million shares outstanding, per-share earnings were up 20 percent. The company expects new products and marketing initiatives to lube the way for revenue growth in the 3–4 percent range in FY2017 and 5–6 percent in FY2018. Profit growth will take a pause in 2017 as the 2016 compare has a nonrecurring component and as the company moves into a new San Diego headquarters (yes, that does have an impact on a company this size), but per-share earnings will resume a modest but accelerating growth starting in FY2018. Healthy dividend increases should come especially in FY2017 as cash flows will remain strong through the period, and the company has authorized another $75 million for buybacks.

## Reasons to Buy

WD-40 has a dominant market position in the US, so expanding geographic reach is a priority. Fortunately (and ironically) the company's product is "sticky"—that is, its customer base is very loyal. Few things work as well for the intended purpose, and lower-cost competitors are few, so market acceptance is high. We like the branding leverage and niche dominance of any business we see like this. Moreover, we like the way this company is run. A visit to their website and their "About Us" page will uncover their view of the world and clearly stated values: This is a leaner and better culture—or "tribe" as they refer to it—than we've seen in most consumer brand companies. Too, a trip through their investor presentations will shed an unusual amount of positive light on their concise management style. Management respects its employees...and respects its shareholders too. Finally—we can't ignore this—it has all the hallmarks of a Buffett acquisition: a simple business model, strong brand, and good management in place.

## Reasons for Caution

The company has stated that the current lineup in the Homecare and Cleaning Products group are "harvest brands" (meaning there will be no further investment here and the brands will likely be sold off). There does not appear to be a replacement strategy for this segment, so revenue growth at WD-40 will have to come from increasing the breadth and/or market penetration/ share of the Maintenance products line. Acceptance of the Specialist line has been good, but the sales decline in Homecare may accelerate as distributors rebalance to more heavily promoted brands.

Finally, the stock price has appreciated considerably, particularly in 2015; it could be a little ahead of the current growth prospects. We seriously considered removing WD-40 from our list due to the high valuation and low near-term growth prospects, but we couldn't walk away from the solid brand marketing model and management style. Not yet, anyway. The choice of a good entry point could prevent rust in your stock portfolio.

**SECTOR: Industrials** ❑ **BETA COEFFICIENT: 0.66** ❑ **10-YEAR COMPOUND EARNINGS PER-SHARE GROWTH: 7.0%** ❑ **10-YEAR COMPOUND DIVIDENDS PER-SHARE GROWTH: 6.0%**

|  | 2009 | 2010 | 2011 | 2012 | 2013 | 2014 | 2015 | 2016 |
|---|---|---|---|---|---|---|---|---|
| Revenues (mil) | 292 | 322 | 336 | 343 | 369 | 383 | 378 | 381 |
| Net income (mil) | 26.3 | 36.1 | 36.4 | 35.5 | 39.8 | 43.7 | 44.8 | 52.6 |
| Earnings per share | 1.56 | 2.15 | 2.14 | 2.20 | 2.54 | 2.87 | 3.04 | 3.64 |
| Dividends per share | 1.00 | 1.00 | 1.06 | 1.14 | 1.22 | 1.33 | 1.48 | 1.64 |
| Cash flow per share | 1.82 | 2.42 | 2.49 | 2.57 | 2.96 | 3.36 | 3.55 | 4.16 |
| Price: high | 34.6 | 41.8 | 48.0 | 54.4 | 79.3 | 87.1 | 105.0 | 125.0 |
| low | 21.6 | 29.3 | 35.4 | 39.4 | 47.0 | 65.2 | 80.0 | 94.0 |

Website: www.wd40.com

---

**GROWTH AND INCOME**

# Welltower, Inc.

Ticker symbol: HCN (NYSE) ❑ Large Cap ❑ Value Line financial strength rating: A++ ❑ Current yield: 4.8% ❑ Dividend raises, past 10 years: 10

## Company Profile

Welltower, our first real estate investment trust choice added four years ago in 2014, invests primarily in senior living and medical care properties mainly in the US but also in Canada and the UK. The business—and we think it's a good business, not just a real estate portfolio—operates in three primary business segments. The first and largest is referred to as the Seniors Housing "triple-net" segment and is involved primarily in owning senior housing properties, including independent, continuing care, and assisted living facilities, and leasing them to qualified operators like Sunrise Senior Living and Genesis Healthcare in return for a steady income stream. This segment currently owns 569 properties in the US in 40 states, but is concentrated in high-cost urban areas mostly on the coasts, and contributes about 28 percent of revenues. There are now also 56 facilities in the UK and six facilities in Canada.

The second and fastest-growing segment is the Seniors Housing Operating segment, which operates some of the facilities owned by the REIT and others owned by third parties. It operates 268 properties in 35 states, 104 in Canada, and 48 in the UK and contributes about 59 percent of revenues. The third major segment is Outpatient Medical, which owns and sometimes operates 258 outpatient medical centers including skilled nursing facilities in 35 states, contributing about 13 percent to revenues. The company sold its last hospital and its life sciences facilities in 2015 and 2016. In total, Welltower owns and/ or operates some 1,414 properties in three countries, housing some 210,000 residents and supporting 16 million annual outpatient visits.

Welltower employs a conscious and stated strategy of being in markets with high barriers to entry and with a more upscale, affluent retiree base—this is part of why we feel it is a good business, not just a real estate play. Markets such as Boston, New Jersey, Seattle, and major coastal California cities are territories for Welltower. The top five markets are New York, Philadelphia, Los Angeles, Boston, and greater London. The average revenue per occupied room in the seniors operating segment is $6,755 per month, some 51 percent higher than the national senior housing industry average. (For the triple-net segment, this figure is $1,331 per bed/unit per month.) In the markets in which HCN operates, the cost of the average single-family home runs 74 percent higher than the national average, and household incomes are 40 percent higher. Eighty-five percent of facilities are in the 31 most affluent US metropolitan areas. FY2016 occupancy rates are 86.5 percent in the seniors housing triple-net segment, 88.7 percent in the seniors housing operating, and 94.7 percent in the medical facilities segments (these figures were 87.2 percent, 91.0 percent, and 95.1 percent respectively in 2015; the decrease reflects a bit of overbuilding and overcapacity in the industry). The facilities are newer, more attractive, and desirable, as a trip through the company's website at www.welltower.com will show.

The strategy and focus are to "differentiate" and to provide an "infrastructure platform that emphasizes wellness and connectivity across the continuum of care,"—or pleasant, well-appointed alternatives to the traditional facilities usually offered to both healthy and less healthy seniors.

REITs, obviously, play on the real estate market, and in the Welltower case, in the high-value-add REIT segment of healthcare. You're also investing in the aging population—which is expected to grow 40 percent by 2024 against a 9.1 percent growth in the population as a whole. In this case in particular, you're investing in the ability and willingness of the more affluent segments of the elderly population to spend for a pleasant retirement.

REITs are typically good income producers, as they are required by law to pay a substantial portion of their cash flow to investors. The accounting rules are different, and REIT investors should focus on Funds From Operations (FFO), which is analogous to operating income; net income figures have depreciation expenses deducted, which can vary in timing and not always be realistic. Funds From Operations (FFO) support the dividends paid to investors.

## Financial Highlights, Fiscal Year 2016

A few minor portfolio sales and acquisitions, and stronger pricing combined with slightly diminished occupancy rates combined to produce modestly higher results. FY2016 revenues rose about 11 percent, while per-share Funds From Operations (FFO) rose about 4 percent over FY2015. The dividend was raised another 4 percent. A steady occupancy rate and slightly increased rents are projected to produce revenue growth in the 3–5 percent range annually through FY2018, while a slight uptick in expenses and in share count will keep per-share FFO roughly unchanged; the REIT expects stronger growth in both categories after the 2018 year. The company continues to add a modest number of shares to fund acquisitions and to approach a goal of 60 percent equity as noted in the following section.

## Reasons to Buy

Welltower continues to be a solid, relatively risk-free, income-oriented way to play the steady growth and trends of the healthcare industry and the aging demographic. Rents—and rent growth—are better than average, and its income payout is stable and growing. Longer term, the company estimates that senior housing rent growth will exceed inflation by 1.7 percent, that the US population over 75 years of age will grow some 86 percent over the next 20 years, and the 85+ population will double—all factors supporting a healthy growth story.

Some 93 percent of revenues were estimated to be derived from private pay sources in 2017, up from 88 percent in 2016, 87 percent in 2015, and 83 percent in 2014. With the concentration on private-pay services, Welltower will avoid some of the exposure to Medicare utilization management initiatives and related cutbacks that many others in the sector are exposed to—and an improving economy will only help further. We like, and most in the industry agree, the expansion into the UK, which positions them well for other fertile pastures overseas. The company also avoids exposure to debt and interest costs better than most REITs, with a target debt of 40 percent of total capital (they have currently managed this down to 45 percent).

In sum, Welltower offers a good combination of high yield and safety with a modest long-term growth kicker mixed in for good measure.

## Reasons for Caution

Because of their differences from ordinary corporations, it may be difficult to understand this investment, particularly the financial performance of REITs, especially a complex REIT such as this one, which has both traditional property investments and operating company investments. There is mounting evidence of competitive pressure and oversupply in the seniors real estate market, but we feel confident that Welltower is playing in the stronger, more exclusive niches and wisely not taking on the "mass market" players head to head. One could also question, going forward, whether retirees will be as well-heeled as they are today, with deterioration in retirement savings and increased costs. Finally, there is some sensitivity to rising interest rates; the modest underlying growth and high yield makes the stock act more like a bond than a stock much of the time.

SECTOR: **Healthcare** ◻ BETA COEFFICIENT: **0.26** ◻ 10-YEAR COMPOUND FFO PER-SHARE GROWTH: **4.0%** ◻ 10-YEAR COMPOUND DIVIDENDS PER-SHARE GROWTH: **3.0%**

|  | | 2009 | 2010 | 2011 | 2012 | 2013 | 2014 | 2015 | 2016 |
|---|---|---|---|---|---|---|---|---|---|
| Revenues (mil) | | 569.0 | 680.5 | 1,421 | 1,822 | 2,880 | 3,344 | 3,858 | 4,281 |
| Net income (mil) | | 162 | 84 | 156 | 295 | 93 | 505 | 884 | 1,078 |
| Funds from operations per share | | 3.13 | 3.08 | 3.41 | 3.52 | 3.80 | 4.13 | 4.38 | 4.55 |
| Real estate owned per share | | 49.3 | 58.4 | 72.5 | 66.9 | 74.9 | 69.5 | 75.8 | 73.3 |
| Dividends per share | | 2.72 | 2.74 | 2.84 | 2.96 | 3.06 | 3.18 | 3.30 | 3.44 |
| Price: | high | 46.7 | 52.1 | 55.2 | 62.8 | 80.1 | 78.2 | 84.9 | 80.2 |
| | low | 25.9 | 38.4 | 41.0 | 52.4 | 52.4 | 52.9 | 58.2 | 52.8 |

Website: www.welltower.com

# Whirlpool Corporation

Ticker symbol: WHR (NYSE) ❑ Large Cap ❑ Value Line financial strength rating: A+ ❑ Current yield: 2.4% ❑ Dividend raises, past 10 years: 6

## Company Profile

Whirlpool is the world's leading home appliance manufacturer in a $120 billion global industry. The company manufactures appliances under familiar and recognized brand names in all major home appliance categories including fabric care (laundry), cooking, refrigeration, dishwashers, water filtration, and garage organization. Familiar brand names include Whirlpool, Maytag, KitchenAid, Amana, Jenn-Air, Gladiator, and international names Bauknecht, Brastemp, Indesit, and Consul. The Whirlpool brand itself is the number one global appliance brand and is number one across all four major world geographic regions. Products are found in 97 million homes worldwide. Seven brands within the branded house generate over $1 billion in annual sales. Based on FY2016 sales, the product breakdown is about 28 percent refrigerators and freezers, 28 percent fabric care, 18 percent home cooking appliances, and 26 percent "other." About 48 percent of Whirlpool's sales come from outside North America. Although results have been mixed, the company has invested heavily in overseas markets especially with the recent acquisition of two moderately sized international firms: Europe's Indesit (another billion-dollar brand) and China's Hefei Sanyo. Latin America is a big emphasis too. The acquisition strategy keys on adjacent businesses, many to open or gain critical mass in international markets. Whirlpool estimates that through its acquisitions it now has access to 90 percent of the world's consumers.

In an industry not traditionally known for innovation, Whirlpool has striven to be an innovation leader in its industry ("Innovation at the Pace of Life" is one slogan). This has manifested itself both in new products, product platforms, and contemporary styling within those platforms; and in manufacturing and supply-chain efficiencies, such as a global platform design for local manufacture of washing machine products, recalling similar achievements in the auto industry. Such gains are key in this competitive, price-sensitive industry. The company also has initiatives to build lifetime brand loyalty and product quality, improve water and energy efficiency and quietness of operation, and add more interesting and decorative colors to some of its products. More recently it has marketed specialized "smart" appliances; one example is the Whirlpool 6th Sense Live app, which allows owners to operate a washing machine remotely for convenience and to save energy ("Innovations That Connect" is another slogan proudly displayed on their website and annual report).

Overall, the strategy is to expand the business through innovation, brand strength, and geographic coverage; then to expand margins through supply-chain and cost-structure efficiency.

## Financial Highlights, Fiscal Year 2016

For several years the company has ridden the coattails of an improving economy, an improved replacement cycle for old units, improved demand for today's more efficient appliances, and operational improvements. Emerging market weakness and currency effects have been the sales bugaboo lately and again in FY2016. Revenues dropped about 1 percent but would have been up 1.6 percent without currency. What really came out good in the wash were earnings, up a full 10 percent, and a 4 percent share buyback led to a 14 percent gain in per-share earnings, mainly on the back of a more favorable product mix, operational improvements, and lower input costs. In fact, net profit margins have doubled in five years from the 3 percent range to around 6 percent now and going forward.

The stated "value creation framework" is to deliver 3–5 percent annual "organic" sales growth, grow earnings per share 10–15 percent annually, and to expand margins and free cash flow. In fact, forecasts call for 3–4 percent annual sales growth through 2018, with per-share earnings advancing 12–14 percent each year—both figures well within their "framework." Mid-single-digit dividend increases look likely after a 23 percent raise in 2015 and a 13 percent increase in 2016; moderate share buybacks add to squeaky-clean returns to shareholders.

## Reasons to Buy

Long a dull, boring business, Whirlpool has made shopping for an appliance more interesting and has profited handsomely from its efforts. If you shop for an appliance today—take washers and dryers, for example—they work better, they're more energy efficient, they use less water, and are more technology enabled. In short, they're better products, and guess what: They're more expensive and more profitable for the manufacturers, too. Operational improvements, higher-product value add, and a gradual increase in premium brands have driven operating and net margins substantially higher. We continue to like the way the company wrings ever more profit out of a modestly growing or even flat sales base.

Now as the economy and employment strengthen globally, Whirlpool is in a particularly good position to capitalize on these tailwinds. Whirlpool used the Great Recession and ensuing recovery as a wake-up call and an opportunity to streamline its businesses and to put some real strategic thought into how to drive its brand assortment and international portfolio to achieve better results.

The company continues to innovate toward better products and internal processes. Long term, we see more opportunities to develop "smart" appliances, which can work together with smartphones and other residential management applications to deliver better, more energy-efficient results. Bottom line: Whirlpool has ever more to compete on than just price.

Too, the company is building critical mass in overseas markets. Cash flows and investor returns are solid and rising. More than most, the management team is a plus with a recognizable pragmatic and strategic approach to managing this business.

## Reasons for Caution

By nature, the appliance business is highly competitive and cyclical. In addition, some consumers with more disposable income have of late been opting for fancier, more expensive foreign brands, like Bosch and LG, a trend that could hurt if it continues. We believe that Whirlpool is countering this trend by adding elegance, advertising, and channel support for its top-tier brands and products—as well as a few "foreign" brands of its own. Too, it looks like the Department of Commerce might crack down on "dumping" of laundry and other products by some foreign competitors. Commodity costs, labor issues, quality issues, and shifts in consumer preferences, while favorable now, are perpetual risks. Weakness in emerging markets has emerged as another. But overall we still don't find much dirty laundry in this story.

SECTOR: **Consumer Durables** ❑ BETA COEFFICIENT: **1.70** ❑ 10-YEAR COMPOUND EARNINGS PER-SHARE GROWTH: **6.5%** ❑ 10-YEAR COMPOUND DIVIDENDS PER-SHARE GROWTH: **6.0%**

|  |  | 2009 | 2010 | 2011 | 2012 | 2013 | 2014 | 2015 | 2016 |
|---|---|---|---|---|---|---|---|---|---|
| Revenues (mil) | | 17,099 | 18,366 | 18,666 | 18,143 | 18,768 | 19,872 | 20,891 | 20,718 |
| Net income (mil) | | 328 | 707 | 699 | 559 | 810 | 907 | 987 | 1,085 |
| Earnings per share | | 4.34 | 9.10 | 8.95 | 7.05 | 10.03 | 11.39 | 12.38 | 14.08 |
| Dividends per share | | 1.72 | 1.72 | 1.93 | 2.00 | 2.38 | 2.88 | 3.45 | 3.90 |
| Cash flow per share | | 11.37 | 16.91 | 16.54 | 14.05 | 17.53 | 18.80 | 21.43 | 23.51 |
| Price: | high | 85.0 | 118.4 | 92.3 | 104.2 | 159.2 | 196.7 | 217.1 | 194.1 |
|  | low | 19.2 | 71.0 | 45.2 | 47.7 | 101.7 | 124.4 | 140.5 | 123.5 |

Website: www.whirlpoolcorp.com

## Appendix A

# PERFORMANCE ANALYSIS: *100 BEST STOCKS TO BUY IN 2017*

ONE YEAR GAIN/LOSS, APRIL 1, 2016 - APRIL 1, 2017,
EXCLUDING DIVIDENDS

| Company | Symbol | Price 4/1/2016 | Price 4/1/2017 | % change | Dollar gain/loss, $1000 invested |
|---|---|---|---|---|---|
| 3M Company | MMM | $167.53 | $191.33 | 14.2% | $142.06 |
| AbbVie(*) | ABBV | $61.00 | $65.16 | 6.8% | $68.20 |
| Aetna | AET | $113.71 | $127.65 | 12.3% | $122.59 |
| Allstate | ALL | $68.23 | $81.49 | 19.4% | $194.34 |
| Amazon(*) | AMZN | $659.59 | $886.75 | 34.4% | $344.40 |
| Apple | AAPL | $109.99 | $143.71 | 30.7% | $306.57 |
| Aqua America | WTR | $31.93 | $32.15 | 0.7% | $6.89 |
| Archer Daniels Midland | ADM | $36.47 | $46.04 | 26.2% | $262.41 |
| ATT | T | $39.05 | $41.55 | 6.4% | $64.02 |
| Becton, Dickinson | BDX | $153.49 | $183.44 | 19.5% | $195.13 |
| Bemis | BMS | $52.16 | $48.86 | -6.3% | $(63.27) |
| Campbell Soup | CPB | $65.16 | $57.34 | -12.0% | $(120.01) |
| CarMax | KMX | $51.75 | $59.22 | 14.4% | $144.35 |
| Carnival Corporation(*) | CCL | $49.05 | $58.91 | 20.1% | $201.02 |
| CenterPoint Energy | CNP | $21.20 | $27.57 | 30.0% | $300.47 |
| Chevron | CVX | $94.26 | $107.37 | 13.9% | $139.08 |
| Cincinnati Financial | CINF | $65.96 | $77.27 | 17.1% | $171.47 |
| Clorox | CLX | $127.38 | $134.83 | 5.8% | $58.49 |
| Coca-Cola | KO | $46.83 | $42.44 | -9.4% | $(93.74) |
| Colgate-Palmolive | CL | $71.20 | $73.19 | 2.8% | $27.95 |
| Columbia Sportswear(*) | COLM | $58.57 | $58.75 | 0.3% | $3.07 |
| Comcast | CMCSA | $30.38 | $37.60 | 23.8% | $237.66 |
| ConocoPhillips | COP | $39.78 | $49.87 | 25.4% | $253.65 |
| Corning | GLW | $20.83 | $27.00 | 29.6% | $296.21 |
| Costco Wholesale | COST | $158.25 | $167.29 | 5.7% | $57.12 |
| CVS Health | CVS | $104.82 | $78.50 | -25.1% | $(251.10) |
| Daktronics | DAKT | $8.03 | $9.45 | 17.7% | $176.84 |
| Deere | DE | $76.50 | $108.86 | 42.3% | $423.01 |
| DuPont | DD | $63.91 | $80.33 | 25.7% | $256.92 |
| Eastman Chemical | EMN | $73.66 | $80.80 | 9.7% | $96.93 |

* = New for 2017

| Company | Symbol | Price 4/1/2016 | Price 4/1/2017 | % change | Dollar gain/loss, $1000 invested |
|---|---|---|---|---|---|
| Empire State Realty Trust | ESRT | $17.59 | $20.64 | 17.3% | $173.39 |
| Fair Isaac | FICO | $108.80 | $128.95 | 18.5% | $185.20 |
| FedEx | FDX | $163.67 | $195.15 | 19.2% | $192.34 |
| Fresh Del Monte | FDP | $42.96 | $59.23 | 37.9% | $378.72 |
| General Electric | GE | $31.93 | $29.80 | -6.7% | $(66.71) |
| General Mills | GIS | $64.96 | $59.01 | -9.2% | $(91.59) |
| Grainger W.W. | GWW | $234.38 | $232.76 | -0.7% | $(6.91) |
| Honeywell | HON | $113.23 | $124.87 | 10.3% | $102.80 |
| Illinois Tool Works | ITW | $103.44 | $132.47 | 28.1% | $280.65 |
| International Flavors & Frag | IFF | $116.38 | $132.53 | 13.9% | $138.77 |
| Itron | ITRI | $41.86 | $60.70 | 45.0% | $450.07 |
| J.M. Smucker | SJM | $132.52 | $131.08 | -1.1% | $(10.87) |
| Johnson & Johnson | JNJ | $109.19 | $124.55 | 14.1% | $140.67 |
| Kimberly-Clark | KMB | $136.20 | $131.63 | -3.4% | $(33.55) |
| Kroger | KR | $38.32 | $29.42 | -23.2% | $(232.25) |
| Macy's | M | $42.96 | $29.64 | -31.0% | $(310.06) |
| McCormick | MKC | $100.53 | $97.55 | -3.0% | $(29.64) |
| McKesson | MCK | $157.41 | $148.26 | -5.8% | $(58.13) |
| Medtronic | MDT | $75.37 | $80.56 | 6.9% | $68.86 |
| Microchip Technology | MCHP | $48.28 | $73.78 | 52.8% | $528.17 |
| Monsanto | MON | $87.87 | $113.20 | 28.8% | $288.27 |
| Mosaic | MOS | $26.84 | $29.18 | 8.7% | $87.18 |
| NextEra Energy | NEE | $118.71 | $128.37 | 8.1% | $81.37 |
| Nike | NKE | $61.59 | $55.73 | -9.5% | $(95.15) |
| Norfolk Southern | NSC | $82.97 | $111.97 | 35.0% | $349.52 |
| Novo Nordisk | NVO | $54.94 | $34.28 | -37.6% | $(376.05) |
| Oracle | ORCL | $41.16 | $44.61 | 8.4% | $83.82 |
| Ormat Technologies(*) | ORA | $43.40 | $57.08 | 31.5% | $315.21 |
| Otter Tail | OTTR | $29.44 | $38.15 | 29.6% | $295.86 |
| Patterson | PDCO | $46.35 | $45.23 | -2.4% | $(24.16) |

* = New for 2017

| Company | Symbol | Price 4/1/2016 | Price 4/1/2017 | % change | Dollar gain/loss, $1000 invested |
|---|---|---|---|---|---|
| Paychex | PAYX | $54.17 | $58.90 | 8.7% | $87.32 |
| Perrigo | PRGO | $126.73 | $66.39 | -47.6% | $(476.13) |
| Praxair | PX | $115.24 | $118.60 | 2.9% | $29.16 |
| Procter & Gamble | PG | $83.53 | $90.03 | 7.8% | $77.82 |
| Prologis(*) | PLD | $45.41 | $51.88 | 14.2% | $142.48 |
| Public Storage | PSA | $275.52 | $218.91 | -20.5% | $(205.47) |
| Qualcomm(*) | QCOM | $50.52 | $57.34 | 13.5% | $135.00 |
| Quest Diagnostics | DGX | $72.57 | $98.19 | 35.3% | $353.04 |
| ResMed | RMD | $58.99 | $71.97 | 22.0% | $220.04 |
| C.H. Robinson(*) | CHRW | $70.97 | $77.29 | 8.9% | $89.05 |
| Ross Stores | ROST | $58.64 | $65.87 | 12.3% | $123.29 |
| RPM International | RPM | $47.94 | $55.03 | 14.8% | $147.89 |
| Schlumberger | SLB | $72.17 | $78.10 | 8.2% | $82.17 |
| Schnitzer Steel | SCHN | $18.94 | $20.65 | 9.0% | $90.29 |
| Scotts Miracle-Gro | SMG | $73.01 | $93.39 | 27.9% | $279.14 |
| Southwest Airlines | LUV | $44.56 | $53.76 | 20.6% | $206.46 |
| St. Jude Medical | STJ | $55.19 | $80.82 | 46.4% | $464.40 |
| Starbucks | SBUX | $61.02 | $58.39 | -4.3% | $(43.10) |
| State Street Corp | STT | $58.95 | $79.61 | 35.0% | $350.47 |
| Steelcase | SCS | $14.93 | $16.75 | 12.2% | $121.90 |
| Stryker Corporation | SYK | $108.52 | $131.60 | 21.3% | $212.68 |
| Sysco | SYY | $47.08 | $51.92 | 10.3% | $102.80 |
| Target | TGT | $82.76 | $55.19 | -33.3% | $(333.13) |
| Time Warner Inc | TWX | $72.99 | $97.71 | 33.9% | $338.68 |
| Timken Company | TKR | $33.67 | $45.20 | 34.2% | $342.44 |
| Total S.A. | TOT | $44.20 | $50.42 | 14.1% | $140.72 |
| Union Pacific | UNP | $78.92 | $105.92 | 34.2% | $342.12 |
| UnitedHealth Group | UNH | $129.82 | $164.01 | 26.3% | $263.36 |
| United Parcel Service | UPS | $104.95 | $107.30 | 2.2% | $22.39 |
| United Technologies | UTX | $99.97 | $112.21 | 12.2% | $122.44 |

* = New for 2017

| Company | Symbol | Price 4/1/2016 | Price 4/1/2017 | % change | Dollar gain/loss, $1000 invested |
|---|---|---|---|---|---|
| Valero | VLO | $62.91 | $66.29 | 5.4% | $53.73 |
| Valmont | VMI | $123.82 | $155.50 | 25.6% | $255.86 |
| Verizon | VZ | $54.01 | $48.75 | -9.7% | $(97.39) |
| Visa | V | $77.59 | $88.87 | 14.5% | $145.38 |
| Waste Management | WM | $59.17 | $72.92 | 23.2% | $232.38 |
| WD-40 | WDFC | $110.69 | $109.00 | -1.5% | $(15.27) |
| Wells Fargo | WFC | $48.45 | $55.66 | 14.9% | $148.81 |
| Welltower | HCN | $69.16 | $70.82 | 2.4% | $24.00 |
| Whirlpool | WHR | $183.31 | $171.33 | -6.5% | $(65.35) |
| Whitewave Foods (*) | WWAV | $40.21 | $56.15 | 39.6% | $396.42 |

* = New for 2017

# THE *100 BEST STOCKS* 2018, DIVIDEND AND YIELD BY COMPANY

| Company | Symbol | 2016 | | 2017 | | Dividend Raises, Past 10 Years |
| --- | --- | --- | --- | --- | --- | --- |
| | | Dividend | Yield % | Dividend | Yield % | |
| 3M Company | MMM | $4.44 | 2.6% | $4.51 | 2.4% | 10 |
| Abbott Laboratories | ABT | $0.98 | 2.2% | $1.05 | 2.4% | 10 |
| AbbVie | ABBV | $2.28 | 3.6% | $2.35 | 3.6% | 2 |
| Aetna | AET | $1.00 | 0.9% | $1.00 | 0.8% | 5 |
| Allstate | ALL | $0.32 | 2.0% | $1.36 | 1.7% | 6 |
| Amazon | AMZN | | | | | |
| Apple | AAPL | $2.28 | 2.7% | $2.28 | 1.6% | 4 |
| Aqua America | WTR | $0.71 | 2.2% | $0.75 | 2.3% | 10 |
| Archer Daniels Midland | ADM | $1.20 | 2.8% | $1.22 | 2.6% | 9 |
| AT&T | T | $1.92 | 4.9% | $1.93 | 4.6% | 10 |
| Becton, Dickinson | BDX | $2.64 | 1.6% | $2.78 | 1.5% | 10 |
| Bemis | BMS | $1.16 | 2.3% | $1.17 | 2.4% | 10 |
| Boeing | BA | $3.62 | 3.2% | $5.02 | 2.8% | 8 |
| Campbell Soup | CPB | $1.25 | 2.0% | $1.35 | 2.4% | 8 |
| CarMax | KMX | | | | | |
| Carnival Corporation | CCL | $1.40 | 2.9% | $1.40 | 2.4% | 4 |
| Caterpillar | CAT | $3.01 | 3.9% | $3.08 | 3.0% | 10 |
| CenterPoint Energy | CNP | $1.03 | 4.6% | $1.05 | 3.8% | 10 |
| Chemed | CHE | $0.94 | 0.7% | $1.02 | 0.5% | 8 |
| Chevron | CVX | $4.28 | 4.2% | $4.30 | 4.0% | 10 |
| Cincinnati Financial | CINF | $1.92 | 2.8% | $1.94 | 2.5% | 10 |
| Coca-Cola | KO | $1.40 | 3.2% | $1.42 | 3.3% | 10 |
| Colgate-Palmolive | CL | $1.56 | 2.2% | $1.56 | 2.1% | 10 |
| Columbia Sportswear | COLM | $0.68 | 1.3% | $0.70 | 1.2% | 10 |
| Comcast | CMCSA | $1.10 | 1.8% | $0.55 | 1.5% | 7 |
| ConocoPhillips | COP | $1.98 | 4.5% | $1.02 | 2.0% | 9 |
| Corning | GLW | $0.54 | 2.6% | $0.56 | 2.1% | 5 |
| Costco Wholesale | COST | $1.80 | 1.2% | $1.80 | 1.1% | 10 |
| CVS Health | CVS | $1.70 | 1.8% | $1.78 | 2.3% | 10 |

| Company | Symbol | 2016 Dividend | 2016 Yield % | 2017 Dividend | 2017 Yield % | Dividend Raises, Past 10 Years |
|---|---|---|---|---|---|---|
| Daktronics | DAKT | $0.40 | 5.0% | $0.31 | 3.3% | 7 |
| Deere | DE | $2.40 | 3.0% | $2.40 | 2.2% | 10 |
| Dentsply Sirona | XRAY | $0.30 | 0.5% | $0.32 | 0.5% | 9 |
| DuPont | DD | $1.52 | 2.3% | $1.44 | 1.8% | 7 |
| Eastman Chemical | EMN | $1.84 | 2.5% | $1.94 | 2.4% | 6 |
| Empire State Realty Trust | ESRT | $0.34 | 1.8% | $0.42 | 2.0% | 1 |
| Fair Isaac | FICO | $0.08 | 0.1% | $0.08 | 0.1% | 1 |
| FedEx | FDX | $1.00 | 0.6% | $1.60 | 0.8% | 10 |
| First Solar | FSLR | | | | | |
| Fresh Del Monte | FDP | $0.50 | 1.0% | $0.58 | 1.0% | 3 |
| General Electric | GE | $0.92 | 3.4% | $0.94 | 3.2% | 8 |
| General Mills | GIS | $1.84 | 2.9% | $1.90 | 3.2% | 10 |
| Grainger W.W. | GWW | $4.88 | 2.2% | $4.80 | 2.1% | 10 |
| Honeywell | HON | $2.38 | 2.1% | $3.45 | 2.8% | 9 |
| Illinois Tool Works | ITW | $2.20 | 2.1% | $2.52 | 2.0% | 10 |
| International Flavors & Fragrances | IFF | $2.24 | 1.7% | $2.50 | 1.9% | 10 |
| Itron | ITRI | | | | | |
| J.M. Smucker | SJM | $2.00 | 2.3% | $2.48 | 1.9% | 10 |
| Johnson & Johnson | JNJ | $2.68 | 2.1% | $2.92 | 2.3% | 10 |
| Kimberly-Clark | KMB | $3.68 | 2.9% | $3.73 | 2.8% | 10 |
| Kroger | KR | $0.42 | 1.2% | $0.47 | 1.6% | 9 |
| McCormick | MKC | $1.72 | 1.8% | $1.77 | 1.8% | 10 |
| McKesson | MCK | $1.12 | 0.6% | $1.12 | 0.8% | 7 |
| Medtronic | MDT | $1.52 | 1.9% | $1.72 | 2.1% | 10 |
| Microchip Technology | MCHP | $1.44 | 3.0% | $2.16 | 1.9% | 5 |
| Mosaic | MOS | $1.10 | 2.9% | $1.10 | 3.8% | 4 |
| NextEra Energy | NEE | $3.48 | 2.9% | $3.59 | 2.8% | 10 |
| Nike | NKE | $0.64 | 1.2% | $0.68 | 1.2% | 10 |
| Norfolk Southern | NSC | $2.36 | 2.4% | $2.39 | 2.1% | 10 |

| Company | Symbol | 2016 | | 2017 | | Dividend Raises, Past 10 Years |
|---|---|---|---|---|---|---|
| | | Dividend | Yield % | Dividend | Yield % | |
| Novo Nordisk | NVO | $0.96 | 1.7% | $1.11 | 3.2% | 10 |
| Oracle | ORCL | $0.60 | 1.5% | $0.60 | 1.3% | 5 |
| Ormat Technologies | ORA | $0.50 | 1.2% | $0.38 | 0.7% | 5 |
| Otter Tail | OTTR | $1.25 | 4.2% | $0.96 | 2.1% | 4 |
| Paychex | PAYX | $1.68 | 3.1% | $1.80 | 3.1% | 8 |
| Perrigo | PRGO | $0.58 | 0.6% | $0.59 | 0.9% | 10 |
| Praxair | PX | $3.00 | 2.7% | $3.04 | 2.6% | 10 |
| Procter & Gamble | PG | $2.68 | 3.3% | $2.68 | 3.0% | 10 |
| Prologis | PLD | $1.68 | 3.5% | $1.70 | 3.3% | 4 |
| Prudential | PRU | $2.66 | 3.5% | $2.85 | 2.7% | 9 |
| Public Storage | PSA | $7.20 | 2.8% | $7.60 | 3.5% | 8 |
| Qualcomm | QCOM | $2.12 | 3.8% | $2.12 | 3.7% | 10 |
| Quest Diagnostics | DGX | $1.60 | 2.1% | $1.65 | 1.7% | 6 |
| ResMed | RMD | $1.20 | 2.1% | $1.29 | 1.8% | 3 |
| C.H. Robinson | CHRW | $1.72 | 2.3% | $1.76 | 2.3% | 9 |
| Ross Stores | ROST | $0.54 | 1.0% | $0.57 | 0.9% | 10 |
| RPM International | RPM | $1.10 | 2.2% | $1.15 | 2.1% | 10 |
| Schlumberger | SLB | $2.00 | 2.6% | $2.00 | 2.6% | 9 |
| Schnitzer Steel | SCHN | $0.75 | 4.7% | $0.75 | 3.6% | 3 |
| Siemens | SIEGY | $1.87 | 3.6% | $5.61 | 7.8% | 8 |
| Scotts Miracle-Gro | SMG | $1.88 | 2.7% | $1.97 | 2.1% | 7 |
| Southwest Airlines | LUV | $0.40 | 0.9% | $1.24 | 1.5% | 4 |
| Starbucks | SBUX | $0.80 | 1.5% | $0.90 | 1.5% | 6 |
| State Street Corp | STT | $1.36 | 2.2% | $1.48 | 1.9% | 8 |
| Steelcase | SCS | $0.48 | 3.0% | $0.49 | 2.9% | 6 |
| Stryker Corporation | SYK | $1.52 | 1.4% | $1.61 | 1.2% | 9 |
| Sysco | SYY | $0.24 | 2.6% | $1.63 | 1.7% | 10 |
| Timken Company | TKR | $1.04 | 3.1% | $1.04 | 2.3% | 8 |
| Total S.A. | TOT | $2.73 | 5.6% | $2.67 | 5.3% | 7 |

| Company | Symbol | 2016 Dividend | 2016 Yield % | 2017 Dividend | 2017 Yield % | Dividend Raises, Past 10 Years |
|---|---|---|---|---|---|---|
| Tupperware | TUP | $2.12 | 3.7% | $2.12 | 3.0% | 6 |
| Union Pacific | UNP | $2.20 | 2.7% | $2.31 | 2.2% | 10 |
| UnitedHealth Group | UNH | $2.00 | 1.5% | $2.50 | 1.5% | 6 |
| United Parcel Service | UPS | $3.12 | 3.0% | $3.17 | 3.0% | 10 |
| United Tecnologies | UTX | $2.64 | 2.6% | $2.64 | 2.4% | 10 |
| Valero | VLO | $2.40 | 4.4% | $2.50 | 3.8% | 9 |
| Valmont | VMI | $1.50 | 1.1% | $2.29 | 1.9% | 10 |
| Visa | V | $0.56 | 0.7% | $0.61 | 0.7% | 7 |
| Vodafone | VOD | $1.53 | 5.9% | $1.60 | 6.4% | 4 |
| Waste Management | WM | $1.64 | 2.7% | $1.66 | 2.3% | 10 |
| WD-40 | WDFC | $1.68 | 1.5% | $1.52 | 1.4% | 7 |
| Welltower | HCN | $3.44 | 5.0% | $3.60 | 5.1% | 10 |
| Whirlpool | WHR | $4.00 | 2.3% | $3.60 | 2.1% | 5 |

# YIELDS, LOWEST TO HIGHEST: *100 BEST STOCKS TO BUY IN 2018*

| Company | Symbol | 2016 Dividend | 2016 Yield % | 2017 Dividend | 2017 Yield % | Dividend Raises, Past 10 Years | Aggressor factor |
|---|---|---|---|---|---|---|---|
| Siemens | SIEGY | $1.87 | 3.6% | $5.61 | 7.8% | 8 | 62.4 |
| Vodafone | VOD | $1.53 | 5.9% | $1.60 | 6.4% | 4 | 25.6 |
| Total S.A. | TOT | $2.73 | 5.6% | $2.67 | 5.3% | 7 | 37.1 |
| Welltower | HCN | $3.44 | 5.0% | $3.60 | 5.1% | 10 | 50.8 |
| AT&T | T | $1.92 | 4.9% | $1.93 | 4.6% | 10 | 43.8 |
| Chevron | CVX | $4.28 | 4.2% | $4.30 | 4.0% | 10 | 47.0 |
| CenterPoint Energy | CNP | $1.03 | 4.6% | $1.05 | 3.8% | 10 | 46.5 |
| Valero | VLO | $2.40 | 4.4% | $2.50 | 3.8% | 9 | 40.0 |
| Mosaic | MOS | $1.10 | 2.9% | $1.10 | 3.8% | 4 | 38.1 |
| Qualcomm | QCOM | $2.12 | 3.8% | $2.12 | 3.7% | 10 | 33.9 |
| Schnitzer Steel | SCHN | $0.75 | 4.7% | $0.75 | 3.6% | 3 | 15.1 |
| AbbVie | ABBV | $2.28 | 3.6% | $2.35 | 3.6% | 2 | 37.0 |
| Public Storage | PSA | $7.20 | 2.8% | $7.60 | 3.5% | 8 | 10.9 |
| Coca-Cola | KO | $1.40 | 3.2% | $1.42 | 3.3% | 10 | 7.2 |
| Daktronics | DAKT | $0.40 | 5.0% | $0.31 | 3.3% | 7 | 27.8 |
| Prologis | PLD | $1.68 | 3.5% | $1.70 | 3.3% | 4 | 33.5 |
| Novo Nordisk | NVO | $0.96 | 1.7% | $1.11 | 3.2% | 10 | 23.0 |
| General Mills | GIS | $1.84 | 2.9% | $1.90 | 3.2% | 10 | 13.1 |
| General Electric | GE | $0.92 | 3.4% | $0.94 | 3.2% | 8 | 32.4 |
| Paychex | PAYX | $1.68 | 3.1% | $1.80 | 3.1% | 8 | 32.2 |
| Caterpillar | CAT | $3.01 | 3.9% | $3.08 | 3.0% | 10 | 25.2 |
| Tupperware | TUP | $2.12 | 3.7% | $2.12 | 3.0% | 6 | 24.4 |
| Procter & Gamble | PG | $2.68 | 3.3% | $2.68 | 3.0% | 10 | 30.0 |
| United Parcel Service | UPS | $3.12 | 3.0% | $3.17 | 3.0% | 10 | 18.0 |
| Steelcase | SCS | $0.48 | 3.0% | $0.49 | 2.9% | 6 | 29.8 |
| Kimberly-Clark | KMB | $3.68 | 2.9% | $3.73 | 2.8% | 10 | 29.5 |
| Honeywell | HON | $2.38 | 2.1% | $3.45 | 2.8% | 9 | 17.6 |
| Boeing | BA | $3.62 | 3.2% | $5.02 | 2.8% | 8 | 28.3 |
| NextEra Energy | NEE | $3.48 | 2.9% | $3.59 | 2.8% | 10 | 22.4 |

| Company | Symbol | 2016 Dividend | Yield % | 2017 Dividend | Yield % | Dividend Raises, Past 10 Years | Aggressor factor |
|---|---|---|---|---|---|---|---|
| Prudential | PRU | $2.66 | 3.5% | $2.85 | 2.7% | 9 | 28.0 |
| Archer Daniels Midland | ADM | $1.20 | 2.8% | $1.22 | 2.6% | 9 | 24.3 |
| Praxair | PX | $3.00 | 2.7% | $3.04 | 2.6% | 10 | 23.8 |
| Schlumberger | SLB | $2.00 | 2.6% | $2.00 | 2.6% | 9 | 25.6 |
| Cincinnati Financial | CINF | $1.92 | 2.8% | $1.94 | 2.5% | 10 | 23.0 |
| Eastman Chemical | EMN | $1.84 | 2.5% | $1.94 | 2.4% | 6 | 25.1 |
| Abbott Laboratories | ABT | $0.98 | 2.2% | $1.05 | 2.4% | 10 | 14.4 |
| Bemis | BMS | $1.16 | 2.3% | $1.17 | 2.4% | 10 | 24.0 |
| Carnival Corporation | CCL | $1.40 | 2.9% | $1.40 | 2.4% | 4 | 23.9 |
| 3M Company | MMM | $4.44 | 2.6% | $4.51 | 2.4% | 10 | 9.5 |
| Campbell Soup | CPB | $1.25 | 2.0% | $1.35 | 2.4% | 8 | 23.6 |
| United Technologies | UTX | $2.64 | 2.6% | $2.64 | 2.4% | 10 | 18.8 |
| Johnson & Johnson | JNJ | $2.68 | 2.1% | $2.92 | 2.3% | 10 | 23.5 |
| Aqua America | WTR | $0.71 | 2.2% | $0.75 | 2.3% | 10 | 23.4 |
| Timken Company | TKR | $1.04 | 3.1% | $1.04 | 2.3% | 8 | 23.3 |
| C.H. Robinson | CHRW | $1.72 | 2.3% | $1.76 | 2.3% | 9 | 18.4 |
| Waste Management | WM | $1.64 | 2.7% | $1.66 | 2.3% | 10 | 20.5 |
| CVS Health | CVS | $1.70 | 1.8% | $1.78 | 2.3% | 10 | 22.8 |
| Deere | DE | $2.40 | 3.0% | $2.40 | 2.2% | 10 | 22.7 |
| Union Pacific | UNP | $2.20 | 2.7% | $2.31 | 2.2% | 10 | 22.0 |
| Medtronic | MDT | $1.52 | 1.9% | $1.72 | 2.1% | 10 | 21.8 |
| Norfolk Southern | NSC | $2.36 | 2.4% | $2.39 | 2.1% | 10 | 21.4 |
| Colgate-Palmolive | CL | $1.56 | 2.2% | $1.56 | 2.1% | 10 | 21.3 |
| Otter Tail | OTTR | $1.25 | 4.2% | $0.96 | 2.1% | 4 | 21.3 |
| Scotts Miracle-Gro | SMG | $1.88 | 2.7% | $1.97 | 2.1% | 7 | 8.5 |
| Whirlpool | WHR | $4.00 | 2.3% | $3.60 | 2.1% | 5 | 14.8 |
| RPM International | RPM | $1.10 | 2.2% | $1.15 | 2.1% | 10 | 10.5 |
| Corning | GLW | $0.54 | 2.6% | $0.56 | 2.1% | 5 | 20.9 |
| Grainger W.W. | GWW | $4.88 | 2.2% | $4.80 | 2.1% | 10 | 10.4 |

| Company | Symbol | 2016 | | 2017 | | Dividend Raises, Past 10 Years | Aggressor factor |
|---|---|---|---|---|---|---|---|
| | | Dividend | Yield % | Dividend | Yield % | | |
| ConocoPhillips | COP | $1.98 | 4.5% | $1.02 | 2.0% | 9 | 20.6 |
| Empire State Realty Trust | ESRT | $0.34 | 1.8% | $0.42 | 2.0% | 1 | 18.4 |
| Illinois Tool Works | ITW | $2.20 | 2.1% | $2.52 | 2.0% | 10 | 2.0 |
| Microchip Technology | MCHP | $1.44 | 3.0% | $2.16 | 1.9% | 5 | 20.2 |
| Valmont | VMI | $1.50 | 1.1% | $2.29 | 1.9% | 10 | 9.5 |
| J.M. Smucker | SJM | $2.00 | 2.3% | $2.48 | 1.9% | 10 | 18.9 |
| International Flavors & Fragrances | IFF | $2.24 | 1.7% | $2.50 | 1.9% | 10 | 18.9 |
| State Street Corp | STT | $1.36 | 2.2% | $1.48 | 1.9% | 8 | 14.9 |
| McCormick | MKC | $1.72 | 1.8% | $1.77 | 1.8% | 10 | 18.1 |
| DuPont | DD | $1.52 | 2.3% | $1.44 | 1.8% | 7 | 12.5 |
| ResMed | RMD | $1.20 | 2.1% | $1.29 | 1.8% | 3 | 5.4 |
| Quest Diagnostics | DGX | $1.60 | 2.1% | $1.65 | 1.7% | 6 | 10.1 |
| Allstate | ALL | $0.32 | 2.0% | $1.36 | 1.7% | 6 | 10.0 |
| Sysco | SYY | $0.24 | 2.6% | $1.63 | 1.7% | 10 | 16.7 |
| Kroger | KR | $0.42 | 1.2% | $0.47 | 1.6% | 9 | 46.2 |
| Apple | AAPL | $2.28 | 2.7% | $2.28 | 1.6% | 4 | 6.3 |
| Starbucks | SBUX | $0.80 | 1.5% | $0.90 | 1.5% | 6 | 9.2 |
| Southwest Airlines | LUV | $0.40 | 0.9% | $1.24 | 1.5% | 4 | 6.1 |
| UnitedHealth Group | UNH | $2.00 | 1.5% | $2.50 | 1.5% | 6 | 9.1 |
| Becton, Dickinson | BDX | $2.64 | 1.6% | $2.78 | 1.5% | 10 | 15.2 |
| Comcast | CMCSA | $1.10 | 1.8% | $0.55 | 1.5% | 7 | 10.2 |
| WD-40 | WDFC | $1.68 | 1.5% | $1.52 | 1.4% | 7 | 9.6 |
| Oracle | ORCL | $0.60 | 1.5% | $0.60 | 1.3% | 5 | 6.7 |
| Stryker Corporation | SYK | $1.52 | 1.4% | $1.61 | 1.2% | 9 | 11.0 |
| Nike | NKE | $0.64 | 1.2% | $0.68 | 1.2% | 10 | 12.2 |
| Columbia Sportswear | COLM | $0.68 | 1.3% | $0.70 | 1.2% | 10 | 11.9 |
| Costco Wholesale | COST | $1.80 | 1.2% | $1.80 | 1.1% | 10 | 10.8 |
| Fresh Del Monte | FDP | $0.50 | 1.0% | $0.58 | 1.0% | 3 | 2.9 |
| Perrigo | PRGO | $0.58 | 0.6% | $0.59 | 0.9% | 10 | 8.9 |

| Company | Symbol | 2016 Dividend | 2016 Yield % | 2017 Dividend | 2017 Yield % | Dividend Raises, Past 10 Years | Aggressor factor |
|---|---|---|---|---|---|---|---|
| Ross Stores | ROST | $0.54 | 1.0% | $0.57 | 0.9% | 10 | 8.7 |
| FedEx | FDX | $1.00 | 0.6% | $1.60 | 0.8% | 10 | 8.2 |
| Aetna | AET | $1.00 | 0.9% | $1.00 | 0.8% | 5 | 3.9 |
| McKesson | MCK | $1.12 | 0.6% | $1.12 | 0.8% | 7 | 5.3 |
| Visa | V | $0.56 | 0.7% | $0.61 | 0.7% | 7 | 4.8 |
| Ormat Technologies | ORA | $0.50 | 1.2% | $0.38 | 0.7% | 5 | 3.3 |
| Dentsply Sirona | XRAY | $0.30 | 0.5% | $0.32 | 0.5% | 9 | 4.5 |
| Chemed | CHE | $0.94 | 0.7% | $1.02 | 0.5% | 8 | 4.0 |
| Fair Isaac | FICO | $0.08 | 0.1% | $0.08 | 0.1% | 1 | 0.1 |
| Amazon | AMZN | | | | | | |
| CarMax | KMX | | | | | | |
| First Solar | FSLR | | | | | | |
| Itron | ITRI | | | | | | |

# Currently available from Value Line for individual investors

**THE VALUE LINE INVESTMENT SURVEY®**
The signature publication from Value Line is one of the most highly regarded comprehensive investment research resources. Published weekly, it tracks approximately 1,700 stocks in more than 90 industries and ranks stocks for Timeliness™ and Safety™.

**THE VALUE LINE INVESTMENT SURVEY® — SMALL & MID-CAP**
The Small & Mid-Cap Survey applies Value Line's data and analysis protocols to a universe of approximately 1,800 companies with market values from less than $1 billion up to $5 billion.

**THE VALUE LINE INVESTMENT SURVEY® — SMART INVESTOR**
This Internet version of The Value Line Investment Survey tracks approximately 1,700 stocks and offers sorting functions and custom alerts.

**THE VALUE LINE INVESTMENT SURVEY® — SAVVY INVESTOR**
The Internet counterpart of the preceding three Surveys, Savvy Investor includes every one of our 3,500 stock reports plus updates during Stock Exchange hours.

**THE VALUE LINE® 600**
Provides stock reports from The Value Line Investment Survey on 600 large, actively traded and widely held U.S. exchange-listed corporations, including many foreign firms, spanning more than 90 industries.

**VALUE LINE SELECT®**
Once a month, subscribers receive a detailed report by Value Line senior analysts, recommending the one stock that has the best upside and risk/reward ratio. A less-seasoned promising issue is sometimes highlighted as well.

**VALUE LINE SELECT®: DIVIDEND INCOME & GROWTH**
A monthly, in-depth report recommending one dividend-paying stock, providing extensive information about the company's finances, prospects, and projected earnings, along with follow-up on numerous alternate selections.

**THE VALUE LINE SPECIAL SITUATIONS SERVICE®**
The Value Line Special Situations Service is designed for those seeking investment ideas in the small-cap arena. It includes both aggressive and conservative selections every month.

Value Line & SELECT® ETFs recommends one Exchange-Traded Fund each month.

A special 14-day trial of The Value Line Investment Survey — Smart Investor is available to individual investors with the code "100STOCKS" at www.valueline.com/100STOCKS.

551 Fifth Avenue, 3rd FL, New York, NY 10176
www.valueline.com
1-800-VALUELINE